Can you smell the roasting peanuts?

The Glosser Bros. Department Store has reopened, just for you, just in the pages of this one-of-a-kind book. For the first time, the whole true story of Glosser's has been told, on the 25th anniversary of the fabled department store's closing. Step through the famous doors on the corner of Franklin and Locust Streets and grab a brown-and-white-striped shopping bag. You're about to embark on a journey from the humble beginnings of Glosser Bros. to its glory days as a local institution and multi-million dollar company…and the thrilling battle to save it on the eve of its grand finale. Read the stories of the executives, the employees, and the loyal shoppers who made Glosser Bros. a legend and kept it alive in the hearts and minds of Glosser Nation. Hundreds of photos, never before gathered together in one place, will take you back in time to the places and people that made Glosser's great. Experience the things you loved best about the classic department store, from the roasted nuts to the Shaffer twins to the Halloween windows and the amazing sales. Discover secrets and surprises that have never been revealed to the general public until now. Relive the story of a lifetime in a magical tour straight out of your memories and dreams, a grand reopening of a store that never really closed in your heart and will open its doors every time we shout…

Long Live Glosser's

Long Live Glosser's

DELUXE EDITION

By Robert Jeschonek

pie press publishing

Other Johnstown and Cambria County
books by Robert Jeschonek

A Glosser's Christmas Love Story
Christmas at Glosser's
Death by Polka
Easter at Glosser's
Fear of Rain
Halloween at Glosser's
Penn Traffic Forever
The Masked Family

DEDICATION

To Leonard Black, Janet Sinberg Dash, Alvin Glosser, Izzy
Glosser, Mark Glosser, Sydney Ossip, Ruby Shaffer, Ruth Shaffer,
Herb Sinberg, Isadore Suchman, and all the others who are gone
but not forgotten, much like the department store whose story
they helped make so compelling.

Introduction

Think of this book as a work in progress.

It tells a story that ended long ago--over 25 years ago--and yet that story goes on today. The Glosser Bros. Department Store closed in 1989, but its influence on our hearts and minds never really went away. Its echoes still ripple out through our lives, and will continue to do so forever. "The Store" was just that big a place, a vision, a way of life.

Is it any wonder that its story is just as big? That as I researched and wrote this book, the story continued to get bigger and bigger?

Each door I opened led to a dozen new doors. Each phone call I made led to a dozen new calls. Each story I heard led to ever more stories, multiplying like snowflakes swirling in a gathering squall.

I learned so much along the way--how the Glosser family first came to America, how The Store first opened, when the escalator was built, why the supermarket was put in the basement. I learned about the delivery trucks, the cafeteria, the Halloween window painting contests, the Gee Bee stores, and the aftermath of the floods (in '36 and '77). Best of all, I learned about all the amazing people who made the story possible, from the Glosser family to the company's employees to the folks who shopped at The Store.

And yet, the biggest lesson I learned is that this story isn't done growing yet.

This is not a definitive scholarly work, set in stone. It is a memory book, meant to entertain and carry the legend of Glosser Brothers forward into the future.

Photo by Robert Jeschonek

Much of the information used in the book came from oral histories--interviews with people who figured prominently, in one way or another, in the events depicted. I was lucky to find so many of them, so many people who remember what happened at The Store all the way back to the 1920s and 30s. It was a gift, to say the least, and I am honored to pass it along to you.

Where possible, I have supported the oral histories with archival research. I made this book as close to true history as I could get...and moved on to put it in your hands as soon as I could.

Remember, as you read, that this is a work in progress. If you have a suggestion for a change or addition, reach out (at glosserbrothers.com), and I'll try to put it in a future edition.

Because you're as much a part of the story as anyone else. Glosser's was *your* store. Its story was the story of *your* life.

I turned that story into this book for you, to help you remember... to learn things you might not have known...and to pass it along to those who might otherwise never have understood just how *special* Glosser's was. I wrote this book for all those reasons.

And I wrote it for me, because I love Glosser's. I love the smell of the roasting peanuts and cashews, wafting through the store. I love the ice cream sundaes in the cafeteria, served up by the famous "Glosser Twins" (aka the Shaffer Twins). I love all the sights and sounds and smells of that one-of-a-kind place, filled with shoppers forever smiling and loading their brown-and-white-striped shopping bags with quality discount merchandise. I love it all.

It's just that simple.

Chapter 1

A Family Reunion

The reunion wasn't supposed to start until ten o'clock in the morning, but the crowd started to form around nine. A small group gathered in the bright morning sunlight in front of the building that had once housed the Glosser Bros. Department Store in downtown Johnstown, Pennsylvania.

It was the first time they'd been there together in at least a quarter of a century.

What brought them there after so long apart? They came for a reunion and photo shoot commemorating the 25th anniversary of the store's closing in 1989. They came for a chance to commemorate a local landmark that had helped define Johnstown, and the lives of its citizens, for more than 80 years.

But more importantly, the people came to visit family. Every one of them, at one time or another, had been an employee of the Glosser Bros. Department Store...and, therefore, a member of the Glosser's family.

Photo by Philip Balko

3

That was one thing they all agreed on: working for Glosser Bros. was like being part of a family. The store might have closed 25 years ago, but the bonds between those who worked there--and shopped there--were stronger than ever.

And on this sunny summer morning at the corner of Franklin and Locust Streets, those bonds would be celebrated and renewed.

A Crowd to Remember

The dozen or so early arrivals gathered around what had once been the corner entrance of the store, now the main entrance of the Press Bistro restaurant. They wasted no time striking up old friendships and reminiscing as they waited for the reunion to begin.

Some wondered how many more people would show up. Would there only be a few, since Glosser's had been gone for so long? It was impossible to say.

As the minutes ticked by, a few more people straggled over to the corner. It looked as if the size of the group would be modest...perhaps because it was Memorial Day Monday, and so many people had holiday plans.

Then, around a quarter till ten o'clock, it became clear that this reunion would not be so modest after all.

Photos by Philip Balko

People poured in from all directions, swelling the crowd with each passing moment. They streamed in from Franklin Street and Locust Street, waving and calling out to each other. They trooped across Central Park, arm in arm, chatting and laughing.

Some came with canes and walkers. Others strolled or trotted without assistance.

And all of them, every last one of them, was smiling from ear to ear.

Ten o'clock came and went, and still they kept coming. There was Ruby Shaffer, who'd worked for decades in the Glosser's cafeteria with her twin sister, Ruth; Bill Hritz, who'd managed the parking lot for many years;

Linda Hockenberry, who'd worked in the advertising department in the 1950s, and her husband Al, whom she'd first met 50 years ago in the store; Joe Kovach, who'd worked for years in the shoe department; Jack and Arlene Goss, who'd also worked a long time at the store; and Bill Glosser, who had managed personnel, security, and financial public relations.

Soon, dozens of former Glosser Bros. employees crowded the sidewalk. We counted over seventy--far more than we had anticipated.

Photos by Philip Balko

For a while, with so many people and so much chatter and hustle and bustle around that building, it was a little like the old days again...the days when the Glosser Bros. Department Store was still open for business, a hive of activity in the heart of the city.

You could practically smell the hot peanuts and cashews again, their sweet fragrance wafting on the warm breeze from the roasters on the first floor.

Photo by Philip Balko

Memory Department

I wish Glosser Bros. was still there.   I remember going downtown on Thursday nights and Saturdays. We would always go to the cafeteria for fries and gravy. You could find anything and everything at Glossers.
  - *Linda Williams*

Whatever you wanted, Glosser's had it! I loved the smell of the fresh peanuts when you walked in the store. It's sad to think of all the kids growing up today who will never feel the excitement of Christmas and the awesome window displays of the season and the paintings of Halloween scenes on the windows. Downtown was a magical place that time of year.
  - *Paul Maines*

I will never forget the happiness of my first Christmas working at Glosser's. I was on my own and had no money to buy anything. Then, when Christmas Eve arrived, each clerk received a gift. Excited? You bet I was.
  - *Carol Lutz*

Glosser's was the greatest place I ever worked. Such wonderful memories of working on the floor as a sales clerk and then working in the offices for a buyer. I still remember what my time card number was. I loved the sidewalk sales, too.
- *Debbie Kmett Spisak*

Photo by Robert Jeschonek

One of my best memories happens to be related to Glosser Bros. Every year, the week before Christmas, my sister and I would wait to see which day our dad would pick to do his shopping for our mom. On that day, we would head down to Glosser Bros. and get her a nightgown and a robe. It was the same gift every year. Our next stop was the cafeteria, where we ordered milkshakes for all three of us. Next stop was the candy department, where we got broken pieces of Clark bars. It was forty years ago, but I still remember it like it was yesterday. Life was so much easier then.
- *Vicki Berkey*

When we were growing up, my dad worked at the Gautier Works of Bethlehem Steel. Every payday, he would stop at Glosser's on the way home from work. He would bring assorted white bags of candy and redskin peanuts home with him.
- *Sandy Seth*

8

Connie was in charge of the nut department located just under the stairs on the first floor. When she roasted the nuts down there, you could smell them the minute you walked into the store!

- *Chris Bittner-Italiano*

Every Fall, we had the Anniversary Sale and Old-Fashioned Bargain Days. I loved it so much because I got to work outside on the sidewalk.

- *Paula Katie Buynack Becker*

Of course I remember the Raining Cats and Dogs sales, when they had puppies and kittens available for adoption at the store. And the colored peeps and ducks at Easter. And the bargain basement!

- *Darlene Lipuma*

I remember the comic books that were sold in the tobacco department--5-cent comics without the covers. I used to spend my allowance on those.

- *Barbara Mattes*

Photo by Robert Jeschonek

Chapter 2

We're All Going to Glosser's

What was so special about the Glosser Bros. Department Store? What made the place so unique that dozens of former employees gathered on the 25th anniversary of the store's closing (and, therefore, the permanent loss of their jobs) to celebrate its memory?

As the employees at the reunion agreed, the feeling of being part of a family was a huge part of the Glosser's mystique. The store was owned and operated by the Glosser family, and they took pains to make employees and shoppers feel as if they were all part of the same family.

But there was much more to it than that. Glosser's Department Store was a giant presence in the community, one that filled a host of needs for masses of people and created ties and a shared mythology that outlasted the store itself.

More Than Just a Store

It's not enough to say that Glosser's was the Wal-Mart or shopping mall of its time...though that was certainly true. In cities and towns across the United States, department stores like Glosser's provided one-stop shopping. Instead of trekking all over town from one specialty shop to another in search of various goods, shoppers could find everything from clothing to furnishings to toys to groceries under one roof. They could save time and fuel and energy by doing all their shopping in one place...and they could save money, too, as Glosser's was able to offer low prices by buying in bulk across multiple categories of merchandise.

The one-stop shopping and low prices drew shoppers from Johnstown and its suburbs as well as other communities in the surrounding region. It wasn't unusual for people to drive to Glosser's from Ebensburg, Somerset, Bedford, or beyond to stock up on merchandise and take advantage of deals that they couldn't find at home.

But coming to the Glosser Bros. Department Store was more than a shopping trip or a necessary nuisance. Glosser's was part of a centralized business and cultural district at the heart of people's lives and activities.

This district included department stores, specialty shops, drug stores, banks, barber shops, restaurants, and theaters. Visitors could drive in or take the trolley or bus and spend the day there, doing everything from getting a haircut to seeing a movie to eating lunch to shopping for clothes, toiletries, cosmetics, and groceries. They could see friends and neighbors and get caught up on the latest news and gossip, strengthening social connections.

How is all that different from going to a shopping mall or a big-box plaza today? We have the same centralization of business, dining, culture, and other services...the same opportunities for entertainment and socializing.

But what we *don't* have is the same level of longevity and tradition. The Johnstown Galleria mall opened in 1992, and the Richland Town Center with its Wal-Mart Supercenter opened in 2004. By contrast, the original Glosser Bros. store opened in 1906; the full-blown Glosser's department store took shape in the mid-1920s. So by the 1960s, the Glosser Bros. Store had been in business in one form or another for over fifty years. By the 1980s, the store had been in business for over *seventy* years.

In other words, Glosser's became an *institution,* deeply rooted in the fabric of people's lives. It seemed like it had always been there and always would be. Local calendars were punctuated by its sales and events; it became an inextricable part of family milestones and holidays.

Photo from Glosser Bros. Annual Report, Jan. 1978

Photo courtesy of Ruby Shaffer

The Personal Touch

While the store established itself as an institution, its owners never forgot the importance of the personal touch. From the beginning, they made an effort to treat their employees and customers alike as members of a family. They worked hard to make them feel welcome and appreciated, to give them a personalized shopping and social experience.

As part of this effort, the Glosser family supported many local charitable causes and provided help in times of trouble. During the Great Depression, for example, they often provided clothes, cash, and hot meals to travelers. They gave bags of groceries to local families in need.

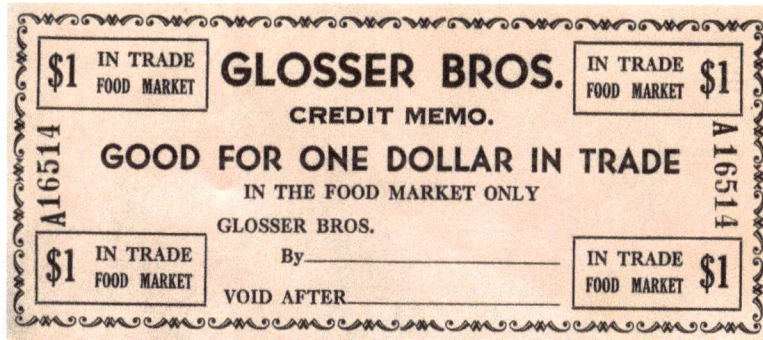

When the banks closed during the Depression, the Glossers continued to cash shoppers' checks and extended credit in the form of in-store currency, or scrip. When shoplifters were caught in the act during hard times, they often went unpunished and were given the items they'd stolen.

People never forgot this legacy of kindness and personal attention. Even decades after the store's closing, they remember what Glosser Bros. did to help them when times were tough. The Glosser family and their store won over the hearts and minds of shoppers, made them feel like they were part of something much more personal than a retail shopping experience and a series of business transactions...and claimed a place in their imaginations, to boot.

Imagining Glosser's

The store's presence as an institution only seemed to grow larger with the passing of years...and it developed an increasingly powerful hold on the public's imagination. Its layout, its ads, its people, its sights and sounds and smells became a part of our collective memory and common dreamscape. Perhaps this was easier to do in the pre-Internet era, when there weren't nearly as many distractions and alternate forms of entertainment as there are now.

Maybe that makes Glosser's even more special, because no brick-and-mortar store in the modern age of limitless distractions--cell phones, the Internet, video games, etc.--would likely be able to seize our imaginations in quite the same way.

Unforgettable Glosserisms

Over the decades, the Glosser Bros. Department Store (or simply "The Store," as the family calls it) loomed as large in local hearts and minds as it did in the downtown landscape. On the day it closed forever--May 25, 1989--it left a vast crater in the collective psyche of Johnstown's people. Nothing would ever fill that hole in quite the same way again, and everyone knew it.

It also left behind a story that we continue to retell to this day, a story of the scenes, songs, images, aromas, and textures of a lost time and place that many of those who experienced it long to revisit.

It seems like the story happened only yesterday when we think of certain unforgettable things that were uniquely Glosser's. We might call them "Glosserisms," and the list might look like this:

- **Glosser Bros. Shopping Bags.** Who can forget the brown-and-white striped shopping bags that so many shoppers carried while trooping out of the store with their purchases?

Photo by Philip Balko

14

Glosser bros

- **Glosser Bros. Logo.** This iconic logo of flowing script text, with or without the stylized flower sprouting out of the letter "G," adorned everything from shopping bags to newspaper ads to delivery trucks.

- **"We're all going to Glosser's..."** Remember the theme song from the TV commercials of the 1960s and 1970s?

- **The Wooden Escalator.** How often did your hand grip the worn rubber rail of the wooden escalator as you rode it up to the second floor?

- **Old-Fashioned Bargain Days.** This sales event included a host of downtown businesses, but Glosser's put its own special spin on it by encouraging employees to dress up in old-fashioned costumes.

- **The Twins.** For many years, the Shaffer twins--Ruth and Ruby--served up snacks and dished out ice cream to hungry customers, always dressing in identical outfits and asking customers the famous question, "And what else?"

- **Roasted Nuts.** During business hours, the smell of roasting peanuts and cashews wafted through the store, emanating from the candy and nut counter on the first floor near the magazine racks and tobacco counter.

All these Glosserisms and more come to mind when we think of the store and its story. They're the things we think of when we think of Glosser's, the things that feel the most familiar to us.

But they're only a *part* of the story. There's so much more to it than most of us know--the kind of vast history that comes to life when a place exists for more than eighty years.

There are so many questions that most of us don't know the answers to, questions that get at the secret heart and little-known facts of a story that's much bigger and more interesting than we ever imagined.

Where did the Glosser family come from? How did they end up in Johnstown? How did they open "The Store?"

When did the store expand? Why was the grocery department located in the basement? How did Glosser Bros. become a publicly traded company on the American Stock Exchange?

What was the store's moment of greatest triumph? Why did it finally close its doors forever? Where did the Glosser family go after that, and where are they now?

Read on, and you'll find out.

16

Memory Department

I remember the candy department and the twins in the cafeteria. Also, the wonderful smell when you walked in the door...and all the windows at Christmas.

- Karen Moore Taleff

Photo by Kasey Hagens

My grandmother used to take me to Glosser's every week on the bus. She used to buy those marshmallow cookies with the jelly inside, and they were really good.

- Arlene Goss

When I went to Joe Johns, we went once a week to Glosser's for the 10-cent special of a Coke and a hot dog.

- Linda Starr O'Brien

Ruth and Ruby Shaffer were the sweetest, kindest people you'd ever want to meet. Some of my fondest memories of Glosser's were my many visits to the cafeteria. Many times, I barely had 50 cents to spend, but I knew I could always go to the counter and get a Coke float for 26 cents and then hang out with my friends at one of the tables before continuing home from school. Almost every day, kids went directly from Joe Johns or Johnstown High to Glosser's Cafeteria before walking home from school. Sometimes, it was so crowded in there that we had to sit on each other's laps. It was THE after school hangout, period.

- Joann Golian Freeman

Photo courtesy of Ruby Shaffer

When I remember Glosser's, my first thought is the smell of the peanut counter. I also remember the check desk where you could check your purchases throughout the day and not have to carry all your bags from department to department. I remember the basement grocery store and the smell of the cheese counter as you went down the steps. Of course I also remember the escalator, but even more than that, I remember the ladies who operated the elevators. As the doors opened to a floor, they would name all the departments on that floor. I also remember the cafeteria and "the twins" who worked at the soda fountain there. I remember buying my wedding gown in the bridal department. Talk about one-stop shopping! We eliminated the department stores and built malls for one-stop shopping but we already had it!

- Thelma Smith

The head of marketing at Glosser's came up with the idea for a Ladies' Day Sale.
During this sale, which was held once a year, each female buyer got to be the president of
Glosser's for the day. When my turn came, I got to participate in commercials for the sale
on radio and TV. Also during my Ladies' Day, Terry Bradshaw and Franco Harris of the
Pittsburgh Steelers came to Glosser Bros. to promote Steelers t-shirts. I got to have lunch
`with them in the Hunt Room restaurant, which was very exciting!

- *Chris Bittner-Italiano*

I still remember the smell of pipe tobacco when I would hang around the comic books across from the tobacco counter. I also remember the water cooler near the elevators and how my mom would take a collapsible metal cup from her purse so I could get a drink.

- *Forrest Batdorf*

Each September, we had a big Anniversary sale for two weeks, which kicked off the Fall selling season and was one of the best sales for our customers among the many that were held throughout the year. The preparation that we, as buyers, put into this event started months in advance and provided our customers with outstanding merchandise at prices that were incomparable anywhere.

- *Jeff Diamond, Glosser Bros. employee 1966-1988 (and son-in-law of Glosser's comptroller Sydney Ossip)*

I worked in the advertising office from 1960 to 1963. Back then, all the illustrations were created with what we called "metal cuts"--metal plates with reverse images burned into them. If we couldn't generate the right picture with metal cuts, I drew it. I ended up being Glosser's first artist, actually, because I could produce good freehand illustrations. Still, everything we published was black and white back then. We had no color in our ads.

- *Linda Hockenberry*

I met my husband, Rick, on the freight elevator at Glosser Bros. in January 1971. We've been married 38 years! We thought the world of all the Glosser Family and will never regret working there!

- *Paula Katie Buynack Becker*

Chapter 3

Roots of the Family "G"

Imagine living in a place where armed Cossacks ride through the streets, looking to cripple or kill you. A place where the non-Jewish peasants sic their dogs on your children. Where the threat of ethnic massacres, or pogroms, constantly hangs over your head. Where your home has a dirt floor, a thatched roof, and no indoor plumbing, and you barely scrape by, selling kerosene, salt, and potato bread in a humble market stall.

Now you know how the Glossers felt before they came to Johnstown...or at least the people who would become the Glossers. We're not sure what last name they had in the Old Country... though members of the family listed the name "Glotzer" on their paperwork when they finally emigrated to America.

Whatever their last name, the husband and wife who were destined to someday become the Glossers of Johnstown were just Wolf Leib and Bessie of the Eastern European town of Antopol, which was part of the Russian Empire.

The Original Glosser Brothers...and Sisters

Did you know that the Glosser brothers of Glosser Bros. Department Store fame all came from the Old Country? There were four of them, the sons of Wolf and Bessie: Nathan, David, Saul, and Sam.

There were three sisters, too: Jennie, Rose, and Bella. And it's safe to say that during their childhoods back in dreary, scary Antopol, neither they nor their brothers ever imagined the prosperous future awaiting them in Johnstown.

Photo courtesy of Ruth Glosser

In the bad old days in Antopol, the kids and their parents were busy just trying to make ends meet...which wasn't going so well.

Often, the family didn't have enough to eat. According to Bella (later Bella Glosser Coppersmith), "At night we used to follow around my mother and keep on saying 'Mom, we're hungry, we're hungry'...and I was always scared and always worried."

As the kids got older, the family's financial situation continued its downward spiral. Two of the girls (Jennie and Rose) were married off, and three of the boys learned trades (Nathan as a tailor, David an apprentice shoemaker, and Saul an apprentice cap maker), but none of it made much difference in the big picture. Business at the family stall was bad, and Wolf was drowning in debt.

Creditors were snapping at his heels, and options were dwindling fast. Bessie was reduced to begging for cash and asking for loans. The future looked increasingly bleak as desperation took hold.

But in the end, it was this very desperation that led to a brighter tomorrow and a classic American success story. If things hadn't gotten so bad, there might never have been a Glosser Bros. Department Store in Johnstown. We might never have had that institution at the heart of our community for eighty years and change.

Because when Wolf bottomed out and realized he had nowhere left to turn, he decided to get out of Antopol. It was the only card he had left to play.

His brother, Moses, had done the same thing before him, leaving Antopol for greener pastures. Now Wolf planned to follow in his footsteps and join Moses in a new country.

The United States of America.

$8.00 in His Pocket

How many of us have some version of the same tale in our family histories? Someone leaves the Old Country (wherever it might be) to escape poverty or persecution or war and comes to America. He or she arrives at Ellis Island (or some other location) with next to nothing, begins a new life in the U.S., and makes enough money to send for the rest of the family.

That was Wolf's story, too. He came to Ellis Island on January 7, 1903 aboard the German ship the S.S. Moltke. According to the ship's manifest, he had a grand total of $8.00 in his possession.

Photos courtesy of Ruth Glosser

And he was alone. He'd left Antopol in the middle of the night, the only way he could escape his creditors--and Bessie and the kids had stayed behind as guarantors that he would repay his debts.

But Wolf wasn't alone for long. His brother-in-law, Schmuel Levine, who lived in New York City, helped him get on his feet. Soon, Wolf was peddling fruit on street corners in New York and sending money home to his creditors.

It wasn't long before one of his sons joined him: Nathan, who left a job in Poland and went to work in a sweatshop in New York. But Nathan and his father weren't together in New York for long.

The first of the Glosser Brothers to arrive in the U.S. was about to become the first to come to Johnstown. But that might not have happened if a certain horse hadn't died at Windber first.

The Horse Died at Windber

Windber was where Nathan Glosser went to visit his Uncle Moses, on a break from working in the New York sweatshop. But Moses would not have been in Windber at all if it hadn't been for the horse.

Moses' journey to Windber had been a convoluted one. He'd fled Antopol to avoid being conscripted in the Russian army. Legend has it he'd dressed as a woman to escape unnoticed on a hay wagon to Bremen, Germany.

After arriving in the U.S., Moses worked in York, Pennsylvania for a while, saving up money to send for his family. When he finally brought his wife and kids over, they settled on a farm in Blossburg, Tioga County.

Eventually, though, they pulled up stakes and headed for Somerset, Pennsylvania, to launch a business selling scrap metal and miners' used rubber boots (which were then turned into automobile tires). Moses had plenty of experience with metals after working as a coppersmith in Europe, so he was a natural for this business.

But Moses and his family never made it to Somerset. Somewhere near Windber, the horse pulling their wagon died, and they could go no further. They set up the business, M. Glosser and Sons, in Windber instead (though it eventually moved to Johnstown).

It was here that Nathan Glosser took the trip that changed his life forever.

Chapter 4

Birth of "The Store"

During Nathan's visit to Windber, he spent time in nearby Johnstown...and something about the place appealed to him. In fact, he liked it well enough to look for work there and found a job as a tailor.

It turned out to be the job of a lifetime, an opportunity that launched a business that would reshape a town and a family forever.

Little did Nathan know, when he went to work as a tailor at Cohen's Laundry-Tailor Shop at 105 Franklin Street, that he would soon own the place.

And that it would be the seed that would someday become the Glosser Bros. Department Store.

The Angel Investor

What kind of downpayment does it take to start a successful future? In Nathan's case, all it took was 200 bucks.

That was the asking price for Mr. Cohen's store. After Nathan had worked for him for a while, Cohen and his wife decided to move to Harrisburg. Cohen liked Nathan and gave him first crack at buying the store for $200.

Nathan knew a good deal when he saw it...but he didn't have the cash. Two-hundred dollars was a lot of money in 1906, and Nathan had been sending most of his paychecks back to his family in Antopol.

Luckily, someone stepped in at just the right time to save the day. Morris Miller, a local businessman who owned Miller's Clothing Store on Main Street, offered to loan Nathan the money...no collateral needed.

They shook hands on it, and the deal was done. Nathan got the $200 and gave it to Cohen, who in turn handed Nathan the keys to the store. The 21-year-old was now the owner of a business, one that was already established and had potential for expansion in a growing town.

Forging a Family Business

From the beginning, Nathan's store--which he called the N. Glosser Store--was all about family...just like the department store it eventually became. It's no accident that over a century later, former employees at the 2014 Glosser's reunion were still talking about the company's dedication to family.

Shortly after buying the store, Nathan brought in his father, Wolf, to work with him. Wolf had left New York City to peddle merchandise in Johnstown with a horse and wagon...but he didn't hesitate to sell them when given a chance to help with the store.

Business kept growing, and Nathan expanded the store's offerings to include second hand clothing. Soon, the place was doing well enough that he could afford to pay for his brother, David, to come to America.

David started out working at Max Weisberg & Son's General Store on Broad Street in Cambria City...but it wasn't long until Nathan hired him to work at the N. Glosser store. With that move, the place was starting to live up to the name it would someday make famous: Glosser Bros.

Now it was just a matter of bringing the other two brothers into the fold.

Photo courtesy of Johnstown Area Heritage Association

Photo courtesy of Ruth Glosser

Completing the Set

The S.S. *Rijndam* arrived at Ellis Island from the port of Rotterdam in the Netherlands on July 9, 1906, carrying the remaining Glosser brothers--15-year-old Saul and 13-year-old Sam. Glosser sister Bella, 9, made the voyage, too...as did mother Bessie, who was 50 by then.

After taking the train from New York to Johnstown, the new arrivals found that their surroundings weren't the only things that had changed. For example, the family's finances had improved; Nathan was able to pay a driver with a wagon to pick them up in style at the train station and take them on a tour of Johnstown.

Thanks to the financial upturn, the family also had a new home waiting for them at 18 River Avenue in the 13th Ward of Johnstown. Unlike the house back in Antopol, this one had wooden floors instead of dirt...and a bathroom inside the house. The place lacked electricity and central heating, but it was still a big step up and a welcome change.

Then there was the change in the family patriarch, Wolf. He had recently become a new man...one with a new name, at least. Wolf Leib Glatzer now went by "Louis Glosser," a new name to commemorate a new beginning with his reunited family in America.

It was the perfect time to celebrate a new start. Now that the Glossers were together (except Jennie and Rose, who'd stayed in Europe with their own husbands and families), and they had a new home and a business on the rise, they could finally put the hardships of the past behind them and focus on their plans for the future.

Now that the four brothers were in town, the stage was set for the next phase of the story.

Welcome to "Glosser Brothers"

Imagine going to school in a place where you don't speak the language. Things could get a little rough, to say the least.

That was how it went for Saul and Sam, the youngest brothers and latest arrivals. They didn't speak much English and were both picked on like crazy. They ended up in one fight after another (though Bella didn't have quite the same trouble). Eventually, they decided enough was enough and dropped out...at which point they went to work at the N. Glosser store.

Saul and Sam scrubbed dirty clothes dropped off for cleaning by local mill workers. It was hard labor but a way to become part of the business, which was growing fast and would soon provide new opportunities for all of them.

In fact, in 1910, Nathan and David bought Jacob Fisher's storeroom across the street, at 118 Franklin Street. They set up a second store location there, as well as a third at 137 Clinton Street.

These new locations went by the same name, one that's still familiar to us over a hundred years later: *Glosser Bros.*

Photo courtesy of Johnstown Area Heritage Association

Memory Department

My grandma Hanzel often spoke of the Glosser boys & their horse drawn wagon selling goods in Cambria City when she was a girl. Ice wagons, too. The Glossers are quite the important family in the story of our city and all of our youthful memories.

- Georganne Hanzel Yurasko

My father, born in 1914, would frequently disappear from the family home near Wood Alley when he was 4 years old or so. When he couldn't be found, my grandmother always headed to Glosser's, which is where she knew she'd find him.

His younger sister Dorothy, born about 1919, got her first job at Glosser's selling ginger snaps. She later became a supervisor for General Telephone, two doors down from Glosser's.

- Marj Fritz

Chapter 5

On the Move and in the Fight

Life had never been sweeter for the Glossers of Johnstown. They were together again after years of separation; they had several thriving businesses and enough money to pay for the necessities of life; and they owned a home complete with amenities they'd never possessed in the Old Country.

Naturally, things couldn't stay the same for long.

For example, Nathan Glosser, the driving force behind the Glosser Brothers businesses, left town and moved to the Bronx. Nathan suffered from asthma, and the air quality in Johnstown made it worse...to the point that he had to get out. Ironically, the very steel industry that boosted the local economy and fueled the success of Glosser Bros. created so much pollution that Nathan could no longer bear to stay in town.

Nathan Glosser

31

Not that the Bronx was without its problems. Soon after Nathan and his family moved into a two-room apartment there, his little son, Gerald, came down with diphtheria.

Nathan, his wife, Fanny, and their kids soon left the Bronx and moved to Detroit, Michigan; they returned to Johnstown eventually, but years had passed by then. The Glosser Bros. businesses were short an original brother until 1920...more than one brother, when all was said and done.

Business Without Nathan

Without Nathan in the mix, the Johnstown businesses might have fizzled... but he'd done such a great job starting them, and his brothers and father worked so hard to keep them going, that the opposite happened.

By 1916, the Glosser Bros. store at 118 Franklin Street had expanded into a second storefront, next door at 120 Franklin. Glosser Bros. expanded its merchandise, too, including women's clothing as well as men's.

Across the street, at 105 Franklin, the cleaning and pressing shop--now known as Louis Glosser and Sons--was doing fine, too. The family did end up closing their third store, the one at 137 Clinton Street...but quickly replaced it with one at 139 Clinton.

Business was great and growing fast, just as Johnstown was growing fast. By 1910, Johnstown was one of the nation's top six steel-producing centers. Between 1880 and 1910, Johnstown's population boomed from 8,000 to over 50,000. In the ten years leading up to 1914, a new post office, city hall, library, railroad station, YMCA, and other structures were added to the city.

There was no reason to expect the upward trend would end anytime soon. All the Glossers had to do was ride the wave and keep providing quality merchandise at reasonable prices.

Though keeping the rest of the brothers from leaving town might have made life a little easier, too.

A One-Eyed Glosser Goes To War

As important as the family businesses were, a historic struggle a world away took precedence. Two Glosser Brothers left Johnstown to fight in World War I...though only the one with the blind left eye got to see any action.

World War I had been raging in Europe since 1914, and the United States entered the conflict in 1917. Saul and Sam got caught up

Saul Glosser

in the patriotic fervor and enlisted...though only one of them made it into the U.S. armed forces. And he *wasn't* the one who ended up in the fight.

Saul was accepted into the U.S. Army and stationed at Fort Lee, Virginia. Later, he was transferred to Fort Drum, New York...but the war ended (in 1918) without him being sent overseas.

Sam, on the other hand, was rejected by the U.S. Army because he was blind in his left eye (the result of a bout of measles in childhood). He couldn't pass the physical; Uncle Sam *didn't* want him.

But the Jewish Legion did.

Organized to fight the Turks in Palestine, the Jewish Legion consisted of five battalions of Jewish volunteers assigned to the Royal Fusiliers of the British Army. Rejected by the U.S. armed forces, Sam enlisted in the Jewish Legion...and made it through the physical by memorizing the eye chart before his optical exam.

For the next few years, retail and Johnstown were far behind him. Sam was stationed in Palestine and Egypt through the end of the war in November 1918. After that, he stayed in Palestine until 1920, serving

Sam Glosser

as part of the British occupying forces. He was discharged on April 20, 1920, by which time he'd received a British War Medal, a Victory Medal, and two blue chevrons.

Not bad for a high school dropout with a retail background who hailed from humble Antopol and Johnstown, Pennsylvania.

Yes, *That* Ben-Gurion

During Sam's tour of duty in Palestine, he traveled extensively, experiencing the country that would one day be part of Israel. He also got to know many Jews who were serving or settling in the region, including his future wife, Pearl Apter...and a man who would someday be instrumental in the formation of the Jewish state: David Ben-Gurion.

Sam and Ben-Gurion stood guard duty together many times; according to Glosser family legend, they had been known to share a tent and became good friends. Ben-Gurion even attended Sam's wedding in 1919.

Years later, Ben-Gurion became Israel's founding father. He helped to write the new nation's Declaration of Independence and was the first to sign it. He also led Israel during the 1948 Arab-Israeli War and became Israel's first prime minister.

Photos on both pages courtesy of Ruth Glosser

Sam and Pearl Glosser's Wedding
Rehovot, Palestine, Feb. 20, 1919

Sam and Pearl Glosser with infant daughter, Freda
Jaffa, Palestine, Feb. 20, 1919

As for Sam, he and Pearl left Palestine in 1920, seven months after the birth of their daughter, Freda. Their plans were not quite so grand as Ben-Gurion's, their destination not so embattled.

Their ship, the S.S. *Philadelphia*, took them to the U.S. And the train they boarded in New York City took them to Johnstown, where they went to live on Sherman Street in Kernville.

Finally, Sam was back in town--and back in business--with his brothers, David and Saul, and his father, Louis. Nathan returned from Detroit that year, too, reuniting all four Glosser Brothers.

It was a good thing, too, because business was still booming. The family needed all the help they could get to meet demand and power the expansion that now seemed increasingly inevitable.

Chapter 6

Ill Repute on the Third Floor?

They say it isn't over until the fat lady sings. In the case of the Glosser Bros. Department Store, things didn't really get off the ground until the fat lady stopped singing for good.

The building we've all come to know as the Glosser Building, the one that housed the department store for so many years, stands on a site that was once occupied by the Johnstown Opera House.

Johnstown Opera House

Inside the Johnstown Opera House (courtesy of BeeMark Publications

The Opera House went up in flames in 1903, then was replaced by a new structure known as the Ellis Building.

Ellis Building (courtesy of Johnstown Area Heritage Association)

In 1910, it was renamed the Franklin Building.

It was this building that housed the central location of the Glosser family's core business, the one that spanned 118-120 Franklin Street. And in 1917, that location expanded to include another storefront. The Glosser family's takeover of the Franklin Building, which someday would be theirs in its entirety, was well underway.

Franklin Building (courtesy of Johnstown Area Heritage Association)

In the meantime, as of 1917, the place was still an amalgamation of enterprises. In addition to the Glossers' storefronts and storerooms, the first floor included a piano store, a meat market, and a Wells Fargo office. The second floor housed phone company and coal mine offices. And on the third floor...

The third floor of what would someday become the Glosser Bros. Department Store featured a house of ill repute. That's right; the third floor was sectioned off into apartments where certain services were provided for a fee. (At least according to word of mouth from certain sources...)

It was an interesting configuration for our dear old Glosser Building... albeit one that wasn't destined to stay in place for long.

Because the takeover of the building was about to shift into high gear.

100% Glosser

The early 1920s were the best times yet for the Glosser businesses. Sales continued to grow, and the upward trend showed no signs of slowing or stopping.

Clearly, the time was right to grow the business. Striking while the iron was hot could lead to big rewards down the line.

And the Glossers didn't hesitate to capitalize on their success. During the early '20s, they expanded the core business from men's and women's clothing to a little of everything. They converted Glosser Bros. to a complete department store, leasing the space to house it in the Franklin Building.

By August 1921, the Glossers were renting the entire first floor. At that point, the family started advertising their growing store as "The Largest One-Floor Store Between Pittsburgh and Harrisburg."

Courtesy of Johnstown Area Heritage Association

Over the next two years, The Store expanded to occupy four floors of the building...and by 1923, the firm had filled the entire building. Its full interior, including the basement, was now 100% Glosser.

The piano store, the offices, even the house of ill repute were pushed out, and the space converted to retail sales. The building was all about the Glossers now.

And further expansion was in the wind. Shortly after taking over the Franklin Building, the Glossers built a small addition to the original structure. The new building was approximately 60 feet square and was attached to the rear of the Franklin Building, along the alley. This addition was built to house the freight elevator, which was needed to take incoming merchandise to the fifth floor for pricing and distribution throughout The Store. The addition also provided space for the men's suit department, the boys' department, and employee and public bathrooms.

Rear of the Glosser Building, 2014, with the "small addition" at center.
(Photo by Robert Jeschonek)

Another expansion had its roots in October 1925, when the Glosser brothers bought a piece of property on the corner of Franklin and Washington Streets. The family planned to use this 128 x 66 square foot lot for a new building that would be located across Good Alley from the rear of the Franklin Building.

Then there was the Parkview Building on Locust Street and the lot behind it, which the Glossers also bought. They tore down the Parkview and started construction soon thereafter on a new five-story addition between the Franklin Building and the offices of the Johnstown Tribune newspaper.

The pace of change and expansion was breathtaking. With so much growth in so short a time, the age of the Glosser Bros. Department Store had begun.

Grocery Store Fever

As the Glossers grew the store, they made local history, of course...but they also made history on a *national* level. In 1916, the family opened the *Glosserteria*, the first grocery store located inside a department store (or one of the first) in the U.S.

The Glosserteria was also unique in that it was one of the earliest self-serve supermarkets in the U.S. Inspired by a similar setup at a Piggly Wiggly market in the South, David Glosser decided the concept might work well in Johnstown, too...and it did.

The Glosserteria only occupied a few hundred square feet on the first floor of The Store, but its impact was powerful. Since customers could select and carry their own groceries to the checkout, fewer employees were needed, reducing labor costs and enabling the Glossers to charge lower prices.

Photo courtesy of Bill Glosser

As a self-serve facility and a grocery market within a department store, the Glosserteria served as the template for other stores elsewhere and helped change the landscape of grocery sales in the U.S. forever. Ironically, it was a direct ancestor of supermarkets and supermarket/department store chains like Giant Eagle and Wal-Mart that eventually helped put the Glosser Bros. company out of business.

Photo courtesy of Bill Glosser

But for a long time, the Glosserteria was a beloved innovation and yet another boost to The Store. Its success set the standard for later growth in the grocery category, in fact. In decades to come, supermarkets would be a key aspect of Glosser's business plan, a plan that would bring the company spectacular success and recognition.

It all started with the Glosserteria in 1916, the product of a vision and a family determined to make it a reality. Sometimes it seemed like they could do anything they put their minds to.

Even bringing the rest of the family back from Hell itself.

Return of the Sisters

Battles raging in the streets. Soldiers torn apart by gunfire and explosives. Houses burned to the ground in scorched-Earth actions by retreating troops.

These were some of the horrors that became commonplace during World War I in Antopol. The village was at the heart of a struggle for regional control between the Russians, Germans, and Poles...with the poor villagers caught in the middle.

That included the two Glosser sisters who had stayed behind when the rest of the family fled the Old Country. Rose and Jennie--Rose Weisman and Jennie Ossip by marriage--lived through years of pure Hell back in Antopol, struggling to survive with their husbands and children.

Photos courtesy of Ruth Glosser

They lived in constant fear and desperation as the Russians and Germans took turns controlling the village. When scorched-Earth fires burned down the Weismans' house, they ended up sharing the Ossips' house, crammed together in that one humble dwelling.

Always, all of them lived on a razor's edge, a hair's breadth away from disaster. Even after the war ended, they still subsisted in deplorable conditions in the war-ravaged landscape of Eastern Europe.

Then, Rose and Jennie and their families finally got out. The Weismans came to Johnstown first, in the spring of 1920, and could hardly believe how wonderful it was compared to Antopol. The Ossips came a little later, in August 1921, and had a similar reaction.

At last, all the Glosser brothers and sisters--all the children of Louis and Bessie--were reunited in Johnstown. Most importantly, they had with them the next generation of Glossers (and Weismans and Ossips), who would carry The Store forward and build on the foundation that their parents had laid.

Memory Department

At age 5, I ate at the lunch counter with my Mom. It never failed: after we finished, my mom would unhook her purse from the cool little portable, folding counter-purse hook she had, remove a dainty hankie, spit on it, and wash my face. Even at that age, I was embarrassed, but it was the price I paid for a burger or other treat. My other favorite Glosser Bros. memory is, finally being old enough to go downtown by myself, including a trip up the escalators and up and down the aisles, looking at all the stuff. Were the floors wooden? I vaguely remember the sound of many feet on wood.

- Daniel Lions-Den

My Mom worked at Glosser's, and she always told a story of her first day there. They were having one of their sales, and prior to opening the doors, the managers walked the main floor and told all the sales clerks to get behind their counters. Mom was working a counter where men's jeans were on sale. She said they unlocked the doors, and women stampeded in. During the sale, two women tussled over one pair of jeans, each holding onto one leg of the jeans. Another lady asked Mom if the jeans on the table were durable. Mom said she looked at the two women fighting over the jeans and looked at the lady asking the question and said, "Ma'am, if they hold up through this sale, they'll hold up for anything else."

- Thelma Smith

I remember when I was a little girl, my father used to take me to the store on Sundays, when it was closed to the public. He let me get free candy from the candy counter and visit the toy department, looking at all the toys. It was great fun getting that candy and seeing all the toys, but what I loved the most was spending time with my dad in that very special place.

-*Freda Glosser*

What I remember most was going shopping with my mother and grandmother in the grocery section in the basement. My grandmother was German and loved their pickled pig feet in a huge jar on top of the meat counter. They'd sell her one, and she'd eat it right there. Also, I remember Aunt Jemima walking around demonstrating her Pancake Mix & Syrup. I also liked the area where you could leave your bags, and they would give you a number for the shelf your bags were put in. Never was anything missing when you returned for them. They didn't charge you for it, either. I would love to have Glossers back in a heartbeat.

- *Romaine Ringler Moran*

Photo courtesy of Bill Glosser

Chapter 7

Let's Not Talk About Pittsburgh

Sometimes it seemed like the Glossers could do anything they put their minds to. Other times...not so much.

For example, did you know there was once an honest-to-goodness Glosser Bros. Department Store in downtown Pittsburgh?

What's that, you say? Never heard of it?

Case in point.

It must have seemed like a safe bet at the time. By 1926, the Johnstown store was going like gangbusters. Clearly, the Glosser brothers had developed a successful retailing formula. And if that formula worked in Johnstown, chances were good it would work elsewhere, too, right?

Right?

Glossers Blocked

Convinced they were making a sound business decision, the family moved forward with Operation Pittsburgh. They found and leased a location at 533-535 Penn Avenue. They made all the necessary arrangements, remodeled the interior and exterior, and stocked and staffed the store. George Ossip, Jennie's son, was given the job of managing the place.

On April 19, 1926, the Glosser Bros. Department Store opened for business on Penn Avenue in downtown Pittsburgh, and curious shoppers poured through the doors. The Glosser magic that had conjured up such great results in Johnstown cast its spell in a first-ever big city location. There was every reason to think the outcome would be the same.

Photo courtesy of Bill Glosser

Except for one little thing...one problem that couldn't be abracadabra'd away.

The local newspapers wouldn't run Glosser Bros. advertising. They flat-out refused, and no amount of money would change their minds.

The other retailers in town had put the squeeze on the papers, threatening to pull their own ads if Glosser Bros. ads made it into print. It was a cutthroat tactic to freeze out the competition...and it worked.

Without advertising, many Pittsburgh shoppers were barely aware of the new store's existence. They had no way of knowing what items were on sale in any given week. Glosser Bros. could have the best bargains and highest quality merchandise in town, and it wouldn't make any difference if shoppers weren't aware of them.

No strategy could overcome this handicap. Locked out of newspaper advertising, Glosser Bros. could make no headway in Pittsburgh. The new store sank like a stone and quickly closed.

Glossered Over?

It was a stinging defeat. The new store could have led to additional expansion in other cities. Glosser Bros. could have grown to become a national department store chain along the lines of Macy's or Marshall Field or J.C. Penney. Now, that dream was over.

But only temporarily. Eventually, it came back around again in a new and different configuration...and this time, the Glosser Bros. company did *not* fail.

The new venture didn't launch until 1962, but it was a solid success. By 1976, there were fourteen new stores across Western Pennsylvania, Maryland, and West Virginia. The new stores boosted the company's sales from $8,213,000 in 1962 to $103,198,000 in the fiscal year ending January 31, 1976.

By the late 1980s, there were 23 of these new stores, carrying the Glosser Bros. magic across five states. So in the end, the Glossers' vision of expansion and success beyond Johnstown came to fruition after all. Perhaps it took longer than expected, but it still came to pass. And some of the stores in the Glosser Brothers' new chain were even located in the Pittsburgh area.

It was true that there was never again a Glosser Bros. Department Store in Pittsburgh. But there *were* stores owned and operated by the Glosser Bros. company.

They were called *Gee Bee* stores.

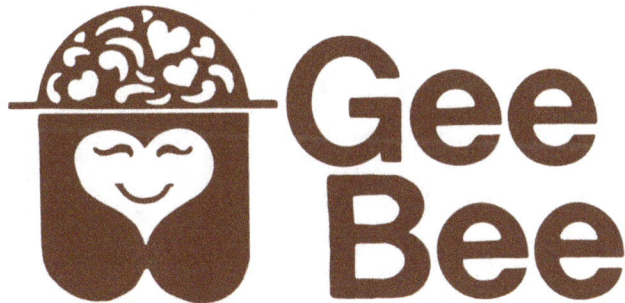

GLOSSER'S BARGAIN CIRCUS

Chapter 8

Brother, Can You Spare a Monkey?

Just imagine: Your family's department store company is going great guns. (Let's not talk about Pittsburgh.) Business keeps getting better and better; the Johnstown store gets bigger and bigger. In 1927, The Store advertises "five floors, 3 modern elevators, 71 departments, and 200 employees." The new basement supermarket is going great guns, bringing in shoppers in droves. A state-of-the art pneumatic tube system whisks money and sales slips through the store to cashiers, then zips change back to customers lickety-split, in a dizzying ballet of modern technology.

Your family's store even features an on-site *optometrist*, of all things. Dr. Rysky has an office on the stairway landing between the first floor and the second (extended back from the flow of pedestrian traffic on a platform supported by special columns). Dr. Rysky's eye chart hangs out over the ground floor, in fact, so folks below can enjoy the sight of eye exams in progress.

You sponsor parades and hold big sales events like the Bargain Circus, where you give away *ponies* to lucky winners. Your motto is "Everybody's Store," and it seems to be true. People flock to your establishment, and the cash registers just keep ringing.

The American dream is within reach. Another immigrant family, starting with next to nothing, has achieved success and made a positive impact on the community.

By the time family patriarch Louis (Wolf Leib) Glosser dies on July 31, 1927, he has seen the enterprise thrive beyond anything he imagined back in Antopol. When his wife, Bessie, dies on October 18, 1929, the company has risen to even greater heights.

Then *boom!* Like a thunderclap heard 'round the world, the U.S. stock market crashes on October 29, 1929. It hardly seems possible after the wild ride of the Roaring Twenties...but a Great Depression descends over the land like a soul-sucking shadow.

What do you do? Allow fear to control your thinking? Focus on cutting corners and avoiding risk as you desperately try to keep your business above water?

Or, having weathered hard times before (remember Antopol?), do you pull out the stops and keep the show going with sheer determination, ingenuity, and generosity?

If you were a Glosser in Johnstown in the 1930s, you chose the latter.

So how did *that* work out for you?

The Greatest Show in Johnstown

How could the Glosser brothers keep sales strong at a time when disposable income had bottomed out?

They put on a show. Throughout the 1930s, the family mounted a series of promotional events that got shoppers' attention and took their minds off the Depression.

Entertainment was almost as important as pricing in those dire times; people needed diversions to survive. Why else would the 1930s become known as the golden age of both Hollywood *and* old time radio? People craved activities that gave them a chance to laugh, socialize, and let off steam...without spending a lot of money.

The Glosser Bros. company set out to give them just that. In the process, The Store became the greatest show in Johnstown.

For example, Glosser Bros. sponsored a series of town dances.

Photo courtesy of Bill Glosser

For 25 cents, folks could dance to their hearts' content at a Johnstown venue known as the Auditorium. The crowds could get pretty big, with a record attendance of 4,500 at one such event.

Then there were the parades, at least one a year, in conjunction with the Bargain Circus and other sales. People came from all over, filling the sidewalks to watch and listen to the spectacle of colorfully costumed performers and musicians marching up Main Street to celebrate the sales at Glosser's.

The yearly Anniversary Sale was always a big deal, the biggest of the year...and the Glossers made sure everyone who wanted to get there could make it. If you couldn't afford a trolley pass, no problem. Glosser Bros. issued free passes to all customers riding in from surrounding neighborhoods. People loved it and came in droves.

Giveaways continued to attract crowds, too...though ponies weren't the prizes anymore. Instead of horseflesh, Glosser Bros. gave away *horsepower*, in the form of automobiles. In 1933, for example, Glosser Bros. chanced off a new Chevrolet; a massive crowd turned out for the drawing at the store on June 28, waiting excitedly to learn who would drive away in the car.

The car giveaway was such a popular promotion that the Glossers brought it back year after year. Long after the 1930s, mobs of people still swarmed The Store on drawing day, waiting to see who the winner would be...and doing plenty of shopping while they were there.

It's Teething Biscuit in the Home Stretch

Another contest that became an annual tradition was Glosser Bros.' Baby Derby, which started in 1931. Every year, Glosser's gave a complete layette set to the first baby born in the region in the new year. Special awards were also given to twins born on New Year's Day, whether or not they were the first babies across the "finish line."

The first Baby Derby winner was Dorothy Helen Urban, daughter of Mr. and Mrs. Francis Urban of Jerome. The first twins to crawl away with the special prize were Jeannie Marie and Joan Martha Rucosky of 153 Marshall Avenue in Johnstown. Later winners came from as far afield as Hastings, Homer City, Lilly, Carrolltown, and Latrobe.

Like so many Glosser Bros. promotions and events, people loved it. The Baby Derby became a longtime annual tradition...unlike the ill-fated Monkey Show.

Monkeys Gone Wild!

File this one under "It seemed like a good idea at the time."

You can just imagine the planning session: "Folks love monkeys, don't they?" "Yes, they do." "So let's get a bunch of monkeys and put them in one of our display windows on Locust Street." "Great idea! They'll cause a sensation! What could possibly go wrong?"

The answer to that question, of course, is "Everything."

The monkeys created a sensation, all right...just not the way they were supposed to.

At first, the Glosser Bros. Monkey Show went off without a hitch. Passersby swarmed the window, watching the monkeys at play, laughing at their antics. Children, especially, were drawn to the little primates behind the glass as they jumped and swung and chattered. It was more fun than a barrel of...*you* know.

At least until the glass broke.

No one quite remembers if human or monkey broke the window, and in the end it didn't matter. As bystanders scrambled to get out of the way, the monkeys sprang from the display area and headed straight for Central Park.

The next thing anyone knew, the trees in Central Park were full of screeching monkeys.

For a while, the park was like a wild jungle. Chaos reigned as the monkeys capered on the grass and leaped from branch to branch and tree to tree. It might have been the craziest, most surreal scene that anyone has ever witnessed in Central Park, before or since.

Then, the Johnstown police showed up. The scene got even crazier as the cops chased the monkeys through the park with nets, trying to round them up.

But in the end, the police got every last of one of them. The monkeys were returned to their cages; their Great Escape was over.

The next day, the Glossers returned the animals to the folks who'd supplied them...and made a promise that they kept for the rest of The Store's lifetime.

No more monkey business at Glosser Bros. Department Store. Ever!

But Was The Chickenfeed Free, Too?

On the other hand, rabbits and chicks were still fair game...and the Glosser brothers made them the stars of their own animal-kingdom giveaways.

In those days, little boys wore suits for special occasions. Around Easter time, Glosser's gave away a rabbit to anyone who bought a suit in the boys' clothing department.

Photos by Philip Balko

Glosser's also gave out free chicks to children who came to The Store with their parents at Easter. The baby chickens were kept in an incubator on the first floor. Passing customers heard the chicks chirping and stopped to admire the cute, fluffy creatures peeping up at them.

According to Fred Glosser, the chicks had a practical purpose, as well. "Back then, lots of people kept chickens in their back yards and got fresh eggs from them. Taking home one of our chicks provided folks with a free future egg-layer...a nice bonus during the hard times of the '30s."

Out-Glossering the Glossers

From circus parades to car giveaways to baby derbies to free chicks, the Glosser brothers were masters of promotional gimmicks in the 1930s. The stream of special events succeeded even when they failed (monkeys, anyone?), getting attention and boosting awareness of The Store. And that built sales in an age of extreme economic distress.

But the ever more outrageous promotions forced the Glossers to work harder to top themselves. They constantly had to raise the bar to ensure they dominated the local marketplace.

Fortunately, rising to the challenge was not a problem for these retail ringmasters. They excelled at showmanship, whether the spotlight was on Chevys or ponies or monkeys.

Though the biggest party of the 1930s had nothing to do with any of those things. And no event before or after could ever quite compare to the spectacle of that one sunny day in November of 1931.

GLOSSER'S ALL-STARS

FRED GLOSSER

In 1929, when Fred Glosser was five years old, the guys in the basement used to put him in the paper baler. He had the best time ever jumping up and down on the piles of paper and cardboard thrown down the trash chute from the upper floors, compressing it so the guys could bind it into bales for disposal.

It was Fred's first job in a career at the Glosser Bros. company that would last all the way until his retirement in January 1986 (with only a short absence during a stint in the Army during World War II).

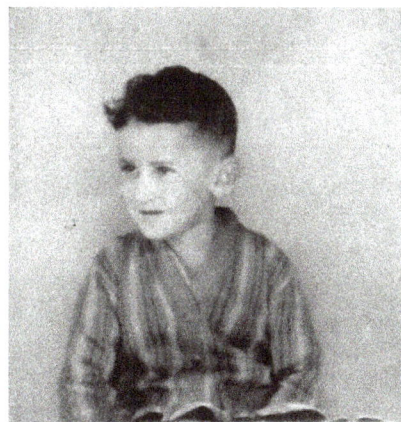

Fred was born in 1924, the youngest of three children of Sam, one of the original Glosser brothers. At the tender age of five, he worked around The Store, picking up scattered paper and cardboard left on the floor by sales associates as well as helping the crew in the basement flatten it for baling.

Photos courtesy of Fred Glosser

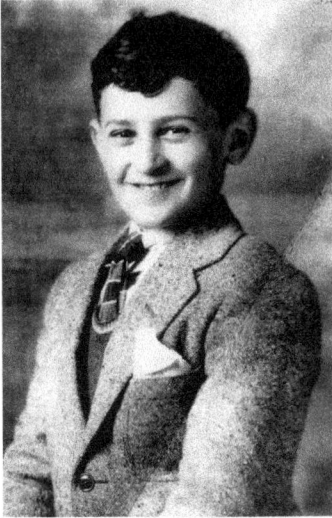

In the years that followed, Fred did various odd jobs around The Store, helping out wherever he was needed. "I did everything from painting to cleaning toilets," says Fred. "There wasn't anything I didn't do. There never was anyone in the store who did everything that I did."

He left in 1943 and spent two years in the army, much of it at Camp Claiborne, Louisiana, a training facility where he taught diesel engine mechanics.

Returning to Johnstown in 1945, he again did an assortment of maintenance-related jobs at Glosser's, then went to work as a stock boy. Eventually, he moved up to work in the notions department, where he was trained by Mr. Bill Wenky. "Bill really knew the retail business, knew how to handle people and get things done. He took me under his wing," says Fred.

A few years later, Fred applied what he'd learned to a new position managing the Infants and Children Up To Age 6 department. But his biggest and most satisfying challenge came in 1962, when Glosser Bros. launched the Gee Bee stores.

Photos courtesy of Fred Glosser

Fred was put in charge of construction and maintenance for the new stores, which eventually numbered 23. All aspects of the stores--everything from fixtures to lighting to cleaning--came under his supervision.

He did the same work for the Dollar Bargain stores, which were also part of

Photo from Glosser Bros. Annual Report, Feb. 1975

Glosser Bros. Inc. and expanded to 44 locations. All storage and shipping for Gee Bee and Dollar Bargain were under Fred's authority, too, including three warehouses and a fleet of 10 trucks and 12 trailers.

These days, Fred lives in Austin, Texas and enjoys working on carpentry and metal sculpture, among other things. But he'll always be a Glosser's All-Star for his key role in building, launching, and maintaining the Gee Bee and Dollar Bargain stores.

Photo courtesy of Fred Glosser

Monday, August 30, 1954   THE TRIBUNE-DEMOCRAT—JOHNSTOWN, PA.   Page 7

Lots of Summer Ahead for You . . . But It's the End of the Season for Us . . . . Final Reductions on Hundreds of Still Wearable Summer Needs. Come Early Tuesday . . . . Buy for Back - to - School Wear!

We're sorry, but no mail or phone orders. No layaways. All sales final.

NOTE:

GLOSSER BROS. *Famous For Savings*

FINAL REDUCTIONS ON ALL 'LEFT-OVERS'

Everything Must Go!

Ladies' Undies

1.98 Rayon Gowns ... 1.09
1.98 Acetate Slips ... 1.09
1.98 Half Slips ... 1.09
3.98 Slips and Gowns ... 2.59
Robes and Dusters ... 3.99

Ladies' Sportswear

Bermuda Shorts ... $1
Up to 3.98 Blouses ... $1
To 7.95 Swim Suits ... $2
To $25 Raincoats ... $13
Summer Blouses ... $1

Hosiery Dept.

Knee-High Nylons ... 49c
White Bobby Socks ... 24c
Boys' Anklets ... 29c
Ladies' Nylon Hose ... 49c

Girls' Dept.

1.99 Dungarees ... 1.47
Plaid Blouses ... $1
2.29 Cotton Slips ... $1

Men's Dress Furnishings

2.98 Summer Pajamas ... 1.59
Summer Robes ... $2
Men's Straw Hats ... 50c
To 1.95 Sport Hats ... $1
To 1.95 Playshirts ... 35c
To 7.50 Felt Hats ... $3

Men's Work Clothes Dept.

To 3.99 Shirts ... 1.44
To 2.39 Dungarees ... 1.59
To 3.49 Pants ... 1.99

Men's, Children's Shoe Dept.

Sneaker Oxfords ... $1
Children's Sandals ... 1.37
Men's to 4.99 Casual Oxfords ... 1.99

400 Ladies' BETTER DRESSES
Values 8.80 to 12.95. 2 Groups—Reduced to
$3 $5
Special Group! ... $6

Boys' Dept.
Nylon Sport Shirts ... 77c
Washable Play Togs ... 39c
To 2.95 Swim Trunks ... $1
To 3.49 Longies ... 1.39
To 4.95 Jackets ... 2.49
Straw Hats ... 29c
Sweatshirts ... 69c
To 3.95 Robes ... 1.69

Main Floor Jewelry and Dress Accessories

1.98 Handbags ... 69c
To 3.98 Wool Stoles ... $1
1.98 Crepe Blouses ... 53c
To 1.98 Babushkas ... 48c
$1 Leather Belts ... 48c
50c Handkerchiefs ... 18c
15c Handkerchiefs ... 8c
2.98 Umbrellas ... 1.69
To 1.98 Jewelry ... 98c
$5 Sun Glasses ... $1
To 35c Table Silver ... 16c
To 1.50 Gloves ... 39c
To 3.98 Handbags ... $1

MEN!
They Must Go Now!
250 Tropical and Year-Round Suits
21.50 to $25 Values Now Reduced to
$10

Women's, Teens' SHOE DEPT.

Huskie Sports
Regularly 5.95 ... 3.99
Sandler-of-Boston Sports
To 8.95 Values ... 4.99
Famous Make Dress Shoes
Regularly 7.95 ... $2
Famous Make Arch Casuals
Regularly 5.95 ... $2
Summer Play Shoes
Regularly 2.99 ... $1
2.99 MOCCASINS ... 1.99

Out They Go! Less Than Makers' Wholesale Cost

50 LADIES' 32.95 to 69.95 SPRING COATS $15 & $20

100 Ladies' 19.95 to 39.95 Famous Makers TOPPERS $10 Sacrifice Low Price

15 Ladies' $25 to 49.95 SUMMER SUITS Drastically Reduced $10 & $15

12 Faille Coats Were 16.95 Fully lined Navy and black Sizes 10 to 18 $10

TOTS' DEPT.
P.J.'s AND GOWNS ... 57c
1.50 DRESSES ... 57c
SUMMER PLAY TOGS — ½-PRICE
1.49 JACKETS ... $1
To 1.99 SLIPS ... 53c

Budget Dress Dept.
400 Ladies' to 5.95 SUMMER DRESSES 1.58
To 7.49 UNIFORMS ... $3
88c COTTON APRONS ... 39c

YARD GOODS and DOMESTICS DEPT.
WINDOW AWNINGS $2
ROLL-UP AWNINGS
PORCH AWNINGS
30-In. WIDE VALANCE ... 59c
PLISSE BEDSPREADS ... 2.99
PUCKERED NYLON ... 49c
COTTON PIECE GOODS ... 29c
PATCHPRINT QUILTS ... 4.99

NOTION DEPT.

19.95 CHILDREN'S PLAY GYMS $10
20" BICYCLES ... $20

Only 10! 5-Pc. Dinette Sets
Values to 79.50 Reduced to $33
FIBER PORCH RUGS
SUMMER FURNITURE
EXTRA SPECIAL!

12 Only ADMIRAL CLOCK RADIOS 19.99

ROOM-LOT WALL PAPER 1.88

Paint Roller, Tray Set 1.17
45-Lb. Roll Roofing 1.97

GLOSSER BROS. *Famous for Savings*

Nationally-Known Electric Fans
REG. 3.95, 8-INCH NON-OSCILLATING ... NOW 3.44
REG. 10.95, 10-INCH OSCILLATING ... 7.88
REG. 17.95, 12-INCH ... NOW 10.80
REG. 29.95, 12-INCH OSCILLATING ... $18
REG. TANG CABINET TYPE ... $21
REG. FAN LABOR TWIN TYPE ... NOW $45

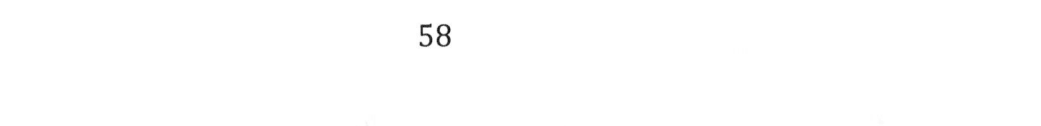

Chapter 9

Rock Star Glosser's

Imagine Wal-Mart constructing an addition to its local store. Would *thousands* of people flock to the grand opening of the addition? Would dignitaries from across the state arrive to help christen the expanded store?

Unlikely, perhaps? Say Wal-Mart sweetens the pot and sponsors a parade. Maybe they throw in some free food, too. What are the chances that *thousands* of people will show up for the celebration?

Somewhere between zero and zilch, right? Times have changed. As much as people like free food and fanfare, it's still just Wal-Mart, isn't it? And Wal-Marts are everywhere, aren't they? The emotional attachment just isn't there for many of us. Maybe if a rock star or celebrity showed up, crowds would follow.

But the Glosser Bros. Department Store was another story in 1931. Back then, for all intents and purposes, Glosser Bros. *was* a rock star.

But Would There Be Crowd Surfing?

It was like Springsteen (or McCartney or Jagger) was coming to town. As soon as the show was announced, excitement raged through the community. Everyone who was anyone made plans to go.

Because this was *big*. In the world of Johnstown in 1931, this was *huge*.

The grand opening of the brand new addition to the Glosser Bros. Department Store was set for November 17, and a good time would be had by all. No one else in town, it's safe to say, scheduled much of anything important that day. Glosser's competitors, like Penn Traffic, might not have expected their biggest crowds of the year, either.

Because everyone was singing the same song: *We're all going to Glosser's.*

59

Dial It Up to "11"

Thousands of people packed the streets of Johnstown on November 17, 1931, roaring with excitement as the festivities got underway.

The Store was decked out for the occasion, of course. The first-floor windows of the main building along Locust Street were bursting with floral displays. And the addition itself gleamed in the sunlight, polished and pristine in its newborn glory.

It stood between the Franklin Building and the *Johnstown Tribune* Building, on the former site of the Parkview Building. The Glosser family had bought the property in the mid-20s and set to work soon thereafter with demolition and new construction...always with this end result in mind. This addition.

Now here it stood, solid and real. Because of it, The Store had roughly doubled in size. Even the Stock Market crash and the onset of the Great Depression hadn't stopped the Glosser Bros. Company from taking the next step in its evolution.

The party was well-deserved, and everyone seemed to feel it.

Photo courtesy of Bill Glosser

Photo courtesy of Johnstown Area Heritage Association

Can I Get an Amen?

Driving through town must have been impossible that day. There was a big parade through town, complete with floats and marching bands. Wall-to-wall spectators mobbed the sidewalks and streets, massing around The Store and elsewhere.

Ceremonies at the new addition on Locust Street and Point Stadium took on a religious fervor. The crowd cheered and applauded as VIPs gave rousing speeches to mark the occasion.

Pennsylvania's Lieutenant Governor, E.C. Shannon, offered up inspirational remarks. So did Judge J.H. McCann. Nathan Glosser presented the key to The Store to Johnstown Mayor O.W. Saylor.

And the crowd loved it. The carnival atmosphere helped them forget their troubles for a little while. The Glossers gave them a big, free show, complete with free food and entertainment, and it was just what they needed.

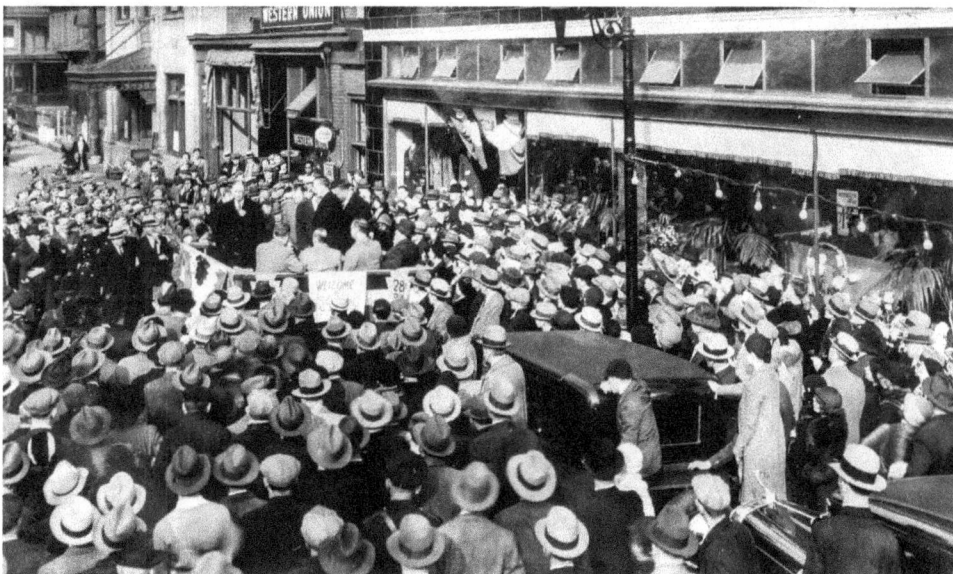

Photo courtesy of Johnstown Area Heritage Association

A Long Way from Antopol

It was what the Glossers needed, too--and not just in terms of promoting the store and goosing sales in difficult economic times. The party was a validation of all their accomplishments, a milestone in their personal rags-to-riches story.

They had come a long way from that single storefront on Franklin Street in 1906. They had come even further from that rundown market stall in impoverished Antopol.

Photos courtesy of Johnstown Area Heritage Association

They had built something new and powerful, carved out a niche in a competitive economy, and paved the way for a brighter future for themselves and their descendants.

And thousands of people turned out to support them and their business. Huge crowds showered them with appreciation and approval. Dignitaries came to give their blessings and curry favor.

And yet...

And yet, there was still an undercurrent that always made its presence felt. Because when it came to being Jewish in America, it seemed that some things never really changed.

Photos courtesy of Johnstown Area Heritage Association

GRAND OPENING PICTURE OF THE EMPLOYEES OF
··· The GREATER GLOSSER STORE ··· ···
··· NOV. 17, 1931 ···

Photo courtesy of Johnstown Area Heritage Association

Chapter 10
Grocery Gold Rush

Once the new addition had been opened, the pieces were in place for the next stage in the development of Glosser Bros.

For this stage, the family set their sights on a part of The Store that had been successful and was showing tremendous potential: the Glosserteria grocery store.

The Glosserteria had turned out to be a bright spot on the balance sheet...so bright that the family decided to expand it. This meant they would have to move it to a new location in The Store, however, as the original first-floor space did not allow for expansion.

After considering the situation at length, the Glossers settled on the perfect location, a place with enough room to accommodate the enlarged supermarket: the basement of the new addition.

But could a basement supermarket possibly succeed? Would shoppers be willing to put up with the inconvenience of hauling their groceries upstairs? Would the Glosserteria's sales continue to grow, or would they wilt and wither away?

There was only one way to find out.

The Underground Supermarket

In 1927, the Glossers bit the bullet and moved the Glosserteria to the basement of the new addition, expanding it significantly in the process.

Meyer Silberstein, head of the company's grocery department (and a son-in-law of Nathan Glosser) spearheaded the effort. Meyer and the other Glosser Bros. executives did everything they could to enhance the new supermarket's appeal, from installing shiny new fixtures, display cases, and checkout stands (located on the first floor) with state-of-the-art cash registers to hiring a small army of new employees to stock the shelves and ring up purchases.

Meyer and his colleagues also set up a meat department on the first floor. The meat department, for all intents and purposes, was an extension of the supermarket, sharing walk-in freezer and cooler space in the basement.

In addition to the obvious physical improvements, Meyer and the rest of the Glosser leadership team took care of what was perhaps the single most important element of their supermarket strategy, the one thing that had been the biggest key to the success of their department store operations.

Pricing.

Turning to Globe Wholesale

Low prices had always been Glosser's trademark...but sustaining a deep discount strategy on the grocery side of the business could be challenging.

Photo by Russell Heffley, courtesy of Johnstown Area Heritage Association

The best way to keep prices at a rock-bottom level was to buy direct from manufacturers. Unfortunately, many manufacturers would only sell to wholesalers. These middle-men would then sell to retailers like Glosser's, adding their own markup in the process.

Trimming off that markup by cutting out the wholesalers would help Glosser's keep grocery costs low. But how could the family do that if certain key manufacturers would only sell direct to wholesalers?

The Glossers wrestled with this question until they found themselves asking a new question, one that pointed the way to a fresh strategy: What if Glosser Bros. could act as *its own* wholesaler?

That was exactly what they ended up doing, creating a new company called Globe Wholesale. Based in a warehouse on Jackson Street in downtown Johnstown, Globe was owned by Glosser Bros. but acted as a separate business entity.

Photo by L.G. Hornick, courtesy of Johnstown Area Heritage Association

Photo courtesy of Bill Glosser

Though the Glosser Bros. company, in its role as a retailer, could not always buy direct from manufacturers, Globe Wholesale could. Buying through Globe, Glosser Bros. could purchase many items at a much lower cost than if a wholesaler not owned by the company had been involved. Then, by keeping Glosser's own markup low, The Store could pass along the savings to customers.

And that, the Glossers realized, would be the absolute best way to ensure the new supermarket's success.

The Biggest Little Warehouse on Jackson Street

Globe Wholesale's headquarters, the Jackson Street warehouse, had plenty of room to handle an influx of groceries and other merchandise. The building had four floors, accessible by freight elevator, all dedicated to Glosser Bros. stock.

Empty lot on site of Globe Wholesale, 2014 (photo by Philip Balko)

The location was perfect, too. Situated along the railroad tracks, Globe had its own siding, a short section of track where freight cars could pull off the main line, then park and unload. At first, the unloading was done "bucket brigade" style, with lines of men passing

67

boxes hand to hand. Later, gravity roller conveyors were installed, allowing boxes to be fed along a metal track, requiring fewer employees to do the work. One man could place items from the freight car on the conveyor, while another man at the other end grabbed and stacked them.

Shipments were also received from tractor trailers at the loading docks. As boxes shipped from manufacturers were unloaded into the warehouse, other boxes were loaded into the trailers for delivery to the Glosser Bros. Department Store.

It was just the right setup to keep the relocated and restructured supermarket supplied for many years to come.

Photo by Morton Glosser, courtesy of Johnstown Area Heritage Association

The Worst-Located Grocery Store Ever

In the weeks leading up to the relocated and expanded supermarket's grand opening, the Glossers did everything they could to generate buzz around town. They posted signs in the store, talked to customers about the new venture, and advertised extensively in local newspapers.

Then, after the gala grand opening, complete with proclamations and a ribbon-cutting, they welcomed their first customers to the basement store. From then on, there was nothing to do but watch and wait, hoping for the best as the new sales figures rolled up to the executive offices on the fourth floor.

Things could still go either way, in spite of all the careful preparations. The Glossers had been in the grocery and retail business long enough to know there were no sure things. The basement location alone might be enough to hobble the new enterprise.

On the other hand, it might not be a problem at all. Because when the figures from the first weeks and months came in, they showed a decidedly upward trend.

People were spending more money than ever on groceries at Glosser's. The new supermarket was gaining customers and sales with each passing week.

Photos by Morton Glosser, courtesy of Johnstown Area Heritage Association

69

People joked that it was the worst-located grocery story ever...but the shoppers kept coming. According to Bill Glosser, the basement supermarket was more successful than ever by the early 1930s. "On a typical Saturday in those days, there were 18 checkouts open, and every one of them was busy.

"Shoppers had to lug baskets of food up 50 steps to the checkout, then through the store, then to a parking lot where they had to pay to park. So why did they keep coming back? Why did those cash registers keep ringing like crazy? *Prices.*

"We had the best prices around, plain and simple. That was the secret of the supermarket's success," says Bill.

Photos by Morton Glosser, courtesy of Johnstown Area Heritage Association

Paper, Plastic, or Crystal Ball?

The location might not have been convenient, but the supermarket's success--and its impact--were undeniable. It set the pattern for further grocery-related achievements by Glosser Bros. in years to come.

The basement supermarket itself expanded multiple times, eventually employing 75 people (18 of them cashiers), and generating huge sales volumes. By 1953, companies such as Campbell's, Heinz, and Procter & Gamble recognized the Glosserteria for selling more of their products than any individual food store in the U.S. in a calendar year.

The buying strategy developed for the supermarket had a long-lasting impact, as well. Globe Wholesale was so effective, Glosser's used it not only to buy groceries for the supermarket, but also cigarettes, diapers, wallpaper, paint, shoes, hardware, and all manner of merchandise for the department store. Eventually, Globe Wholesale even sold merchandise to other retailers in the Johnstown area, leading to another new revenue stream for Glosser Bros..

Globe Wholesale and the basement supermarket were real game-changers for Glosser's, in the short term as well as the long one. Further down the line--much further--they would even make help to make possible the creation of a grocery division in the company, led by the hybrid half-supermarket/half-department stores of the suburban shopping center-based Gee Bee chain.

Photos by Morton Glosser, courtesy of Johnstown Area Heritage Association

71

72

Chapter 11

When the Sun Went Down

What was it like to be a member of a prominent Jewish family in Johnstown in the early and middle decades of the 20th century?

In the case of the Glossers, life was good. Their business was thriving...and beloved, for the most part, by the community. The Store was especially popular with blue collar customers, who shopped there for quality merchandise at affordable prices.

During the 1920s and 30s, Glosser Bros. events like the Bargain Circus, town dances, and giveaway contests helped take people's minds off their worries. The Store became a local institution, an important part of the fabric of local lives, culture, and families.

Shopping at The Store became a tradition for many families, strengthened by the Glosser brothers' family-grounded philosophy. Throughout the growth of the company, the Glossers maintained the same focus on family that they'd had at the start. They went out of their way to make shoppers and employees feel like they were all part of the same family.

Photo courtesy Ruth Glosser

73

But were they? As friendly and supportive as everyone was, as strong as their connection through The Store, there was always a hidden tension between them.

There was always an awareness that the Glossers were Jewish, and most of the community was not.

"That Ended At Sundown"

Bill Glosser, son of original Glosser Brother Saul, knew that anti-Semitic attitudes were a part of life in those days. The Glossers and their customers were friendly and familiar in their dealings at The Store. "A lot of people shopped every day, just to come in and say hello," remembers Bill.

During the day, Jews and Gentiles got along as if there were no differences between them. But according to Bill, "That ended at sundown." Outside the context of business hours at The Store, attitudes toward the Glossers weren't always so congenial.

Bill remembers hearing people make anti-Semitic remarks--calling him a "dirty Jew," for example. And Jews were excluded from certain organizations.

The North Fork Country Club was closed to Jewish members until the mid-1940s. Even then, Jews admitted to the club (including Bill's father, Saul) could only join as Class B members who lacked voting privileges for the Board of Governors. Sunnehanna Country Club didn't open to Jewish members until much later, in the late 1960s. There were still restrictions, though; only a few golfing memberships were available to Jews, along with a handful of social (non-golfing) memberships.

But during the years of rejection, the Glossers and their friends still wanted access to the kind of recreational opportunities that the clubs offered...so they founded their own. Izzy and Fred Glosser and Herb Sinberg established a new venture, the Menoher Heights Swim Club, on Ligonier Pike, complete with swimming pool, tennis

Menoher Swim Club 2014 (photo by Philip Balko)

courts, picnic area, and lunch counter. From then on, the Glossers and their partners could spend hot summer days at the new club, which was also open to the public regardless of race or religion.

"They Wouldn't Rent to Us"

Country club rejections and anti-Semitic bad-mouthing weren't the only forms of discrimination faced by Jews in the Johnstown area. Just finding a place to live could often be a struggle, in fact.

Ruth Glosser recalls facing this very issue in the late 1940s, when she and her husband, Izzy, were looking for an apartment. "A lot of people wouldn't rent to Jews," says Ruth.

"We had that experience several times, where we saw an ad in the paper, and we'd go to look, and they'd say, you have to stay with your own people, you don't want to live here. And they wouldn't rent to us."

Eventually, Ruth and Izzy found an apartment near the Masonic Temple. A widow named Mrs. Smith agreed to rent the second floor of her home to them...but the arrangement was far from ideal.

"It wasn't until we moved in that we discovered she also had a renter on the third floor," says Ruth, "and he had go through our apartment and up and down our stairs to get in or out. It was a bit of a shock."

But Ruth and Izzy just had to make the best of it. As Jews--even members of the prominent Glosser family--their choices were limited in that day and age.

"A Full Schedule of Fights"

Some of the worst treatment, though, was handed out in childhood. Bill remembers battling his way home from grade school many times in the 1930s, fighting off bullies who taunted him for being Jewish.

Bill's cousin, Fred, had similar experiences. "I had a full schedule of fights," says Fred. "I fought someone every day at morning recess, noontime, afternoon recess, after school, and after dinner. I used to have to fight every day except Saturday and Sunday, sometimes even on Saturday.

"There was a lot of anti-Semitic name-calling and abusive behavior in those days. I didn't like it, and I fought back."

The constant fights lasted all the way through grade school before ending in seventh grade for Fred. By then, he'd gotten big enough not to be intimidated by his tormentors. The abuse died down...but the anti-Semitism continued to rear its ugly head in years to come.

For example, Fred joined the junior varsity basketball team in school, and Izzy was on the varsity team. The same man coached both teams and told Fred and Izzy the same thing: "Why don't you go home? I'll never let you play." Fred ignored the advice. A substitute coach played him in some of the team's out-of-town games, and Fred ended up earning his letter, after all.

Fred also ran up against anti-Semitic attitudes from two of his high school teachers, but he refused to let it get him down. The approach served him well when he left Johnstown and encountered similar prejudice elsewhere in his travels.

Big Mouth in the Barracks

During his time at Camp Claiborne, Louisiana in the 1940s, Fred encountered his share of trash talk from his fellow men in uniform. One time, in particular, he fought to stop the abuse, just like he'd done in childhood.

The incident happened in a barracks at Camp Claiborne, where Fred and other servicemen were spending an evening. "A young guy from Chicago kept needling me with anti-Semitic remarks," remembers Fred. "He just kept at me and wouldn't let up."

Fred hesitated to lash out, since he could have gotten in big trouble for fighting... but eventually, the big mouth crossed the line with his comments. "I had had enough," says Fred. "I walked over and said 'You stand up. I'm not taking this anymore.' The guy stood up, and I let him have it. I knocked him out."

The other men in the barracks congratulated Fred. "They said 'We were wondering how long you were going to take that crap from him.' A lot of the fellas were from big cities and had Jewish friends, so they were my friends, too."

Not everyone took Fred's side in the service, though. When Fred attended religious services on Friday evenings, some of the men didn't like it. "They had to stay and clean up the barracks while I was away. They had to clean windows and scrub floors. I knew from the way the sergeant acted toward me that it was a problem."

To keep the peace, Fred stopped going to Friday services and stayed to help clean the barracks. That solved the problem...but there were others.

When Fred was in the signal corps, his sergeant gave him a hard time. "Once, he was showing a kid how to fix a guardrail using a wrench," says Fred. "The sergeant came over and said 'Glosser, why don't you go find a left-handed wrench?' In other words, he wanted me to get lost.

"I didn't argue with him. I just went and sat behind a building for a while."

He never forgot the negativity he encountered...but he never let it poison him or keep him down for long.

The other Glossers followed the same approach. They went right on being successful, contributing to the community, and embracing their faith instead of pushing it away.

Chapter 12

Cafeteria Days

Glosser's without the cafeteria would be like French fries without gravy, wouldn't it?

The two were so closely entwined, it almost seems they were always together. But the truth is, the cafeteria wasn't there from the start. We know that much.

So when did the cafeteria first open? It depends on whom you ask. Which maybe is only fitting for a place we can't imagine wasn't there all along.

A place that for many of us has become a kind of legend... like Camelot, but with meat loaf and mashed potatoes.

A Magical Beginning

The most likely date for the start of Glosser's cafeteria might be in the early 1930s, around the time of the Locust Street addition. Glosser veterans seem to agree on that much.

Where did the magic begin? The same place it kept happening for decades afterward--in the top floor of the Annex. The Glossers bought this two-story building on the corner of Franklin and Washington streets at some point in the 1920s or 30s.

Though the ground floor of the Annex was rented by a variety of businesses for many years, the Glosser family decided to convert the second floor to a cafeteria.

The new cafeteria followed Glosser's credo of selling quality merchandise (in this case, prepared food) at a discount, while providing excellent service. Soups, sandwiches, salads, and entrees like meat loaf and baked chicken were all on the menu, along with desserts like ice cream and pie.

Glosser's customers gobbled it up. The cafeteria appealed to shoppers looking for a quick bite, as well as people who worked downtown during the day and wanted an inexpensive lunch.

Photo by Albert's Photography, courtesy of Johnstown Area Heritage Association

The revenue from the cafeteria was a bonus for Glosser Bros., of course--but there was a secondary benefit that wasn't as directly measurable. If customers didn't have to leave for lunch, they might be more likely to extend their shopping day and spend more money at The Store.

In the Hunt Room

The Glossers knew a good thing when they saw one...and they knew how to capitalize on it.

The original cafeteria was such a hit that the family added a second restaurant alongside it. The restaurant, called the Hunt Room, shared the same kitchen--and some of the same personnel--as the cafeteria, but with a focus on table service.

Instead of ordering and receiving food and beverages while moving along a cafeteria line, customers ordered from wait staff while seated at tables. It made for a more formal dining experience.

78

The sense of formality was reinforced by the entry fee that patrons paid at the door. From at least the early 1950s through the 80s, customers had to pay a quarter just to walk in and get a table. It made the place seem just a bit more high-end, which was perfect for local business people, doctors, attorneys, and VIPs.

The attraction extended to Glosser Bros. managers and executives, who often ate in the Hunt Room and sometimes conducted business meetings there. The Hunt Room was also a favorite place for visiting Glosser family members to have lunch...though one Glosser, at least, ended up being banned.

"My little grandson, Eli, couldn't sit still in the Hunt Room," remembers Fred Glosser. "My wife and mother used to take him there for lunch, and he'd run all over the place and throw food all over the floor. Finally, the Hunt Room manager said, 'You're not allowed to bring him in here anymore. He annoys everybody and makes too much of a mess.'" Fred laughs. "These days, Eli's a lieutenant commander in the Navy Air Force."

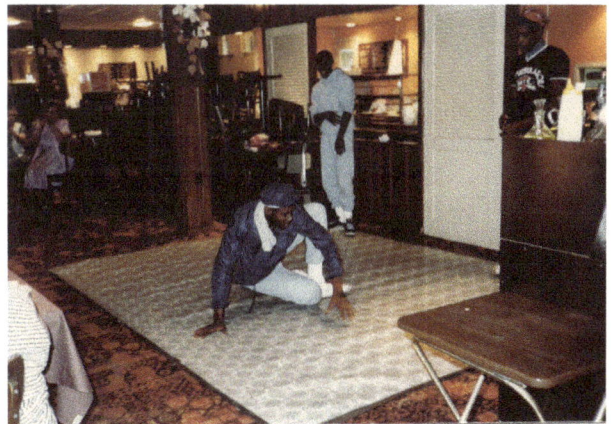

Photos by Margie Hagerich

79

Sundae, Sundae

The Hunt Room went over well, but the most popular addition to the cafeteria might have been the soda fountain.

Soda fountain customers could order sweet treats to their hearts' content, everything from ice cream sodas to sundaes. It was the perfect place to finish off a cafeteria meal or enjoy a midday snack.

It was also home to two of the cafeteria's star attractions--Ruby and Ruth Shaffer. The Shaffer girls, who came be known as the "Glosser twins," (though they weren't Glossers at all) served up goodies at the soda fountain for 38 years, starting in 1951.

Photos by Margie Hagerich

CAFETERIA DAYS

People still remember the Glosser twins fondly for their sweet personalities, identical outfits, and classic catch phrase: "And what else?"

Together with the other employees of the cafeteria and Hunt Room, they helped create a memorable dining experience, a Johnstown signature tradition as beloved as banana splits and open-faced hot turkey sandwiches with fries and gravy.

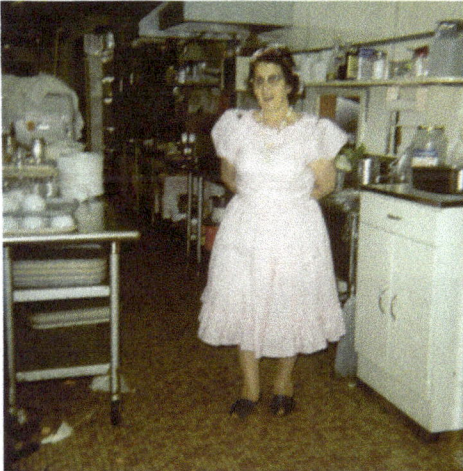

Photos by Margie Hagerich

CAFETERIA STAFF

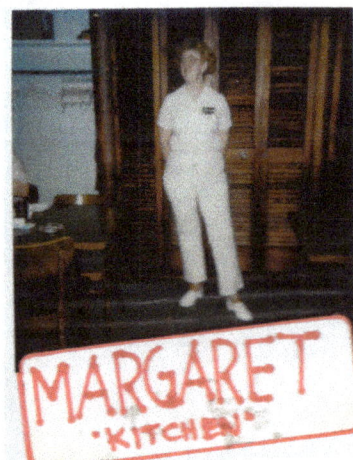

BILLIE
CHOW LINE

CAROL
"BUS GIRL"

CHARLOTTE
"KITCHEN"

GEORGANN
"KITCHEN"

GUILDA
SHORT ORDER COOK

JUDY
CHOW LINE

JULIA
"CASHIER"

MARGARET
"KITCHEN"

Photos courtesy of Margie Hagerich

CAFETERIA STAFF

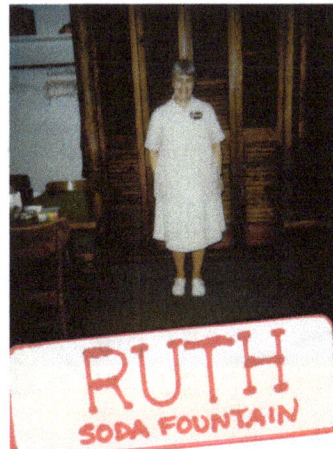

MARTHA
HEAD "BUS GIRL"

MARY ANN
HUNT ROOM WAITRESS

MICHELLE
"BUS GIRL"

NANETTE
"KITCHEN"

NATALIA
"BUS GIRL"

SANDY
SECOND COOK

RUBY
SODA FOUNTAIN

RUTH
SODA FOUNTAIN

Photos courtesy of Margie Hagerich

HOLDFAST!
Thursday—Our Great July Clearance With A Super
Dollar Day
Window Screens 2 for $1
Girls' Play Suits 2 for $1
GLOSSER BROS
JOHNSTOWN, PA.
EVERYBODY'S STORE
6x9 Grass Rugs $1
Boys' 69c Unionalls 2 for $1
Women's Sweaters, 2 for $1
5x8 Rag Rugs $1
Zipper Jackets . . $1
O. N. T. Crochet, 12 for $1
Wash Day Outfits $1
Suedine Jackets $1
Axminster Carpet, yd. . . $1
$1.49 Pajamas . . $1
Wo's Summer Belts, 2 for $1
Wo's Acetate Dresses . . $1
Wo's 2-Pc. Gingham Suits $1
Kidney Benches $1
Muslin, 10 yds. . $1
Women's Slips, 2 for . . . $1
Uniforms and Aprons . . $1
Women's Play Togs, 2 for $1
Metal Sweepers $1
Silk Pongee, 7 yds $1
All-Silk Slips $1
Sample Dresses, 2 for . . $1
Silk Crepes, 2 yds. $1
Tots' $1.95 Sweaters . . $1
Cretonnes, 8 yds. $1
Women's Summer Hats $1
Covert Work Shirts, 2 for $1
Tots' $1.95 Dresses $1
Crash, 8 yds. $1
Star Overalls $1

SPRING GLOSSER BROS. SALE
Ladies . . . You Get Spectacular Savings In Our Great Lingerie Extravaganza!
It's A Record Shattering Purchase! Styles You Want! Prices You'll Like!
NYLONIZED SLIPS and GOWNS
NYLONIZED FINISH MEANS EXTRA WEAR, EXTRA STRENGTH, EXTRA BEAUTY! ACETATE TRICOT, IT'S MUCH FASTER DRYING
The Greatest Lingerie Scoop Ever! Don't Miss It!
$1.99
Buy Generously! Use Our Layaway!
Luxury Lavished With Nylon Lace Trim!
Wonderful Companion Purchase!
NYLONIZED LACE LAVISHED TRICOT PANTIES
59¢
SLIPS
PETTICOATS
GOWNS
Here are the "dress buys" you've been waiting for! Fresh new Spring styles!
500 RAYON and COTTON DRESSES
Up to 5.95 Values
$3
ALL SIZES
BUY NOW . . . USE GLOSSER'S CONVENIENT LAY-AWAY PLAN . . . A SMALL DEPOSIT IS ALL YOU NEED!

Here are Extraordinary Spring Fashion Buys in Sportswear Dept.!
Makers' "Fashion Firsts"
Sample Spring SUITS
$12
Terrific Savings on Crisp New
Blouses—Skirts—Sweaters
1.99
BLOUSES
SKIRTS
SWEATERS
100 Smart, New 'All-Weather' COATS
Best Seller Style "Hits" Values to 22.95
$10
SPRING GLOSSER BROS. SALE
New Spring Handbags
1.59
Famous Make DuPont Nylon CARDIGANS
3.99
Makers' Samples Spring HATS
$2
Pigskin! Capeskin! Spring Gloves
1.98
"Miss George" Umbrellas
2.67
SAVINGS are EXCITING on New Spring SHOES!
Sensational Low Price! Soft Kidskin ARCH SHOES
2.99
Nationally Advertised 4.95 "PLAYMAKERS"
Superb Styling! Choice Leathers!
2.99
Extraordinary Sale! Famous Make Ladies' Shoes
2.99
BUY NOW . . . USE GLOSSER'S CONVENIENT LAY-AWAY PLAN . . . A SMALL DEPOSIT IS ALL YOU NEED!

Chapter 13

Faith and Charity, Glosser Style

After living through brutally hard times in Antopol, Louis, Nathan, and the rest of the family knew what it was like to suffer and do without. They also knew what a difference it could make to receive help when it was most needed, and they wanted to do for others the kind of good works that had been done for them. Their personal experience demanded it, and so did their faith.

The Jews have a tradition of *tzedakah*, a commitment to charitable giving that helps the condition of fellow human beings without judging them or putting them in a subservient or inferior position. The Glossers practiced this from the start in Johnstown, donating to local charities and causes. As far back as 1905, for example, Louis and Nathan Glosser supported relief for victims of pogroms in Russia--this at a time when both men were still struggling financially.

Why Is "Tomato Soup" In Quotes?

The Glossers continued the *tzedekah* tradition through the 1930s, when so many people were down on their luck.

To help hungry neighbors keep body and soul together, the Glossers gave out free "tomato soup"--bowls of hot water and ketchup, supplemented by oyster crackers.

The Glosser family did much more than that, though. Fred Glosser remembers helping hobos--homeless, jobless men who were passing through town on a search for survival.

"These traveling men didn't have any money, and they'd come to the store," says Fred. "Sometimes it was cold outside, and they didn't have a coat. Or they had no shoes.

"We'd fit them up with a coat and a pair of shoes. We'd give them a good dinner in the cafeteria and some money so they could go on to the next town."

Fred's brother, Izzy Glosser, agrees. "They would never leave the store empty-handed, that's for sure. It was a tradition for us. It was how we were raised."

And the tradition extended beyond transients, including anyone who seemed to have fallen on hard times. "I remember one time a paint manufacturer came to the store in the middle of winter," says Izzy. "He didn't have on a warm coat, and my dad said 'Mr. Miller, it's wintertime, it's cold out there. Where's your coat?'

"The paint manufacturer, in jest, said 'Well, I'm not doing enough business.' My dad believed him. Mr. Miller was busy with me for a while, arranging our supply of paints, and pretty soon the loudspeaker came on, saying 'Mr. Miller, please come to the men's suit department.' He went down there, and my dad had gotten him a new coat.

"From then until the day he died, Mr. Miller never forgot that. He and my dad became the best of friends and visited each other often," says Izzy.

According to Fred, these charitable acts were paid for out of The Store's profits...but the expenditures were never questioned or discouraged.

"We were all doing well," says Fred. "We made a good living. But we also helped other people. That's the way we were brought up."

They Came to the House

According to Izzy Glosser, people in need did more than go to The Store in search of help. They also came right to his home.

"People knew where we lived and came to the house once in a great while," says Izzy. "We would give them some of the groceries we had in the house."

It was a way for the family to give something back as The Store continued to thrive. "We never lost money in the worst of those days. We had very loyal customers. They wouldn't go anywhere else."

Money for Nothing

The Glossers helped travelers in dire straits, but they also continued to look for creative ways to assist local residents. One of those ways was providing credit by printing their own in-house money.

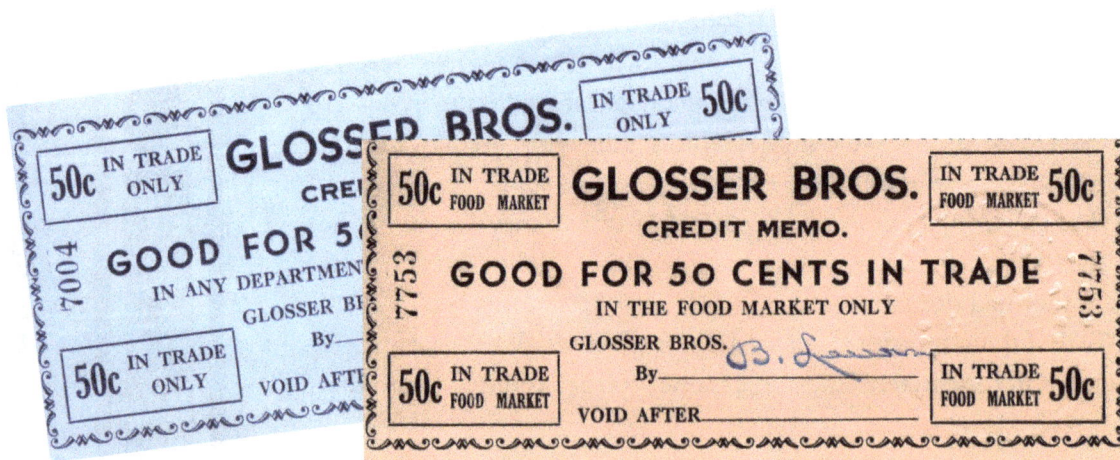

ALWAYS CARRY THIS BOOK WHEN SHOPPING

ACCOUNT NO. _____

GLOSSER BROS.
Famous for Savings

GLOSSER BROS., INC. assumes no liability or responsibility to the purchaser if book is lost, stolen or destroyed.

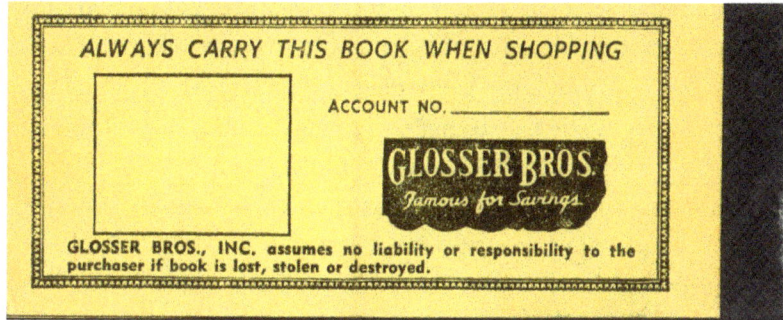

Use your GLOSSER Credit Coupons like cash. They are good in all departments except food and tobacco. They are not acceptable as payment on credit coupon books.

Coupons are not good if detached. Salesperson will remove coupons having a total face value nearest to the amount of your purchase. All Taxes payable in cash.

This book is not transferable.

When people couldn't access their bank accounts because of bank "holidays" or lost their cash-flow due to unemployment, the Glossers made their own money available. This "scrip" amounted to a no-interest loan that customers could spend in the store.

"People didn't have any money, and they didn't have anything to eat," says Fred Glosser. "We had to help them."

A borrower could get up to $25 in scrip just by signing his or her name and promising to pay the money back whenever they could. There were no consequences for failing to pay back the loans, but almost everyone repaid them sooner or later.

"Ninety-nine percent paid them back," says Bill Glosser. "We trusted them, and they lived up to their agreements."

This coupon good for 014540

$2.00

in merchandise at

GLOSSER BROS.
Famous for Savings

Subject to conditions on inside front cover. Coupon not good if detached.

This coupon good for 014540

$2.00

in merchandise at

GLOSSER BROS.
Famous for Savings

Subject to conditions on inside front cover. Coupon not good if detached.

Fred Glosser recalls the story of another kind gesture that helped area residents during the Depression. One autumn night, an early frost struck a field of cabbage on Sam Glosser's farm. Though the cabbage was damaged and couldn't be sold as usual at The Store, it could still be eaten. Sam knew there were lots of hungry people around who could benefit, so he drove to Cresson to make an offer.

"A woman sent me a letter years later, telling me how, when she was a little girl, Sam approached her father in Cresson," says Fred. "Sam told her father he could come out to his farm with as much help as he needed and cut that whole field of cabbage. They could take it all home and use it for cooking or to make sauerkraut.

"In the end, that cabbage helped to feed many families, and it didn't cost any of them a penny," says Fred.

In all these ways, plus a long list of generous philanthropic acts supporting local causes and those in the Old Country, the Glossers lived up the *tzedakah* tradition. They reinforced the beliefs that had guided and nourished them all along, though this was not the only way they kept their Jewish faith front and center.

Seders at The Store

The Glossers took their religion seriously, honoring its traditions and living by its precepts. They attended temple or synagogue weekly and gave regularly to charitable causes.

The Store was geared toward its clientele, most of whom were followers of Christian denominations. The big front windows on Locust Street were decorated for Christmas, not Hanukkah. There were Christmas sales, not Passover sales...Santa Clauses--not Stars of David or menorahs--on the walls.

But Jewish holidays were an important part of life at The Store just the same. Each year, Glosser Bros. Department Store was closed for Rosh Hashanah and Yom Kippur. The firm ran multiple ads in local newspapers well in advance, announcing the closings.

But Passover was the only Jewish holiday that the Glossers actually celebrated *at* The Store. Annual Passover Seder dinners were held in the cafeteria, because it was the only space big enough to hold the growing Glosser family.

During the 1930s and 40s, if a Glosser Seder was limited to family, there would be 80-100 people in attendance. Sometimes, the entire local Jewish community was also invited, in which case, the cafeteria in the Annex was filled to capacity.

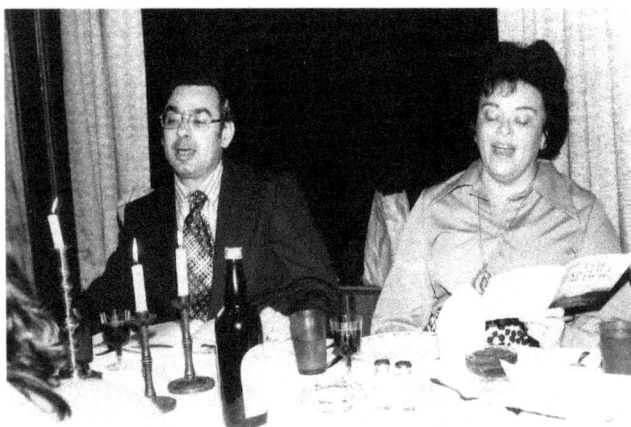

Louis and Bernice Coppersmith (photo courtesy of Ellen Ossip Sosinski)

Izzy Glosser, Sydney Ossip, and Bess Silberstein (photo courtesy of Ellen Ossip Sosinski)

The menu was always the same: gefilte fish, chicken soup with matzo balls, matzo farfel, chicken, stewed fruit, matzo, and macaroons for dessert. The Seder ceremony, likewise, remained the same from year to year.

The Glossers honored the traditions of their faith just as they always had. Local people might have had mixed feelings about their Jewishness, even kept them

Steve Eiseman and Susan Black (courtesy of Robin Eiseman)

from the complete acceptance they felt they had earned, but the Glossers went right on worshipping as if none of that mattered. Around them, the store was closed and silent, populated only by mannequins.

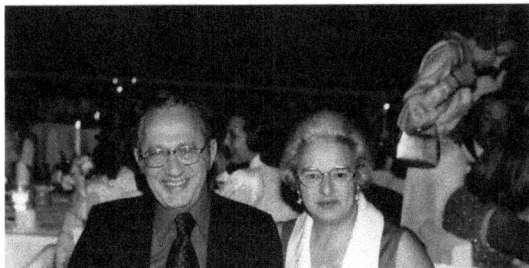

Sydney and Molly Ossip (photo courtesy of Ellen Ossip Sosinski)

But in the cafeteria on the second floor of the Annex, by the glow of flickering candles, the family talked and ate and sang and listened to the holy stories that had been told since the time before time.

Herb Sinberg and Bess Silberstein (photo courtesy of Ellen Ossip Sosinski)

89

Chapter 14

Troubled Waters

Remember the big celebration for the new Locust Street addition to the Glosser Bros. Department Store in 1931? The moment of glory when the lieutenant governor, the mayor, and thousands of people joined together to mark the expansion of The Store that had started 25 years before with one humble shop? Well, guess what happened five years after that?

The Franklin Building, home of the Glosser Bros. Department Store, was *condemned*.

It was a stunning reversal of fortunes, a major blow to the local retail giant. And it was all because of some rainfall and snowmelt that changed the face of Glosser's and Johnstown forever.

Photo by Russell Heffley, courtesy of the University of Pittsburgh Archives

A Soggy St. Patrick's

It was Tuesday afternoon, March 17, 1936--Saint Patrick's Day. Twelve-year-old Fred Glosser looked out the window at school in Southmont, watching the rain pour down and pelt the melting snow. Playing outside after school wasn't in the cards, not the way it was coming down out there. His brother Izzy and cousin Bill were no doubt thinking the same thing.

Down the hill in Johnstown, Fred's father, Sam, must have been thinking gloomy thoughts of his own as he gazed at the rain. It put a damper on business, most likely, and made deliveries, shipping, and receiving inconvenient...especially because it had been raining for two days by then. Temperatures were in the 50s, making the snow thaw fast. There was a lot of water on the roads, what with the rain and all the snow melt left behind by the sudden thaw.

As for the customers, they slogged in with boots and raincoats, shaking umbrellas in the foyer at the corner of Franklin and Locust. People laughed about the rain and wondered when it would stop. Maybe some of them even joked about having another Johnstown Flood.

But did any of them really think that another flood was on its way? Did anyone that day suspect that the valley was about to fill with water, lives were about to be lost, and destruction was about to run roughshod over a town that had already been laid low by flooding 47 years earlier, in 1889?

One thing's for sure. They figured it out soon enough.

Not The Good Kind of Thaw

None of it would have happened without the unseasonable thaw and late-winter rains.

The warm-up melted much of the snow pack blanketing the area, which amounted to between 4 and 10 water-equivalent inches. The rush of snowmelt combined with over 7 inches of rainfall over a four-day period...and by Saint Patrick's Day, the ground was saturated.

To give you some perspective, during the Great Johnstown Flood of 1889, a maximum of 7.9 inches of rain fell in the immediate area--without the snowmelt, but over a shorter period of time.

So yes, this was a disaster in the making. If a dam had given way (as it was rumored that the Quemahoning Dam might), it could have rivaled the toll of 1889.

As it was, things were bad enough for Johnstown...and Glosser's.

Waterlogged Dreams

With the ground saturated and the rain and snowmelt still flowing, water started to rise ominously in downtown Johnstown. The Stonycreek and Conemaugh Rivers climbed to a height of 18 inches in one hour. By mid-afternoon, both rivers had jumped their banks.

Suddenly, the possibility of a flood was all too real. The water wasn't just inconvenient anymore; it was life-threatening.

A general flood warning was issued at 3:00PM. Glosser Bros. closed early for the day, and its employees and customers hurried toward higher ground. By then, water was rising fast all over the city and its boroughs, including Hornerstown and Moxham.

Soon, the streets were filled with cars, abandoned by their owners and quickly disappearing under sloshing brown water. People fled on foot to the Inclined Plane, which carried them to emergency centers in Westmont.

Before long, with the streets flooded to the point of being impassable, even that escape route was cut off. Those who remained behind sought refuge in the upper floors of office buildings, watching from lit windows as the flood waters continued to climb around them.

But as the night dragged on, those windows all went dark. The water had shut down the power plant and toppled utility poles throughout the city.

Still, the rain continued to fall. Somewhere in the pitch black murk, water poured in around the doors and windows of the Glosser Bros. Department Store, tossing merchandise and mannequins as it rolled across the first floor and gushed into the basement supermarket.

It was like a living thing reaching into the stronghold of the Glossers, the heart of their dreams and success, to drown it. For better and worse, The Store and the town had been intertwined from the start; now, it seemed, they would go down together.

14 Feet, $41 Million

The floodwaters peaked around midnight at 14 feet...then slowly receded as the rains finally slowed. And stopped.

Photo by James DuPont, courtesy of Johnstown Area Heritage Association

By the time it was all over, two dozen lives had been lost, and over $41 million in property damage had occurred. Seventy-seven buildings had been destroyed, and 3,000 more had suffered severe damage.

The Franklin Building was among them.

When the water had gone down enough the next day to get to The Store and step inside, the Glossers were stunned. The first floor was a world of wreckage and filth, a jumble of soaked merchandise and debris. Mud and muck were everywhere, coating the warped floors and fouling every crack and crevice.

Then there was the supermarket downstairs. The stench of ruined and spoiled food mingled with raw sewage blasted up from the basement, a sickening reek. Waterlogged packages floated in the slimy brown soup that still lapped at the basement stairs, the market's once-fresh stock reduced to bobbing, rotting garbage overnight.

Photo by Rock-Photo, courtesy of Johnstown Area Heritage Association

The upper floors of the building were intact, but the first floor and basement had been devastated. The Store as the Glossers and Johnstown had known it was no more. It would have to change to survive.

But just how extensive that change was going to be would come as a shock.

Condemned

The city inspectors shook their heads and scribbled on clipboards as they walked through The Store, inspecting it in the wake of the flood. The damage to the first floor and basement was even more disastrous than it had seemed on the morning after the deluge. Not only had the water wrecked the flooring and infiltrated the walls, but it had undermined the structural integrity of the Franklin Building. Not only was the place closed for business, but it was no longer safe for human habitation.

The city inspectors *condemned* the entire property. It would have to be demolished unless significant renovations and reinforcement were undertaken.

And the clock was ticking. The building's owners couldn't wait forever to repair the structure...or tear it down.

Chapter 15

Sink or Swim

The Glosser Bros. Department Store saga was about to be cut short. It came *thisclose* to ending forever. The building, which the Glossers were renting, had been condemned, and the property owners had no intention of making costly repairs to shore it up.

The Glossers, however, were not about to say die. Instead of salvaging what they could and abandoning the building, they came up with another option.

The building's owners seemed content to write the place off rather than invest in repairs. Maybe, if they were so willing to unload it, they might *sell* it to someone more committed to keeping it alive. Someone who'd poured their sweat and blood into the place for decades, who'd made it a thriving business and a pillar of the community. Someone who saw it as so much more than a flood-ravaged liability.

Someone like the Glosser brothers.

The Benefits of Being Condemned

The Glossers made an offer, and their landlord was interested. The two sides came to terms, and the historic transaction commenced.

When it was over, the Glosser family owned the condemned structure, which would henceforth be known as the Glosser Building. And they wasted no time reviving and remaking it. Buying the building and being forced to remodel it gave them an opportunity to lay the groundwork for a modern new era for The Store.

The Glossers hired engineers and worked with them to devise and implement a sweeping plan. The plan revolved around one key change in the building's layout: moving the elevators from the middle of The Store to the Locust Street side.

95

As work crews tore out the original two elevators in the heart of The Store, they opened up floor space on every level. When they installed a bank of four new elevator shafts on the Locust Street side, they doubled passenger capacity while providing the structural reinforcement required by the city inspectors.

Additional reinforcement was supplied by new concrete buttresses installed around the bases of the columns in the Franklin Building basement. The buttresses were big, but making room for them wasn't a hardship; no sales floor space was lost, since that part of the basement was used as a stockroom for the supermarket, shoe department, men's furnishings department, and ladies' hosiery department. (Coffee was also ground down there, then packaged and sold as "Glosser Coffee.")

With the added reinforcement in place, workmen were able to move forward with putting in new flooring for the entire first floor. Fred Glosser, who was 12 years old at the time, remembers watching the men work, ripping out the ruined linoleum and underlayment and installing new materials in their place.

Not all the scraps discarded by the workmen went to waste, thanks to Fred. "One night, I picked up some scraps of wood and a hammer and a saw and made a nice little table and took it home," says Fred. "My parents were surprised with what I did there."

A Johnstown First

The new elevators and open floor plans went a long way toward changing the look of The Store...but another addition was even more innovative.

The Glossers had an Otis brand wooden escalator installed on the first floor, the first of its kind in Johnstown and the only one between Pittsburgh and Harrisburg. It would carry customers only as far as the second floor, where they'd have to switch to elevators or plain old non-moving stairs to go further...but the then-futuristic device was bound to make an impression. And a statement.

The Glosser Bros. Department Store was coming back better than ever, looking to the future instead of dwelling on the past.

What's That Moving Staircase Thingy?

When Glosser's reopened for business, customers poured through the doors like the floodwaters had done just a few months earlier. The rush was on to see first-hand if the place would measure up to the rumors about its remodeling.

The gawking shoppers were greeted by what looked like a brand-new store--one that was bright and shiny and overflowing with new merchandise. One that looked so much *bigger* now that the elevators had been moved off to the side. One that had an honest-to-goodness *escalator*, which some folks had never even *seen* before.

It was the Glosser Bros. store of the future...but with the same selection of quality merchandise at discount prices. Would shoppers come to love it as much as they had the old Glosser's, the one from before the flood of '36?

Only time would tell. But the ringing cash registers and loaded shopping bags flying out the doors suggested things were headed in the right direction.

Echoes of '36

The 1936 flood changed Glosser's and Johnstown in ways that still echo into the 21st Century.

Take a look at the sloped concrete river walls along the Stonycreek and Conemaugh Rivers. They were built by the Army Corps of Engineers to prevent future flooding after the events of Saint Patrick's Day 1936. President Franklin Delano Roosevelt himself spearheaded the construction after visiting Johnstown to see the flood damage first-hand.

Along with the river walls, the new configuration of the Glosser Building proved to be a lasting change. The restructured interior of the building provided a framework for the future of The Store. The layout didn't change much, in fact, until the next flood in 1977. Even then, the basic floor plan remained the same.

That basic plan is still intact today. The Glosser Building has been divided into offices and courtrooms, with a restaurant and retail space on the first floor, but three of the elevators are still on the Locust Street side, where they've been since the renovations of 1936 (though one elevator is currently closed off).

The changes to the building so long ago have long outlived The Store, just as memories and dreams of that place likewise refuse to die in our hearts and minds.

Photo from the Beers Collection, courtesy of Johnstown Area Heritage Association

20 BIG HOURS
SATURDAY
8 A.M. 'til 10 P.M.
SUNDAY
11 A.M. 'til 5 P.M.

Glosser's
DOWNTOWN JOHNSTOWN

FREE
3-HOUR PARKING
IN BOTH GLOSSER LOTS
AND BOTH CITY GARAGES
ALL DAY SATURDAY AND
SUNDAY WHILE SPACE IS
AVAILABLE.
BUS SERVICE AVAILABLE
SATURDAY UNTIL 10:15 P.M.

SATURDAY ONLY
2-HOUR DOORBUSTERS

8 A.M. UNTIL 10 A.M. ONLY!

A FREE INSTANT LOTTERY TICKET TO THE FIRST 100 CUSTOMERS AT OUR THIRD FL. LAYAWAY DEPT.
From 8 a.m.-10 a.m. No purchase necessary. Glosser Bros./ Gee Bee/Dollar Bargain employees are not eligible.

MEN'S OCEAN PACIFIC® SPORT SHIRTS
$6
Nationally Advertised At $20.00
No-iron fabric featuring Ocean Pacific® fashion styling. Stripe patterns with printed backs. Sizes S,M,L,XL. While quantities last. **Main Floor**

MISSES' MANUFACTURER'S SAMPLES
50% OFF
Mfr. Sugg. List $24.00 to $90.00
NOW $12 TO $45
Choose from blouses, pants, skirts and sweaters. Misses' sizes 8-10. **Third Floor**

LADIES' "SLIPPERSAURUS" SLIPPERS
3 49
Reg. $6.99
Plush, over-sized slippers styled like dinosaurs. Padded soles. Available in blue or lilac. Sizes 5-10. **Main Floor**

LADIES' COMFORT PUMPS
4 88
Compare at $26.00
Full-cushioned insole and arch. Fall and winter colors. Limited quantities. Broken sizes Mostly narrow widths. **Main Floor**

LADIES' PARIGI® WARM-LINED BOOTS
6 88
Mfr. Sugg. List $42.00
Pull-on style with water-proof uppers. Royal blue. Limited quantities. Ladies' sizes 6-9. **Main Floor**

½ OFF LADIES' AND GIRLS' HOSIERY GIFT BOX SETS
2 50 TO 3 75
Reg. $4.99 to $7.49
Choose from 2 and 3 pair hosiery gift sets in assorted styles and colors. Sizes 9-11. **Main Floor**

½ OFF LADIES' TOTES® TOASTIES™
$5
Reg. $10.00
Special traction sole helps you keep your footing on smooth surfaces. Assorted colors to choose from. Washable. One-size-fits-all. **Main Floor**

LADIES', MEN'S AND CHILDREN'S UMBRELLAS
1 88
Reg. $2.97
Choose automatic fold for Ladies' in fashion colors or Men's in black. Children's styles available in colorful prints. **Main Floor**

EMERSON® AM/FM DUAL CASSETTE STEREO
34 97
Reg. $46.97
Continuous play & dubbing. With AM/FM stereo tuner. AC/DC operation & built-in condenser microphone. (532) **Fourth Floor**

KODAK® ALKALINE BATTERIES
97¢ PACK
Reg. $1.49 Pack
Choose from "C" or "D" 2-packs or 9-volt single pack. **Fourth Floor**

SUAVE® SHAMPOO, CONDITIONER OR HAIRSPRAY
89¢ EA.
Reg. $1.49
Choose 16-oz. shampoo, 16-oz. conditioner or 8-oz. hairspray. **Lower Level**

CLARK BAR OR ZAGNUT BAR BITES
99¢ LB.
Reg. $1.89 lb.
Great-tasting treats the whole family will enjoy. **Main Floor**

8 P.M. UNTIL 10 P.M. ONLY

A FREE INSTANT LOTTERY TICKET TO THE FIRST 100 CUSTOMERS AT OUR THIRD FL. LAYAWAY DEPT.
From 8 p.m.-10 p.m. No purchase necessary. Glosser Bros./ Gee Bee/Dollar Bargain employees are not eligible.

MEN'S RUSTLER® JEANS
9 99
Reg. $14.97
Straight leg or boot cut prewashed denim, straight leg corduroy in popular colors. Both 4-pocket basic models in waist sizes 32-38. **Main Floor**

LADIES' TEDDY BEAR FUN FUR COATS
$25
Reg. $125.00
100% acrylic pile fun fur pastels and bright colors from America's fun fur manufacturer Hiller Bros./ Sizes S,M,L. **Third Floor**

MEN'S LEATHER FAMOUS NAME CASUAL SHOES
9 99
Reg. $25.99 to $39.99
Choose from Giorgio Brutini,® Hippopotamus® and Nunn Bush.® Sport unit soles. Men's sizes in the group. **Main Floor**

14K GOLD DIAMOND EARRINGS
$5
Reg. $20.00
2-pt. genuine diamond earrings set in a 14K gold buttercup mounting. Only 100 pairs to sell! **Main Floor**

COSMO® DIGITAL ALARM CLOCK
$3
Reg. $7.97
Digital display, snooze bar Top panel controls. Perfect for kitchen, bedroom or den. **Main Floor**

SELECTED GROUP DELUXE LUVS® DIAPERS
$6
Reg. $9.99
Leak-resistant fit, no tear taping surfaces. Choose: Small 66's, Medium 48's, Large 33's, X-Large 28's **Third Floor**

I.M.A.® PUSH BUTTON TELEPHONE
Reg. $12.97
Sale 6 97
Mfr. Mail-in Rebate $5.00
FINAL COST After Mail-In Rebate 1 97
Features include last number redial. (TP-3) **Fourth Floor**

I.M.A.® ELECTRONIC KEYBOARD
9 97
Reg. $19.97
Piano or organ selection with 9 pre-programmed songs. AC/DC. tempo control. 33 keys, 2½ octaves. (KB-1) **Fourth Floor**

TURBO DUSTER® RECHARGEABLE CORDLESS VACUUM
Reg. $19.99
Sale $10
Mfr. Mail-in Rebate $5.00
Bonus Mfr. Mail-In Rebate $5.00
FINAL COST After Mail-In Rebate .... **FREE**
Rechargeable, always ready when you need it. **Lower Level**

WINDSHIELD WASHER SOLVENT
77¢ GAL.
Reg. 99¢ gal.
1-gallon size. Protects to 20 degrees below zero. **Lower Level**

ZEREX® ANTIFREEZE
4 97 GAL.
Reg. $6.97 gal.
For extreme conditions Limit 2 gallons per customer. **Lower Level**

SPECIAL PURCHASE FRESH ROASTED CASHEWS
2 99 LB.
Reg. $6.49 lb.
Great-tasting, fresh roasted cashews the whole family will love. Limit two pounds per customer. **Main Floor**

Get your share of the savings ...
CASH·BACK
Frequent Shopper Plan
Get up to 5% Cash Back · Details in Store.

DISCOVER VISA MasterCard Glossers

JUST SAY "CHARGE IT!" APPLY FOR YOUR GLOSSER'S CHARGE CARD TODAY. STOP AT OUR THIRD FLOOR CREDIT AND LAYAWAY DESK.

GLOSSER'S ALL-STARS

IZZY GLOSSER

Izzy Glosser remembers standing on the second floor landing in Glosser's Department Store, looking for a shiny bald head.

It's one of Izzy's childhood memories of The Store, from when he was growing up in the 1920s. In those days, he attended Hebrew school every afternoon after public school, then walked to The Store to go home with his father, Sam Glosser.

Izzy's father was never hard to find. "All I had to do was stand on the second floor landing and look over the crowd below. Whenever I saw that shiny bald head, I knew it was him."

Photo courtesy of Izzy Glosser

Izzy, like his brother Fred and cousin Bill, was a son of the original Glosser brothers, part of the first generation of Glosser kids to grow up with The Store in their lives. He spent a lot of time there from an early age, learning the ropes, having fun, and making memories.

"My dad used to take Freddie and me with him to the store on Sunday to make sure the watchmen, Felix and Sam, were on duty," remembers Izzy. "Dad opened the door with his key, and we walked into the store. I can still hear him calling out *'Shmoyal! Shmoyal!'* That was Sam the watchman's Hebrew name. While Dad was doing that, Freddie and I went up to the toy department on the fourth floor and played with the toys."

Izzy also remembers being pushed around the basement supermarket on carts by the workers who stocked the shelves with groceries...and making the most of produce-related accidents. "Sometimes a truckload of watermelons would arrive in the alley behind the store," says Izzy. "The fellas would roll the watermelons down a sliding board to the basement, where other fellas would catch them and haul them out to put them on display.

"Once in a while, a melon would get dropped and bust open. The fellas in the basement would eat it right up, and I would join them."

The Store was always a big part of Izzy's life, from childhood to college and beyond. After graduating high school in 1939, he left Johnstown to attend Temple University in Philadelphia, then transferred to the University of Pittsburgh at Johnstown after one year. While studying business administration at UPJ, he met his future wife and fellow student, Ruth Taubman, and worked part-time as a salesman in the men's furnishings department at Glosser Bros. He also worked at a Glosser warehouse, loading and unloading trucks.

Izzy completed his bachelor's degree at Pitt's main campus in Pittsburgh, graduating in 1943, at the height of World War II. He tried to enlist in the armed forces but was rejected because of poor eyesight.

Fred, Freda, and Izzy

Fred, Freda, and Izzy

Turned down by Uncle Sam, Izzy went to work full-time at The Store and ended up making a career of it. He became a buyer and manager for the "hard lines" departments, which included hardware, paint, wallpaper, housewares, furniture, rugs, auto accessories, and toys. "Anything you didn't wear or eat, basically," says Izzy.

As a buyer, Izzy bought merchandise from wholesalers and manufacturers for resale in The Store. "I used to go to the wholesale houses and factories from time to time and buy merchandise for Glosser Bros. We negotiated reasonable prices for merchandise, and Glosser's passed along the savings to shoppers. It helped that I got to be good friends with some of those wholesalers and manufacturers."

Working at Glosser's suited Izzy so well that he never left the company. "We had a whole bunch of compatible people working at Glosser Bros. There were lots of cousins and aunts and uncles and friends, and we got along well together."

Izzy went on to work in the Gee Bee division, traveling from store to store to ensure they were being properly managed. He also served on the Glosser Bros. board of directors for many years.

By the time he retired in 1977, he had worked for the company for 34 years. His long career and commitment to volunteer work (the American Cancer Society, Junior Achievement, United Jewish Appeal, Catholic Charities, etc.) make him a Glosser's All-Star...with special recognition for preserving the past.

In May 1989, after The Store closed its doors for the final time, Izzy had the foresight to take one last tour with his camera. He shot a remarkable series of photos, capturing The Store's departments in that one historic moment in time before they were emptied of merchandise and fixtures forever. Thanks to Izzy, we are able to open a window on yesterday and see Glosser's Department Store as it once was, as if time itself had frozen, and the fateful final chapter had never been written.

Photo courtesy of Izzy Glosser

Memory Department

My earliest memory of Glosser Bros. goes back to the years when I was an underclassman at Jr. Pitt. To earn some extra income, I worked Saturdays at Glosser's--sometimes in the notions department and sometimes in the grocery department, where I bagged the items the clerk had rung up. When one of the customers asked me for a "poke," I was dumbfounded. Surely she didn't want me to poke her. When I hesitated, she reached under the counter and pulled out a big paper bag. And that was my introduction to the Pennsylvania-Dutch phraseology common in the area. Some of the other phrases I soon learned included "red up the house" and "papa is all."

Shortly after Izzy and I were married, he made me an offer I couldn't refuse. He offered to pay me $2.00 for each breakfast that I made for him. Now, during World II, that was a worthwhile sum of money. I would have made his breakfasts without any payment but I accepted his offer. What he didn't tell me was that the Glosser Bros. managers who breakfasted in the Hunt Room had made bets about how long it would be before Izzy joined them for breakfast. Before too long the breakfast payments stopped, but I've been making breakfasts for Izzy for the past 70 years.

Photo courtesy of Ruth Glosser

I have so many memories of Glosser Bros. During World War II, I remember women waiting in long lines to buy a pair of nylon hose. I remember that at Halloween, each school district painted one of Glosser Bros.' windows with a Halloween motif. I remember the ponies that Glosser Bros. brought to the Franklin Street side of the store to give pony rides to children. I remember the buyer of the infants' department predicting the sex of each expectant mother's baby as she came to Glosser's to buy infant's wear. I remember the Passover Seders that the family held each year in the cafeteria. Those years flew by quickly, but they have left us with many happy memories.

- Ruth Glosser, wife of Izzy Glosser

103

LONG LIVE GLOSSER'S

I was privileged to have the experience of growing up at Glosser's. I can still recall the wonderful aroma of hot roasted nuts that wafted through the first floor. There are many other wonderful memories, many of them revolving around visiting my father (Izzy Glosser) in the store.

Photo courtesy of Ruth Glosser

In addition to his managerial responsibilities for the downtown store and the Gee Bees, my father managed several departments...but by far the most enjoyable from my point of view was the toy department. Checking out what was new on the shelves was always a highlight of a trip to the store. However, my favorite time to be in the store was closing time. On our way out to the parking lot, my father would let each of us children raid the candy department. Who could resist a handful of M&Ms with some nonpareils thrown in?

Another treat was helping Margie the elevator operator. In the days before the elevators were automated, Margie would let me sit on her little stool and push the handle up and down and call out the floor numbers and departments at each stop.

Other favorites memories include inspecting and selecting each month's new editions of favorite comic books, which were displayed near the highly decorated cigar boxes. Looking at the cigar box lids was also a great deal of fun.

Another treat was joining my Dad for dinner in the store cafeteria on some of the nights when he worked late. It was one of my few opportunities to eat French fries.

I remember, as preteens, my cousin Patti and I decided to print a weekly newspaper which primarily featured gossip (mostly made up) about our cousins and kids in our Sunday school classes. That great opus was printed on the store mimeograph machine with the help of friendly cousins and store employees.

We did all of our shopping at Glosser's, and I worked in the lingerie department part-time after school. It was a great adventure and an excellent way to learn about excellent customer service.

It was a great sadness to me when Glosser's closed, even though I had moved to California by then. I still miss it.

- Miriam Glosser Miller

When I was a long distance operator back in the day, Dave Glosser would come on my line and with his deep voice say, "Dave Glosser, 81296." It still rings in my ears like it was yesterday.

- Pat Regan Haer

My first job in Johnstown (after shoveling snow, of course), was working at Glosser's parking customers' cars. They had two parking lots. I think the fee was 25 cents an hour. After that, I graduated to the notions department, working for Willy Eichenberg. I also worked in the grocery department, which was downstairs below level one. There was no elevator, so we had to help the old folks up the stairs with their bags. All in all, I learned how to be responsible and maintain a job. It was a good part of my early life.

- *Richard Chill*

One time, I was riding the escalator to the second floor, and a little boy was in front of me in his bare feet. His toes went right under the teeth at the top, and he was caught. I can to this day see his face and hear his screaming. They got the escalator shut off almost immediately and got his foot out. He was cut and scared, but not hurt too bad, and those employees were wonderful.

- *Darlene Lipuma*

I loved riding the elevators in Glosser's. The metal gate that they pulled across to close the elevator was the best part!

- *Jennifer Renee*

| Every Morning At Your Door | THE JOHNSTOWN DEMOCRAT | Complete News Coverage |

THE WEATHER — Snow   JOHNSTOWN, PA., TUESDAY MORNING, DECEMBER 9, 1941   THREE CENTS

WAR DECLARATION UNITES U. S. FOR TOTAL VICTORY

American Targets of Japanese Bombs in Pacific, Enemy Aircraft Carrier

Shown above are the targets of Japanese bombers that winged in to sudden attacks on United States Pacific outposts. At upper left is the Japanese aircraft carrier Kaga, which possibly may be among those from which the Japanese were believed to have launched their attack on Hawaii. Pearl Harbor, the powerful American naval base near Honolulu, which the Japanese bombed, is pictured upper right. Approximately 350 soldiers were reported killed by a direct bomb hit on a barracks at Hickam Field, Hawaii, lower right, principal U. S. Army air base from which planes took off to fight the attackers. Part of the U. S. Asiatic Fleet is shown, lower left, at anchor in Manila Harbor in the Philippines, also reported bombed.

BURST OF UNANIMITY MARKS 476-TO-1 VOTE IN REPLY TO FDR PLEA

NATION TO HEAR WAR SITUATION IN FDR ADDRESS

Chief Executive to Bare Facts of Jap Conflict Tonight in Radio Talk; Information Expected

DESIRE PRESS FREEDOM

Navy Seeking to Avenge Jap Killing of 1,500; Germany Is Accused of Instigating War Move; Lend-Lease Continues

WASHINGTON, Dec. 8—(AP)—A Grim-visaged Congress, united by the shock of battle and aroused by startling losses to America's own armed forces, quickly and all but unanimously declared war today upon Japan.

Nippon's Bombers Pound Manila

GREAT BRITAIN DECLARES WAR

Japs Claim Reduction Of U. S. Pacific Fleet

NAZIS ACCUSED BY WHITE HOUSE

U. S. FIGHTER PLANES ENGAGE JAP RAIDERS

Attack Confined to Military Objectives; Nichols Field, Fort McKinley Are Hit; Six Hospitals Are Jammed to Capacity

BRITISH BLAST JAPS IN MALAYA

Baering Down On the News

By ARTHUR (BUGS) BAER

The Weather

CONGRESSMAN ASKS FOR ACTIVE DUTY

LEWIS JOINS IN SUPPORT OF GOVERNMENT IN WAR

HITLER'S MOVE UNKNOWN; SPOKESMEN BLAME FDR

Chapter 16

War and the Store

Seven years after the Johnstown Flood of 1936 nearly shut down the Glosser Bros. Department Store for good, Izzy Glosser looked out through the display windows at the line of shoppers waiting outside. It was a long line that sunny Monday morning, winding along the sidewalk from the front door to the end of the block...and it didn't stop there.

When Izzy opened the door and stepped out on the corner of Franklin and Locust, he saw that the line wrapped all the way around the block and kept going. Where the end was, he couldn't tell from that corner.

But he knew why the shoppers were there. It wasn't an uncommon sight in those days, at the height of World War II. People got there early, before the doors opened, and formed lines that seemed to go on forever. They were all there for the same thing, too, as much as they could get of it.

Had they come for a big sale? Had the Glosser brothers bought yet another bulk shipment of merchandise at a low, low price and stocked mountains of it so they could pass along the savings to shoppers?

Actually, the opposite was true--the opposite of Glosser Bros.' usual marketing strategy--as was often the case in 1943. The shoppers hadn't come to buy up overstocked merchandise from a big lot snapped up for pennies on the dollar from some wholesaler.

As the customers took off their hats and jostled through the door past Izzy, they all wanted something that was in short supply. They wanted something that had been rationed because of wartime shortages.

They wanted *cigarettes*, and Glosser's had them...but not for long. There probably weren't enough to go around, judging from the length of that line.

Whoever missed out would just have to get there earlier the next time a shipment arrived.

Empty Shelf Syndrome

Cigarettes weren't the only items in short supply at Glosser's during the war years. Izzy remembers crowds lining up to buy butter, sugar, coffee, cheese, shoes, and nylon stockings. With a war on, the shelves designated for these products were often empty; The Store was understocked except when shipments of the scarcities arrived...though they never lasted long.

Glosser Bros. put a system in place to try to ensure fair distribution, mailing out special numbered cards on which ration items were printed. When a shopper's card number appeared in the newspaper, he or she could purchase the rationed items...if they were in stock.

Even then, people didn't always get what they wanted. When shoppers did manage to

fill their carts, they could only buy what they wanted if they had enough ration stamps. Each individual was eligible for a certain number of stamps per month, issued in booklets by local rationing boards.

When the ration stamps ran out for the month, there were no more to be had until *next* month...meaning shoppers had to plan their purchases carefully.

"If I wanted a can of pineapple, I hesitated to buy it," recalls Izzy's wife, Ruth Glosser. "I knew when I ate that pineapple, I was eating ration stamps that I might need later for something else."

If a *Glosser* was thinking that, and she was part of the family that owned and operated The Store, what does that tell you? That plenty of other shoppers must have been thinking the same way, right?

And that wouldn't have been good for business, would it? If everyone was hesitating to use their ration stamps, Glosser Bros. Department Store *must* have been hurting. No retail business could thrive under those conditions, could it?

Guess again.

The War Dividend

Rationing or no rationing, Glosser's kept right on booming even as the heavy artillery kept booming on battlefields around the world.

The Store's shelves might not always have been well-stocked, but plenty of Johnstowners had plenty of cash to flash around. It was all thanks to the town's thriving steel industry, which was working overtime to supply the war effort.

"The steel mills were always the major source of income for families in Johnstown," says Ruth. "During the war, business was exceptionally good. Lots of local people had jobs...*good* jobs.

"I remember the mills closing each day at 3:00, and these huge *rivers* of men would pour out. They would roar across the bridges on their way home, so very many men with their hard hats and lunch pails. It was really something to see."

And all those men and their families were likely to have money in their pockets when they walked into a store. And they were likely to walk into Glosser's because it had a reputation as a blue collar establishment, the home of great bargains.

And when they walked in, they'd be more inclined to spend some of that hard-earned money. If some products were out of stock, they would buy other things that they needed.

"People still loved to shop at Glosser Bros.," remembers Izzy. "They could get good quality merchandise and make their money go pretty far."

Where some businesses might have struggled in the era of shortages and belt-tightening, Glosser Bros. continued to succeed, just as it had during challenging times in the past.

Fred remembers something his father used to tell him. "Even in the worst of times, the store never lost money."

And it never forgot to give back to the community. Glosser Bros. made sure to put some of its profits to use for the war effort, sponsoring events like the Civil Defense benefit dance held in Johnstown in 1942.

Photo courtesy of Bill Glosser

From the Sales Floor to the Battlefield

Johnstown's economy soared during the war, and Glosser's bottom line rose right along with it. But not everyone in The Store's extended family got to enjoy the windfall, because they left their jobs for other commitments that had nothing to do with retailing.

"A lot of our employees went to war," recalled Sydney Ossip, longtime comptroller of the Glosser Bros. company (and youngest son of original Glosser sister Jennie). "Not all of them returned. But we managed to carry on."

Not that carrying on was always easy. New hires filled open positions and kept The Store running...but the absence of familiar faces left a void, whether they were hired help or part of the Glosser family by bonds of blood or marriage.

In fact, there were a number of Glosser family members and relations who left The Store to help with the war effort in one way or another. Fred, for example, taught diesel mechanics at Camp Claiborne, Louisiana for several years.

According to Fred, Camp Claiborne was a multidisciplinary educational and training center for Army personnel. "Fellas could learn just about any trade at Claiborne," says Fred. "We had a tank school, a machine shop school, a blacksmith school, a carpentry school, a foundry and pattern school, even a school for working on road grading equipment. You name it.

"The instructors mostly came from the biggest industries in the U.S. They were key men in their 30s, 40s, and 50s who trained the troops to do what they could do best."

Many of the students at Camp Claiborne were African-American, says Fred. "They were separated from the whites in those days," he recalls. "But we made sure they all got a good education and learned an excellent trade. We helped them learn the skills they needed for the war effort and hoped they could use them to get good jobs when they left the service after the war."

While Fred did his part in Louisiana, Herb Sinberg, husband of Freda Glosser (Fred and Izzy's sister), served in the U.S. Navy in the Pacific theater. Herb was the paymaster, disbursing officer, and supply chief for a Navy flotilla that fought among the Pacific islands from New Guinea to the Philippines.

Fred, Izzy, and Freda's cousin, Alvin Glosser (son of original Glosser Brother Saul) also served in the military during the war. Alvin was part of the Medical Administrative Corps, which provided administrative support for Army doctors. He moved from Little Rock, Arkansas to Oregon to Newcastle, Delaware, always proud to serve his country though his duties kept him stateside.

The same was true of Leonard Black, who didn't work at The Store before the war but would become an important figure in its future. Leonard, the husband of another cousin, Betty (daughter of Glosser Brother David), served as a Navy supply chief in San Francisco for three years. Eventually, he attained the rank of lieutenant commander.

Then there was Sydney Ossip, who contributed in a non-military capacity. Sydney went to work for the Office of Price Administration (OPA), a federal agency dedicated to preventing economic upheaval on the homefront. Ironically, the OPA was the very agency responsible for the rationing that was causing the empty shelves and long lines of shoppers at Glosser's in Johnstown.

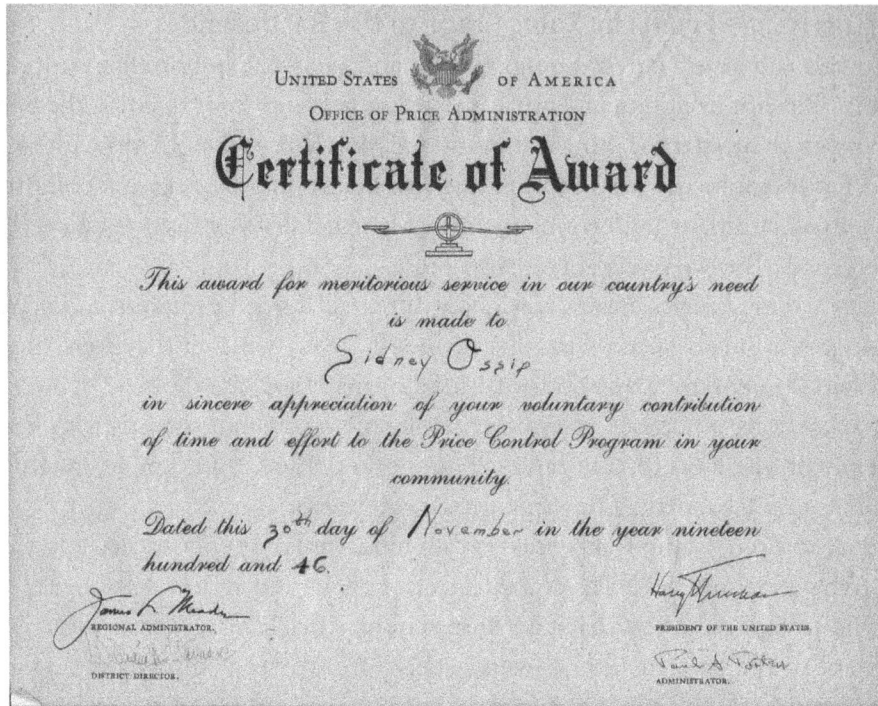

UNITED STATES OF AMERICA
OFFICE OF PRICE ADMINISTRATION

Certificate of Award

This award for meritorious service in our country's need is made to

Sidney Ossip

in sincere appreciation of your voluntary contribution of time and effort to the Price Control Program in your community.

Dated this 30th day of November in the year nineteen hundred and 46.

REGIONAL ADMINISTRATOR.

DISTRICT DIRECTOR.

PRESIDENT OF THE UNITED STATES

ADMINISTRATOR.

Holding Down the Fort

What about Izzy? What path did he take while Fred, Herb, Alvin, Leonard, Sydney, and so many others left Glosser's to help the war effort in one way or another?

Izzy ended up staying behind to hold down the fort. He tried to enlist but failed the physical because of poor eyesight. He couldn't even get limited duty, though his father had tried pulling strings to make it happen.

So Izzy--a tall, muscular man who might have been the one Glosser best equipped to fight a war, physically speaking--spent the war years working at The Store, helping to fill the gaps left when other Glosser's staff went off to do their part.

It wasn't the fate he would have chosen, but he accepted it without complaint--and his wife, Ruth, considered it a kind of blessing. "Izzy Glosser" was one less name she had to look for on the daily casualty lists in the local newspaper.

Life and Death in Print

During the war, Ruth Glosser remembers watching the newspaper every day to see if any of her friends had been killed.

It was a daily routine, one that everyone in the country had in common. With American forces in peril around the globe, everyone knew *someone* who was part of the action in one way or another.

"So many people we knew were in the service," says Ruth. "We checked the casualty lists in the paper every day to see who'd been spared and who hadn't."

The stress took a visible toll on Ruth's family and friends. It broke her heart watching others suffer like that...and she decided to do something about it.

Ruth volunteered as a Red Cross Home Service worker, helping local families deal with the challenges of having loved ones serving in the armed forces during wartime. "We did what we could to help families and servicemen," remembers Ruth. "We were the ones on the home front who made special arrangements and took care of emergencies. If a family member had a health crisis, for example, we could arrange for a loved one in the service to get a pass and come home as needed.

"We helped people keep track of loved ones overseas and helped them stay in touch. And when there was a death in the family, or a serviceman was killed in action, we were there to help and heal."

Ruth's work with the Red Cross Home Service kept her busy during the war and gave her insight into the suffering that was going on around her. "It was a very tense time. A lot of women didn't get their husbands or brothers or sons back."

Back at the Big G

Among the men who did come back were the members of the Glosser family--Fred, Alvin, and Gerald (Nathan's son), along with Herb and Leonard, who'd married into the family. And they came back changed, as many men did in those days.

In years to come, they would all go on to play important roles in The Store, bringing sensibilities shaped by conflict and military bureaucracy to the competitive retail industry. Every one of them would someday sit on the Glosser Bros. Board of Directors.

Gerald became general merchandise manager of Glosser Bros. Department Store. Fred became an influential force in launching and growing the Gee Bee empire. Herb and Alvin became vice presidents of the company, and Leonard became president. (Sydney became treasurer, in the years after he returned from his job at the OPA.) When Leonard retired and moved on to become Chairman of the Board, Alvin took his place as president.

Their experiences had given them the resourcefulness and strength of character they would need to become leaders of the Glosser company of tomorrow. They would be the ones who took the company to new heights, transforming it in ways that had not yet been imagined. Together, they would preside over an unprecedented expansion, making Glosser Bros. more profitable than it had ever been, making it a publicly held company on the American Stock Exchange, bringing in hundreds of millions of dollars a year.

And they would also face the greatest disasters that the company had ever known. They would need their strength and perseverance, honed in wartime, for the battles ahead.

Glosser Bros.' darkest hours were still decades away, but they would not be able to avoid them.

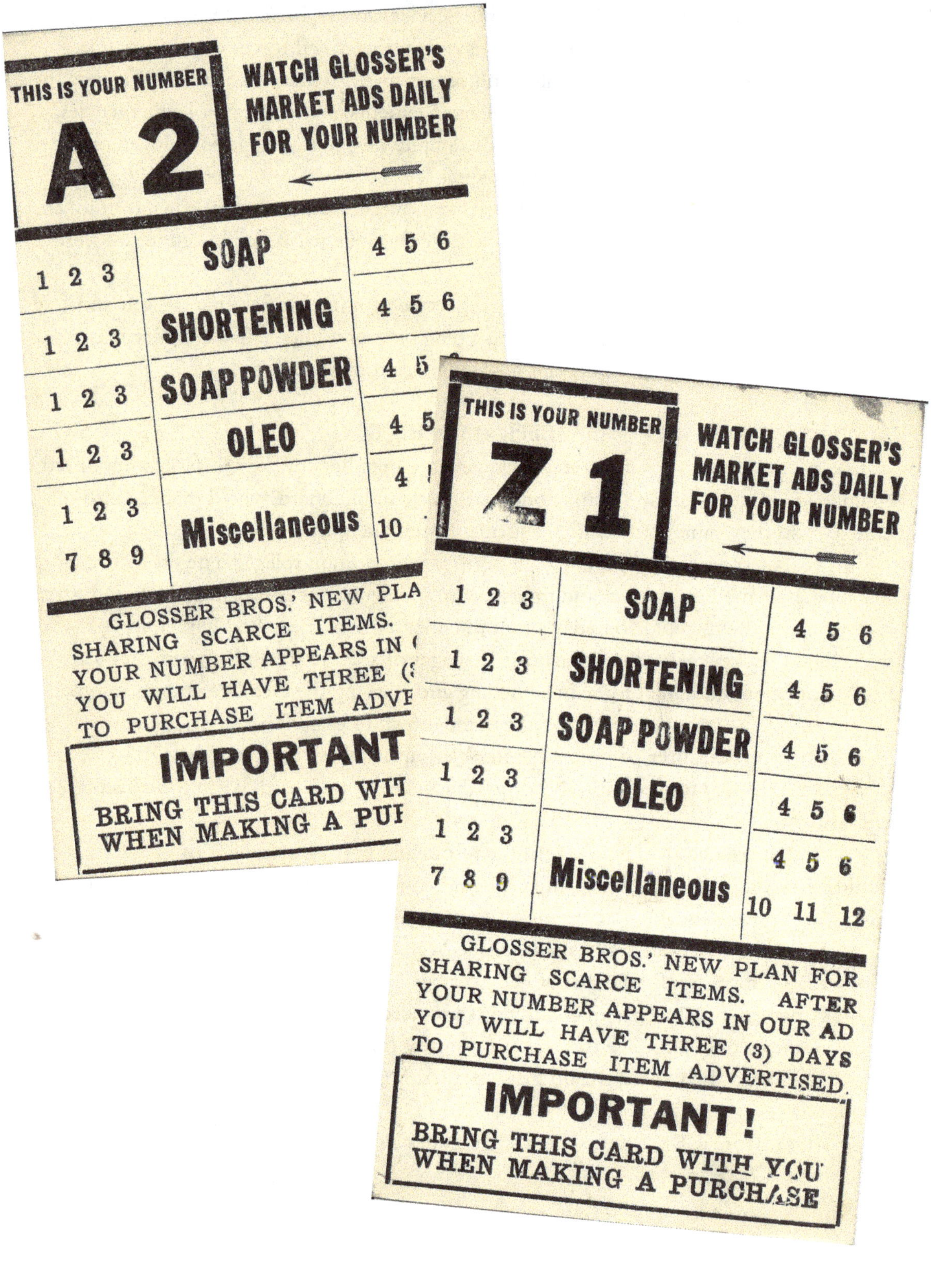

Card A2:

THIS IS YOUR NUMBER

A 2

WATCH GLOSSER'S MARKET ADS DAILY FOR YOUR NUMBER

←

1 2 3	SOAP	4 5 6
1 2 3	SHORTENING	4 5 6
1 2 3	SOAP POWDER	4 5
1 2 3	OLEO	4 5
1 2 3 7 8 9	Miscellaneous	4 10

GLOSSER BROS.' NEW PLAN SHARING SCARCE ITEMS. YOUR NUMBER APPEARS IN YOU WILL HAVE THREE (TO PURCHASE ITEM ADV

IMPORTANT

BRING THIS CARD WIT WHEN MAKING A PU

Card Z1:

THIS IS YOUR NUMBER

Z 1

WATCH GLOSSER'S MARKET ADS DAILY FOR YOUR NUMBER

←

1 2 3	SOAP	4 5 6
1 2 3	SHORTENING	4 5 6
1 2 3	SOAP POWDER	4 5 6
1 2 3	OLEO	4 5 6
1 2 3 7 8 9	Miscellaneous	4 5 6 10 11 12

GLOSSER BROS.' NEW PLAN FOR SHARING SCARCE ITEMS. AFTER YOUR NUMBER APPEARS IN OUR AD YOU WILL HAVE THREE (3) DAYS TO PURCHASE ITEM ADVERTISED.

IMPORTANT!

BRING THIS CARD WITH YOU WHEN MAKING A PURCHASE

GLOSSER'S ALL-STARS

SYDNEY OSSIP

Is it true that everyone at Glosser's loved Sydney Ossip? It sure seems that way, once you start asking around.

Employees and customers alike tell stories of how nice Sydney was, how he always went out of his way to talk to them and take an interest in their lives.

"There wasn't an employee who didn't love and respect him," remembers his middle daughter, Janet Schwartz. "Every person has told me that he *always* made them feel that they were not working *for* him but *with* him.

"To my dad, everyone was on an equal plane," says Janet. "He never got angry with them if there was a problem, and he was always there to help them when they needed help. There was always a smile on his face, and he always dealt with everything in an extremely gentle way. He was like that as a father as well."

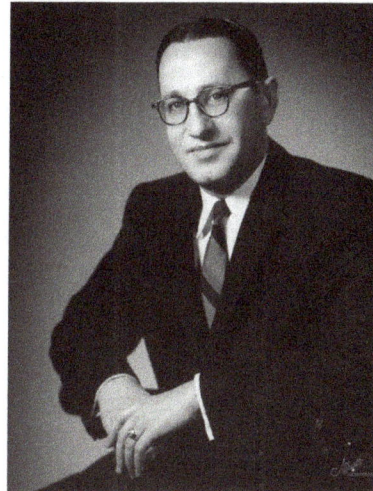

Sydney, for his part, seemed to enjoy being a part of their world. "I got along well with the employees and customers at Glosser's," he said. "I always treated them nicely, and they did the same for me. I enjoyed having so many friends."

And he got to see them quite often during his 44 years as comptroller of Glosser Bros., beginning in 1938. Though his story actually started in Antopol, Russia.

Photos courtesy of Ellen Ossip Sosinski

115

Born in 1916, Sydney was the youngest son of Jennie Ossip, sister of the original Glosser brothers. His family emigrated to Johnstown, then moved to New York City because of his mother's asthma.

Sydney studied accounting at the City College of New York, then eventually moved back to Johnstown to work for Glosser Bros. His first job was in sales, to learn the business.

"For several weeks, I worked on the sales floor," remembered Sydney. "I needed to get a feeling for what customers were like and how they had to be treated."

Shortly after that, Sydney moved into the job of comptroller for the Glosser Bros. company. "Being the comptroller was a very responsible job," said Sydney. "I had to monitor all departmental income and expenses. I had to process all financial statements from departments within the store as well as from all our vendors.

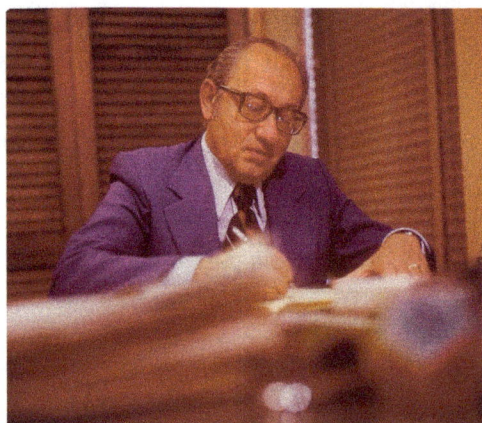

"I also had to make sure we were working on a decent markup. Glosser Bros. offered more of a discount than other department stores, which the public appreciated, but we still had to make a profit."

In the 1960s, Sydney's workload grew dramatically, reflecting the expansion of the Gee Bee stores. Instead of managing income and expenses for just one store, he had to do the same for multiple department stores and supermarkets.

But Sydney handled the increased workload with grace, as he seemed to handle everything. He did his part to propel Glosser Bros., Inc. to new heights, all the way to becoming a publicly traded company eventually listed on the American Stock Exchange in 1971.

"It was very exciting to go public and let the shareholders have our reports and watch the earnings increase as we opened more stores," said Sydney.

After 44 years as comptroller for Glosser Bros., Sydney retired in 1982. He remained on the board of directors for a bit, then left that behind, as well.

But his heart always stayed with Glosser's, and the people who worked and shopped there.

"I was very happy working for Glosser Bros., and I still think about it every day." That was what he said at age 97, long after his retirement. "It was a very pleasant place to work, and it was full of people whose friendship has always made me feel like a lucky man."

Photos courtesy of Ellen Ossip Sosinski

Chapter 17

Back to Business as Usual

Had World War II even happened? Sometimes, when Fred was putting cans on shelves, driving trucks, or doing maintenance work at The Store, he felt like maybe it hadn't.

When he returned to Glosser Bros. after the war, after years in the Army, he was right back where he started. Before the war, he'd performed maintenance duties, worked as a stock boy, driven delivery trucks, and worked in the warehouse. When he came back to Glosser's in 1945, he was doing the exact same work--painting, cleaning toilets, scrubbing floors, driving trucks, stocking shelves, completing maintenance tasks, and the like.

His career had been frozen back in 1943, when he'd gone off to Camp Claiborne. How many men had he taught while he was there? How much of a difference had he made in their lives? How much had he contributed to the war effort?

None of it seemed to matter anymore. At Glosser's, he was back to square one.

His reentry took some adjustment, and he wasn't alone in that regard. "All the employees who went to war and survived the experience came back to Glosser's," said Sydney Ossip. "They were welcomed with open arms and given whatever jobs were available."

For Herb Sinberg, that meant working as a buyer of ladies' shoes. "When it came to ladies' shoes, he knew the right from the left, and that was about it," says his wife, Freda. "But he was glad to have a job. He was happy to be back at Glosser's."

So was Fred, in spite of the strangeness of being back in his old low-end job after years of higher responsibility at the Army training center. He didn't have it in him *not* to love The Store and the team of family and good friends who made it run.

The way things worked out, he didn't have to stay in his old job for long, anyway. Soon enough, he was in a new position at Glosser's with a new set of challenges and improved prospects for his career at The Store.

All he had to do to get there was create his own department from scratch.

Hardware From Thin Air

"Do it yourself" is a mantra often applied in the hardware business. Many people who shop for hardware are "do-it-yourselfers," buying tools and supplies they can use to repair or improve their homes and properties. So it's only fitting that Fred applied the "do it yourself" philosophy to starting the very first hardware department at Glosser Bros..

His father, Sam, gave him the idea. Since there weren't any job openings for buyers or managers at the time (thanks to all the war veterans returning to The Store), maybe Fred could *create* one. Why not start a new department at Glosser's, one he could call his own?

Since The Store didn't have a hardware department, and there was a strong demand for hardware merchandise, that seemed like the perfect choice. With Sam's blessing, Fred set out on a mission to build just such a department.

The first thing he did was find a table in The Store and haul it upstairs to an available space on the fourth floor. He set up the table between the elevators and the money office, then went downstairs to find some stock.

Fred hiked from department to department through the store, gathering up items that belonged in Hardware. He found hammers and screwdrivers in Housewares, tacks in Notions, and cans of 3-in-1 oil in the supermarkets. He scavenged everything he could find that might fall under the heading of Hardware, then hauled it to the fourth floor and laid it out on the display table.

It was a humble start for an unproven department, and Fred wondered if it could possibly succeed. It was new, and off the beaten path, and understocked. Would it take a miracle to draw shoppers and generate a profit that might justify its continued existence?

In a word, no. "I sold $45 worth of merchandise on the first day," says Fred. "And it only went up from there. Before you knew it, I had four tables on the fourth floor. Pretty soon, I was traveling to wholesalers' warehouses and buying up what merchandise I could find to sell in Hardware."

The new department made a big impression and turned into a solid profit center for Glosser's. It showed everyone what Fred could do, how he could basically make money out of little more than thin air.

So why was it suddenly taken away from him and given to somebody else?

Birth of a Notions Buyer

Not long after Fred created Glosser's new Hardware department, he was told he would have to give it up. Another employee who'd returned from the war needed a job, and Sam Glosser had decided Hardware was the best place for him.

Once again, Fred was a man without a department. After all his work building Hardware out of thin air, he was back to maintenance and stock boy work. He wasn't the kind of guy who was prone to sour grapes, he never had been, but still...it was a setback.

Luckily, it didn't last long. A position opened up for a buyer/manager in the Notions department, and Sam asked Fred if he was interested. Fred said yes in a heartbeat.

He applied and got the job, which paid a whopping $35 a week. But the experience and opportunity were more important than the pay To Fred. What mattered most was that he had another chance to break free of his stock boy/maintenance man job, a chance to show just how capable he could be in a responsible position.

He rolled up his sleeves and dug in, determined to prove himself. It didn't hurt that he had a little help along the way. "I had a really good trainer, Mr. Bill Wenky," says Fred. "He was the merchandise manager for several departments, and he really knew the retail business. He knew how to handle people and get things done. He took me under his wing and taught me everything."

Soon, Fred was going on buying trips with Bill, learning on the job as they met with wholesalers and manufacturers in the never-ending quest to stock The Store. "We would buy large quantities of greeting cards, sewing supplies, cosmetics, gift items, whatever," remembers Fred. "We came back with so much stuff that the stock room was overflowing. I'd ask him, 'Where are we going to put all of this stuff?'

"Bill always said the same thing. 'We're going to put it in people's homes.' And we did!"

Working with Bill Wenky was an education and a half...and it inspired Fred to come up with moneymaking ideas of his own. One idea, in particular, caught on fast and became a Store staple through the late 1940s.

Who would have thought a 4-cent sale could be so profitable? Besides Fred Glosser, that is.

4-Cent Fortune

It all started with a supplier in New York City who had a unique specialty. "When I found out he specialized in merchandise that you could sell for 4 cents per piece with a one or two cent profit, the wheels started turning," says Fred.

After talking to the supplier and crunching the numbers, Fred came up with a plan. "I decided to buy a couple thousand dollars worth of items at 2 or 3 cents per piece.

"Then, I set up some tables on the first floor of Glosser Bros. and loaded them with 500 or 600 of these items, all priced at 4 cents each. We had four tables, and we left them up for 4 or 5 days."

The sale was wildly successful. Hundreds of people crowded The Store each day to rummage through the 4-cent items...and they didn't leave much behind. "We sold what we put out, almost to the last item. People just loved it."

The first 4-cent sale was such a hit, Fred ran another one a month later. That was a smash, too, and led to many more 4-cent sales in months and years to come.

"I would go to New York and buy more stuff and put it out for 4 cents. If there was ever anything left, I just used it for the next sale."

Fred and Bill also bought merchandise for the sale from local suppliers. "We went to Roaring Spring, near Altoona, to a paper manufacturing company," says Fred. "We bought a truckload of tablets, note books, typing paper, and many other paper products that they made. We bought it by the pound, and it worked out to be very profitable on the 4-cent sale table.

"That sale was always a real crowd-bringer. We didn't make a lot of money on it, but we didn't lose money, either. We always made a profit, and it brought people into the store."

The 4-cent sales continued through the rest of the 1940s, cementing Fred's reputation as a savvy buyer and department manager--keeping Notions a busy place even as Fred moved on to greener pastures at The Store.

Retailing 101

When the buyer for the Infants and Children Up To Age 6 Years Old department retired in 1946, Fred had the chance to bid on his job.

He jumped at it. If he wanted to keep climbing the career ladder at Glosser's, he needed a job with more responsibilities and opportunities...both of which could be found in the Infants and Children department.

Fred's success in Notions served him well, and he got the job. When he stepped into his new position, he even got some office space--though he had to share it with the store nurse, Alberta Raab.

This turned out to be a lucky break for Fred. "Alberta was a great help to me," he says. "When she wasn't tending to her duties as Glosser Bros.' nurse, she took care of the control tickets for everything that was sold in my department. I couldn't have succeeded in my job without her help."

Before long, he was going on buying trips with Mr. Strump, The Store's general merchandise manager. "Sometimes, we went to Pittsburgh," says Fred. "In those days, manufacturers would send their representatives to town at certain times of the year. They would rent a whole floor of a hotel and fill it with samples of the merchandise they had for sale. Then we would come in and look it over and place orders for what, if anything, we wanted to sell at Glosser's.

"Sometimes, we would just meet with individual salesmen in a single hotel room in Johnstown or an office at Glosser Bros. The salesmen would open up their bags and trunks and hang up everything they were selling. Then we would place our orders based on that."

There were also plenty of buying trips to New York City and other locations. "In those days, everything we sold was made in the U.S., often in New York City," explains Fred. "There were also many small manufacturers in towns around Johnstown that we visited, where we could buy children's clothing at very low prices.

"We went to the main offices of the manufacturers and talked directly to the owners of the companies to get the best deals. They liked Glosser Bros. because we paid quickly, and they treated us better than Sears Roebuck."

During their visits to manufacturers, Fred and Mr. Strump often bought end-of season merchandise. "We liked to buy closeouts," says Fred. "Near the end of the winter season, for example, there would be a lot of winter merchandise left over--coats, boys' clothing, sleepers, and what have you. We could buy it for maybe 50 cents on the dollar. The manufacturer just wanted to get rid of it."

After buying up end-of-season merchandise, Fred kept it boxed up until the next season when it would be in demand. "If we bought winter merchandise on closeout, we held it until the next fall, when we had our big anniversary sale. It was brand new merchandise in the original packaging, so the quality was high, but the prices were very low.

"If something originally sold for $2.99, we sold it for $1.99. We still made a profit, and the customer got a beautiful item, such as a beautiful piece of clothing, for a third off what he would've paid before, when it was first in season.

"Many times, we could sell something at our cost or less, just to bring the customer into the department to buy something else that was on sale at a real bargain."

Coming up with pricing could get complicated because Fred sometimes bought assortments of items for the Infants and Children department that had different wholesale costs and relative values. "Some items I could make a profit on, while with others I could only break even. To price them, I multiplied each price by the number of items it applied to, then added up all the subtotals I got from that and divided that number by the total number of items. That's how we averaged it out and came up with individual item prices. Then we added our markup and had a sale.

"The same rules applied to pajamas, dresses, underwear, any kind of clothing," says Fred. "We paid closeout wholesale prices and kept our markup low, and that kept our prices down. The customers would benefit, getting a good value for the kids."

1950s-Bound

Fred Glosser had come a long way. That much was obvious, as the 1940s drew to a close.

He had gone from Army instructor to stock boy/maintenance man to Notions buyer... and now to buyer/manager in Infants and Children Up To Age 6.

The Store had changed, too. Employees who'd joined the war effort had come back to reclaim their positions. Wartime shortages had been replaced by postwar plenty.

And in 1946, the company had taken a big step that would better position it for future growth. After decades as a partnership, the company had incorporated in the state of Pennsylvania. The resulting entity would be known forever after as Glosser Bros., Inc. That much of the future, at least, had been decided...though so many other questions remained.

What would the next decade bring? Tremendous expansion for Glosser's? Career advancement for Fred? Extreme peaks for them both in an era of boundless prosperity?

It didn't seem to matter much at the time. Glosser's kept rolling along, bringing in the customers the way it always had. In 1948, The Store marked its 42nd anniversary with the usual anniversary sale; customers could get free inbound bus and streetcar rides to the sale, and they could take a chance at winning a free Chevrolet. It was business as usual, with sales and promotions to keep the public entertained and the cash registers ringing.

Meanwhile, the future lay ahead like a bank of fog, keeping its secrets until it was good and ready to clear away and reveal them.

Photo courtesy of Johnstown Area Heritage Association

MEMORY DEPARTMENT

Glosser's had the best snack bar, where the Shaffer twins would make the best banana splits, cherry Cokes, and sandwiches. The cafeteria featured a special every day. Tuesday was Chinese, Wednesday was spaghetti, and so on. I remember the won ton soup! The end of the cafeteria line had glasses so you could get yourself as much water as you liked.

- Paula Katie Buynack Becker

My friend Terry and I would walk from Lorain Boro into town to save money. When we were done with our 7 Up and sherbet floats at Glosser's, we would have just enough money to take the bus home. Such wonderful memories.

- Catherine Blaschak-Karwoski

I got my first job at Glosser's in 1956. I was 16, and they stuck me in the shoe department, and I didn't know the first thing about fitting shoes. Then, I was put in the candy department. That job, I could do.

- Romaine Ringler Moran

I started working as a part-time employee at Glosser's in the mid 1940s. In the early 1950s, I became full-time as assistant manager in the notions department, and later was offered the manager/buyer job in the Record Department, which became the Book, Record, and Stereo Department. It was something, getting the Top Ten records as soon as they came out. Every Friday at 5:10, I named the Top Ten records for that week over the radio.

- *Helen Harteis Schad Bowman*

Photo courtesy of Helen Harteis Bowman

Photo by Russell Heffley, courtesy of Johnstown Area Heritage Association

In the 1940s and early 50s, my folks did all their grocery shopping at Glossers. Dad would park in the penny meters next to the Post Office, and we kids fed the meter while Mom went shopping and Dad disappeared up the block to a beer joint. We got a quarter for hot cashews for us three kids to share. Then, Mom would appear at the curb with the bags of groceries, and Dad would bring the Buick around, and away we went, back up the hill to Richland.

- *Donald J Bukovec*

I cherish my memories as a child in the mid-50s. My grandfather, Sam Glosser, would take some of us grandchildren down to the store when it was closed on Sunday mornings. We were allowed to be elevator operators, get a bag of candy from the candy department, talk to the night watchman, and run up and down the escalator! We had so much fun!

- *Janet Sinberg Dash*

Glosser Bros. and Johnstown! What HAPPY memories!

My grandmother, Jenny Ossip (nee Glosser) was a sister to the Glosser brothers—David, Sam and Saul—who were my great uncles. When my father, George Ossip, came to this country as a Russian immigrant, the Glosser brothers gave him his first job in the Glosser Bros. men's department. His brother, Sydney, later became the Glosser Bros. comptroller for many, many years.

Having gained valuable retail experience at Glosser Bros., my father and David Glosser's wife's nephew, Moe Sacks, moved to Cumberland, Maryland, and opened a department store there. Unfortunately, the Cumberland flood wiped them out, and they ended up opening the Public Service Food Markets. The original market was later to become the building for the Gee Bee store in Cumberland.

I was born and reared in Cumberland (which is about 60 miles from Johnstown) but made many trips to Johnstown with my family. When we visited Johnstown, shopping at Glosser Bros. was always a memorable experience. The clothes were so different from those available in Cumberland. We always managed to fill the trunk of the car with many boxes containing the latest fashions at least four times a year. While we were in the store, we had lunch in the cafeteria and visited with our many relatives who worked there. Those trips were always a wonderful family reunion and a fantastic boost to our wardrobes. Glosser Bros. was definitely THE place for up-to-date fashions!

- *Bobbi Ann Ossip*

When I was small, I was afraid to go into the women's restroom at Glossers. In the restroom stall, you had to step up, and there was this toilet seat that was lit up with blue lights. It was supposed to kill germs on the toilet seat. It scared the heck out of me.

- *Barbara Schonhardt*

This scale once stood outside the ladies' restroom at Glosser's. Now, it can be found in the home of Anne Zurilla.

Photos courtesy of Anne Zurilla

I remember the man who sat in the elevator all day and pushed the button for everyone. That must have been a boring job, but I guess it had its ups and downs.

- *David P. Campbell*

GLOSSER'S ALL-STARS

BILL HRITZ

Bill Hritz managed both Glosser's parking lots for 13 years, starting in the early 1950s. Customers in those days could get valet parking--two hours for 25 cents. But parking was free if the driver's only destination was Glosser's.

"When they pulled in, I asked where they were going," remembers Bill. "If they were only going to Glosser's, not the bank or drug store or wherever, I put a special tag on the car instead of the usual ticket. Then, when the person came back for the car, they just showed me the receipt for what they'd bought in Glosser's, and I refunded their 25 cent parking fee."

Photo courtesy of Bill Hritz

There were two lots at the time, one behind The Store facing Washington Street, and the other on the corner of Franklin and Washington, beside the current location of the Post Office. Even with all the available spaces, though, there wasn't always enough room for everyone. "Cars lined up down Washington Street, all the way to City Hall, waiting to get in the Glosser Bros. lots," says Bill. "The cops didn't like it much, because of the traffic, but the customers liked being close to the store."

Bill, who was born in 1934, worked six days a week and loved his job...even when people argued about paying a quarter. "When folks didn't want to pay, I'd give them a talking-to and straighten them out. The bosses on the fourth floor leaned out their windows and clapped when I did it, too."

Bill also drove the delivery trucks when the regular drivers couldn't make it to work. He did his share of entertaining, too, playing his accordion in the cafeteria every morning for an hour or two.

As for his own lunch, he liked to get a hot dog or hamburger at the lunch counter on the first floor, then eat in Central Park with his co-workers. "Everyone who worked there, whether they were part-time or full-time, was like family. It was a great group of people, and a great place to work.

"I loved Glosser's. It was my heart," says Bill.

It was a sentiment shared by many people, one thing that would remain constant even as The Store and company continued to evolve.

Photos courtesy of Bill Hritz

Chapter 18

The Countdown Decade

Ten...nine...eight...

As Izzy Glosser counted down the last seconds until midnight on December 31, 1949, he wondered what the new decade had in store for The Store.

Seven...six...

Other members of the Glosser's family had similar thoughts-- from those in the first generation of Store operators (David, Sam, and Nathan) to those in the second generation (Fred, Izzy, Bill, Alvin, Paul, Gerald) and beyond.

The truth, if they had known it on that night, would have shocked them.

Five...four...

It would have shocked them because great things were coming, *incredible* things, but not until the next decade, the 1960s. And not all of them would live to *see* the 60s.

Three...two...one...

The 1950s would set the stage for the great things to come. The great things would have their start then...but the years and months and days themselves would be largely uneventful. The decade itself would be less of a turning point...

Zero!

...and more of a countdown.

Generation Milkshake

When it comes to listing the ways for setting the stage for the future, raising the next generation has got to be right up there in the top five at least. Better make that the top *three*.

And that was exactly what the extended Glosser family did in the 1950s. The families of Fred and Izzy's generation--those born in the teens and 1920s, primarily--had been having babies since the 40s and kept at it well into the 50s. A whole new wave of Glossers, the second generation to grow up with The Store in their lives, began to make its presence felt.

This batch of kids, like their parents before them, had a common Jewish heritage and a Glosser's Department Store legacy that kept them close. Their childhoods had so many shared experiences: picking treats from the Glosser Bros. candy counter; playing with toys in the toy department; making ice cream sundaes in the snack bar; celebrating Seder with dozens of relatives in Glosser's cafeteria. These kids knew what it was like to grow up a Glosser in Johnstown, and this understanding forged strong bonds between them.

Some bonds were stronger than others, though. The children of Fred, Izzy, and Freda, for example, developed a special connection. They spent more time together than they did with other cousins, in part because Fred, Izzy, and Freda were all siblings, the offspring of Sam and Pearl Glosser.

Photos courtesy of Patti Glosser Rudick

"The children of Sam and Pearl and their spouses and children were more one big family than three individual families," remembers Izzy's wife, Ruth Glosser. "We went on vacations together, had holiday meals together, took Sunday drives together, you name it. We were an incredibly close-knit family."

The kids formed an alliance that would last a lifetime, one that even had its own special symbol: *the milkshake*.

"We often had dinner together," says Ruth. "But the kids were such finicky eaters, they barely touched their food. So we started taking them out for milkshakes after dinner, just to get something in their stomachs.

"Pretty soon, it became a tradition. And the kids started calling themselves the Milkshake Club."

Born in the mid-1950s, the Milkshake Club included Izzy and Ruth's kids (Mark, Miriam, and David), Fred and Betty's kids (Patti and Daniel), and Freda and Herbert Sinberg's kids (Matthew and Janet).

Every time they posed for a photo, the Milkshake Club lined up in the same order, from left to right: Daniel, Patti, Mark, Matthew, Janet, Miriam, and David. It was a tradition they followed all through adulthood, an expression of their deep connection, a gesture of their abiding love for each other.

And *milkshakes*.

Photos courtesy of Janet Sinberg Dash

Last of the Brothers

Even as a slew of shiny new Glossers stepped into the spotlight, a group of older ones stepped aside to make way. They weren't just *any* old Glossers, though. They were the *originals*.

The original Glosser brothers.

Saul had been the first to pass away, in 1944. The other three all lived to see The Store's 45th anniversary, in September 1951...but the years continued to take a toll.

David died next, in 1954, while serving as president of the company. Nathan died shortly thereafter, in 1955.

When David passed away, Sam stepped into the presidency, which he held for four more years. Then, on August 14, 1959, Sam died, too.

By the turn of the decade, the start of the 1960s, all four of the original Glosser brothers were gone. None of them lived to see the company's glory days, the big expansions and record profits and stock offerings that were yet to come. But none of that would have been possible without the brothers. They wouldn't see it or share the rewards, but their influence would always be felt.

GLOSSER BROS.
"In the Heart of Johnstown"

45 YEARS IN THE HEART OF JOHNSTOWN

Once again the inevitable has taken from Johnstown another staunch champion of this great community. We extend our heartfelt sympathy to the family and friends of

DAVID GLOSSER

His warm and friendly smile and hand clasp will be greatly missed by all who shared his acquaintance and his absence from the Johnstown scene will be sorely felt by all.

MILLER'S

PENN FURNITURE

joins the many thousands in mourning the death of

David Glosser

...a fine citizen
...a great leader
...a true Johnstowner

David Glosser

David Glosser's keen business ability contributed much during the last half-century to build up one of the largest independent merchandising houses in the state. And his sound judgment was frequently sought, and always freely given, to the civic enterprises of this community.

Just four years ago he received the Good Neighbor award of the Good Cheer Club of Johnstown. He had served as a trustee and honorary vice president of the Community Chest, and was active in the YMCA; and he was a member of the board of Lee Hospital, the Red Cross, the Family Welfare Society, the Salvation Army and the Jewish Home for the Aged in Pittsburgh.

Always interested in the community's youth, Mr. Glosser was a member of the Johnstown Oldtimers Baseball Association and one of the incorporators of Johnnies, Inc., which sponsored professional baseball here for a number of years; as well as a sponsor and backer of other recreational activities.

Mr. Glosser rarely missed a Good Will Tour of the Chamber of Commerce through this area, and he usually took part in the Good Roads Tour of the Johnstown Motor Club. A friendly man, he showed a warm interest in the problems of others; and his interest in the progress of Johnstown was always evident.

In nearly half a century of business activity since, in 1906, he joined his father and an older brother in the operation of Glosser's Store—subsequently becoming president of Glosser Bros. Store following its incorporation—Mr. Glosser became known as one of the state's most enterprising merchants. He was one of the group of men whose foresight and ability built the business center that Johnstown has become.

OUR DEEPEST SYMPATHY . . .

to the family of
DAVID GLOSSER
Johnstown has lost a valuable leader and friend

Management and Employes Of
SWANK HARDWARE CO.

With deep regret we note the passing of
DAVID GLOSSER
Pres. Glosser Bros. Store

We shall long mourn the death of this great community leader and gentleman. We shall long remember him for his kindly wisdom, his unselfish service to every worthwhile community project. He shall serve as a continuing source of inspiration to us for many, many years.

Cambria Equipment Co.

SEARS

extends its deepest sympathy in this hour of sadness as we note the passing of

DAVID GLOSSER

Our deepest sympathy to his family, friends and store personnel. His passing is a grievous loss to the civic and business life of this community.

We deeply mourn the loss of
DAVID GLOSSER

A good citizen, a good neighbor and a good friend who faithfully preserved and honored the traditions entrusted to him.

HOME FURNITURE CO.

We extend our deepest sympathy to the family, friends and business associates of

DAVID GLOSSER

whose death is a severe loss to the civic and business life of this community.

The Nathan and Elsasser Families

Bella on the Board

Courtesy of Ruth Glosser

At least one of the Glosser sisters took up the reins and continued to make the first generation's influence felt. Bella Glosser Coppersmith kept up the tradition of having an "original" Glosser in the board room after her brothers had passed away. Bella served until the early 1970s as honorary chairman of the board of directors of Glosser Bros., helping to ground the company's progress in the wisdom of the generation that had risen from hardship in the Old Country and made The Store possible.

For years, Bella's husband, S.G. "Coppy" Coppersmith, was head of the women's departments at Glosser's. Their son, W. Louis Coppersmith, would make an impact of his own by serving as a Pennsylvania state senator from 1969 to 1980.

Free Deliveries...For Real

According to Sydney Ossip, The Store thrived in the 1950s. "Business was very good then. Glosser Bros. was very profitable in those years."

The post-World War II economy was booming, and Glosser's basked in the halo effect. Wartime shortages and rationing were over, and shoppers were happy to be able to get what they wanted. Thanks to the Baby Boom, there were plenty of young families in need of life's necessities and simple pleasures, and Glosser's had plenty of both in stock.

In 1953, the City of Johnstown installed improved lighting in the central business district, encouraging stores to stay open later and shoppers to take advantage of extended hours. Downtown businesses did well, and Glosser's was no exception.

The company's delivery trucks always seemed to be busy, rushing merchandise to shoppers' homes--always free of charge. "Any time someone bought something, they could have it delivered at no additional cost," remembers Fred. "A shopper could buy something for a dollar, even, and have it delivered for free."

Glosser's fleet of five trucks delivered to outlying communities, sometimes traveling as far as Cresson and beyond. The more often they were gone from their garage across Franklin Street from The Store, the better business was...and in the 50s, they weren't in the garage very much.

Photo from Glosser Bros. Annual Report, Jan. 1976

Why Anticipation Is A *Good* Thing

Actually, Glosser's was a standout not only on the local level, but the national level as well. The business reporting company Dun and Bradstreet gave Glosser Bros. a credit rating of AAA1, its highest, in the 50s. According to Fred Glosser, this was made possible by the Glosser company's system of paying its debts as early as possible.

"We used to pay our bills before we even got the merchandise we'd purchased," says Fred. "We made sure we paid early enough to get what's called an anticipation discount."

"Here's how it worked. If you bought merchandise from a wholesaler or manufacturer, and you paid your bill within ten days, you could take a 2%, 3%, or 8% discount. For clothing, the discount was often 8%, though there were lower discounts for other items.

"Most retailers paid within ten days but not right away. They waited a few days, until they'd sold some of the merchandise, and then they paid the bill.

"But if you paid the bill within one or two days of receiving it, you could take an extra 1% off. That was called the anticipation discount, and we always got it.

"So Glosser's got the usual 8% discount for paying within ten days, plus the 1% anticipation discount, and it really added up. When you're doing 100 million dollars in business a year, that 1% is a lot of money. And that was our profit at the end of the year.

"The credit discounts are where we made our money. It made up for the fact that not all our merchandise sold equally well. Sometimes, we had to sell items at cost or below cost. If we sold half our merchandise at a profit, then sold the other half at a loss, we only broke even. But the credit discounts put us over the top again."

Fifty Candles on the Cake

As the decade of the 50s progressed, The Store continued to post strong earnings--and marked a series of milestones that were a testimony to its longevity and promise.

On September 21, 1956, Glosser Bros. Department Store celebrated its 50th Anniversary. It was the biggest party of the year in Johnstown, even if the exact date of the store's founding was up for debate. The year was correct, at least; everyone agreed that the Glosser Bros. store had opened in 1906. As for the month and day, the Glossers had chosen it for a very good reason: a sale and promotional event in September would be good for business. Anniversary sales had always been held in September, and this one would be no exception.

The family made the 50th Anniversary an occasion to remember, complete with a parade, a giant cake, and a huge sale with tons of discounted merchandise. If The Store hadn't been an official institution before, it was now; 50 years in business had cemented its place in the community and the hearts of shoppers.

Photos courtesy of Bill Glosser

16—Johnstown Tribune-Democrat, Sat., Sept. 15, 1956   (Advertisement)

Glosser's Enjoys Steady Growth in 50 Years

Father, Eldest Son Started Store Company

City Firm Expands Quickly Following Founding in 1906

Glosser Market A First

25 YEARS LATER

Winner of First Glosser's Baby Derby Is Now Mother

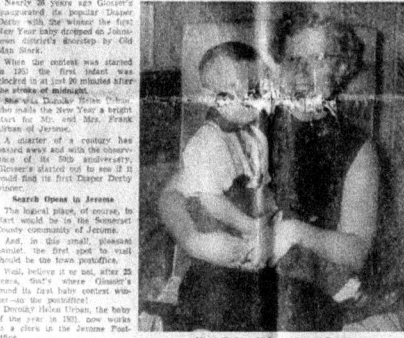

Mrs. Walter Kohs and son, David

THIS GLOSSER'S DEPARTMENT ONE OF BUSIEST

Unlabeled Cans Sold After Flood

Cafeteria Popular Lunchtime Spot

A THANK YOU FROM GLOSSER'S

An anniversary statement from Gerald Glosser, general manager of Glosser Bros.

Hat Time Near

Busy Glosser Counter

The following join in a salute to a Great Store — Glosser Brothers of Johnstown, Pa.

A. ELGART & SONS	BERKLIFF UNDERGARMENT	CHESTER H. ROTH CO.	FELCO ATHLETIC WEAR	H. H. BROWN SHOE CO.	KAUFMAN, FIRST & ROSENKRANTZ
ADAM HAT MANUFACTURERS	BERKSHIRE HOSE	CUMBERLAND MACARONI MFG. CO.	FLAUM'S	H. J. HEINZ CO.– 57 Varieties of Pure Food	KENMORE GARMENT CO.
ALPAGORA–Outercoats and Sportcoats	BESTFORM FOUNDATIONS	D & H DISTRIBUTING CO.	FLAGG ROMAN CO.	HAMILTON CURTAIN CORP.	KICKERINOS
AMERICAN FOAM RUBBER CORP.	BETTY ANN HATS, INC.	DANFORTH CORP.	FLORIE DIEBOLD & CO.	HARRY IRWIN CO.	KINGSLEY CO.
AMERICAN JUNIORS SHOE	BIDDLE PURCHASING CO.	DENTON SLEEPING GARMENT MILLS	FORDHAM-BARDELL SHIRT CORP.	HENSEL & SONS	KIRBY, BLOCK & CO., INC.
ANN REVERE LING, INC.	BIFLEX FOUNDATIONS	DEXTON CLOTHES	FREEMAN SHOE CORPORATION	HERSHEY CLOTHES, INC.	KIRSCH COMPANY
ARIA LINGERIE	BIG TOP-STURDIBOY-COLLEGIATE	EAGLE CLOTHES	G. H. HAMMOND CO.	INTERNATIONAL LATEX	KLEIN CHOCOLATE COMPANY
ARMOUR & COMPANY	BOURJOIS, INC.	EBERHARDT MANUFACTURING CO.	G. K. DRUG & CIGAR CO.	J. P. STEVENS CO.	KRAFT FOODS CO.
ARTCRAFT VENETIAN BLIND CO.	BROOKFIELD CLOTHES	EDWARD HAHN PACKING	GARFIELD AND ROSEN	J. PUMA COMPANY, INC.	LA PREMIATA MACARONI CORP.
ATLAS PASTE CO.	BROWN BROS. POTATO CHIP CO., INC.	EMPIRE SPECIALTY FOOTWEAR CO.	GEORGE COHEN CLOTHING	JACK SPIRO & CO., INC.	LAD 'N' DAD SLACKS, INC.
AUGUST F. NIELSEN CO.	BURLINGTON HOSIERY CO.	ELI A. ALBERT CO.	GENERAL MILLS, INC.	Lily Bee Frocks	LADY ANDREA, INC.
BAAR & BEARDS	C. H. PAGE BEDDING CO.	EVERRIGHT DRESS CO.	GIBBS UNDERWEAR CO.	JOHNSTOWN SANITARY DAIRY CO.	LINDY ALLEN
BABYKNIT CO., INC.	CAMBRIA HOME BAKERY	EXQUISITE FORM BRA	GLOBE VARNISH CO., INC	JOLLEY METAL COMPANY	LO-BEL COMPANY
BARKEN & LEVIN CO.	CAMPUS GIRL ROBES	FAIRTEX UNDIES, INC.	GLORIA GAY COATS, INC.	JOLLY KIDS TOGS	LOOMCRAFT FAMOUS SLIPS
BEAVER MEADOW CREAMERY, INC.	CAMPUS SPORTSWEAR CO.	FEDERAL SWEETS & BISCUIT CO., INC.	GOLD SEAL RUBBER CO.	KAHN-LUCAS-LANCASTER, INC.	M. ARON CORP.
BELL TEXTILES	CANNON MILLS, INC.		GOOD LUCK GLOVE CO.		M. C. RUSSIC CO.
	CAROLYN CHENILLES, INC.		GOULD BROS.	KAMLER DISTRIBUTING CO.	M. G. KINSLER CO.
	CHARM UNDERGARMENT		GRIFFON CUTLERY CORP.		MA-RO HOSIERY CO., INC.

135

(ADVERTISEMENT)   Johnstown Tribune-Democrat, Sat., Sept. 15, 1956—17

Glosser's women's and men's clothing departments are among the largest in Western Pennsylvania.

38 LOCAL BUYERS

4 Buying Firms Aid Glosser's

A staff of 38 local buyers working with four large buying firms assure Glosser Bros. a front row seat in the mercantile marts. Glosser's employs the services of Weisberg-Jaffe Co. Inc., millinery specialists in New York; Kirby, Block & Company Inc., with offices in New York, London and Paris; Puddle Purchasing Company, New York, Chicago and San Francisco, and Johnny Conen, shoe specialists, Boston.

The 38 local buyers work in cooperation with these purchasing houses in making the wide selection of items for the Johnstown store.

Praises Long Association

Says Weisberg-Jaffe on the occasion of Glosser's 50th anniversary:

"We have been associated with

this great store for over 32 years, considering the fact that we are, so to speak, in business 12 years this year. Glosser is one of our oldest and, I add, very fine accounts."

Kirby, Block states in a congratulatory message:

"We have been associated with this fine store for over 23 years at their New York market representatives. Their buyers work with our staff to obtain for the customers of Glosser Bros. the best fashions and values obtainable.

"We are proud to participate in this anniversary and to have been associated with Glosser

Bros. for these many years."

New Maternity Shop

One of the smartest and newest departments in Glosser's is the Maternity Shop, offering a wide selection of all styles of sports and dress clothing.

The women's clothing department is one of the largest in Western Pennsylvania.

Not to be outdone is the large selection in the men's department with a full selection of all kinds of suits.

In the shoe department, a wide range is carried in the kiddies, growing tots and adult sizes.

These are just examples of the cooperation of the store, its local buyers and the four large buying firms whose services it employs.

Make Many Trips

During the past several months the buyers have been working tirelessly in preparation for the 50th anniversary event.

A busy department is one that offers the check-cashing service with over 2,000 salary checks cashed a day. The department, located on the fourth floor of the store, is directed by Miss Bertha Lewis, one of the store's earliest employes.

Checkouts for store's modern grocery department in foreground. In back, portion of Glosser's large meat department, can be seen.

The Maternity Shop is one of Glosser's smartest and newest departments.

From this large cooler comes the delicious cuts supplying Glosser's customers.

Glosser's Aids In Baby Beef

The fall season of county fairs always finds Glosser Bros. playing a leading role in one of the feature attractions.

That is the famed baby beef competition in which youths from Cambria and adjoining counties vie for the blue ribbon.

Months of preparation are spent carefully grooming animals for the contest.

When the judges have carefully weighed each animal according to the rule and the ribbons are awarded, the beef goes on the block.

Many buyers from Glosser's are among the top purchasers of prize stock. Purchase of these events.

The policy of Glosser Bros. serves a dual purpose.

First, it is in line with the established policy of purchasing only the top animals for its meat counters.

Second, Glosser's is happy to help in rewarding the untiring efforts of hundreds of youngsters who have devoted their skill and patience to preparing prize stock.

GLOSSER'S CASHES AS HIGH AS 2,000 CHECKS IN DAY

One of the busiest spots in Glosser Bros. store is the check-cashing service on the fourth floor.

On certain days the store cashes over 2,000 individual salary checks at a single day.

Miss Bertha Lewis, one of the earliest employes of the store, is in charge of the cashier office.

Glosser Bros. inaugurated one of the first self-serve grocery departments in the country. The department grew quickly to its present spacious quarters.

Glosser's Once Had Own Money

There was a time when Glosser's scrip was printed its own "money." Actually, legal tender in all departments of it was scrip. During the bank's closing holidays of 1933 when security found they had trouble cashing their checks because bank funds were frozen, Glosser's cashed the checks, paying off partly with cash and partly with them.

Well, one day they got loose and ran wild in the store. That was of monkeyshines ended the showing of the animals by Glosser's. The store found milder displays at store windows ever ago in the days did not result in such wild windows. Whatever happened to possession.

Remember This Display at Store?

Remember the live monkeys the store displayed years ago in its windows?

Store Put Up Big Balloon

As a promotion stunt, the department store formerly kept a big balloon tied to the top of the store with air either to 12-number rides unfailing. On a certain date it would ask for a festival at night.

It would be released. The finder would be rewarded, were merchandise.

However, Glosser's found balloon couldn't be kept tied up too long.

The reason: Holiday-making profits from the air which filled the balloon started a period of 4,500.

Store Dance Feature

Glosser's sponsored monthly teen dances at the old Auditorium during the early 1930s for an admission charge of 25 cents per person. One of these dances attracted a crowd of 4,500.

Sale in the infant and children's department, 1956 (Tribune-Democrat photo courtesy of Johnstown Area Heritage Association)

Annexation

The Store reached another landmark when it completed its first notable expansion since the opening of the Locust Street addition in 1931. This time, Glosser's took over the lower level of what would come to be known as the Annex, a building on the corner of Franklin and Washington Streets behind The Store.

Glosser Bros. had owned the Annex for many years, actually. The cafeteria had been located on the second floor since at least the 1930s, in fact. But the ground floor had been occupied by various tenants, an array of small businesses including the Star Barber Shop, Romanoff's Bar and Restaurant, a shoemaker, a Republic gas station, and a seasonal garden shop next to the alley between the Annex and The Store.

Instead of renewing the leases of these tenants when they expired in the mid-1950s, Glosser Bros. took over the space they'd occupied, converting it into an extension of The Store. Sections of the Annex's ground floor became the locations of the paint, hardware, outdoor furniture, and garden supplies departments. As for the gas station, Fred had it torn down and built a two-story addition to the Annex in its place to house the automotive service department.

In one broad stroke, the company had increased its square footage considerably, creating new retail opportunities in the Annex itself and the space opened up in the main store by moving out certain existing departments.

Promotions, Anyone?

Life after the 50th Anniversary was different at Glosser's. Times were changing, as the Annex expansion suggested, and the leadership of the company was changing with them.

The new group of leaders had been in development for quite a while, working their way up through The Store's chain of command. As the old the guard retired, these younger faces moved into the upper echelons, forming the team that would carry Glosser's, Inc. into the future.

Alvin Glosser and Sydney Ossip had been directors and vice presidents since 1946. Leonard Black and Paul Glosser had received the same titles in 1954.

But it wasn't until the passing of the last of the original Glosser Bros. in 1959 that the new head honchos were given the keys to the kingdom.

Fred, Izzy, and Herb Sinberg were promoted to vice presidents...and an existing vice president moved even higher. Leonard Black was elected to the position of president, succeeding the late Sam Glosser. For the first time, a man who had not been born a Glosser, who had no Glosser blood in his veins and arteries, would steer the destiny of the Glosser Bros. company.

With his promotion, the new leadership team was in place. From that point onward, into the 1960s and beyond, Leonard and his colleagues would play key roles in moving the company forward, meeting new challenges in ways that would promote growth and enhance profitability. They would stay together for decades to come, united by family ties and a shared love for The Store and company that had been at the center of their lives for as long as they could remember.

Meanwhile, just as Glosser, Inc.'s new leadership team took shape, the economic landscape

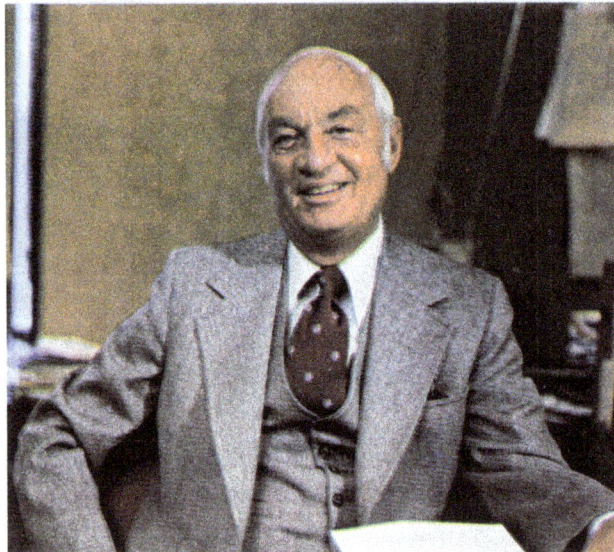

Leonard Black (photo from Glosser Bros. Annual Report, Jan. 1978

they would navigate, which would lead to their bold new plans and successes, was taking shape around them.

Big Buck 'Burbs

Life was good for Glosser's Department Store in the 50s, but warning signs were visible. The suburbs had been growing since the end of the war, as servicemen and their families bought homes away from downtown areas. As new businesses sprouted up in suburban shopping centers to support these residents, the focus of economic activity began a slow but inexorable shift from downtown to the 'burbs.

"We saw other retailers opening up stores in shopping centers," remembers Izzy. "We decided we'd better do the same thing, or we'd be left out in the cold eventually. Our downtown store was still doing great, but we realized that might not last forever if trends continued the way they were going."

The seeds were planted for the company's next move. In the closing years of the 50s, the leadership team relentlessly studied the changing retail climate, gathering data on which to base their own plans. They met with experts, crunched numbers, and toured competitors' stores in other towns and cities to see exactly what they were doing.

They also hired an advertising agency to come up with a name for the new venture. It took many meetings between the agency, Glosser Bros. executives, and Glosser's own display advertising department to come up with what seemed like the perfect name: *Gee Bee.*

The result of all these efforts, the first Gee Bee Discount Department Store, wouldn't be built until the early 1960s. But it was a child of the 50s, just as surely as so many of the Glosser kids who were born and raised in that decade.

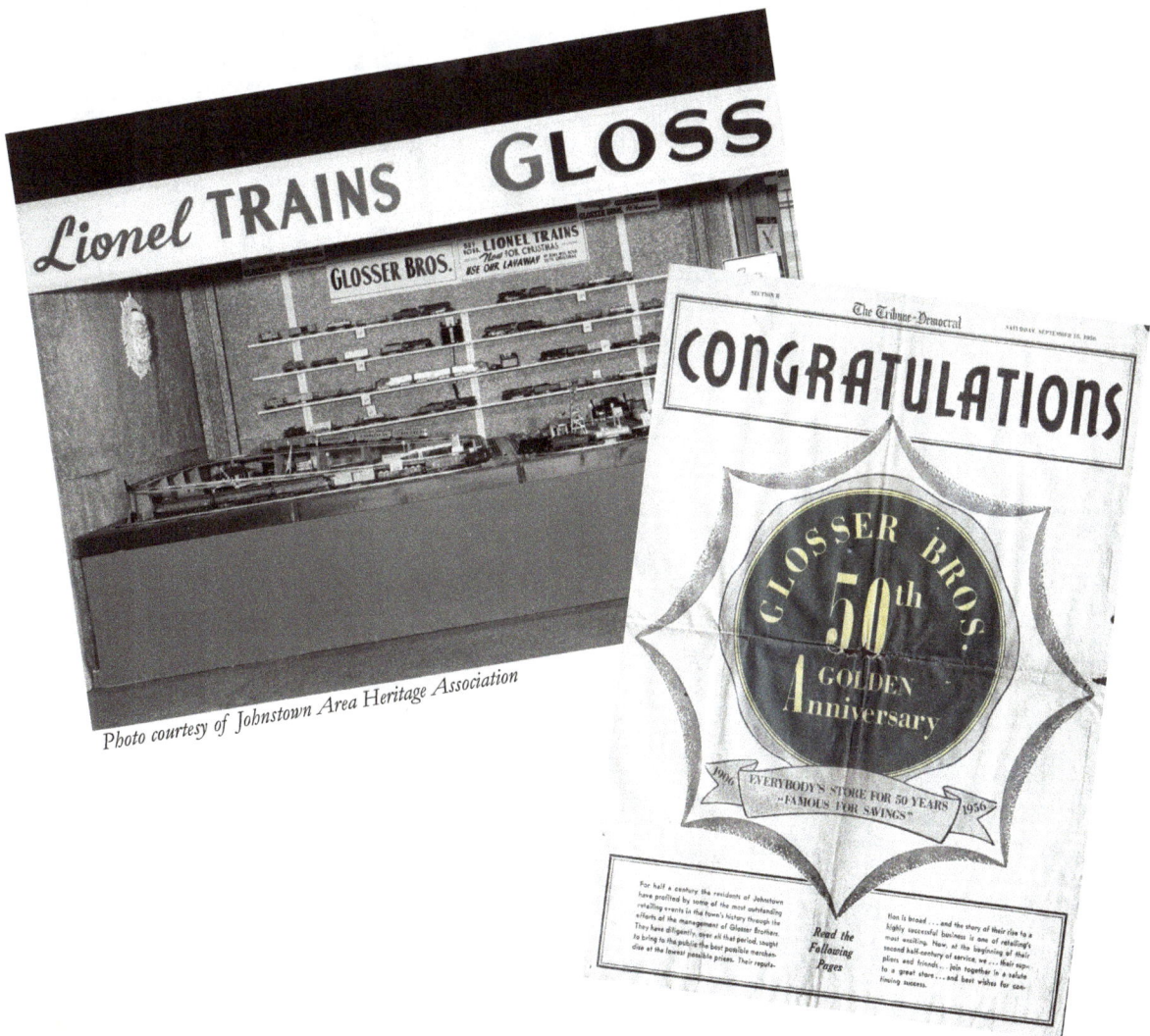

Photo courtesy of Johnstown Area Heritage Association

GLOSSER'S ALL-STARS
THE SHAFFER TWINS

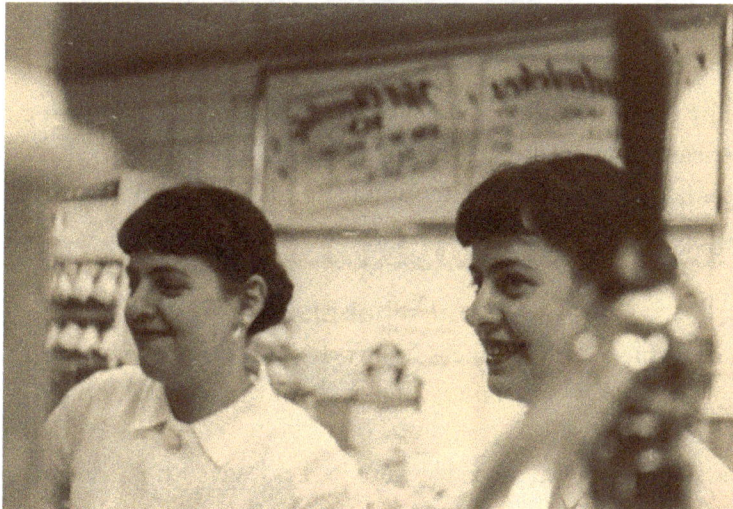

Photo courtesy of Ruby Shaffer

The women who became forever known as "the Glosser Twins" weren't Glossers at all.

"We said, 'We're not the Glosser twins, we're just the *Shaffer* twins," remembers Ruby Shaffer. "But folks just went on calling us that.

"We weren't even the only twins in the store. There were five sets of twins at Glosser's...but for some reason, folks singled us out as the Glosser twins.

"We'd walk down the street, and people would say, 'Here come those Glosser twins. They're always jolly, walking to work.' And the name just stuck," says Ruby.

38 Years at the Soda Fountain

Ruby and her sister, Ruth, became local legends while working for 38 years at the Glosser Bros. Department Store. Their careers started when they dropped out of high school after their father, a miner, was injured on the job.

At first, Ruby and Ruth worked in the main section of the cafeteria. When the hot dog counter opened on the ground floor, Ruth moved there, but the sisters reunited before long.

141

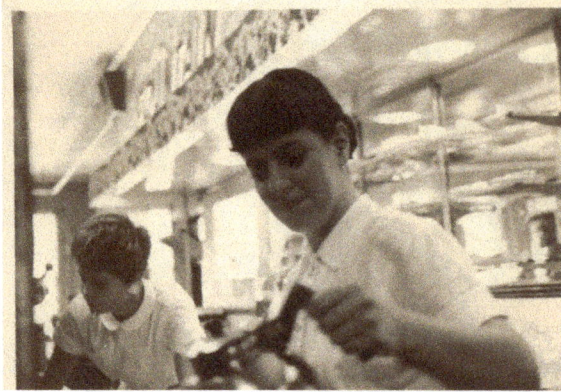

Photo courtesy of Ruby Shaffer

When the two girls working at the soda fountain quit, Ruby and Ruth stepped into their jobs...and didn't leave for over three decades. That's where they became known as the Glosser twins, serving up ice cream sundaes with unfailingly sunny dispositions.

"Ruth and I were taught to be pleasant to people, respect our elders, and do what we could do to help," says Ruby. "Our parents raised us to be good to everyone."

Once, Ruby remembers, a customer told her he couldn't afford to pay for the lunch he'd just eaten. Instead of calling in security, Ruby told him she would pay for his food. "I said, 'Don't even think about paying me back. It's just a gift. Go ahead and enjoy your meal.'"

"And What Else?"

Treating customers with kindness wasn't the only common thread that endeared the twins to generations of customers. They also wore identical outfits every day, right down to their jewelry.

"We always dressed alike, since we were babies," says Ruby. "We wore the same dresses, shoes, nightgowns, hair clips, everything.

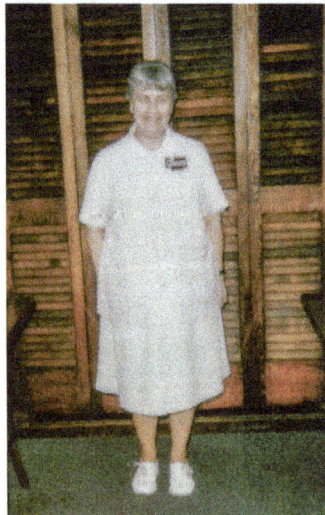

Photo courtesy of Margie Hagerich

Photo courtesy of Margie Hagerich

"At Glosser's, we wore identical white dresses as uniforms. Sometimes, we got to wear white slacks instead."

Ruby and Ruth also used the same catch phrase whenever they waited on customers. "'And what else?' That was what we always said when we were taking people's orders. 'And what else?'" says Ruby.

Maybe it was the catch phrase that made people order so much from the soda fountain and cafeteria--or maybe the food was just that good.

Ruby and Ruth certainly loved it and ate their share for lunch during their work-day shifts. "We never brought a lunch, we always just ate in the cafeteria. We were allowed to have the food, as long as we didn't waste it.

142

"We loved having a big order of French fries with gravy over them. The spaghetti dinner with meatballs was one of our favorites, too. It was delicious.

"Sometimes we'd have a meat loaf dinner with gravy and French fries. And sometimes we'd just get ourselves a sundae."

"Here Come Those Twins"

Ruby and Ruth's sweet treats, and even sweeter personalities, won them many friends among Glosser's customers. "We got to be close with the regulars," says Ruby. "When people came in a lot, we got to know all about them. As soon as we saw them walking down the steps, we got their food ready, because we already knew what they liked."

Ruby and Ruth also enjoyed spending time with their co-workers in the cafeteria and the Hunt Room table service restaurant. "When the soda fountain wasn't busy, we helped out in the kitchen, doing dishes or prepping food. We helped in the Hunt Room, too, putting placemats on tables or cleaning up or serving orders to customers.

"We just liked helping everybody and enjoying their company. We'd even kid around some when we could. Sometimes we'd give somebody a broom and say, 'you sweep and I'll watch you for a while,' and we'd laugh. Sometimes they'd do the same thing to one of us, instead."

The twins also visited fellow employees throughout The Store on their lunch breaks. "They were nice, all of them. Down in the supermarket and meat department, they were all nice. Upstairs in the other departments, they were the same way. If Ruth and I wanted to buy something, and they didn't have it in stock, they'd order it for us.

143

Photos courtesy of Ruby Shaffer

"The ladies in the offices on the fourth floor were good to us, too," says Ruby. "We'd take up a cup of coffee, and they were always nice to us. They'd say, 'Here come those twins.'

"If we had trouble with our register, they'd come help us out and explain things. They'd tell us a little bit of change wasn't anything to worry about, as long as it wasn't *all* the money."

The Glosser Twins and the *Real* Glossers

Ruby and Ruth might not have been actual Glosser twins, but they did have a special place in their hearts for the members of the Glosser family who ran The Store. "They were wonderful to work for. Very nice, pleasant people. Honest people.

"They helped you out if you needed help. If you needed something and couldn't afford it, they let you have it and said 'Pay when you can pay.'

"They also sent us a discount card on our birthday. I think it was for 25% off. They always seemed to remember," says Ruby.

Birthdays were special for the Glosser twins...and so was the Christmas season. Ruby and Ruth loved the decorations, especially in the display windows, and the holiday music playing over the PA system.

"We had special meals in the cafeteria," remembers Ruby. "Sometimes they'd make up special plates of goodies and pass them around the store for employees and customers alike.

"People were always happy at Christmas time. Sometimes, they'd even sing in the store, and we'd join in with them.

"Then there was Santa Claus. He'd walk around and pass out little candy canes to the kids. Sometimes he'd hand out little baskets with candy, prizes, and toys."

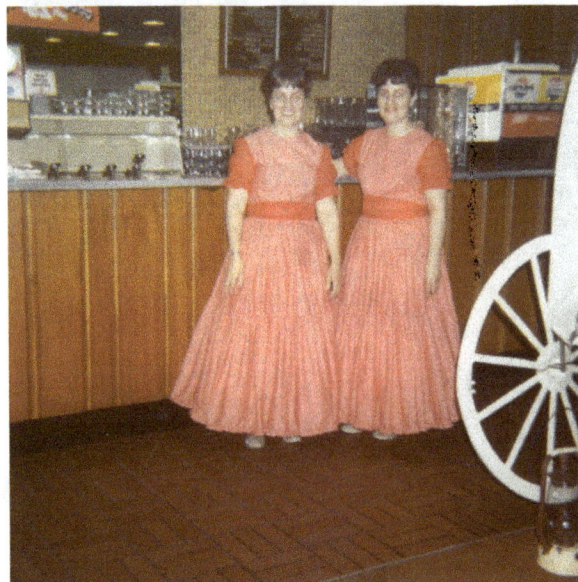

"I Want My Banana Split"

Unfortunately, the good times at Glosser's ended in the late 1980s. When The Store closed for good, the curtain fell on the Glosser twins' careers at the soda fountain. It's a loss that haunts Ruby to this day.

"Every day, I think about Glosser's," she says. "Every time I go down to the dollar store that's in there now, I look at that building and say, 'Remember how busy that place was?' I look through the windows and say, 'I wish that store was still open.'

"But I know it's gone, and I have to accept it. We really enjoyed it, Ruth and I, but it's over. At least I have the memories."

So do Ruby and Ruth's many friends. To this day, they often recognize Ruby and talk to her about the old days.

Ruby Shaffer 2014 (photo by Robert Jeschonek)

"I can't go walking down the street to go to the store, without someone stopping and saying, 'I want my ice cream soda,' or somebody else comes along and says, 'I want my banana split.' Or somebody else will come along and say, 'I want my good bag of popcorn you always made me.' Every time I go somewhere, they stop me," says Ruby.

They did the same for Ruth until she passed away in late 2013. Things haven't been quite the same since, but Ruby's other two sisters, Diana and Audrey, still share a house with her and keep her life interesting.

And her Glosser's fame keeps leading her in surprising new directions.

"There was a big reunion downtown for the 25th anniversary of the store's closing," says Ruby. "At first, I didn't want to go. But then my sisters talked me into it, and I enjoyed it so much.

"I saw some old friends and talked about old times at Glosser Bros.. It was so nice to see them again.

"And I thought, 'Oh, I'm glad I did come. I'm so glad I didn't miss this.'"

Photo courtesy of Ruby Shaffer

Photo by Philip Balko

MEMORY DEPARTMENT

I had the honor and pleasure to work with Ruth and Ruby Shaffer at Glosser's! I learned more about how to treat people than how to serve food. They were blessings!
- *Joella Bobak*

My Mom didn't drive, so we would take the bus into town and go to Glosser's for lunch and get French fries and gravy and a real cherry coke. I remember watching the twins get my Coke and then add cherry juice and then say "anything else?" I remember sitting at a window seat and spending time with my Mom, enjoying my cherry Coke and her company. These memories might be simple, but they are so precious to me.
- *Sherri Angel*

My wife, Marianne, worked at Glosser Bros. when she was 16, both during the summer and over the winter holidays. She worked the sports department on the fourth floor and remembers eating at the cafeteria many times. I also worked at Glosser Bros., but for a contractor, Carstensen's Construction, as a laborer assisting the carpenter in remodeling the grocery section on the first floor. That was the summer of 1957 when I was still in high school.
- *Barry Van Scoyoc*

147

I worked at Glosser's in the jewelry, handbag, and wedding departments. During my time there, I became very good friends with certain co-workers, especially Fritzie, Pauline, and Mrs. Psinakis. I also fondly remember Iz Suchman, who worked in the shoe department. And I loved visiting my dad (Bill Glosser) and other relatives in their offices.

I remember the escalator, the candy department, and the painted Halloween windows. My favorite memories include the special Sundays when I was a kid, when I got to create delicious ice cream sundaes in the cafeteria...and, of course, holidays with the entire family clan gathered in the cafeteria...the moms, grandmas and aunts cooking all the food.

- Alix Paul

I liked the special sales like Old Fashion Days when the employees dressed in old-fashioned clothes. I made my own clothes to wear for that sale. We would visit the other departments to see how our friends were dressed. Working at Glosser's was like being part of a big family. Everyone was friendly.

- Helen Harteis Schad Bowman

I grew up near South Fork. In the late 1950s and early 1960s, we had a Saturday routine: catch the Blue & White bus at Rager's Corner at 11 a.m., eat lunch at either Glosser's, Grant's, or Woolworth's lunch counter or Penn Traffic, followed by a movie at one of the downtown theaters (State, Embassy, or the third one, all on Main Street, I think), or shopping for something (clothes, drug store, shoes, whatever was needed) or a dentist appointment. Then we'd go to Glosser's again and buy warm nuts at the candy counter (I always got Spanish peanuts!) and catch the bus at 5 p.m. to go back home.

- Carla Davis

My friend Betsie Walls Mack and I used to ride the bus from Seward to downtown Johnstown to go to Glossers. We were probably in the sixth grade when we started. I remember Glossers most at Christmas time with the window displays. I also remember when we shopped for Easter shoes, how we both got this pair of sandals that had a hole in them. We also had boots that laced up in the front which we remember getting at Glossers.

- Carrie Duncan Walker

148

My Dad, Sydney Ossip, was the comptroller at Glosser Bros. Being a part of the Glosser family made for a wonderful childhood, because of the many fantastic hours spent at Glosser Bros. department store, both when the store was open and when it was closed.

For example, my Dad usually went to the store on Sunday afternoon when it was closed to do some work, and many times, I was fortunate enough to go with him. While he worked, I would pretend that I was one of the elevator operators. Sitting on the pull-down seat, I would welcome imaginary shoppers when they got into the elevator. Then, I would stop on every floor (by using a lever to go from floor to floor; there weren't any buttons!) and announce what departments were on that level. It was so much fun, and I felt like a real grownup.

Photo courtesy of Ellen Ossip Sosinski

I became friendly with many of the employees and would go to the store just to visit them. When I was ten years old, Connie Pingatore LaBuda was hired to be my Dad's secretary. I became close to her, and she would even take me to her house on weekends every so often to spend time with her family. She worked in the store for five years, and I am still close to her today.

When I became old enough to work in the store, I worked in two different departments. I would either work in the candy department or the record department. The store lost money on me when I was in the candy department because I would eat a lot of the malted milk balls! When I worked in the record department, I would dance with the students who came in from the Johnstown schools. As you can imagine, I loved my job!

The holiday of Passover was the best, though. Our entire family would have the Seder in the store's cafeteria. My father would lead the Seder, all of the women in the family would make the food, and the cafeteria employees would serve the food and clean up. What a fabulous evening!

I can't imagine a better way to grow up. I often wish that our sons could have had the experience that I was fortunate to have in my life.

Sydney and Molly Ossip (photo courtesy of Ellen Ossip Sosinski)

- *Janet Schwartz*

On Sundays, I would often go to "the store," as Glosser's was referred to by the family, with my Dad (Fred Glosser). Usually, there was a cousin or two to go along. What a wonderful place the store was when it was closed. It was a great place for hide and seek, making ice cream sundaes in the cafeteria, and eating all the candy and nuts you could eat in the candy department. Running up and down the escalator when it wasn't moving held a huge attraction for some reason. The really big deal was operating the elevator. Back in those days, an elevator operator ran the elevator. Dad always held my hand to be sure I was doing it correctly.

As a teenager, I used to work in the store. I started sorting tickets until I was old enough to work in one of the departments. Women's Sportswear was my favorite. I worked Thursday night and Saturday. I also remember, as a small child, standing downstairs at the front door at closing time and helping Charlie mark the employee bags with a red marker as they left the store. He always wore a white shirt and suspenders.

Another really special memory was the annual store picnic at Fun City. I don't remember when it stopped or why but I do know they were fun while they lasted.

The people who worked at the store were always special people to me. When I left for college, and later, after I moved to Texas, going back to the store was something I couldn't wait to do. Everyone who worked there always made you feel like they were so glad to see you, and they were genuinely pleased to see you back.

Several of my friends at school had parents who worked at Glosser's. Karen Alwine (Shirly Alwine, sportswear) and Poppy Psinakis (Mrs. Psinakis in the bridal department) were two. Isadore Suchman worked in the shoe department, and I played with his daughter, Joan. Roz, his wife, was one of my mom's best friends. Mrs. Bishop, one of the nurses, stayed with us when my parents traveled and put up with all my rowdy friends. She was a very special woman!

Glosser's wasn't about employer vs. employee; it was about relationships. I remember as a child calling the store and asking to talk to my "Daddy" Mr. Glosser. Dorothy, the operator, would just laugh and ask "which one?" I'll bet she got asked that question several times a day and never lost it once.

So many people who worked at Glosser's worked there for years and years. I see them like another family. How lucky were we, the Glosser children, to have this legacy and to have had the opportunity to grow up surrounded by cousins and the Glosser Employee Family.

- Patti Glosser Rudick (daughter of Fred Glosser)

Chapter 19

A Club of Their Own

Izzy Glosser worked up a sweat as he dragged fire hoses across the Ligonier Pike.

He'd borrowed the hoses from local fire departments for a special job, a pet project that the family and their partners had been working on for a while.

Now, as he and his helpers hauled hoses across the road, it was almost finished.

Cars rolled up from either direction and stopped to let him pass. One of the drivers leaned out his window and shouted, "What're you doing with the hoses?"

The answer was twofold, though Izzy only told him one part of it: "Filling a swimming pool!"

The other part, the part Izzy didn't tell the driver, was this: "Thumbing our noses at anti-Semitism!"

How The Glossers Rolled

To say the least, the Glosser family had been prominent in the Johnstown area for decades. By the late 1950s, they had celebrated their company's 50th anniversary, converted the company to a corporation, and begun laying plans for a major expansion.

But local country clubs still kept them at a distance. Jews could only join the North Fork Country Club as Class B members without voting privileges. Sunnehanna Country Club didn't exactly encourage Jews to apply for membership, either.

151

The rejection had to sting. The Glossers were local success stories and pillars of the community. They had always given back to the community through philanthropic support of worthwhile causes. Not to mention all the little kindnesses they'd performed through the years, from giving out hot meals and liberal credit during the Depression to putting bags of free groceries on the doorsteps of needy families.

Photo courtesy of Menoher Swim Club

But certain doors were still closed to them, just because they were Jews.

So what did they do? Make a stink about it? Fight the power until they got what they wanted?

Not at all. What they did was build their own club.

"We got a number of people involved who were willing to back us," remembers Ruth Glosser. "We brought in an advisor who had experience with this sort of thing. And we started our own club."

If You Build It, They Will Swim

The group that took on this project included Izzy and Fred Glosser, their cousin, the attorney Louis Coppersmith, Louis' fellow attorney Gus Margolis, and Herb Sinberg. Herb was one of the few family members who'd managed to join Sunnehanna, but he still supported the dream of a new club and wanted to do his part to make it a reality.

Commitment was important, because this was no small project. The group had to find a suitable location, negotiate its purchase, get all the right permits, draw up blueprints, solicit bids from contractors, oversee construction, and take care of all the million-and-one other little tasks that came up along the way.

They started in the late 1950s, choosing a site along the Ligonier Pike in Somerset County and laying all the necessary groundwork. Construction ended in 1960, which is where the fire hoses came in.

The focus of the club was an in-ground swimming pool. Family members had always wanted a place to take their kids to swim in the summer, since they couldn't use the pool at Sunnehanna.

Filling the new pool seemed like it was going to be a challenge, though. "The city of Johnstown didn't have running water out that far at the time," remembers Izzy. "We couldn't just tap a water main and run a line up to the pool."

It was the one problem the Glosser team hadn't fully worked out in advance. How could they bring in the thousands of gallons of water they needed in a way that was cost-effective and relatively trouble-free?

Izzy stumbled upon an answer when he was exploring the surrounding area. Across the road and down the hill from the new club, a clear mountain stream ran through the woods, glittering in the patches of sunlight that dappled its rippling surface. It was a perfect source of water for the pool...with just one problem.

How could they get the water up the hill, across the street, and into the pool?

Just Add Water

After thinking it over a bit, Izzy dreamed up a solution. All it would take was some fast talking, a couple of strong backs...and a big ol' pump.

"What I did was, I went to various fire departments around Johnstown," explains Izzy. "They all knew the Glossers and shopped at the store, and I was able to talk them into lending me some fire hoses.

The Menoher Swim Club in 2014 (photo by Philip Balko)

"We ran the hoses from the swimming pool across Ligonier Pike and down the hill to the stream, which was pretty active. There was a large volume of water available with a nice, strong flow.

"Next, we set up a big water pump," says Izzy. "We pumped water from the stream through the hose, up the hill, across the Ligonier Pike, and into the pool.

"It was an unusual way to fill a pool, that's for sure. But it worked perfectly.

The Menoher Swim Club in 2014 (photo by Philip Balko)

"Later, we put in a pond on the property, and we could filter the water from that if we needed to refill the pool. But for that first time, the fire hoses, pump, and stream really did the trick."

Just like that, the club's centerpiece was ready for action. And the Menoher Heights Swim Club was ready for its big debut.

Splashing Away Discrimination

When the new club opened in the summer of 1960, it was really *open*. Instead of being exclusive like other clubs in the area, it was *in*clusive. No one was barred from membership.

153

"The idea all along was to have a place people could join regardless of race or color," says Izzy. "And that was exactly what we created. Anyone could join, and did."

Members had access to the pool, tennis courts, picnic areas, and a lunch counter. The sprawling, grassy grounds provided an idyllic setting for families to lay out a beach blanket and picnic basket and while away the hot summer days.

"Children splashed in the water and ran around on the grass, playing and laughing," recalls Izzy. "Gangs of women put up bridge tables around the pool and played bridge. I loved seeing everyone enjoying themselves."

Izzy spent a lot of time at the club, in part because he loved playing tennis. "Also, it was a business enterprise. I needed to make sure the lunch counter was stocked with enough hamburger meat, rolls, soda, and other supplies. I needed to see if any repairs or painting had to be done, and I saw to it that it was taken care of. I was pretty interested in the whole process."

Sunnehanna Going Down

The Glossers hired local college students on summer break to staff the lunch counter and serve as lifeguards. But young people were also front and center when it came to boosting club pride.

Each year, the best young swimmers in the membership joined the club's swimming team. A coach from the Johnstown YMCA led the team as it competed in meets with teams from other clubs and organizations.

According to Izzy, Menoher Heights had a pretty good team. "They won meets regularly," he remembers. "We used to look forward to those competitions, especially when we were up against Sunnehanna Country Club."

The Menoher Heights swimmers didn't always win, but they had their share of hard-fought battles against Sunnehanna.

Ruth Glosser remembers one such occasion, when she watched as the Menoher Heights kids flew across the pool, swimming with that extra bit of determination they always had against Sunnehanna. She remembers the crowd cheering louder than usual as the race neared the end, as a Menoher Heights swimmer charged neck-in-neck through the final lap with a Sunnehanna opponent.

Then, as the Menoher Heights swimmer--a Glosser, no less, one of Izzy's three aquatically-inclined kids--tagged the wall a split-second before the Sunnehanna swimmer, Ruth leaped to her feet. She and every Glosser in the crowd cheered and clapped *much* louder than usual for a Menoher Heights win.

And when the kids from Menoher Heights and the kids from Sunnehanna shook hands after the race in a gesture of mutual respect, maybe, just maybe, Ruth's eyes even glistened with a tear or two.

GLOSSER'S ALL-STARS

LEONARD BLACK

Photo from Glosser Bros. Annual Report, Feb. 1975

If you were a top manager at Glosser Bros. back in the day, chances are good that you had some Glosser blood flowing through your veins.

Yet the man who presided over the company's glory days had none of that. Sure, he'd married into the family, but he wasn't a Glosser by birth.

Yet somehow, he ascended to the throne, becoming company president ahead of multiple direct descendants who were already in line, men with more time at the company than he had. Which has to make you wonder, doesn't it?

What was so great about this guy? What did Leonard Black have going for him?

Whatever it was, original Glosser Brother David spotted it right away. He recruited Leonard to move to Johnstown and work at the store straight out of the Navy, after the war.

Leonard married David's daughter, Betty, it's true. They met in July 1941, at a bridge game in Atlantic City. Leonard was on leave at the time, and Betty was on vacation. They got engaged in December, then married in June 1942.

155

After living for a while in Washington, D.C., they moved to Berkley, California. For the next three years, Leonard worked as a supply chief at the Navy yards in San Francisco. By the end of the war, he had attained the rank of lieutenant commander.

It was then that his father-in-law, David, offered him a job at Glosser Bros.. Did he hire Leonard just because he was married to David's daughter, Betty? It seems unlikely that the shrewd businessman would have brought Leonard into the fold solely on the basis of that.

Did David hire Leonard because he had a degree in business administration from the University of Pennsylvania? Or because he had experience as a supply chief at the San Francisco Navy yards?

It probably didn't hurt...but isn't it more interesting to think that David sensed something special about Leonard? That he picked up on the kind of leadership qualities it would take to guide the company through the challenges of changing times and unforeseen disasters?

Whatever the reason, David hired Leonard as a sportswear buyer soon after the war. As it turned out, he never regretted the decision.

Leonard had sound business instincts, a charismatic personality, and plenty of determination. "He got along well with employees and co-workers," remembers Betty Black. "He worked hard, and everyone respected him. He was quite a guy."

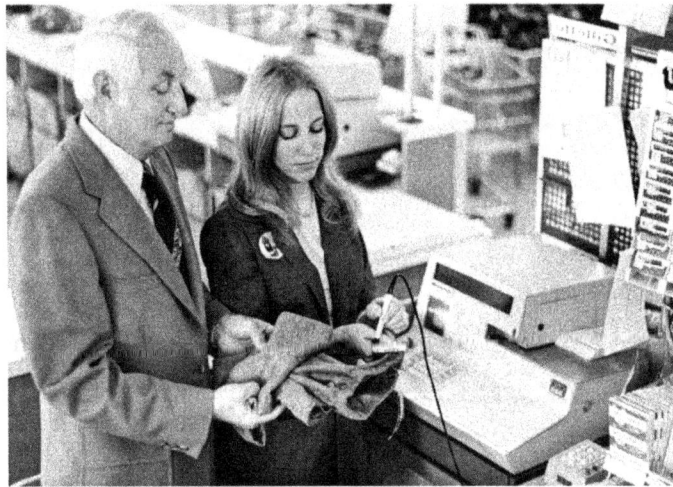

Photo from Glosser Bros. Annual Report, Feb. 1975

During the next few years, he rose through the ranks, building a reputation and gaining support among the company's directors. By 1954, he was assistant secretary-treasurer to the Board of Directors...but his biggest successes were yet to come.

In 1959, Leonard was named president of Glosser Bros., Inc. His greatest achievements followed, as he was instrumental in launching and expanding the Gee Bee stores, which started in 1962. He played a big role in selecting Gee Bee store locations and expediting construction, ensuring rapid growth and building momentum.

The company reached new heights of profitability in the 1960s, thanks to the Gee Bee chain. By the late 60s, another venture was in the works, one in which Leonard was also a key player. Glosser Bros., Inc. was in the process of becoming a publicly traded company on the American Stock Exchange. The first public offering of its stock would happen in 1971, after which the company's fortunes rose even higher.

Photo from Glosser Bros. Annual Report, Feb. 1975

For the most part, Leonard's presidency was distinguished by continual growth and record success--though it was also marked by calamity when the third Johnstown flood struck in 1977. Leonard, and Glosser's, rose to the occasion, though. Under his leadership, The Store reopened in a few short months, sparking an outpouring of unity and optimism in a town laid low by natural disaster.

After retiring as president in 1980, Leonard served as Chairman of the Board of Directors of Glosser's until 1984. He was also very active in the community. "He was on the board of directors of Memorial Hospital and several banks," says Betty. "He also worked with the Chamber of Commerce and various charitable organizations."

Leonard died in 2007 but will always be remembered as a true Glosser's All-Star. By the time he retired as president, he had shepherded Glosser Bros., Inc. through a golden age in which even a devastating flood couldn't cramp the company's style. He left the company bigger and better than he'd found it, positioned for greater things to come.

The fact that they didn't necessarily come as expected doesn't diminish his accomplishments. The fact that the company imploded in 1989 doesn't make him any less a great leader or his term as president any less an amazing run.

Chapter 20

It's Got To Be Gee Bee

Fred Glosser walked through the empty building, checking what he saw against the blueprints he held out in front of him.

His footsteps echoed as he paced through the newly-constructed space. There were no racks for merchandise yet, no counters or signs or checkouts. No shoppers had strolled through the doors, and not a thing had been bought or sold.

But the place was alive in Fred's mind as if he'd been there a million times. He knew every inch by heart, because he'd studied the plans as if his life depended on them.

It might as well have. A big part of the Glossers' new expansion, their hope for the future, rested on his shoulders. He was in charge of construction and maintenance of the new chain of suburban-oriented stores, the ones that took their names from the initials of the company's flagship department store in downtown Johnstown.

They were called *Gee Bee* stores.

The Reason "Stores" Was Plural

Gee Bee had been in the works since the late 1950s. It was the Glosser company's bid to stay competitive, its response to retail's gradual shift from traditional downtown business zones to suburban shopping centers.

As part of the preparations for the new initiative, President Leonard Black and his team set up a corporate entity to manage them. The team applied to the state of Pennsylvania for approval of the new corporation, Glossers Stores, Inc., which would be a wholly owned subsidiary of Glosser Bros., Inc. The state approved the request, and Secretary of the Commonwealth E. James Trimarchi, Jr. issued a certificate of incorporation dated March 7, 1962. From that point on, all Gee Bee-related activities would fall under the auspices of Glossers Stores, Inc., which in turn would be controlled by the parent company, Glosser Bros., Inc.

159

Courtesy of Johnstown Area Heritage Association

Management of the Gee Bee enterprise would be based in the same executive offices where the rest of the company was managed, on the fourth floor of the Glosser Building. Additional space was needed to house other Gee Bee operations, though.

To provide that space, Glosser Bros. rented the third floor of the next-door *Tribune-Democrat* building. "We knocked a hole in the wall between the Glosser Building and *The Tribune-Democrat*," remembers Fred Glosser. "We put in a doorway, plus two steps leading down from the level of our third floor, which was higher than the floor in the *Tribune-Democrat* building.

"When the work was done, our people could walk from the third floor of the Glosser Building, behind the layaway department, right into the third floor of the *Tribune-Democrat* building," says Fred.

Tribune-Democrat Building 2014 (photo by Philip Balko)

With the new corporation and dedicated offices in place, the way was clear for a formal rollout of Gee Bee...and the name of the subsidiary provided a clue to the scope of the project. The fact that the "Stores" in "Glossers Stores, Inc." was plural told the tale; the Glosser team had multiple new retail outlets in mind, not just one.

As for the specific details of the new outlets, the public would not have to wait long to find out what they would be. A few months after the state of Pennsylvania approved the Gee Bee subsidiary's incorporation, the first of the new stores opened for business.

The Gee Is For "Greens" And The Bee Is For "Burg"

Glossers Stores, Inc. opened the first Gee Bee Discount Department Store in October 1962 (during the Cuban Missile Crisis, actually). This first store, located in the Eastgate Center in Greensburg, Pennsylvania, set the template for Gee Bees to come.

Based on the Glossers' exhaustive research and planning, the first Gee Bee combined a 68,000-square foot department store with a 20,000-square foot supermarket. Putting the two side by side in a suburban shopping center environment was still a novel idea in 1962...an idea that the public quickly embraced.

The Greensburg store was a test, and it succeeded in every way that mattered. Foot traffic was strong, and sales were excellent. People seemed to like everything from the suburban location to the discount prices to the side-by-side department store-supermarket concept.

The results were so encouraging, in fact, that Leonard and his team decided to forge ahead with another Gee Bee store. This one would be located closer to home, in Richland Township, a Johnstown suburb on the rise.

This new store would represent a second test, to determine if additional expansion would be sufficiently profitable. It would also be the next step in developing a system for building and opening new stores, a system that would be vitally important if the company pulled the trigger on further expansion.

To make it all work, the leaders of Glosser Bros., Inc. decided they needed a dedicated Gee Bee construction czar, one man who would manage all facets of building new stores.

They needed to look no further than the one and only Fred Glosser.

The Right Man For The Job

Fred was in the Gee Bee loop from the start, though his role in the early going was very different from the one he took on later.

When the Greensburg Gee Bee opened in 1962, he went to work as a buyer for that store's Infants and Children Up To Age 6 department. It was a natural extension of his work in the same department at the original Glosser's store in downtown Johnstown, so it seemed like a perfect fit.

At least until Fred got bumped out of the job to make room for Sydney Ossip's son-in-law, who'd recently moved to town. Suddenly, Fred was a man without a home, cut out of the Gee Bee action.

But his time as a nomad didn't last. As the company geared up for its next store opening, Fred got the nod to oversee construction and maintenance for the Gee Bee chain. That meant, at the time, that he would be responsible for supervising all maintenance activities for one store and all construction for a store to be built later.

Little did he know that before he was done, decades down the line, he would be working with 23 Gee Bee Discount Department Stores and dozens of stores in other chains operated by Glossers, Inc.

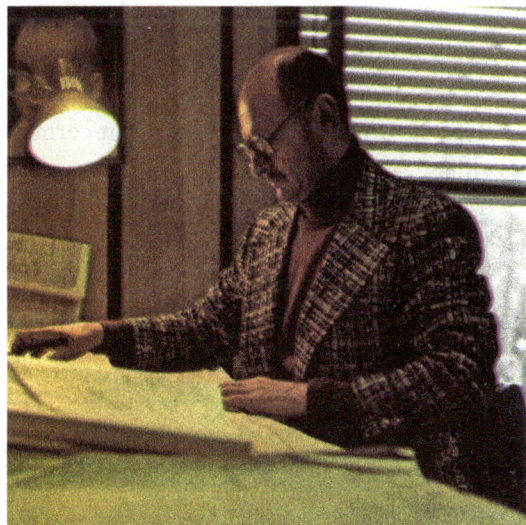

Fred Glosser (photo from Glosser Bros. Annual Report, Jan. 1978)

161

Groundbreaking for Gee Bee Richland (photo courtesy of Johnstown Area Heritage Association)

Details, Details

The second Gee Bee store, which would be located along Scalp Avenue in Richland Township, just past the Route 56 interchange, gave Fred the chance to show what he could do. Methodical and practical-minded as he was, he soon developed an effective system for bringing a new store into existence.

First, Fred worked with architects and engineers to draw up the plans for the new Gee Bee store. Then, he oversaw the laying out of fixtures. "Fixture placement was determined by the fixture manufacturers and the store's merchandise managers," says Fred. "The fixtures had to be laid out in certain ways so they wouldn't require posts or electric outlets in the middle of the aisles.

"All the outlets on the floor had to be in certain places so the fixtures would receive electricity. That was one of my responsibilities--making sure the outlets were properly positioned."

When the plans were done and marked with fixtures and outlets, Fred had to go through and double-check every page. "I had to make sure every measurement was exactly right, that whoever drew up the plan didn't get the scale wrong," says Fred.

"I had to scale everything with a ruler to make sure it measured exactly right for each fixture, each outlet, each door swing. Every column had to be in the right place.

"Everything had to fit together perfectly, like a puzzle. I had to check the specifications of every component, right down to the smallest detail.

"The engineers would give me a book listing the exact specs of everything that went into the building--every fixture, every screw, every piece of hardware, what bulbs to use with the lights. I had to read that book from cover to cover and make sure everything was exact and according to plan.

"Everything had to be exactly right. Once I signed my name on a drawing, if anything was wrong, Glosser's had to pay for any changes made in the field. If the steel was wrong, the builder would have had to order all new steel. If an electrical outlet was out of place, we would have had to change all the electrical plans. I was responsible for all that."

It was a time-consuming, eye-straining process, but it worked. According to Fred, there were no increased costs resulting from planning errors in the construction of the Richland Gee Bee store...or any other Gee Bee store, for that matter.

"We never had to pay one penny of extra expense for putting up a building," says Fred. "Everything was always done exactly the way the plans dictated."

Gee Bee Rising

The new Gee Bee store in the University Park Shopping Center in Richland opened in August 1964 and quickly became a success. Suburban shoppers flocked to it as they had the Greensburg store, enjoying the closer-to-home location and the shiny new building and fixtures. It didn't hurt that it was the creation of the beloved Glosser's company, either, with a discount pricing strategy that was even better than the original. Prices were lower than ever at Gee Bee, as Glosser Bros., Inc. slashed their markups to the bone.

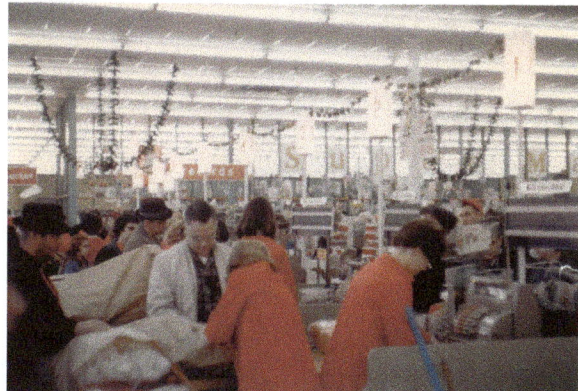

Photos courtesy of Bill Glosser

Photos courtesy of Bill Glosser

Photos courtesy of Bill Glosser

Photo courtesy of Bill Glosser

Leonard Black and the rest of his team could see they had a hit on their hands. As the numbers from the Richland store rolled into the Gee Bee offices, it was more a matter of *when* and *where* the next store would be built than *if*.

"The Gee Bee stores worked out very well," remembered Sydney Ossip, who became the comptroller for Gee Bee as well as the Glosser Bros. Department Store. "We knew a good thing when we saw it, and we built on our success."

New H.Q. O.K. for Gee Bee

As the scope of the Gee Bee project continued to grow, so did the support system that operated and supplied the new stores.

Around the time of the Richland store's opening, the Gee Bee team outgrew the offices in the *Tribune-Democrat* building. More space was needed, and Glosser Bros. found it on the other side of Central Park, in the Park Building (perhaps best remembered as the home of the Hello Shop in later years).

Glosser Bros. bought the Park Building, designating the upper floors as the new headquarters of Gee Bee. Once the lease was signed, the Gee Bee accounts receivable and credit departments were moved to the Park Building's second floor. The accounts payable

Park Building 2014 (photo by Philip Balko)

department was located on the third floor, and corporate accounting was handled on the fourth.

Meanwhile, new warehouse space was also needed to handle the merchandise ordered from wholesalers to stock the new stores. Glosser Bros. already operated a warehouse on Jackson Street, but that wasn't enough to handle the volume needed for the two new stores, plus all the stores yet to come.

To supplement the Jackson Street facility, Glosser's opened a new warehouse in Windber, along state route 160, also known as Pomroys Drive. The company's growing fleet of trucks traveled between the Windber and Jackson Street warehouses and the stores in Richland and Greensburg, ensuring the Gee Bee shelves were always well-stocked.

The additional warehouse and office space positioned Glosser Bros., Inc. for the next phase of expansion envisioned by the company's leaders...though that phase ended up being delayed.

Photo by Philip Balko

Despite Gee Bee's momentum, various issues got in the way of the next store's launch. The third Gee Bee didn't end up opening until almost a full five years after the second.

Photo by Philip Balko

A Store A Year Is Not Enough

When the time finally came for the next addition to the Gee Bee chain, Herb Sinberg, who was in charge of selecting new store locations, recommended a site in the Monroe Plaza in Monroeville, Pennsylvania. Leonard and the other top brass approved the location, though it took a while to get the ball rolling and start converting the existing building on the site into a Gee Bee store.

This delay was due to a problem with the building's small size. It would have to be made larger, but the lower level housed a bowling alley that was owned by the owner and developer of the property. Glosser Bros. would have to construct an addition without interfering with parking for the bowling alley.

There was a meeting to discuss the problem, and Fred sat in on it. "I suggested that columns be drilled into the ground in the back of the structure," remembers Fred. "I proposed that the addition be built on the columns so it wouldn't interfere with the bowling

167

alley's parking. This solved the problem, and the owner agreed to let us move ahead with construction."

This Gee Bee would be a little different, as the Glosser team experimented with new strategies. When it opened in July 1969, it included a 67,500-square foot discount department store but no supermarket, unlike the first two Gee Bees.

The Monroeville store may have been smaller than its predecessors, but its numbers were solid, and it kicked off a new phase of rapid expansion. There'd be no more waiting five years to open a new Gee Bee store.

The next store was scheduled to launch a year later, in 1970. Two stores would open in 1972, and three in 1973. And the expansion wouldn't stop there.

The company that had stood pat for 56 years with just one department store location in downtown Johnstown was about to open 6 new stores in the span of just four years.

The Gee Bee concept and system had proven its profitability, demonstrating a simple theorem with a far-reaching impact: the faster Glosser's put up Gee Bee stores, the faster its bottom line shot upward.

Gee Bee Richland
(Photos courtesy of Bill Glosser)

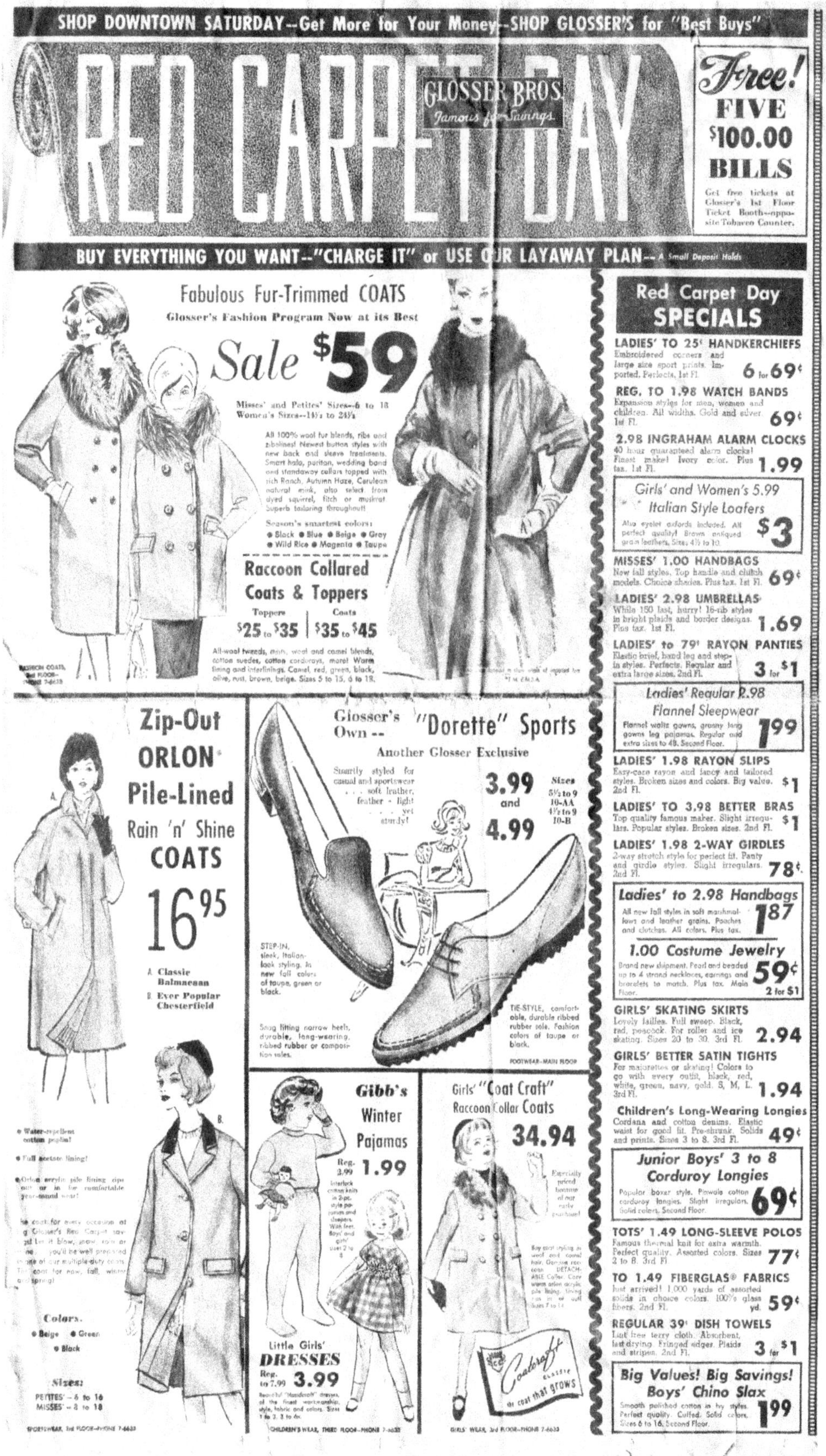

SHOP DOWNTOWN SATURDAY--Get More for Your Money--SHOP GLOSSER'S for "Best Buys"

RED CARPET DAY

GLOSSER BROS
Famous for Savings

Free! FIVE $100.00 BILLS

Get free tickets at Glosser's 1st Floor Ticket Booth--opposite Tobacco Counter.

BUY EVERYTHING YOU WANT--"CHARGE IT" or USE OUR LAYAWAY PLAN-- A Small Deposit Holds

Fabulous Fur-Trimmed COATS

Glosser's Fashion Program Now at its Best

Sale $59

Misses' and Petites' Sizes--6 to 18
Women's Sizes--14½ to 24½

All 100% wool fur blends, ribs and zibelines! Newest button styles with new back and sleeve treatments. Smart halo, puritan, wedding band and standaway collars topped with rich Ranch, Autumn Haze, Cerulean natural mink, also select from dyed squirrel, fitch or muskrat. Superb tailoring throughout!

Season's smartest colors:
● Black ● Blue ● Beige ● Grey ● Wild Rice ● Magenta ● Taupe

Raccoon Collared Coats & Toppers

Toppers $25 to $35 | Coats $35 to $45

All-wool tweeds, mohair, wool and camel blends, cotton suedes, cotton corduroys, more! Warm lining and interlinings. Camel, red, green, black, olive, rust, brown, beige. Sizes 5 to 15, 6 to 18.

FASHION COATS, 2nd FLOOR—PHONE 7-6633

Zip-Out ORLON* Pile-Lined Rain 'n' Shine COATS

16.95

A. Classic Balmacaan
B. Ever Popular Chesterfield

● Water-repellent cotton poplin!
● Full acetate lining!
● Orlon acrylic pile lining zips out or in for comfortable year-round wear!

Colors:
● Beige ● Green ● Black

Sizes:
PETITES' – 6 to 16
MISSES' – 8 to 18

SPORTSWEAR, 3rd FLOOR—PHONE 7-6633

Glosser's Own -- "Dorette" Sports

Another Glosser Exclusive

Smartly styled for casual and sportswear . . . soft leather, feather - light . . . yet sturdy!

3.99 and 4.99

Sizes 5½ to 9 10-AA, 4½ to 9 10-B

STEP-IN, sleek, Italian-look styling. In new fall colors of taupe, green or black.

Snug fitting narrow heels, durable, long-wearing, ribbed rubber or composition soles.

TIE-STYLE, comfortable, durable ribbed rubber sole. Fashion colors of taupe or black.

FOOTWEAR—MAIN FLOOR

Gibb's Winter Pajamas

Reg. 3.99 **1.99**

Interlock cotton knits in 2-pc. style pajamas and sleepers. With feet. Boys' and girls' sizes 2 to 8

Little Girls' DRESSES

Reg. to 7.99 **3.99**

Beautiful "Handcraft" dresses, of the finest workmanship, style, fabric and colors. Sizes 1 to 3, 3 to 6x.

CHILDREN'S WEAR, THIRD FLOOR—PHONE 7-6633

Girls' "Coat Craft" Raccoon Collar Coats

34.94

Especially priced because of our early purchase!

Coatcraft Classic, the coat that grows

GIRLS' WEAR, 3rd FLOOR—PHONE 7-6633

Red Carpet Day SPECIALS

LADIES' TO 25¢ HANDKERCHIEFS — Embroidered corners and large size sport prints. Imported. Perfects. 1st Fl. **6 for 69¢**

REG. TO 1.98 WATCH BANDS — Expansion styles for men, women and children. All widths. Gold and silver. 1st Fl. **69¢**

2.98 INGRAHAM ALARM CLOCKS — 40 hour guaranteed alarm clocks! Finest make! Ivory color. Plus tax. 1st Fl. **1.99**

Girls' and Women's 5.99 Italian Style Loafers — Also eyelet oxfords included. All perfect quality! Brown antiqued grain leathers. Sizes 4½ to 10. **$3**

MISSES' 1.00 HANDBAGS — New fall styles. Top handle and clutch models. Choice shades. Plus tax. 1st Fl. **69¢**

LADIES' 2.98 UMBRELLAS — While 150 last, hurry! 16-rib styles in bright plaids and border designs. Plus tax. 1st Fl. **1.69**

LADIES' to 79¢ RAYON PANTIES — Elastic brief, band leg and step-in styles. Perfects. Regular and extra large sizes. 2nd Fl. **3 for $1**

Ladies' Regular 2.98 Flannel Sleepwear — Flannel waltz gowns, granny long gowns leg pajamas. Regular and extra sizes to 48. Second Floor. **1.99**

LADIES' 1.98 RAYON SLIPS — Easy-care rayon and fancy and tailored styles. Broken sizes and colors. Big value. 2nd Fl. **$1**

LADIES' TO 3.98 BETTER BRAS — Top quality famous maker. Slight irregulars. Popular styles. Broken sizes. 2nd Fl. **$1**

LADIES' 1.98 2-WAY GIRDLES — 2-way stretch style for perfect fit. Panty and girdle styles. Slight irregulars. 2nd Fl. **78¢**

Ladies' to 2.98 Handbags — All new fall styles in soft marshmallows and leather grains. Pouches and clutches. All colors. Plus tax. **1.87**

1.00 Costume Jewelry — Brand new shipment. Pearl and beaded up to 4 strand necklaces, earrings and bracelets to match. Plus tax. Main Floor. **59¢, 2 for $1**

GIRLS' SKATING SKIRTS — Lovely failles. Full sweep. Black, red, peacock. For roller and ice skating. Sizes 20 to 30. 3rd Fl. **2.94**

GIRLS' BETTER SATIN TIGHTS — For majorettes or skating! Colors to go with every outfit, black, red, white, green, navy, gold. S, M, L. 3rd Fl. **1.94**

Children's Long-Wearing Longies — Cordana and cotton denims. Elastic waist for good fit. Pre-shrunk. Solids and prints. Sizes 3 to 8. 3rd Fl. **49¢**

Junior Boys' 3 to 8 Corduroy Longies — Popular boxer style. Pinwale cotton corduroy longies. Slight irregulars. Solid colors. Second Floor. **69¢**

TOTS' 1.49 LONG-SLEEVE POLOS — Famous thermal knit for extra warmth. Perfect quality. Assorted colors. Sizes 2 to 8. 3rd Fl. **77¢**

TO 1.49 FIBERGLAS® FABRICS — Just arrived! 1,000 yards of assorted solids in choice colors. 100% glass fibers. 2nd Fl. **yd. 59¢**

REGULAR 39¢ DISH TOWELS — Lint free terry cloth. Absorbent, fast drying. Fringed edges. Plaids and stripes. 2nd Fl. **3 for $1**

Big Values! Big Savings! Boys' Chino Slax — Smooth polished cotton in Ivy styles. Perfect quality. Cuffed. Solid colors. Sizes 6 to 16. Second Floor. **1.99**

Friday, November 22, 1963
Shop Today -- 9:30 a. m. to 5 p. m. -- Saturday 9 a. m. to 5 p. m.
Glosser's
wonderful world of Christmas
Add elegance and beauty to your winter wardrobe with our precious
Cashmere Coats Collared with MINK
Reg. to 119.95 values!
$99
Coats of precious imported cashmere with elegant mushroom and wedding band luxurious natural mink collars. Choose yours in beige, blue, sable, nude, black, bamboo or butter-cream. Sizes 6 to 16.
CHARGE IT No Money Down
FASHION COATS—THIRD FLOOR
Choose for yourself, for gifts . . . from our
INTERNATIONAL COLLECTION of
Fashion Handbags
priced at just . . . . 7.95 and up
Expertly crafted handbags from France, Belgium, Canada and England. Soft polished calfskins with full leather lining, gleaming brass locks, plus superb detailing. Plus tax.
HANDBAGS—MAIN FLOOR
Sure-to-delight!
Children's WATCHES
by Elgin
7.95 plus tax
Favorite character styles:
•Barbie •Yogi Bear •Roy Rogers •Petite Ballerina •Huckleberry Hound •Space Explorer •All-Star Baseball •More
WATCHES—MAIN FLOOR
It's the newest . . . .
The "POUFF" for Young Juniors
10.95
Others 8.95 to 13.95
Stunningly styled free-flowing dress in 100% wool. Attractively designed with smocked bodice, smart jewel neckline, 3/4-length sleeves and low, low placed pockets. Wear it loose or belted . . . great either way! Black, blue, pink, yellow, turquoise. Sizes 6 to 14.
GIRLS' WEAR—THIRD FLOOR
For the girl who knows clothes . . . . .
Feminine Chiffon by R&K
24.95
Completely unforgettable! Totally feminine. Unconditionally well bred! That's you in this beautiful rayon chiffon by R&K Sizes 10 to 18.
Complete collection of other R&K Originals for daytime and datetime!
FASHION DRESSES—THIRD FLOOR
Skirts to give or to wear . . . all wonderfully styled and wonderfully priced!
All Wool Walker Skirts
by Summit of Boston
All styles priced at a low . . . 8.95
A. Imperial Walker. Slim-line styling with back kick pleat and slit side pocket. Lined seat. Leather belt.
Black, brown, gray, and loden green.
Sizes 10 to 20
Also a complete selection of American and Town & Country Walker Skirts in stock.
SPORTSWEAR—THIRD FLOOR
Gay Holiday Charmers for the younger set!
Little Girls' Gift Dresses
2.95
Others 1.95 to 9.95
Beautiful, holiday cottons in bright solids and prints. Gigantic assortment of styles and colors. All famous makes. Sizes 3 to 6x.
Little Boys' SLACK SUITS
By famous Stevie Togs and Health-tex
3.95
Washable Rayon flannels and china slacks with coordinating shirts in plaids, solids, prints and cotton knits. Sizes 2 to 4, 3 to 7.
Others 2.95 to 4.95
CHILDREN'S WEAR—THIRD FLOOR
Give her warmth and beauty . . . give her this heather-toned spun rayon
AUTUMN WONDER
with fashion button front coat styling, 3/4-length sleeves and slash pockets.
3.99
Sizes 14½ to 24½
The dress she'll wear constantly all winter long. A neat, beautifully styled dress in washable, crease-resistant spun rayon. Light-weight yet warm. Charming gay prints in gray, blue, navy and rosewine.
Mail and Phone Orders Filled Dial 536-6633
DAYTIME DRESSES—SECOND FLOOR
Delightful for gift giving!
Girls' Smart KNIT HATS
1.95
Smartly styled pill-boxes, pokes, pixies and hood models in soft, fluffy wools and Orlon acrylic. White and colors.
Our own famous
No-Seam Sheba Nylons
3 prs. 1.75
Sizes 8½ to 11
HOSIERY—MAIN FLOOR

GLOSSER'S ALL-STARS

HERB SINBERG

Photo from Glosser Bros. Annual Report, Jan. 1978

Did you know that a Glosser Bros. executive had a sandwich named after him in the Hunt Room restaurant at The Store?

The man was Herb Sinberg, and the sandwich was called...wait for it...

The *Sinburger.*

It was a unique claim to fame, but it certainly wasn't Herb's only contribution to the Glosser Bros. empire. Herb was a key figure in the Glosser Bros. leadership team for decades, supporting numerous initiatives that helped the company grow and thrive.

So how did the Sinburger's namesake get his start? How did he begin his climb to the top?

Herb grew up in Allentown, Pennsylvania and earned a bachelor's degree in business administration at Temple University in Philadelphia. His Glosser connection began when he met and married his wife, Freda, while going to college. Freda's father, Sam Glosser, was one of the original Glosser brothers.

After marrying Freda, Herb enlisted in the U.S. Navy and served overseas during World War II. He spent two and a half years as supply chief of a flotilla that was stationed in the South Pacific.

Returning from the war, Herb joined Freda in Johnstown and got a job as a ladies' shoe buyer at Glosser's.

In his early days at Glosser's, Herb carpooled to work with Fred Glosser, who lived next-door, and Izzy Glosser, who lived a block up the street. "They loved doing that," says Herb's daughter, Jan Dash. "Our families all had one car each, so it really helped the wives and kids have some mobility when the three men carpooled. But I think Dad, Fred, and Izzy just liked having the excuse to drive together."

171

In the years that followed, Herb worked as a buyer for the domestics department. He also became the personnel director and went on to set up The Store's credit system.

But Herb's biggest claim to fame occurred after he was promoted to Head of Special Projects in the early 1960s. "Special projects turned out to be expansion," he said.

In other words, he went to work setting up the Gee Bee Discount Department Stores.

"Herb was in charge of finding locations for the Gee Bee stores and getting them built," remembers his wife, Freda. "He worked with my brother, Fred Glosser, to oversee everything from ordering fixtures to hiring employees."

Photo © The Tribune-Democrat

Herb--and his family--were even involved in naming the Gee Bee stores. "I remember sitting around the dining room table with Dad, my brother, and my mother," says Jan. "We were all suggesting names for the new chain of stores, which the company hadn't finalized yet. They didn't use our suggestions, but we had a lot of fun coming up with them."

As the Gee Bee stores took shape and opened for business, Herb visited them often to check on their status. "He traveled to the stores every week to see what was happening, talk with the managers, and make sure everything was running smoothly," says Freda.

Working on the Gee Bee stores kept Herb in the heart of the action for years...but his biggest challenge might have been the 1977 Johnstown Flood.

Herb worked on the cleanup, and said it was more grueling than his service in World War II. "Going through the flood was one of the worst experiences of my life," he said. "For two and a half years, I was in battles and landings overseas, but the flood was more traumatic.

"I went through New Guinea, Okinawa, Saipan, you name it. Kamikaze planes diving on our ships. Suicide swimmers planting explosives. Yet the flood seemed to bother me more-- the cleanup, the dirt, the evacuations because of the threat of gas explosions."

Herb thought it was worth it in the end, though. He was willing to pay the price if it meant reviving The Store.

Photo courtesy of Janet Sinberg Dash

"He loved working for Glosser's," remembers Freda. "He absolutely loved it."

Herb retired on January 31, 1985, after 39 years at Glosser Bros. He served on the board of directors a while longer, then gave that up because of health problems and moved to Lake Worth, Florida with Freda.

But his love of Johnstown never faltered. "There is no place else where you find such loyalty and friendship," he said.

And his love of Glosser Bros. also stayed strong. "He loved the whole Glosser's organization," says Freda. "He loved the people in the family he worked with. He loved the employees.

"He loved everything about it," says Freda.

172

Memory Department

As much as my dad (Herb Sinberg) loved his work, he always took the time to take my brother and I skiing on Friday afternoons and Sundays. He was so athletic, and in addition to skiing, he was an awesome golfer! He had three holes-in-one in his golf career!

- Janet Sinberg Dash (daughter of Herb Sinberg)

Photo courtesy of Janet Sinberg Dash

My dad worked at Glosser's in the 60s. He was night maintenance. One night, as he was cleaning up on the floor where the cash office was located, he found a bag in the trash. When he opened it, he found there was a lot of money in the bag. He turned it in, and I think they gave him a 50 dollar reward. That was my Dad, honest till the day he died.

- Mike Prazinko

My aunt, Virginia Milazzo, worked downstairs in the cheese department for many, many years. It was always fun to stop in to see her on my way home from school. There was always a little "sample" for me to try. What a treat! I also remember decorating the windows for Halloween. Each school was given their window to decorate, and all were judged.

- Rosina Burke

173

My father, Sydney Ossip, was comptroller of Glosser Bros. I have great memories of going to the store with Dad on Sunday mornings in the 50's and 60's, during which time I was able to operate the old-time elevator, visit the candy department, etc. As many have mentioned, I loved the roasted nut smells and the wonderful people who worked there. When I was old enough, I started working there on school vacations and weekends.

When I was home from vacation or breaks from college in the early 70's, I worked on entering data in the "books" under the direction of the wonderful Marie Novak. Also, another wonderful woman, Dorothy Allendorfer, trained me to work the switchboard. It was the kind with plugs, just like the one that Lily Tomlin used as "Ernestine" on *Laugh-In*. Though I didn't treat customers badly, as Ernestine did, or say "one ringy-dingy," I did inadvertently disconnect people by pulling the wrong plug. Good thing that the executives whom I disconnected were close relatives of mine!

The best part of working at Glosser's on school vacations was getting to take my breaks with my then best friend, Tim Sosinski. We would meet in the cafeteria and indulge in French fries and gravy and compare our days. (Tim later became my husband. We both share great memories of our times at Glosser Bros.)

My cafeteria memories also include going to meet Dad for dinner on Monday or Thursday nights in the Hunt Room. And, for several years, our family had a huge Passover Seder in the cafeteria. The kids were so happy to be able to explore the store and get some candy. I remember one Seder in April, facing the large picture window, and watching snow come down. That's Johnstown for you!

A tough memory was being in a quiet store on a Friday afternoon, November 22, 1963, and hearing a mournful scream come from the elevator. It was the day that JFK was shot. It was comforting to be in a place with caring people who were all sharing the same pain, though.

I think that the best memory that I have is, even after the store had been closed for many years, how many people would come up to my dad when we were out and tell him how they remembered him and how wonderful he was to them. Dad was always so humbled at the wonderful things that people said and how much they truly enjoyed their experiences at Glosser Bros.

- *Ellen Ossip Sosinski*

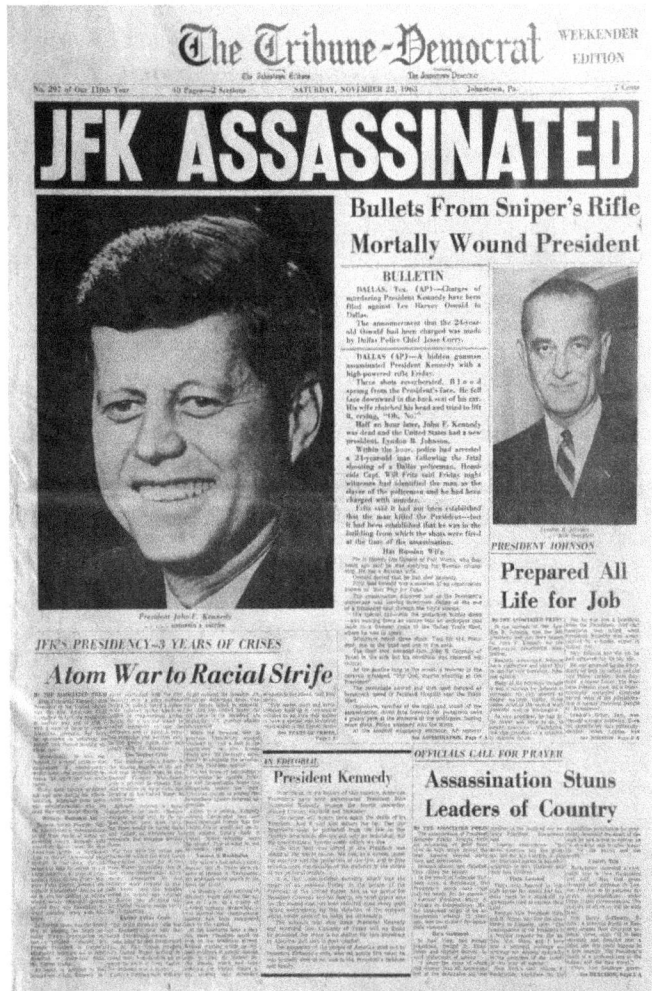

I worked in the infants' department from the end of 1965 until May of 1966. During that time, Fred Glosser was the head of this department. One day, I had a sore throat, and I went to see the nurse, whose office was where our department was. She gave me some medicine and told me to lie down on a cot for an hour. I also remember a Mrs. Roveder who worked there and was very helpful to me while I was learning the job. I'll never forgot her kindness to me, since I was the youngest person in the department. I enjoyed working at Glosser's, and everyone in my department was easy to get along with.

- *Charles Rametta*

My main memories are of our family's huge Passover Seders in the cafeteria. After we searched for the afikomen, my uncle Sydney would give us each a silver dollar and a small white paper bag. The kids would all go downstairs and stuff our bags from the candy counter.

- *Robin Eiseman*

I worked in the Hunt Room from June of 1968 until school started in September of 1968. I was pretty young and just remember that I waited on tables, as the food was served at tableside instead of offered cafeteria style. I also remember only men eating in the Hunt Room, and I believe I was the only waitress.

I made out very well as the diners were generous tippers...but minimum wage back then for waitresses was only about 50 cents an hour. There was a cafeteria which was open to all employees, but the section where I worked was not. I also worked in the candy department for about a month in 1965. Those roasted peanuts and the wonderful aroma were the best part of that job.

- *Debbie Adams Clifford*

Photo by Margie Hagerich

175

Chapter 21

Frightening Traditions

Beginning in the 1960s, Halloween became a real Glosser Bros. time of year.

Even as the company charged down a road of growth and change, it established Halloween traditions that would endure for decades.

Windows of Terror

In 1961, Glosser Bros. launched its first Halloween window painting contest, inviting students from area elementary, junior high, and senior high schools to paint scary images on the ground floor display windows of The Store.

Each 7 foot by 8 foot window was assigned to a different group of contestants from a different division: Elementary, Junior, and Senior. Depending on the division, each group had one to two days to finish painting its window.

Photo © The Tribune-Democrat

Photo © The Tribune-Democrat

After the Halloween-themed paintings were finished, contest judges awarded first, second, third, and honorable mention prizes in each division. But the real prize went to shoppers and passers-by, who got to enjoy the window paintings throughout the Halloween season.

The 1961 event was such a success that Glosser Bros. brought it back in '62...and '63...and every year thereafter until The Store closed in 1989. It became a much-anticipated tradition for local students, who saw it as a chance for their artwork to reach a wider audience.

"My art teacher picked me to paint a picture on one of Glosser's windows for Halloween one year," remembers Catherine Blaschak-Karwoski. "I was so honored. It was a big deal back then."

"I remember painting the windows at Halloween as a member of the Ferndale High School art team," recalls another former window painter, Barb High-Holland.

Photo by Ruby Shaffer

Photo by Ruby Shaffer

178

Furious Competition

Another onetime contest participant, Donald Peters, also has fond memories of his window-painting days. "In my eighth grade year, we were able to go to Glossers Brothers to paint the windows for Halloween. We won first place in the Junior division that year. It was more than just painting a window, though, it was meeting all the others who were invited to paint. The competition seemed furious, but looking back now it was so much fun. And getting out of school was great, too."

Photo from Glosser Bros. Annual Report, Jan. 1976

The window painting contest continued for decades. In 1987, the contest was still popular, with 29 six-person teams competing from 21 area senior high schools, junior high schools, and elementary schools.

Photo by Ruby Shaffer

The tradition became so popular, in fact, that it refused to stay dead for long. Years after Glosser's closed, local organizers revived the idea, inviting area students to paint the ground-floor windows of the Glosser Building just as so many students had done before them.

A Fearful Procession

A few years after the window-painting contest launched, Glosser Bros. started another October tradition that caught on quickly: the annual Halloween parade.

Beginning in 1965, Glosser Bros. sponsored the parade of Halloween floats, costumed characters, marching bands, fire companies, Boy Scouts, Girl Scouts, and other local organizations handing out candy to kids along the parade route. The event was a hit from the start and continued for decades, just like the window-painting contest.

Every year, local groups competed to see who could come up with the best float and win the cash prizes offered by Glosser Bros. Spectators crowded the sidewalks along Main Street, vying for the best view of the elaborately decorated creations.

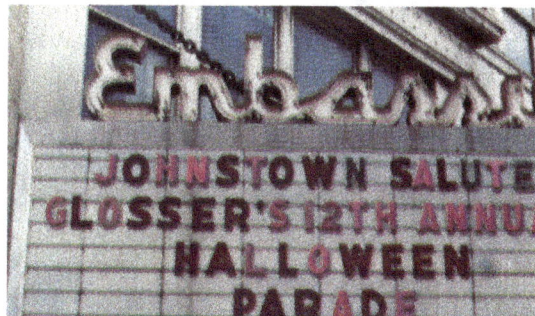

Photo from Glosser Bros. Annual Report, Jan. 1978

179

Photo from The Happy Times newsletter, Fall 1987

The parade became a tradition that was as beloved by members of the Glosser family as those who weren't part of that group.

Diane Glosser Rosenthal, daughter of Alvin Glosser, still remembers the parade with great affection. "My memories of Halloween are filled with watching the parade, admiring the store's painted windows by local students, and finally ending up back at the store after the parade, where my cousins, siblings and I were able to raid the candy department or go make sundaes in the cafeteria."

Photo from Glosser Bros. Annual Report, Jan. 1976

The parade continued for 25 years as a Glosser Bros. event. Even the 1977 Johnstown Flood couldn't keep it down. Though the city of Johnstown--and Glosser's--were still in a rebuilding mode after the July disaster, Glosser Bros. made sure the parade took place as it did every year.

"Everyone's been working hard for a bigger and better Johnstown!" read the flyer advertising the event. "This year we have another good reason to hold our parade with one big evening of entertainment and celebration!"

The community sent thank-you letters and turned out in force, glad to have a favorite event restored in a year of upheaval and loss.

Years later, in 1987, the parade was still going strong. The '87 edition featured the Peanuts gang and

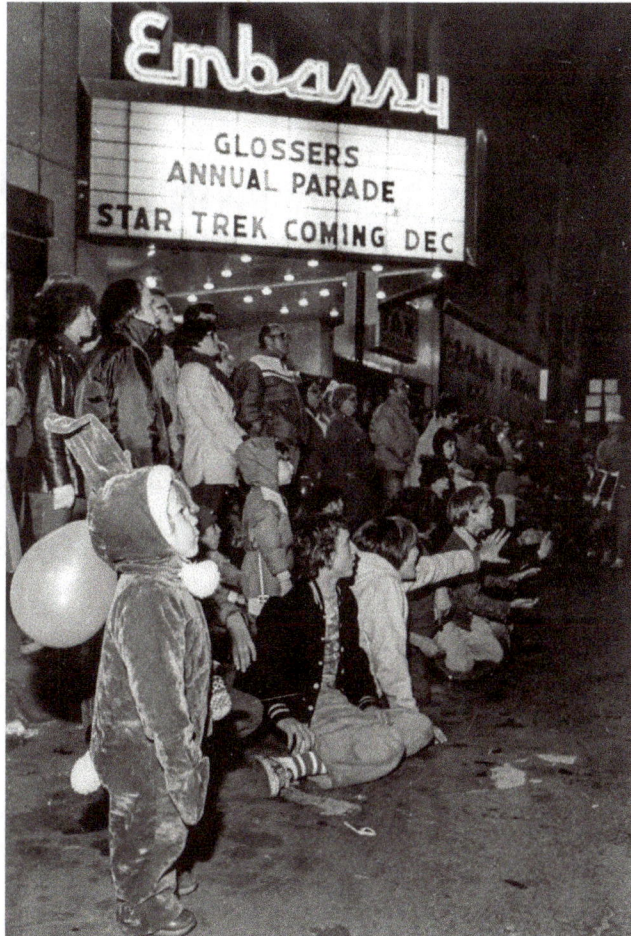

Photo © The Tribune-Democrat

the Great Pumpkin, Mother Goose, characters from *The Wizard of Oz*, and a special Glosser Bros. float starring Spuds McKenzie, the "party animal" bull terrier popularized in Bud Light beer commercials at the time.

Photo courtesy Wendy Dolges

The Parade That Would Not Die

When the Glosser Bros. Department Store closed, and the company entered Chapter 11 in the late 1980s, it seemed the parade might finally be doomed. But by then, it had taken on a life of its own.

WGLU radio and WWCP-TV 8 took over sponsorship of the event, then handed it off to WJAC-TV. WJAC kept it rolling until 2008, when Forever Broadcasting took over. As of 2014, the parade is still a Johnstown Halloween mainstay, 46 years old and showing no signs of slowing down.

In a few more years, the parade will reach the half-century milestone, a testament to the ingenuity and foresight of the Glosser team in creating an event that outlived their own organization.

181

EVERYONE'S BEEN WORKING HARD FOR A BIGGER AND BETTER JOHNSTOWN!

This year we have another good reason to hold our parade with one big evening of entertainment and celebration!

RESERVE THE DATE! IT'S COMING!

Glosser bros 12th ANNUAL
JOHNSTOWN, PA.

HALLOWEEN PARADE

We Will Rebuild TOGETHER!

Please Return Enclosed Entry Card at Once!

7:30 p.m. TUESDAY OCTOBER 25
RAIN DATE OCT. 26
OVER $1,200⁰⁰ IN CASH PRIZES!

Floats and heavy equipment will form on Baumer St. in Honerstown. Marching units and mummers will form in Somerset St. area of Kernville.

- FLOATS • BANDS • MUMMERS
- FIRE COMPANIES • FIRE AUXILIARIES
- MAJORETTES • DRUM CORPS
  - BOY SCOUTS
    - GIRL SCOUTS

If you have any questions please contact:
Debbie LaRue
Glosser Bros.
Phone: 536-6633 Ext. 329

GLOSSER'S ALL-STARS
HUNT ROOM MARY

The woman they called Hunt Room Mary knows one thing for sure: If the Hunt Room restaurant at Glosser Bros. Department Store was still open, she'd still be working there.

So what if she's 87 years old? If there was still a Hunt Room to work in, she'd be hanging on to her old job for dear life.

Hunt Room Mary 2014 (photo by Philip Balko)

Hunt Room Mary--aka Mary Schuster of Johnstown--loved the place *that much*.

"At Glosser's, we were names, not numbers," remembers Mary. "I loved it there. I loved every minute of it."

A Splashy Beginning

Born in 1927, Mary started working at the Hunt Room in 1944, when she was 17 years old. Her Glosser's career could have ended right there, thanks to a bumpy start.

"There was a beer garden called Romanov's downstairs below the cafeteria," says Betty. "I went down there for lunch with some of the girls who were old enough to buy alcohol. They hid me in the middle of the group since I was too young, and they ordered a bunch of drinks. We all had a good time.

"When we went back up to work, I was pretty tipsy. I had to clear the silverware off the tables, putting it in a pail of water on a cart I pushed around...but when I threw the silverware in, I splashed people by accident. I just kept splashing them.

"My boss, Mr. Snodgrass, called me over and said, 'Don't you ever, ever do that again.' But I was lucky, because he didn't fire me."

Mary left a few years later anyway, at age 20, when she got married...but couldn't stay away for long. After her hiatus as a newlywed, she returned to the Hunt Room again.

This time, she stayed for 28 years. Even after all that time, she only left when Glosser Bros. and the Hunt Room went out of business for good.

Where Everybody Knows Your Name

Mary's longevity and friendly disposition made her a well-known and much-loved figure among the crowd of professionals and VIPs who often dined at the Hunt Room.

"Our regulars included attorneys, bankers, doctors, Bethlehem Steel bosses, Crown American executives, you name it," says Mary. "Plus the managers and executives at Glosser Bros..

"Whoever they were, we made sure we took good care of them. We had everything ready so they could just sit down, eat, and leave.

"We knew what everybody drank, whether it was coffee, tea, or water, and we had it poured and ready as soon as they walked in the door," says Mary. "It really was like walking into a place where everybody knows your name."

Kindness Repaid

During her decades at the Hunt Room, Mary served everyone from movie stars to professional athletes. Once, she even waited on the Pittsburgh Steelers' own Franco Harris.

Just as she worked hard to treat her customers right, they repaid her with kindness of their own.

"One time, when I was in the hospital, they had to open another room to put all the flowers in," says Mary. "Then they had to stop bringing in the flowers because they were putting too much oxygen in the room."

At Christmas time, Mary's loyal customers and co-workers never failed to shower her with gifts. "Every one of the Glossers gave me something," she recalls. "Mr. Bill (Bill Glosser) would give me $25. So would Mr. (Sydney) Ossip.

"My manager bought me a turkey. The grocery department sent a basket piled high with all kinds of fruit to my house.

"And every buyer in the store brought me something, too. I remember they gave me gift certificates, leather gloves, all kinds of nice things. It was fabulous."

Special Events and Menu Specials

In addition to her usual duties, Mary helped out with special events throughout the year.

"I took care of all the coffee and doughnuts for the annual coat sale," she says. "I wheeled a little cart over to the display area and served coffee and doughnuts to the customers."

Mary also worked on Buck-a-Cup days with WJAC-TV sports announcer Tim Rigby. "Tim and I served coffee to raise money for the American Cancer Society. We sold buttons for a buck, and you could come in and drink coffee all day with that button if you liked."

But serving lunch in the Hunt Room was always her main job. She still remembers the daily specials as if she had served them just last week. "Monday was split pea soup. We had Chinese and Spaghetti Tuesday and Turkey Thursday. Then there were the half-chickens with mashed potatoes for $1.49."

The Most Wonderful Days

In later years, after Glosser's closed, Hunt Room Mary went to work at the Capri restaurant on Main Street. But her Hunt Room days were never far from her heart.

"When Mr. Bill saw me working at Capri, he said if he ever started another business, he'd buy a chair and put me at the register. I told him I'd take him up on the offer, and I would.

"The days when I worked there were the most wonderful days of my life," says Mary.

Hunt Room Mary 2014 (photo by Philip Balko)

CASH & CARRY

Some Items in Limited Quantity--Be at Glosser's at 12 Noon

Hurry, they'll go fast at low, low price!
Values to 5.98 Record Albums
48¢ ea.
Stereo and Hi-Fi Big selection.
98¢ 45-RPM Records favorite sides . . . 10 for 99
RECORDS—FOURTH FLOOR

Extra Special Savings! Over 80 choice patterns!
To 8.65 Room-lot Wallpaper Sale
Group 2.69
• Group 2 3.69 • Group 3 4.69
Room-lot includes 10 single rolls wallpaper and 18 yds. border. Annex.

Big Toy Dept. "Cash & Carry" Special!
To 8.95 Lionel Freight Cars
$2
Wide selection to choose from! Lumber, chemical, liquefied gas cars, more! For "027" sets. 4th Fl.

Another Super-Toy Special!
Gilbert All-Metal Erector Sets
99¢
While they last, better hurry! Buy now for Christmas gift giving. 4th Fl.

"Cash & Carry" Closeout Special!
10.88 Automatic Elec. Percolator
$5
9-cup. Fully automatic. Shuts off when coffee is ready. Keeps coffee hot. 4th Fl.

Extra Big "Cash & Carry" Savings!
Fiberglas® Dust-Stop Air Filters
41¢
100% glass fibers. For tops in comfort and healthful living all season long. 4th Fl.

Children's --"Cash & Carry"

3 BIG GROUPS
Little Girls Famous Make
SCHOOL & PARTY DRESSES

Values to 2.95	Sizes to 4.95	Values to 9.95
$1	**$2**	**$3**

Come in and see a closetful of these low priced. Assorted colors or styles. Sizes 1-3, 3-6x.

TrimIie Baby Baths

Regular 1.95	Regular 22.99
Floor sample. Only 1, hurry! **$11**	Floor sample. Only 1, hurry! **$14**

• LITTLE GIRLS' BETTER SLIPS . . . . 77¢
Expensive cotton and nylons. All white, snap, sizes 6 to 8.
• CHILDREN'S 3.99 BEDROOM LAMPS . 2.40
Attractively designed to suit many kiddies room decor.
• CHILDREN'S WARM SWEATERS 1.33
Assorted colors and covers for boys and girls. Sizes 2 to 6x.
• LITTLE BOYS' PAJAMAS . . . . 71¢
Heavy warm cotton flannels. Popular styles, 3 to 8.
• CHILDREN'S to 5.95 JACKETS 1.99
Warm, waterweight nylons. Popular styles and colors. 3-6x.
• CHILDREN'S to 7.95 SNOW SUITS . 2.99
Quality styles for boys and girls. Sizes 2 to 4.
• CHILDREN'S to 9.95 SNOW SUITS . . 4.99
Famous styles for boys and girls. Sizes 3 to 6x. Hi mat to match.

INFANTS'--"CASH & CARRY"

• ORLAN CRIB BLANKETS $2
Warm, fluffy. Orlon acrylic. 36x50 size. Snap.
• 1-PC. STRETCH TERRY SLEEPERS . . 73¢
Lightweight stretch terry. Assorted colors.
• to 2.99 INFANTS' WEARABLES . . . . 66¢
Wide selection of shirts, crib sets, more, etc. Big savings.
• INFANTS' PLASTIC PANTS . . . . . 16¢
Soft, waterproof. Popular styles. Sizes S, M, L, XL.
• INFANTS' 1.95 TOWEL SETS . . . . . 99¢
So handy! Contains towel and wash cloth. Assorted.
CHILDREN'S DEPT.—THIRD FLOOR

FASHION SUITS & COATS

ONE- or FEW-of-a-KIND
CASH & CARRY SENSATIONS!

Item	Regular	SALE
(4) Cotton Suits	10.95	$3
(7) Cotton & Rayon Suits, soiled	to 29.95	$5
(3) Handkerchief Cotton Suits, soiled	to 39.95	$8
(2) Famous-Name Wool Suits, soiled	to 59.95	$10
(3) Rainwear Wool Coats, soiled	59.95	$5
(2) Famous Name Wool Coats, soiled	to 39.95	$3
(2) Wool Suits		$10
(4) Wool Laminated Knit Coats	to 29.95	$5
(4) Wool Laminated Knit Coats	to 38.95	$10
(5) All Wool Topper	19.95	$3
(6) Raccoon Collared Coats	29.95	$10
(5) Orlon-Type Coats	49.00	$20
(5) Genuine Leather Suede Coats	29.95	$20
(5) Fake Leopard Toppers	25.00	$8
(4) Fake Leopard Toppers	to 39.95	$10
(17) Fake Leopard Coats	to 29.95	$10
(5) Fur Trim Fake Leopard Coats	to 39.95	$15

Broken sizes for juniors and misses.
FASHION COATS & SUITS—THIRD FLOOR

FOOTWEAR--"CASH & CARRY"

Women's & Girls' 2.99
WARM SNOW BOOTS
1.77
Choose from several popular snap and strap-type styles. Water-repellant, long-wearing vamize-hyde uppers. Crepe soles. Sizes 4 to 10.

WASHABLE WHITE LEATHER
NURSE & DUTY SHOES
Values to 7.99!
2.47
Choose these comfortable and easy to clean styles. With baby ridge soles. Slight irregulars. Sizes 4 to 10 in group. While they last.

Women's Cotton Terry Slippers . . . . . . 67¢
Hurry styles with crepe soles. White with red or blue trim. 5 to 9.
Reg. 12.99 Kickerino Boots $5
Discontinued styles. Just 50 pairs, hurry. Crepe sole styles.
Women's to 7.99 Better Shoes . . . . . 97¢
Dress and sport styles in heels and flats. Broken sizes.
FOOTWEAR—MAIN FLOOR

Sportswear --"CASH & CARRY"

Scramble Racks
Ladies' Sportswear

Regular to 10.95	Regular to 16.95
$3	**$5**

• Slacks • Suits • Car Coats
• Rain Coats • Skirts / Blouse Sets
• Storm Coats • Kookie Coats
Scramble tables piled high. Broken sizes.

3.95 Ban-Lon® Cardigans $2
Non-pill textured nylon. Pastel shades. Sizes 34 to 40.
To 3.99 Sportswear 1.19
Blouses, sweaters, shirts, slacks. Some things.
To 7.95 Famous Sweaters . . $3
Famous Name cardi and bulky styles. 36 to 40.
1st Fl.--Sportswear . . . . 69¢
Sample shirts, tops. Many styles and colors.
SPORTSWEAR—THIRD FLOOR

"CASH & CARRY"--TOILETRIES

• $2.50 Natural Bristle Shaving Brushes . . . . 88¢
• Regular 1.00 Bowles Dusting Powder . . . . 37¢
• 21.95 Famous Riviera Hair Dryers 12.88
• 14.95 Electric Automatic Toothbrush 2.88
• Regular 19 DuPont Sponges . . . . 1¢
• 8MM Movie Film, with developing . . . . . 99¢
• Regular 49¢ Verigon Roll Film . . . . 9¢
• $2 Big 26-ounce Trol Shaving Cream . . . . . 77¢
• $2 "Nice & Clean" Compact Size Cleansing Pads . . 40 for 44¢
• Regular to 1.00 Quality Lipsticks . . . . . . 19¢
DISCOUNT TOILETRIES—MAIN FLOOR

Just 150
Better Dresses
drastically reduced!
Values to 12.95
$2 - $3 - $5
For Juniors, Misses, Women
Some slightly soiled. Hurry in for best selection.
BETTER DRESSES—THIRD FLOOR

"CASH & CARRY" Housewares

Item	Reg.	SALE
BRASS FINISH METAL WASTE BASKETS . . .	88¢	59¢
23-PC. CHINA TEA SET, service for 6 . .	9.95	4.99
10" CHROME CHICKEN FRYER	2.98	1.22
SWING-A-WAY AUTOMATIC CAN OPENER . .	22.47	6.97
"COSCO" DELUXE STEP STOOLS	11.95	7.97
GLASBAKE OVEN-to-TABLE BAKEWARE . .	to 99¢	28¢
4-PC. GLAS-BAKE MIXING BOWL SETS . . .	4.95	1.97
UNIVERSAL 1-PT. THERMOS BOTTLES . .	1.49	87¢
IRONING SLEEVE BOARDS	89¢	57¢
45-PC. DINNERWARE SET, service for 8 . .	14.95	6.88
LARGE HOLIDAY-COLOR GLASS TUMBLERS .	12¢ for	68¢

HOUSEWARES—FOURTH FLOOR

FURNITURE "CASH & CARRY"

• (11) To 10.95 Samsonite Bridge Tables $5
• (1) 24.90 Metal Wardrobe, 36", scratched . . $15
• (2) 16.90 Double-Door Linen Cabinet, 24" . . $10
• (6) 7.95 Hard Plastic Bowling Ball Bags . . . $4
• (2) 29.90 Green Tweed Foam Back Rug, 9x12' $20
• (1) 29.90 Plain Taupe Color Rug, 9x12' . . . $20
• (1) 69.90 Gold Tweed Rug, 12x18' $38
• (2) 39.90 Solid Gray Color Rugs, 10x12' . . . $25
• (1) 26.90 Upholstered Spring Seat Chairs . . $15
• (2) 10.90 Maple Finish Slat Seat Rockers . . 7.50
• (1) 29.90 Black and Gold Boston Rocker, damaged $15
• (1) 69.90 Tapestry Upholstered Sofa Bed . . $50
• (2) 19.90 Metal Kneehole Desks, floor sample $10
• (200) To 1.49 Shag Rugs, odds and ends . . 59¢
• (50) 2.99 Ivory Venetian Blinds, 18, 19, 26" widths 50¢
• (90) 3a 3.99 Oval Hook Rugs $2
• (2) 16.95 Sewing Rockers, maple & mahogany $10
• Rug Border Remnants, 2 and 3-ft. wide. yd. 25¢
FURNITURE—FOURTH FLOOR

HARDWARE & AUTO SUPPLIES

• 14.95 McGraw-Edison Electric Sanders 5.99
• 24.95 McGraw-Edison 7" Power Saw 18.95
• 19.95 Famous Thor 3/8" Electric Drill 9.95
• Regular 39.95 AM-FM Radios 29.95
• 9.95 6-Transistor Radio with battery, earphone, carry case . . 7.99
• Famous Dry Gas "Gasoline Anti-Freeze" . . . . . 8 for $1
• Regular 1.49 Booster Cables . . . . 99¢
• 30 Everready D-Size Batteries, limit 12 . . . . ea. 13¢
• 9.95 Double Stock Outside Antennas 4.97
HARDWARE—FRANKLIN ST. ANNEX

NEW TREAD
WINTER TIRES
Buy Now at a
Big 40% Savings!

MONDAY ONLY	**$8**	Plus tax and exchangeable casing.

All these sizes: 600x13, 640x13, 670x15 and 750x14.
AUTO SUPPLIES—FRANKLIN ST. ANNEX

PAINT DEPT. -- ANNEX

SPECIAL-PURPOSE
PAINTS
Reg. 2.19 Royal Economy Paints
Your Choice **1.87** gal.

• DECOR: flat vinyl latex for walls, wallpaper, masonry & colors, white.
• FLATWALL for interior walls and woodwork. 6 colors and white. Oil base.
• PORCH & FLOOR ENAMEL, for wood or concrete floors, wood trim. 6 colors.
• READY MIXED: All-purpose paint. 6 colors and white.
PAINTS—FRANKLIN ST. ANNEX

• 2.95 WOOD 4-ft. STEPLADDERS 2.77
With bucket platform and skid-resistant non-slip steps.
• 1.19 SPRAY ENAMEL PAINTS . . . . 57¢
Big 14-oz. size. Choice of 12 washing colors.
• REG. 3.59 ROOF COATING 2.44
Big famous 5-gallon bucket. Buy now at big savings.
• 59¢ PAINT ROLLER COVERS . . . . . twin-pack 44¢
Two covers to a pack. Quality Devel, big value.
PAINTS—FRANKLIN ST. ANNEX

TOYS--"CASH & CARRY"

• 88¢ TV's FAVORITE SPARKLE PAINTS . . . . 69¢
• 4.95 GIVE-A-SHOW PROJECTOR, 112 slides . . 2.99
• 3.95 BONANZA DELUXE HOLSTER SET 2.88
• 2.95 TRUE VUE LOOK 'N' LEARN COLORING PAK 1.44
• 12.95 LIONEL MOTORIZED TURNTABLE . . . 4.99
DISCOUNT TOYS—FOURTH FLOOR

"CASH & CARRY"--HOSIERY

INFANTS' ANKLETS
Slight imperfects of a very famous make. Soft, purish and all white. Sizes 3½ to 5½.
12 prs. 88¢

• GIRLS' BOBBY SOCKS . . . . 5 prs. 97¢
Reg. 49¢ if perfect, heavy slound cuff. White and colors.
HOSIERY—MAIN FLOOR

"CASH & CARRY"--NOTIONS

• 2.99 ELECTRIC PENCIL SHARPENER . . . . 99¢
Combines fast, easy, accurate. Heal gift.
• To 69¢ BETTER QUALITY YARNS . . . . . 33¢
Soft. Assorted wools, nylons and Orlon acrylic.
• 10.98 KRAFT PAPER WARDROBES 4.83
40x20x21 size. 2- 3/4 top, double doors. Durable.
• REG. 25¢ PENCIL TABLETS . . . . 17¢
8x10" size. Choice of white or yellow sheets.
• 99¢ INSTANT SEWING IN TUBE . . . . . 31¢
Giant size tubes. Adhesive formula.
NOTIONS—SECOND FLOOR

No Mail or Phone-No Layaways-Open Monday 12 noon until 9

Items On Sale Monday Only

GLOSSER BROS.
Famous for Savings

MEMORY DEPARTMENT

I worked in the Advertising Department located behind the record department two different times. The first time was right after I graduated from the Art Institute of Pittsburgh. I did the layouts for Glosser's ads and some copywriting from 1968 to 1972. I came back to work in the Advertising Department again in the 80s, doing copywriting. Alvin Glosser's office was across the hall from our department, and he used an intercom to communicate with us. He especially

1971 Advertising Department. Back row going up steps, l. to r.: Ed Craine, Nancy Acitelli, Kathy Orlosky. Front row, l. to r.: Barb Ripple, Patti Macik (Photo courtesy of Nancy Acitelli)

loved to embarrass me over the intercom when calling me into his office.

One summer, I asked for a leave so I could go to State College while my husband took some grad courses. When I told Alvin the date I would return, he sent me a hilarious letter about how he had alerted the cafeteria workers, the night cleaning crew, the drivers, and all the other departments he could think of! Also, the day I got married, I received a telegram delivered to my house congratulating us on our marriage. A real telegram! I loved doing the ads and the people I worked with. I am in contact with a couple of co-workers on Facebook and e-mail now.

- *Nancy Acitelli*

When I started at Glossers, I had to have working papers because I had just graduated from high school at the age of 17. I worked anywhere they needed me until I got a full-time position on the fourth floor with Rose Mary Hicks in the Music department, which was my favorite job of my retail career. I worked there until 1976, when I got married to my wonderful husband, Rick Becker.

Rick worked as a floater for the receiving department on the fifth floor. He turned down a job at Bethlehem Steel because they wanted him immediately, and he wanted to give Glosser's a two-week notice. Thank goodness he stayed at Glosser's and remained working in the Jackson Street warehouse for six months, then was transferred to the Windber warehouse, where he remained for 23 years.

- *Paula Katie Buynack Becker*

I worked at Glosser's in 1971-72 as a secretary for the housewares buyers. It was my first job. For $1.60 an hour, they got a secretary, fill-in cashier on the floor, stock room girl, and model for the advertising department! A bargain!

- *Mary Petro Himlin*

When I first arrived in Johnstown in September of 1966, I spent a couple of months working in the men's clothing department with Ben Issacson, who was the buyer. He had established quite a substantial business selling hunting supplies and clothing. Having had no knowledge of hunting prior to moving to Johnstown from New York, I was quite impressed with what he had created. During that hunting season, I urged him to put in a small hunting department in a separate area, and he went to management and got their blessing to do so.

The following year, we had a beautiful little hunting department in the basement with a separate room for hunters to try on the Safety-Back pants & jackets that we sold. We also sold ammunition. This was one example of how Glosser's went the extra mile to accommodate these specialized customers.

When I took over the infants department, within two years I had put in the largest selection of juvenile furniture in western Pennsylvania. I promoted cribs and mattresses, strollers, newly invented car seats and swingomatics, porta-cribs, and all kinds of other juvenile products. I did this with my associate, Joe Muha, who worked with me for eight years. Fred Glosser, who was in charge of building, maintenance, etc. was instrumental in helping design and construct these two new departments that helped Glosser's become even more unique in its merchandising prowess.

- *Jeff Diamond, Glosser Bros. employee 1966-1988 (and son-in-law of Sydney Ossip)*

I was home from Penn State for the month of December and was excited to land a job working in Glosser's. Having money coming in at the end of the year meant that my combination of work and study during the regular school year might be less challenging. I might even get to take time off or have some money for some other pleasure. Like most people, I found the sounds and smells of Glosser's to be magical in December. To this day, I can close my eyes and hear the bells from the Salvation Army booth on the corner. I can hear the hubbub of the first floor blended with a Bing Crosby version of "White Christmas." I can feel the warmth of those holiday lights and tightly packed shoppers around "Sale" racks. I remember the fragrance of Old Spice cologne with overtones of roasted nuts and chocolate.

When the sparkling Marie Novak interviewed and hired me, she asked if it would be okay with me to work in the parking lot. I immediately thought of two things. Ten hours of standing outside in a Johnstown December was not appealing. I had been a paperboy for the Tribune-Democrat and had done a fair amount of snow removal and many other Western Pennsylvania outside jobs while growing up. I knew that the beauty of large early snowflakes diminishes after a few minutes when the wind tops 30 miles per hour. The second thought was MONEY. All of my potential placements at Glosser's were at the low end of the pay scale. Working in the parking lot was going to be cold, but working out there did have one great bonus: harvesting tips. Those tips became my focus.

While the other two parking attendants were happy to huddle around the heater in our tight little standup pay booth and enjoy the entitlement of a job at Glosser's, I tried to be near the lot entrance. I figured that the more cars I parked, the more I hustled, the more I smiled, the greater my opportunity to climb and the greater my tips. After parking one car, I would jog back to the front of the lot to park the next car. It kept me warm. The mothers with pretty daughters seemed to especially appreciate my enthusiasm. The $0.35 parking charge was often paid with two quarters and a smile. In this small but high turnover parking lot, getting twenty $0.15 tips meant an extra $3.00 per hour or $24 per shift. It was some real money in the days when a Coke cost $0.10. I was getting a lot more tips than the other guys. That did not make me real popular with them. But, I was having fun in finding a way to get ahead while I made people's shopping experience better. I think that was the amazing fundamental feeling in the air at Glosser's. The vast majority of the staff carried that Johnstown ethos of doing good while doing well.

Another element of that Glosser's/Johnstown approach was expressed in generosity. My days in the parking lot coincided with the prime years of the Greatest Generation. Those who spent their formative years on Iwo Jima, Omaha Beach, or the Mountains of Asia were a special breed. Knowing that their friends saw an early end of life made them uncommonly generous. One snowy afternoon, I hustled out of one parked car and ran up to a fellow in a nice cloth coat. He looked solid but not rich. I got his ticket and moved quickly to get his car out of the narrow space where we had sandwiched it. The spaces were sometimes so tight that opening a window was the easiest way to squeeze into the driver's seat.

Upon moving the car to the front of the lot to get his payment, he handed me his yellow ticket and a $20 bill. I moved toward the pay booth to get his change and heard him say "Merry Christmas." I turned to say, "Sir, it is a twenty." He smiled the smile of a fellow who knew that a young hustling fellow used to be next to him in a trench on some Pacific Island and simply said, "I know. Merry Christmas."

Tim Sosinski (son-in-law of Sydney Ossip)

As a teenager, I worked during the summers in the men's work clothes department in the back corner of the first floor of Glosser's. And it really changed my life. Watching other employees in the store, how they handled things and dealt with customers, taught me workplace and social strategies that I still use to this day.

- Daniel Glosser (son of Fred Glosser)

Chapter 22

A Glosser's Revolution

In the late 1960s, Operation Gee Bee was in full swing...but new store openings weren't the only changes happening at Glosser Bros., Inc.

New opportunities and advances in technology were reshaping the company in exciting new ways. Even the downtown department store, an institution for decades, was transforming and would never be the same.

There were revolutions underway across America--and around the world--in those days, challenging the status quo and reshaping the course of the future. Glosser's, in its own way, wasn't going to be left behind.

Chill Out, G

What do you get when you keep your store cool by blowing in dirty steel town air from outside? *A very dusty store.*

Which is exactly what Glosser Bros. had for the first 60 years of its existence. In all that time, The Store had never been air conditioned; instead, the Glossers had used powerful fans all over the building to bring in outside air.

And that, of course, brought in lots and lots of dust from the steel mills. So when a long, hot summer settled in, and the fans were running hard, the cleaning crews had their hands full sweeping up all the dust. Clearing dust from the merchandise, so shoppers wouldn't reject it for being dirty, occupied many man-hours.

Finally, in 1967, company management decided to spring for air conditioning. Keeping The Store cool and clean on hot days might help encourage customers to linger longer and buy more stuff.

Naturally, the job went to the companywide construction and maintenance czar, Fred Glosser, who performed his due diligence research and came up with a plan.

"I used all local contractors to do the work," remembers Fred. "They worked at night and on Sundays to avoid disrupting business in the store.

"The air conditioning system was designed, engineered, and put into operation by the Snavely Air Conditioning Co. The related plumbing was designed and installed by Smith Plumbing. Andrew Kindya and Son, Inc. did all the electrical work.

"Strayer and Co. installed the roof compressor, the water chillers, and all the air handlers on each floor. The construction of the roof platform to house the compressor and the chillers was handled by Carstensen, Inc.

"When it was all done, the system worked perfectly. I closed up all the windows with panels and kept the store cool and clean at the same time from then on," says Fred.

Booting Up Glosser's

Another big change came to Glosser's around the same time as the air conditioning--and this one was even more revolutionary.

By the mid-1960s, computers were becoming an important part of big business. They were still physically huge and very expensive compared to computers today, with limited processing power--but the advantages of using them could not be ignored.

Glosser Bros., Inc. decided it was time to put those advantages to work for their company. After weighing the costs and benefits, Leonard Black and his team decided to go in on a joint venture with a local engineering and design firm, H.F. Lenz.

In 1968, Glosser Bros. and Lenz created a new company to handle Glosser's data processing. The company, Data Consultants, Inc., set up shop in the Westwood Plaza, on the ground floor of what was then the local office of H.F. Lenz. Glosser Bros., Inc. owned a 37% stake in the new venture, with the rest owned by Lenz.

Data Consultants Building 2014 (photo by Philip Balko)

Once the company had moved into its new digs, the hardware followed. Data Consultants purchased a new mainframe computer system from the leader in business computing at the time, IBM. The system, like its potential to transform Glosser's, Inc., was enormous. "When IBM installed the computers, they took up a 50-foot by 50-foot room," remembers Fred. "They occupied most of the first floor of the H.F. Lenz building."

The computers enabled Data Consultants personnel to track Glosser's sales, inventory, and expenses

Photo by A. Church Photographers (courtesy of Johnstown Area Heritage Association)

at what was then consider blinding speed. Data Consultants could generate detailed reports in nothing flat, detect sales trends and changes over time, and expedite the processing of credit, payroll, and purchasing. Glosser's decision-makers could have data in their hands much sooner, enabling them to be better-informed of the big picture as they charted the organization's destiny.

Strategically, there could not have been a better time to plug in the new system. Glosser's, Inc. was ramping up its expansion in a big way, preparing to roll out a slew of new stores. Managing the downtown department store plus Gee Bees in Greensburg and Richland was enough of a challenge; add four or five or ten more stores into the mix, and it would be challenging indeed to juggle all their numbers and make smart decisions without help from computers.

It was the right move at the right time, another piece of the puzzle...and only the beginning of the company's use of computers. There would never be *fewer* computers in Glosser's operations; there would always be a need for more computing power, for better, faster ways to track and keep records and generate reports.

These were the days before desktop computers or laptops or the Internet or touchscreens...but Glosser's, Inc. had still taken a giant leap forward. The company was riding the wave of a technological revolution, one that was just in time for the changes that were coming.

One of which would signal Glosser's rise into a whole different level altogether.

From Franklin Street to Wall Street

By 1969, Leonard and his team were already deep into preparations for one of their biggest plays yet. This one would change the company's fate forever, bumping it into the corporate big leagues...if it all worked out.

The plan was this: to sell stock in Glosser Bros., Inc. The management team wanted to make Glosser's a publicly held company, traded on the American Stock Exchange.

It would be a big gamble, but the payoff could be bigger still. Investors could give the company the cash it needed to grow faster than expected, to ascend, perhaps, into the ranks of great American publicly-held corporations.

Glosser Bros., Inc. had an ambitious business plan, an ongoing and successful expansion program, and proven business processes enhanced by state-of-the-art computing technology wielded by experts in the field. Pulling off an initial public offering (IPO) on the American Stock Exchange seemed like a natural next step.

In just a few years, the company that started with a little shop on Franklin Street could become a genuine powerhouse on Wall Street.

Glosser Bros. Board of Directors 1972 (photo by Albert's Photography)

MEMORY DEPARTMENT

I remember driving to work in a vehicle called a Pacer (a bubble car). I came to work one evening and parked the Pacer near a cart drop-off. One of the employees who happened to be out in the parking lot gathering up shopping carts saw me get out of it. He began laughing hysterically. Well, if you could have seen this car, you would have been cracking up, too. I looked at my car and then at him and just lost it. We ended up laughing so hard, we were both crying. You just had to be there.

- *Carla Thomas Sorber*

I was a loss prevention operative at Glosser's. I clearly recall the day after Thanksgiving of 1971 when the store offered cans of fruitcake at the first opening of the doors. Dozens of elderly women crowded around outside and then fought and struggled to get in. At one point, a woman knocked a colleague into the glass door. Another put up a huge fuss because she desired a blue container instead of a red one.

I also fondly remember an African American colleague named Mr. Hill. I don't know if I ever learned his first name, but he was a well-loved and respected man.

- *Thomas J Koharchik*

In late September 1966, I started working at Glosser's after having been employed by Abraham & Straus Department store in Brooklyn, New York. After a brief training period of approximately two months, I took on the job of infants' department buyer from Fred Glosser, who was going to devote his full time to store maintenance and operations. I worked as the buyer for infant & children's wear for over ten years.

A highlight of this experience was recognizing that working for this organization was like becoming a new member of the Glosser family. (I knew how that felt because my wife, Carol, was the daughter of a full-fledged family member, Sydney Ossip.) I think I would have felt that way even if I had just gone there to work without knowing anyone because of the spirit and closeness that all of the store employees felt. There were store picnics each summer out at Fun City/Ideal amusement Park (which was lost in the flood of 1977). Store talent shows periodically featuring anyone who dared show off their talents. And a special store newspaper featured employees from around the store who were deserving of acclaim.

All of these activities, together with the monthly promotions that took place, only strengthened the harmony that existed and made the bond between Glosser management and its employees that much stronger. Bill Glosser, who was in charge of all personnel, made sure that all of these things happened in a timely manner and in good spirit.

- Jeff Diamond, Glosser Bros. employee 1966-1988 (and son-in-law of Sydney Ossip)

Photos by Margie Hagerich

My childhood seemed different than that of many of my friends because so many of my memories revolved around Glosser Bros.

For example, I remember that there were seven male family members running the store, and all the employees called them "Mr." and their first name. So my father was referred to as "Mr. Alvin." What struck me was that the employees were always comfortable around the family and vice versa.

Our family ate dinner in the Hunt Room many Thursday evenings, since my father worked late. It wasn't unusual for me to run through the store visiting with many of the employees either before or after dinner. After all, they were my extended family.

My memories of Halloween were filled with watching the parade, admiring the store's painted windows by the local high schools, and finally ending up back at the store after the parade where my cousins, siblings, and I were able to raid the candy department or make sundaes in the cafeteria.

I also remember traveling to the Gee Bee stores with my father. He told me that once he arrived at the first store, the other store managers would call the subsequent stores to alert them that he was on his way. I learned a lot from listening to the comments my father made to the store managers. One in particular always remains near and dear. It was a hot summer day when we traveled to one of the stores. My father commented that fans should be in the front of the store because of the heat. Fans were an item that would really sell in the hot summer months, yet there wasn't even one in the front of the store plugged in. My father commented, "How do you expect to sell fans if they are not displayed and plugged in?" This made an impression on me since I, too, was interested in retail. I never forgot it!

Glosser Bros was not only a family business, but was entrenched in the Johnstown community. It supported local schools, downtown businesses, and many charities.

After all these years, it's hard to believe that the current generation does not know that the business even existed. All they see is the building on the corner of Franklin and Locust Streets. But he memories of that magical place will always be a very special part of my life!

- *Diane Glosser Rosenthal (daughter of Alvin Glosser)*

GLOSSER'S HAS SO MUCH to CHOOSE for SPRING and EASTER . . . for so very, very little!

SHOP THURSDAY 9:30 'til 9:00
OPEN A GLOSSER CHARGE ACCOUNT
CREDIT DEPT.—THIRD FLOOR

Stuffed EASTER BUNNIES!
78¢ to 1.68
Big, beautiful, cuddly soft 9" to 14" high bunnies in a colorful assortment!

regular 29¢ Easter Grass, 2½-oz. bag .... 21¢
NOTIONS—GLOSSER'S SECOND FLOOR

Great Glosser spring collection . . .

BOYS' Permanent-Press SPORT and DRESS TROUSERS
5.99
others 2.99 to 8.99

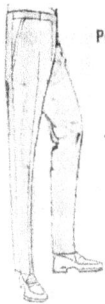

The American Girl SHOE

PUMPS and MORE PUMPS!

We've the newest in shapes and shades, in heels and textures. But how can they cost so little? For the same reason they fit so well. They're American Girls!

Charlotte—10.99
Loretta—12.99

See our complete selection of styles!

Real swinging fashion . . . "Dorette" Debs for Teens

For Boys and Girls . . . "Scuff Tuffs" and "Traveloy Juniors"
5.00
most styles

Spring's prettiest pumps, straps and bow trims in black, blue, pink, white, gray and bone! sizes 4 to 10.
5.99
most styles

her's *styled for the very young lady!*
Sizes . . . widths . . . and lasts especially designed to fit young feet and to please the very sophisticated tastes of today's junior miss!
9.99
Featuring bold toes, "up-front" details and sling backs in black, navy, bone, and white patents. Sizes 4½ to 9, AA to C.
FOOTWEAR—GLOSSER'S MAIN FLOOR

EASTER CANDY!
Individually Boxed!

Milk Chocolate Fruit and Nut or Coconut Cream Eggs
43¢ 1-lb. size

$1.59 Milk Chocolate SOLID RABBITS
99¢

Milk or White Choc. EASTER NOVELTIES
89¢ lb.

5 Brach's Assorted CREAM EGGS
6 for 29¢

Marshmallow CHICKS and RABBITS
39¢ ea.

Chocolate Marshmallow FOIL WRAPPED EGGS
39¢ ea.

Milk Choc. Hand Rolled PEANUT BUTTER EGGS
3 for 29¢

Easter Butter Creams .... lb. 39¢
Brach's Malted Milk Eggs .... lb. 79¢
Brach's Jelly Bird Eggs .... lb. 33¢
CANDY—GLOSSER'S MAIN FLOOR

All from famous makers!

Fabulous value!
BOYS' 10-WAY EASTER SUITS
at an incredible low . . .
$12
Snappy 4-piece suit precision tailored in smooth 70% rayon/30% acetate! Two-button Ivy jacket with flap pockets keyed to match and harmonize with 2 pairs of slacks and reversible vest! Royal blue, olive or brown. Sizes 6 to 12.
(note the number of ways in one outfit it!)
BOYS' WEAR—GLOSSER'S SECOND FLOOR

Li'l Girls' EASTER DRESSES
Beautiful nylon organzas, crisp Dacron® polyester/cotton voiles, permanent-press leno, and sheer cottons in pretty Easter dress-up styles!
Look at this line-up of famous names . . .
● Cinderella ● Li'l Bee
● Kate Greenaway
● Miss Quality
● plus many, many others
5.95
others 3.95 to 10.95
Easter egg colors in flattering solids, stripes and prints. Sizes 1 and 4 to 6x.

OMEGA . . . the last word in BIBLES!
reg. $19.95
15.99
The greatest story ever told, now available in the most comprehensive edition ever sold. 100 full color pictures. Protestant or Catholic edition. White or black, gold-edged pages.
BOOKS—GLOSSER'S FOURTH FLOOR

Jr. Boys' $3.99 PERMA-PRESS SLACK SETS
Washable Fortrel® polyester cotton home slacks with coordinating knit shirt in "Wear Dated" Acrilan acrylic! Handsome spring shades. 2 to 4, 3 to 7.
2.99
CHILDREN'S WEAR—GLOSSER'S THIRD FLOOR

Just arrived . . .
our last-minute shipment of all the fashions you love best!

EASTER DRESSES

Latest spring styles you've seen in leading fashion magazines priced at dollars more than our low . . .
8.80
Youthful-as-spring shifts, sheaths, sleeveless and full skirts, dresses in bonded Orlon® acrylic, new miracle blend sheers, rayon chiffons and other wanted fabrics! Gather up several in pretty solids, stripes, checks and novelty prints. Sizes 8 to 11, 7 to 15, 10 to 20, 14½ to 32½, 46 to 52.
DAYTIME DRESSES—GLOSSER'S SECOND FLOOR

198

199

GeeBee GeeBee GLOSSER'S

Both Gee Bees OPEN 10-10

OPEN
Wed.-Fri.-Sat. 9:30 to 5
Thurs.-9:30 to 9

food markets

✓ fresh ✓ young ✓ tender
ROASTING CHICKENS
4-6 LBS. 49¢ LB.

✓ MAYROSE FINEST REGULAR SLICED
✓ HICKORY HILL THICK SLICED
✓ SURREY FARM MAPLE SUGAR CURED
SLICED BACON
69¢ LB.

Oscar Mayer
sliced BOLOGNA
and
sliced COTTO SALAMI
12-oz. pkg. 65¢

WHOLE or HALF
With the aitch and shank bone removed for easy carving!

Victory Brand fully-cooked
SEMI-BONELESS HAMS
14-16 LBS.
59¢ LB.

from our DELICATESSENS
at Gee Bee RICHLAND & WALNUT STREET!
DELI-DELIGHTS
delicious HOT "ready to eat" FRIED FISH ...69¢ LB.

ICEBERG LETTUCE
SOLID HEADS of California ICEBERG LETTUCE for your EASTER TABLE!
17¢ hd.

HAM 'n' YAMS
Southern YAMS
10¢ LB.

Sweet 'N Large 88 Size Calif.
NAVEL ORANGES
59¢ doz.

solid GREEN
NEW CABBAGE
10¢ LB.

Fresh from our in-store bakeries at Gee Bee RICHLAND & WALNUT STREET!
Easter bakery favorites
Take home a fine assortment for your Easter table!
● twist or round PASKA BREAD
● bunny cakes ● filled danish ● Easter egg rolls
● Easter layer cake ● small Easter baskets

NUT or POPPY SEED LOGS
special price!
49¢ ea.
(reg. 63¢)

Check AND COMPARE

JUST AN EXAMPLE OF OUR "NEW" EVERYDAY LOW PRICES!

Heinz TOMATO SOUP	10½-oz. can 10¢	Fresh GROUND BEEF	LB. 49¢	H-C DRINKS	3 1-qt. 14-oz. cans 89¢
Personal Size IVORY SOAP	4-bar pak 28¢	Zestee SALAD DRESSING	qt. jar 29¢	Waldorf TOILET TISSUE	4-roll pak 37¢
Laundry Powder TIDE	king size 5-LB. 4-oz. 1.15	Kraft MIRACLE WHIP	qt. jar 38¢	ScotTOWELS	jumbo roll 31¢
Morton SALT	1-LB. 10-oz. box 12¢	Hellmann's MAYONNAISE	qt. jar 69¢	Argo PEAS	1-LB. 1-oz. can 12¢
Gee Bee LIQUID BLEACH	gal. 37¢	Ritz or Hi-Ho CRACKERS	1-LB. box 43¢	Crisco OIL	1-pt. 8-oz. bottle 49¢
Clorox BLEACH	gal. 49¢	NESCAFE	10-oz. jar 1.47	Beech-Nut Strained BABY FOOD	jar 8¢
Kellogg's RICE KRISPIES	13-oz. box 49¢	Libby's TOMATO JUICE	1-qt. 14-oz. can 35¢	Carnation CANNED MILK	4 14½-oz. cans 65¢
CHEERIOS	15-oz. box 45¢	Campbell's TOMATO SOUP	10½-oz. can 11¢	Chicken of the Sea CHUNK TUNA	6-oz. can 35¢

GLOSSER'S ALL-STARS

BILL GLOSSER

Photo from Glosser Bros. Annual Report, Jan. 1978

"Home is a place where you go, and they have to take you in." That's what Bill Glosser says about home... and to him, home will always be Johnstown.

Bill lives in the same house where he grew up on Luzerne Street in Westmont. It's a place he's always come back to, even after living five years in Florida in the 1950s, where he practiced as an attorney.

"Miami wasn't a great place to raise kids," says Bill. "I didn't like my clients or colleagues there, either. It was a place where you couldn't trust the word of another lawyer over the phone. I never felt at home like I did in Johnstown."

When Bill returned to Johnstown in 1961, the Glosser Bros. company was ramping up for a major expansion--the opening of the Gee Bee stores. Bill joined the organization as a buyer, then moved up within four years to Director of Personnel.

Part of his job was overseeing security company-wide. When the Gee Bee expansion was at its height, he managed a force of 50 full and part-time people who circulated between the Glosser Bros. Department Store and the Gee Bee stores.

"The thing about security was you were always worried about a false arrest suit," says Bill. "So if there was the slightest problem, the security personnel were told to call me, and we would resolve it."

For example, when 17-year-old Dick Boyle was falsely accused, Bill smoothed things over by hiring Dick for his team. Dick turned out to be a master of disguise, one of the most effective security officers in the company.

"Dick would hide in boxes in the elevator," remembers Bill. "He would dress up as a carpenter, a priest, whatever. He was amazing, and went on to become a respected lawyer."

201

Bill was also in charge of labor negotiations. He had to deal with five different unions between the Gee Bee stores and warehouses, plus a meatcutters' union at Glosser Bros. Department Store.

As the company continued to grow, so did Bill's responsibilities. In addition to serving as Director of Personnel, he became Corporate Secretary. When Glosser Bros. became a publicly-traded company in 1971, Bill started handling financial public relations. He presented the annual report and other financial reports to company shareholders.

And he was there when times got tough, as well. In 1977, he was instrumental in cleaning up flood damage and reopening The Store. He was also involved with The Store's battle to avoid bankruptcy and collapse in 1989.

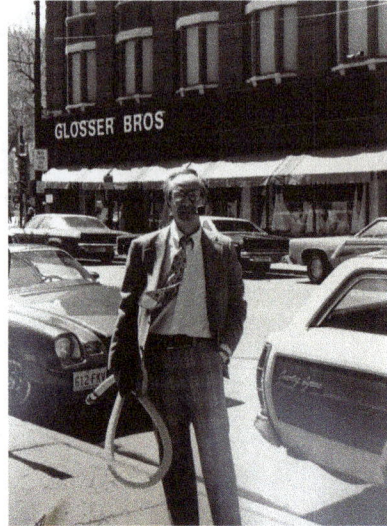

Photo courtesy of Jill Glosser

In the midst of all this, he kept practicing law. He served as a federal magistrate judge for 24 years, from 1965 to 1989. He still works as a lawyer to this day, at the age of 85.

But he'll always be a Glosser's All-Star for his key role in reopening The Store in '77 and trying to keep it alive in '89. When others had given up hope, Bill circulated petitions to save The Store. He reached out to business leaders in the region for help and refused to give up until the bitter end. He couldn't bear to give up on the business that his family had built from a single storefront into a $300 million a year empire over 83 years.

Because to Bill, and so many others in the community, Glosser's was *home*.

Photo from Glosser Bros. Annual Report, Feb. 1975

Chapter 23

That '70s Glow

Bill Glosser couldn't stop smiling as he read the letter from the U.S. Securities and Exchange Commission. Everyone who read the letter or heard it read aloud seemed to have the same reaction, whether it was company President Leonard Black or any of the other members of the Board of Directors.

Their shared vision, the one they had worked so hard for, had become a reality. Guided by an outside legal firm with all the right experience, the Glosser's team had jumped through every hoop without missing a step. Now, after a year of intense preparations and a grueling application process, Glosser Bros., Inc. had received the seal of approval.

Glosser's could sell stock to investors. What had been a privately-owned corporation could become a publicly-held company.

Over-the-Counter Days

"It was an exciting time," remembers Bill. "There were lots of possibilities."

The door was finally open for Glosser Bros., Inc. to seek the funding it needed to finance its next round of expansion. An influx of capital from the sale of stock would enable the company to build Gee Bee stores faster...and the chain's continued success could lead to yet more investment.

But first, Glosser Bros., Inc. had to jump through a few more hoops. "We weren't listed on an exchange right away," explains Bill. "It took a little time to make that happen.

"We started out over-the-counter, meaning we were selling stock without going through an exchange. This went on for about the first year."

Meanwhile, the Glosser team forged ahead with their application to the American Stock Exchange, also known as the ASE. Again working with outside advisors, team members gathered information on all financial aspects of the company, everything from earnings to properties to long-term debt.

Next, outside auditors Alexander Grant and Company performed an audit of Glosser Bros., Inc.'s financial statements related to the ASE application. Grant and Company audited Glosser, Inc.'s consolidated balance sheet, as well as related consolidated statements of earnings, stockholders' equity, and changes in financial position for the past three years.

When the auditors' report arrived, dated March 23, 1972, Leonard and his directors were all smiles again.

"In our opinion," read the report, "the financial statements...present fairly the financial position of Glosser Bros., Inc. and Subsidiaries at January 29, 1972, and the results of their operations and changes in financial position for the three years then ended..."

Life was good. With the auditors' okay, the way was clear to take the final step.

The Glosser team submitted their listing application, dated July 24, 1972, to the American Stock Exchange. Then, as the application--number 9996--worked its way through the ASE hierarchy, Leonard, Bill, Herb, Alvin, Sydney, Paul, Fred, Izzy, and all the rest went about their business back in Johnstown, waiting for the verdict.

With their fingers crossed, of course.

GEE, That Stock's A Winner

The finger-crossing--and the years of planning and effort--paid off. The American Stock Exchange approved the application on August 17, 1972. From that point on, Glosser Bros. stock could be sold through the exchange, giving it a much higher profile with which to attract investors.

The days of over-the-counter selling were gone. Glosser stock would be tracked on the ASE stock ticker, labeled with a distinctive symbol that spoke to the company's recent success and hopes for the future: *GEE*.

"We were on the American Stock Exchange," says Bill. "The importance of that simply cannot be overstated.

"We had the potential for tremendous success beyond the regional level. And we were determined to realize that potential."

The Gee Bee Big Bang Theory

The next phase of corporate growth was already underway by the time Glosser's was listed on the ASE. A new Gee Bee Discount Department Store opened in the Northgate Plaza Shopping Center in Washington, Pennsylvania in March 1970.

In March 1972, a Gee Bee department store opened in the Highlands Mall in Natrona Heights, Pennsylvania, with another Gee Bee following suit in the Uniontown Mall in Uniontown, Pennsylvania in August of that year.

Two stores in one year was a record for Glosser's, Inc., but the record didn't last long. In 1973, the year after the company was first listed on the ASE, no fewer than *three* new Gee Bee Department Stores and one new Gee Bee Supermarket opened their doors to the shopping public.

The four-store speed round started in August of 1973, when Glosser Bros., Inc. opened a new Gee Bee department store on Queen City Boulevard in Cumberland, Maryland.

Photo from Glosser Bros. Annual Report, Jan. 1973

Just two months later, in October 1973, the next new Gee Bee department store debuted in Monaca, Pennsylvania, just as a new Gee Bee Supermarket opened on Osborne Street in Johnstown.

The record fourth store in one year opened just one month later, in November 1973, in the Eastland Shopping Center in North Versailles, PA.

As the dust settled and receipts poured in from the new locations, no one could deny that all the planning and preparation were starting to pay off. The infusion of investment capital was rolling in, providing the needed funding for fast expansion. The system of rapid-fire store construction

Osborne St. Supermarket 2014 (photo by Philip Balko)

and launch spearheaded by Fred Glosser was making it possible to plan, build, staff, and stock multiple stores concurrently, with grand opening dates staggered only one or two months apart.

The 1973 growth spurt kickstarted the Gee Bee chain, generating interest in the company's stock and proving what Glosser's, Inc. was capable of...though the rapid pace would not always be sustained in years to come.

Happy Gee Beecentennial

After the quadruple openings in 1973, was it any wonder that Glosser Bros., Inc. took a year off from introducing new stores?

In 1974, the company paused to consolidate its gains and plan its next moves. Leonard and his team shopped for new sites, ramped up new store construction, and crunched the numbers to choose the best schedule of openings to maximize earnings.

By the time 1975 rolled around, the pieces were in place for another Gee Bee Big Bang. In the space of a single month--April 1975--Glosser Bros., Inc. opened three new stores: a Gee Bee Department store in the Middletown Mall in Fairmont, West Virginia; a Gee Bee Supermarket on Lyter Drive in the Westwood Plaza; and a Gee Bee Home Improvement Center in Richland Township.

Photo from Glosser Bros. Annual Report, Feb. 1975

As expansion phases go, it was a record-setter in its own right--the first time Glosser Bros., Inc. had opened three stores in one month. It was a nice rebound from the zero-store year in 1974, and set the tone for another strong phase in the year to come.

Westmont supermarket 2014 (photo by Philip Balko)

As America celebrated the Bicentennial in 1976, Glosser Bros. celebrated the opening of two new Gee Bee Department Stores. One opened for business in the Nittany Mall in State College, Pennsylvania in July 1976, while the other opened in August in the Park Hills Plaza in Altoona.

That same year, Glosser Bros. purchased the Park Building in downtown Johnstown, which housed the Gee Bee chain's accounting offices and the headquarters of the supermarket division.

But those weren't the biggest events of 1976 for Glosser's, Inc., not by a long shot.

Photo from Glosser Bros. Annual Report, Feb. 1975

Photo from Glosser Bros. Annual Report, Jan. 1976

Park Building 2014 (photo by Philip Balko)

Something with more of a lasting impact happened that same year, though it's possible no one involved with The Store realized just *how* lasting it would turn out to be.

Slap Shot Spotlight

On a sunny afternoon in downtown Johnstown in 1976, crowds lined the streets around Glosser's Department Store--but they weren't there for the usual reason, to make the most of a big sale. Instead, they were fighting for a glimpse of one man, a movie star--one of the greats--who was shooting a scene in front of The Store. Who could blame them?

After all, it wasn't every day that *Paul Newman* came to town.

Newman was the top-billed star of the movie *Slap Shot,* a hockey comedy that was filming in Johnstown that year. The movie, about a minor league hockey team that brings new meaning to the phrase, "There was a fight, and a hockey game broke out," was based on the real-life Johnstown Jets, who'd won the North American League championship in 1975. *Slap Shot*'s Charlestown Chiefs use over-the-top violence to win a championship of their own, in the hope of staving off the sale of the team to an out-of-town buyer.

Director George Roy Hill (who'd helmed Newman's previous Oscar-winning hits *Butch Cassidy and the Sundance Kid* and *The Sting*) made the most of local landmarks like the War Memorial Arena, Central Park, Aces Lounge...and the Glosser Bros. Department Store.

During one scene, Newman and co-star Jennifer Warren have a conversation on the sidewalk along the Locust Street side of the store. (It happens around 1 hour and 14 minutes from the start of the movie, if you'd like to see for yourself.) For that scene and others, fans and curiosity seekers crowded around, just outside camera range, to steal an up-close peek at Newman and watch the filming process in action.

It's a safe bet that none of them knew the true significance of the scene in progress, though. Paul Newman and company weren't just shooting a movie that would play in theaters a while and fade into obscurity. They were creating a time capsule of The Store just one year before it fell victim to another disaster, the Flood of 1977. Glosser's would never

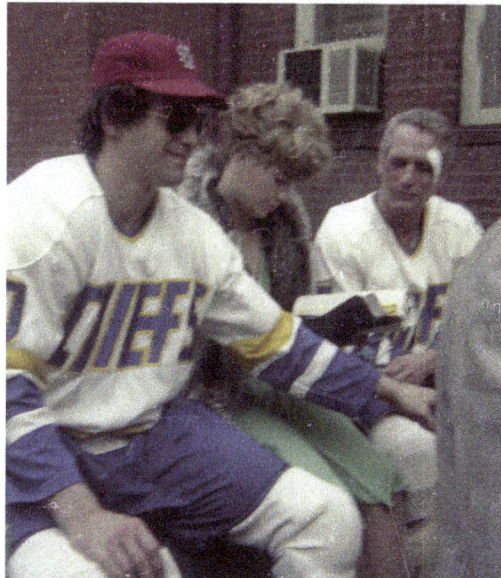

Photo by Mary Kabler, courtesy of Brad Jones

be the same after the '77 Flood, but the way it looked in 1976 would be captured forever by the movie.

207

In the scene with Newman and Warren, for example, you can see the old red, white, and black awnings over the display windows facing Locust Street. Mannequins and sale signs are visible inside the windows, and a Glosser's logo can be seen on the wall. The Locust Street entrance, with a pair of steps leading up to the door, is visible in Warren's cutaway shot, located right behind her as she talks to Newman.

Later, around one hour and 29 minutes from the beginning of the film, a view of the corner of The Store on Franklin and Locust Streets shows up, big as life in the windshield of Newman's car as he speeds down Franklin. Again, Glosser's is captured in all its pre-flood glory, the way it looked for decades to countless multitudes of local shoppers.

Years later, when Glosser Bros., Inc. ran into financial troubles and a final reckoning, the images in *Slap Shot* would take on added significance. The film had captured not only the pre-flood store, but the pre-closing one as well. Watching *Slap Shot* today is like opening a window in time, taking a look back at a place that meant so much to so many of us though it no longer exists.

And millions of other viewers get to share the experience. Though *Slap Shot* wasn't a hit when first released, it became a cult classic and steadily increased in popularity and reputation. It was named "the best

sports film of the past 50 years" in GQ magazine in 2007, and has spawned a pair of sequels.

In years to come, many more viewers will likely see *Slap Shot*, drawn by the comedy, violence, foul language, and Paul Newman's performance. And when they see it, they will also get a glimpse of Glosser Bros. (and Johnstown) in its heyday.

In this way, Glosser's will continue to survive, long after The Store--and all the Gee Bees and supermarkets and other spinoffs that once seemed so important--have closed their doors forever.

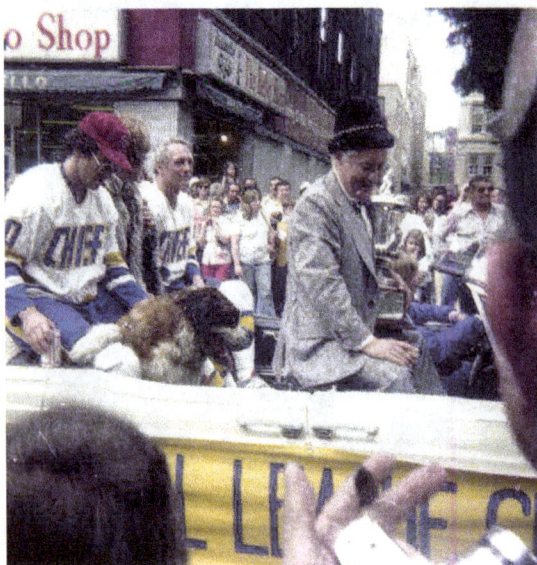

Photos by Mary Kabler, courtesy of Brad Jones

Memory Department

Photo by Chris Bittner-Italiano

When the movie *Slap Shot* was filmed in Central Park with Paul Newman, they were doing an early scene in the center of the park with the store in the background. I was walking from the parking garage to the front of the store to go to my office, not paying attention, thus walking by the windows on the park side, and I heard someone yell "CUT!" I saw the crew staring at me, since I'd walked into the shot, and with a red face, I hurried out of the way.

- *Chris Bittner-Italiano*

I started working at Glosser's in August of 1974. I was one of eight people hired to clean the grocery department. We "cleaned" some of it with hammers and chisels. We went to lunch the first day, and seven of us came back. The next day, five reported for work, and by the end of the second week, there were three of us left, and we all got permanent positions. I was sent to be the Assistant Manager of Toys, Sporting Goods and Giftware. Since there were only three of us in the department, we all had titles but still made the then-current minimum wage of $1.90 an hour.

- *Marty Erdley*

My mother, Alexandra Psinakis, worked as the manager of Glosser's Bridal Boutique from at least 1970 through the Flood in 1977. Her business card read "Madame Alexandra." During her "reign," Glosser's carried the best wedding dresses available, including Priscilla of Boston. She also organized the annual January Wedding Fashion Shows. I loved helping her out when I was home for visits.

- *Poppy Psinakis Patterson*

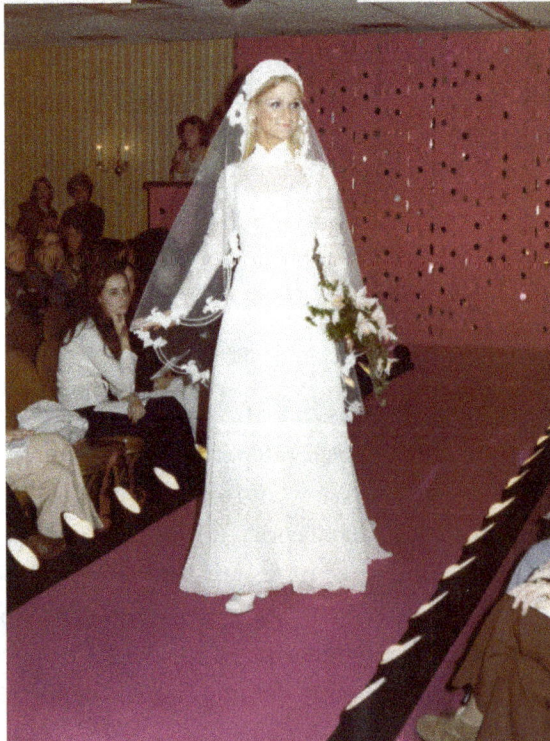

Glosser bros

BICENTENNIAL BRIDAL SHOW

Show Coordinators ... Madame Alexandra
Diane Clites
Bridal Commentator............... Jenifer Vamos
Flower Commentator ...... Thomas O'Brien
Pianist .... Esther Michaud

MODELS

- Mrs. Marie Barnhart
- Chris Bittner
- Diane Clites
- Diane Glosser
- Jill Glosser
- Nancy Rizzo
- Elizabeth Springer
- Lori Weaver

FLOWERS COURTESY of
THE FLOWER BARN
Millcreek at Bucknell Ave.
Phone: 536-7888

Glosser bros
BRIDAL BOUTIQUE
3rd FLOOR

Photo courtesy of Chris Bittner-Italiano

Glosser bros

salutes

THE BICENTENNIAL BRIDE
1776 - 1976

Two hundred years ago, our founding fathers brought forth a new system of government based on freedom, justice and individual rights. Their declaration of liberty has been our historical heritage.

Glosser's Bridal Fashion Show is dedicated to the individualistic gal of today. For the contemporary lifestyle, figure-flattering lines in supple fabrics . . for the traditional gal, ruffles and lace.

The new Bicentennial Bride can select a beautiful gown that is just right for her. It will be young in style because she is young in her thinking. You'll find all the exciting new innovations for 1976 are available for you at Glosser's Bridal Boutique.

SELECT FROM THESE FAMOUS DESIGNERS—

- Priscilla of Boston
- Bridal Couture
- Campus Bridals
- Alfred Angelo
- Piccione
- Bianchi
- Pandora
- And many others

LET GLOSSER'S HELP YOU WITH YOUR WEDDING—

Glosser's Bridal Boutique on the 3rd floor can help you with your complete wedding so that this joyous time is one that you will happily recall. Glosser's qualified staff will gladly assist you with the many details that will result in a wedding you and your family will always cherish.

GREAT SELECTIONS—

See for yourself the wonderful selection of bridal gowns in Glosser's Bridal Boutique. Exquisite gowns from the nation's top designers. Beautiful traditional styles . . . lovely contemporary designs . . . and the prices are right! Choose from bridal gowns starting at $99.95. Bridal veils and headpieces are exclusively at Glosser Bros. from Marie for T & G, Priscilla of Boston, Lounette.

GLOSSER'S CHARGE ACCOUNT MAKES SHOPPING EASY—

One of the first things you need after the wedding is a Glosser's Charge Account, available in the Credit Dept. on the 3rd floor. The convenient payment plan . . . the ease of shopping will help you and your future husband prepare your home! It's so easy when all you have to say is "Charge it!"

MADAME ALEXANDRA
Glosser's Bridal Consultant

Madame Alexandra cordially invites you to visit our Bridal Boutique on the 3rd floor where you'll find an excellent selection of bridal gowns, veils, bridesmaid's attire, flower-girl dresses and gowns for all members of the wedding party. Also a complete selection of going-away outfits, lingerie, wedding gifts and important trousseau items. Let Madame Alexandra help you plan the perfect wedding!

BRIDAL BOUTIQUE—
GLOSSER'S THIRD FLOOR

Both my mom and sister worked at Glosser's for many years. If you got married in the 1970s and bought your gown at Glosser's, my mom probably did the alterations on it. My sister worked in cameras and then notions until Glosser's closed. I used to love going to the basement for groceries. Once I got older, I would sometimes take my mom for lunch in the Hunt Room. They had the best Greek salad. I know it wasn't fancy, but I still can't quite duplicate it.

- *Teri Aveni*

In the 70's, they had Western Days in downtown Johnstown, one of the forerunners of Thunder In the Valley. One year, they shut down Locust Street and had what they called bed races. I was the "bed jockey" for the Glosser entry. We didn't win, but we had a lot of fun.

- *Randy Rudge*

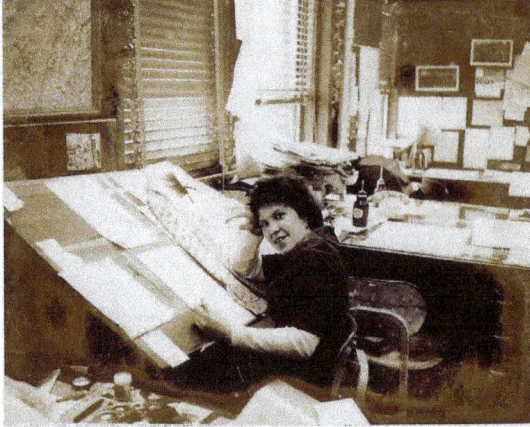

Kip Solomon at work

I began my career in the adv. dept. right out of the Pittsburgh Art Institute in 1969. I worked until 1976 and then again from about 1982 until 1986.

I always enjoyed the annual June Old Fashion Bargain Days promotion. Employees dressed up in costumes, usually themed by dept. I have a few photos of some of the adv. dept. employees dressed up.

A funny story I can relate was of the time Sydney Ossip, the store comptroller, stopped in the advertising dept. and noticed I was pregnant. He congratulated me, and mentioned that, I believe it was his daughter, was also expecting. When I added that I was due within about a month he was quite surprised. Keep in mind that in the 60s, women didn't work up until their delivery date; rather, you went on a "maternity leave." Shortly after

Photos courtesy of Kip Solomon

that, I was told that I would need to begin my leave immediately. I guess Mr. Ossip knew something I didn't, because within a week of beginning my leave, I delivered my first son, one month early!

- *Kip Solomon*

I remember one trip with my mom. We went Christmas shopping without my brothers, just her and I, and I couldn't have been more than 6 or 7 years old, so I guess we're talking 1973 or 74. I know we entered Glosser's through the entrance on the Central Park side of the store, because she knew I would ask for comics from the newsstand, and she could use the promise of new comics to make sure I would behave while shopping. Of course, as soon as we walked into the store itself, the smell of roasted peanuts from the candy counter hit, and I can still smell it even now. I loved that about Glosser's, that smell.

Anyway, we shopped for what seemed like days to a kid but was probably no more than an hour or two, and Mom took me up to the cafeteria for a piece of pie.

We sat and talked about movies, the same topic we always talked about, and after finishing our pie, we went out to sit in the park and have a hot chocolate. We sat there, people-watching, with all the lights around, and now I swear it was like a moment from a movie. Perfect weather and perfect setting. The reason I remember this night so well is what happened in the park. Some guy came up and asked my mom for some spare change. Mom was a very shy and nervous person, so she didn't make eye contact with the guy, and he walked away.

I asked her about it. In fact, I kind of bugged her about why she didn't help the guy, and I think I might have embarrassed her, because we went back into the store and she bought a bag of those roasted peanuts and then walked us back out into the park to find that guy. We found him, and she handed him the peanuts as well as a couple of dollars. My very shy mother shocked me by actually speaking to a stranger when she smiled at the guy and said, "Merry Christmas" before taking me back to the newsstand to get my comics.

She passed away a couple of years ago, and now I think of that night quite often. Funny how that works.

- *Paul Mastovich*

Photo from Glosser Bros. Annual Report, Feb. 1975

My first job ever was as a stock boy in the furniture department at Glosser's in 1970. It was memorable for so many reasons ($1.60 an hour!), including Steve Edelstein, one of the funniest guys I ever met.

- James Finkelstein

I loved sitting in the bleachers with my family (the Glossers) and watching the Halloween parade each year. I particularly enjoyed grabbing the candy thrown at us as we watched. Afterward, my siblings and cousins went to the store and proceeded to have a field day in the candy department. This did not last too long, however, as the buyer alerted our father that we had taken too much candy out of the department with little left to sell. Oh well; we then proceeded to the cafeteria to make very large sundaes instead.

Another fun experience when the store was closed was having cart races in the grocery department located in the basement. We also were asked not to do this anymore because we knocked down too many items from the shelves, causing a real mess! These were fun times in our early grade school years.

Photo from Glosser Bros. Annual Report, Jan. 1976

Whenever I went to the store, I truly felt the employees were my family. I would spend hours walking each floor, visiting with everyone. Eventually, I would show up for dinner in the Hunt Room or go to my dad's office, but mainly I socialized with all the people I became friendly with over the years.

My father expected me to work whenever I had free time, so I would not be watching TV or getting into trouble. Therefore, when I turned 12, I spent the summer working in the cosmetic department. I think I used more products than I sold, but I learned a lot and loved going there to work and visiting with all the customers.

To this day, I still think about the employees who worked there, and I get a real thrill when I see someone in Johnstown from Glosser's. My parents received lots of calls over the years from past employees, buyers etc., and it always put a smile on their faces and brought warm memories that they cherished.

I still love driving by the store!

- *Mindy Glosser Conklin (daughter of Alvin Glosser)*

One of our promotions was the "Beautiful Baby" contest that ran for a month and culminated with prizes for the baby judged cutest by the salespeople in our department. I personally initiated that one.

Jeff Diamond, Glosser Bros. employee 1966-1988 (and son-in-law of Sydney Ossip)

Courtesy of Jeff Diamond

THESE PRICES IN EFFECT THURS. and FRI.
Thurs. 10 to 9; Friday 10 to 5
Glosser bros JOHNSTOWN, PA.
CLOSED SATURDAY FOR RELIGIOUS HOLIDAY
70th Anniversary
DOLLAR DAY BUYS
2 AMAZING DAYS OF SAVINGS! -- JUST SAY CHARGE IT!
MEN'S CREW NECK SWEATSHIRTS $3
LADIES' 100% COTTON FLANNEL SHIRTS 2 for $9
LADIES' NO-IRON COTTON DUSTERS $5
MEN'S WINTER OUTERWEAR $26

Glosser bros JOHNSTOWN, PA.
These Prices In Effect Thurs. & Fri.
Anniversary SALE
$-Days Annex Specials
VIGORO FERTILIZERS
U.L. APPROVED PERFECTION KEROSENE HEATER 19.99
GROUP 7 FILTERS by Purolator
1.59
2.39
THURS. 10 to 9; FRI. 10 to 5; CLOSED SAT.

$-DAYS
Charge It or Use Layaway!
THURS. 10 to 9; FRI. 10 to 5
Closed Sat. for Religious Holiday
RICH FABRIC COATS
48.90
LADIES' COORDINATES
1/2 OFF!
PLAYWEAR AND DRESS SAMPLES
DRESSES $20
LADIES' SCARF HATS $1
HAND-CRAFTED WOODEN CUCKOO CLOCKS $29

Glosser bros JOHNSTOWN, PA.
Anniversary
Men's Long Sleeve No-Iron FLANNEL SHIRTS $4
MEN'S U.S. NAVY LAST OXFORDS $10
Men's Long Sleeve Perma Press KNIT SHIRTS $2
MEN'S DRESS SHOES $3
BOYS' PITTSBURGH STEELER JACKETS $15
BOYS' FAMOUS MAKER RUGBY SHIRTS $6
HOODED PITTSBURGH STEELER SWEATSHIRTS $7
BOYS' FAMOUS MAKER WESTERN SHIRTS $7
Girls' SPORT & DRESS SHOES $10
G.E. DELUXE AM/FM DIGITAL RADIO $36
SOUNDESIGN STEREO SYSTEMS $175
GIRLS' PUFF OXFORDS $8

GeeBee AND The Values
SAVINGS NEVER LOOKED BETTER!
MONDAY, TUESDAY AND WEDNESDAY! WHILE QUANTITIES LAST!
FAMOUS MAKER FASHION SHIRTS or POLY FLANNEL PANTS
Your Choice 5.44
SAVE UP TO 20% ON EVERY SKI JACKET IN STOCK
Heavy Cotton Denim WORK JACKETS 11.90
TAKE ADVANTAGE USE OUR FREE LAYAWAY!
GIRLS' SOFTEE SPORT OXFORD 4.97
WIN $2,000 IN CASH
AND $50 IN FREE MATTEL TOYS
"FREE SPREE ON ME" SWEEPSTAKES
GeeBee
$2,000 "FREE SPREE ON ME" SWEEPSTAKES
UNIVERSITY PARK SHOPPING CENTER Rt. 56 Johnstown-Windber Rd. Open 10 A.M. to 10 P.M.

We CARE
MORE SAVINGS THAN EVER BEFORE
At Gee Bee and Glosser's SUPERMARKETS
Gee Bee and Glosser bros SUPER MARKETS
U.S.D.A. CHOICE WESTERN BEEF SALE
Well Trimmed BONELESS
CHUCK ROAST
89¢ LB.
Corn King FRANKS
79¢
Young Tender VEAL SALE!
SHOULDER VEAL CHOPS
1.19 LB.
LAMB SALE!
LEG OF LAMB
1.59 LB.
POLSKA KIELBASA 1.39
PORK SAUSAGE 1.09
BEEF LIVER 59¢
CHICKEN
MAPLE NUT LAYER CAKES 2.39
YAMS 19¢
PRUNE PLUMS 89¢
CARROTS 19¢
SPANISH ONIONS 15¢
PASCAL CELERY 29¢
SERVING YOU IN JOHNSTOWN FOR 56 YEARS
USE ALL 3 SUPER COUPONS WITH ONE $5.00 OR MORE FOOD PURCHASE
SAVE 60¢ SLICED BACON 1.19
SAVE 30¢ Bounty TOWELS 29¢
SAVE 20¢ A-1 BLEACH 49¢
SQUIRT or Sanders FLAVORS 8 89¢
KEG 'O KETCHUP 79¢
Argo PEAS 4 89¢
AMERICAN CHEESE 99¢
DRINKS 2 89¢
CUT BEETS 4 $1
USE THESE 3 COUPONS WITH ONE $5 OR MORE FOOD PURCHASE
TOMATO SOUP 6 for $1.00
Ivory LIQUID 99¢
KEG-O-KETCHUP 89¢
SPAGHETTI SAUCE 99¢
AJAX CLEANSER 2/45¢
AJAX Window Cleaner 2/99¢
SPAGHETTI 2/79¢
SHOP 5 GREAT LOCA

USE ALL 3 SUPER COUPONS WITH ONE $5.00 OR MORE FOOD PURCHASE
Gee Bee and Glosser bros SUPER MARKETS
PARKAY
Studio Towels
69¢ 39¢ 19¢
WITH COUPON
BEEF SALE
Center Cut CHUCK ROAST
Super Low Price 67¢ LB.
CHUCK STEAK 75¢
ROAST 89¢
Gee Bee QUALITY GROUND BEEF only 69¢ LB.
STAYMAN APPLES 3 59¢
TOMATOES 49¢
COLD POWER
JOY
2 89¢
39¢
4 $1
3 $1
R.C. COLA
DIET RITE
8 89¢
Star-Kist TUNA 49¢
SUNDAE CUPS
5 GREAT LOCATIONS

Get Into Gee Bee And You'll Get More Out Of It. For Less!
SAVE ON FAMILY TOILETRIES!
Dollar Days at GeeBee
LADIES! HAVE YOUR EARS PIERCED
6.99
3-BIG DAYS!
Thursday, Friday, Saturday
PRESTONE II Winter Summer ANTI-FREEZE 3.32 GALLON
GeeBee GIVES YOU MORE THAN JUST A DISCOUNT ... WE GIVE YOU SOMETHING GOOD...

Chapter 24

One Night in 1977

Fred Glosser should have had déjà vu. It was raining so hard that July night in 1977, the wipers on his car windshield were having trouble keeping up.

Then again, it wasn't exactly unusual to have heavy rains in Johnstown, PA. Getting dumped on like that came with the territory and wasn't anything to get excited about.

Usually.

Fred came downtown that evening to inspect the Landmark Building on Main Street that he and his wife Betty owned, to check the roof that he'd just had installed that day. The roof was holding up fine under the heavy summer rain, though water was coming into the basement, seeping in from some ground-floor windows.

Seeing that water pouring in made him think about another time, 41 years ago, when water had forced its way through ground-level vents and rushed into a basement. Which was why, though his own building was taking on water, Fred got in his car and headed up Main Street, then made the turns that took him to the corner of Franklin and Locust Streets.

To the Glosser Building.

Trickle-Down Disaster

When Fred jumped out of his car in front of Glosser Bros. Department Store, his feet splashed in the inches-deep water that was already rushing down the street. As he ran for the door, he was instantly soaked to the skin; it was more like running under a waterfall than through a cloudburst.

Fred dashed under the awning over the Franklin Street entrance and jammed his key in the front door lock. Looking inside the door as he worked the key, he felt a surge of relief. There were always lights on inside at night, and he could see by their illumination that the floor was dry.

If water wasn't visible on the ground level, it likely hadn't infiltrated the basement in sufficient volume to overtax the sump pumps. Maybe he'd been worried for no reason.

Or maybe not.

As soon as Fred opened the door and stepped into The Store, the night watchman called out to him from across the ground floor. "Fred, we've got trouble!" he yelled. "Water's coming in on the fifth floor and into the money offices on the fourth!"

Fred's heart raced as he realized the implications. Leaping into action, he ran up the stairs to the fourth floor, avoiding the elevators in case there was a power failure.

Running into the money office, he soon saw that the watchman was right. "Water was pouring into the money office," remembers Fred. "Other offices were getting it, too. The watchman had put lots of buckets around, but they weren't enough to catch all the water."

Why exactly the water was coming in, Fred didn't know...but one thing was certain. There was only one direction to go if he wanted to stop the flow.

And that direction was up.

A Lake Above The Fifth Floor

If Fred's shoes hadn't already been soaked, they would have been when he stepped out on the fifth floor. Everywhere he looked, the floor was covered with water, fed by a heavy stream gushing down from the ceiling into the display department.

This was where the water running into the fourth floor was coming from...though Fred knew it wasn't the starting point. He had to go up one set of stairs to get there, to the part of the building that was feeding this deluge.

Adrenaline burned in Fred's bloodstream as he raced across the fifth floor to the stairway, then hurried up the stairs to his last stop: the roof of the Glosser Building.

At the top of the stairs, he pushed the door open, then quickly climbed the short stairs to the roof of the new addition. By the glare of the flickering lightning, he saw that the roof had turned into a lake.

The water was at least two feet deep...just below the top of a three-foot-high parapet on the deepest end of the roof. And the level was rising with each passing minute.

As Fred waded out into the rooftop lake, the water was up to his knees. The roof was completely submerged, and the rain was still blasting down with epic force.

Fred was taking his life in his hands, and he knew it...but he had to see if there was anything he could do. He knew the roof better than almost anyone; if anyone could save The Store, it was him.

But how?

One Lightning Bolt Away From Death

There were two big drains on the roof that should have taken away the water. They must have been the root of the problem, though Fred had just checked them recently and knew they were clear. Apparently, though the guards were big enough to let an ordinary rain pass through, the freakish downpour that night was so heavy that the water couldn't go down fast enough.

Fighting through the knee-high water, he realized just how dangerous his situation was. "The lightning was so bright and frequent, you could read a newspaper by it," he remembers. "All it would take was for one bolt to hit the steel beams supporting the air conditioning unit platform on the roof while I was standing in all that water, and I'd be electrocuted."

The water on the roof made it hard to see the drains; so did the water streaming into Fred's eyes. But he knew the layout by heart and finally found what he'd been looking for...though that was just the beginning of the battle.

"Over each drain, there was a dome-shaped steel guard to keep out leaves and paper," says Fred. "These guards were tarred right into the roof, so they were firmly in place."

As lightning kept cracking around him, Fred knew he didn't have time to figure out what was clogging the screens and clear the blockage. The best strategy was to tear them off first and worry about repairing the damage later.

"I grabbed hold of the steel framework of the dome-shaped guard on the first drain," says Fred. "Then I pulled as hard as I could. I really had to put my back into it, but the guard finally tore free.

"As soon as I got the guard off, water rushed down the drain. I heard it hit the bottom of the downspout, and I hoped it didn't smash the pipe. The downspout was inside the building, leading all the way down to the basement supermarket. If the downspout broke, water would surge into the basement in a torrent."

Suddenly, though, the downspout was the least of Fred's worries. The force of the water siphoning into the drain was so great, it dragged his arm in with it.

"The draining water yanked me down hard," says Fred. "It was pulling my arm into the pipe, and I knew I was in trouble."

Drowning on a Roof

Fred fought with all his strength against the tide flushing into the drain pipe. If he didn't free himself, the current would pull his arm into the drain up to his shoulder, pinning him underwater, and he would drown.

Lightning flared, and thunder boomed. With every muscle in his body, Fred fought the mighty pull of the water, desperate to survive.

Finally, he broke free.

He stumbled away from the cleared pipe, stunned by the close call...and then, he quickly shook it off. Opening the first drain had started the process of siphoning off the roof, but his work wasn't done.

Fred waded to the second drain and repeated the process, tearing off the domed guard that covered it. This time, he braced himself better and pulled back faster so the current didn't nearly drag him down.

Opening the second drain speeded things up considerably. The water on the roof quickly subsided, and Fred was able to get a clearer picture of why the fourth and fifth floors had been flooded.

"There was an air vent on the roof to let heat out of the fifth floor, which wasn't air-conditioned," says Fred. "Because the drains were obstructed, the water level had risen above this roof vent, which was about a foot and a half high. With the vent completely submerged, water had poured down through it and into the fifth floor. From there, it had leached through non-watertight floor seams and joints into the fourth floor."

Now, at least, the flow had stopped--but the crisis wasn't over. Fred's work on the roof was done, but with the rain still blasting down, he knew he needed to check on another vulnerable part of The Store.

The Worst Was Not Over

Fred hurried from the highest part of the building to the lowest--the basement. As hard as it was raining, he thought there had to be water down there.

On his way down, he saw signs that he was right. When he reached ground level, water was coming in from the front doors and running across the floor. Fred knew there was one likely place where it would go.

Sure enough, there was water on the stairs to the basement, and then on the basement floor. "It was flowing down from the ground floor and seeping in through the foundation," says Fred. "But the sump pump was running fine, and the water level stayed relatively low."

The basement didn't seem to be in imminent danger, and Fred thought the rain was bound to stop soon. "I told the watchman there was nothing we could do but let the sump pump work," says Fred. "In the morning, I'd come back with a crew and clear out whatever water was left in the basement."

Convinced the worst was over, Fred left The Store for the night and started driving toward his home in Westmont. After jump-starting the fire chief's car at the scene of a lightning-in-duced building fire on Levergood Street, Fred headed out of town around 1:30 in the morning, continuing through the rising water on his way to higher ground.

At the time, he didn't know just how wrong he'd been about the rain stopping anytime soon.

No Ordinary Storm

During the Great Johnstown Flood of 1889, 7.9 inches of rain fell on the Johnstown area. More than 7 inches fell during the Saint Patrick's Day Flood of 1936, supplemented by heavy snowmelt.

But the night of July 20, 1977 outdid them both in terms of rainfall. A full *foot* of rain drenched Johnstown and the surrounding area that night, putting the storms of 1889 and 1936 to shame.

The torrential downpour reached its peak hours after Fred had returned safely to his home in Westmont. Swollen streams and creeks and rivers overflowed their banks, and sewers gushed into the streets. Basements and ground floors of buildings and homes filled with inch after inch of roiling water. By midnight, Mayor Herb Pfuhl Jr. had declared a state of emergency.

Then, when the Laurel Run Dam burst at 2:15 a.m., a tidal wave roared into the Conemaugh River, wiping out the town of Tanneryville along the way. The wave of water from the dam added 15 to 17 feet to the Conemaugh, which then blasted its way through downtown Johnstown and beyond.

By the time it was all over, 85 lives had been lost, including that of one Glosser's employee--Thelma Ressler, a cashier in the basement supermarket. In addition to the human cost, millions of dollars in damage had been inflicted for the third time on what had once been declared a flood-free city.

The Morning After And The Morning After That

The mess that was left behind was truly epic. Fred couldn't even get downtown to see it on the morning after the flood.

"I tried to drive down, but the water was still two feet deep at the bottom of the Easy Grade," he recalls. "I thought about walking, but I didn't want to take a chance in all that water. If a manhole cover was off, I wouldn't be able to see it, and I'd fall right in."

Fred had to wait till the next day, when most of the water had subsided, to drive to The Store. What he saw when he got there brought a lump to his throat. "It was a pitiful sight," he says.

"All the windows were broken. Telephone poles were piled inside the building. It looked like an atomic bomb had hit."

Stepping inside The Store made his eyes water even more, for reasons other than sadness. "The smell was unbelievable. There was sewage everywhere on the ground floor. It had just washed up out of the sewers and accumulated in there."

As Fred walked through the ground level and inspected the damage, he started to get a grasp of the enormity of the cleanup ahead. In addition to the shattered windows and telephone poles and sewage, there were piles of ruined merchandise, broken fixtures, and overturned furniture.

Photo © The Tribune-Democrat

Walls and flooring were buckled and stripped and splintered. The meat department at the back of the ground floor was a tumble of smashed display cases and mangled equipment. The legendary wooden Otis escalator that had been installed after the last flood, in 1936, was intact but ruined beyond repair.

And then there was the basement, where the sump pumps had failed after all. Standing at the

Photo by Fred Glosser

top of the stairs, looking down, Fred saw murky brown water almost up to the basement ceiling, adrift with soaked and rotting groceries. Below that surface, the contents of an entire supermarket bobbed in rippling, rancid darkness, mountains of food reduced to filth-encrusted garbage.

Fred swallowed hard and shook his head. How could this ever be put right? How could so much work ever be finished? How could Glosser's ever come back from all this and reopen?

For a long, dark moment, gazing down at that shivering brown cesspool in the basement, he wondered if it ever would.

221

The Tribune-Democrat

Johnstown, Pa.   Wednesday, July 20, 1977

City Flooded Again;
Areas Devastated
2 Dead, 5 Missing

. . . Walnut Grove damage

Looters Roam Streets

— Full Report Inside

Photo by Fred Glosser

Photo by Fred Glosser

Photo by Fred Glosser

Photo by Fred Glosser

Cameras, Jewelry

Looters Hit Business

Bethlehem Plant
Damaged Extensively

. . . looking at Franklin Street church

Reports Received of Fires,
Motorists Being Swept Away

*Weather
Forecast*

Memory Department

It was about 9:10 PM on July 19th 1977. My mom and I were in Gee Bee getting groceries, including ingredients for my 12th birthday cake. My birthday was the next day. The heavens opened and the white hot lightning cracked the sky. We were in the checkout line and the electricity failed. About 20 minutes later, we were still in line, hoping that we could eventually check out.

Meanwhile, my father pulled up to the exit in our 1970 AMC Hornet. As we drove home, we could see the rocks washing off the hillside above Gee Bee. The power lines and the safety lights at the airport were snapped and flailing about. We went home, and I was instructed to go to bed. At about 2 a.m., I awoke to water rushing into the basement, and, thankfully, rushing out. My parents told me to go back to sleep, even though the thunder was deafening. When I awoke, there was ten feet of water in Johnstown. I always liked going to Gee Bee on a Friday. It was a cool family thing to do...and I always got a cup of soda out of the machine. But after the night of the Johnstown Flood, it never was the same.

- Kathleen Bohachick Trautz

Photo by Fred Glosser

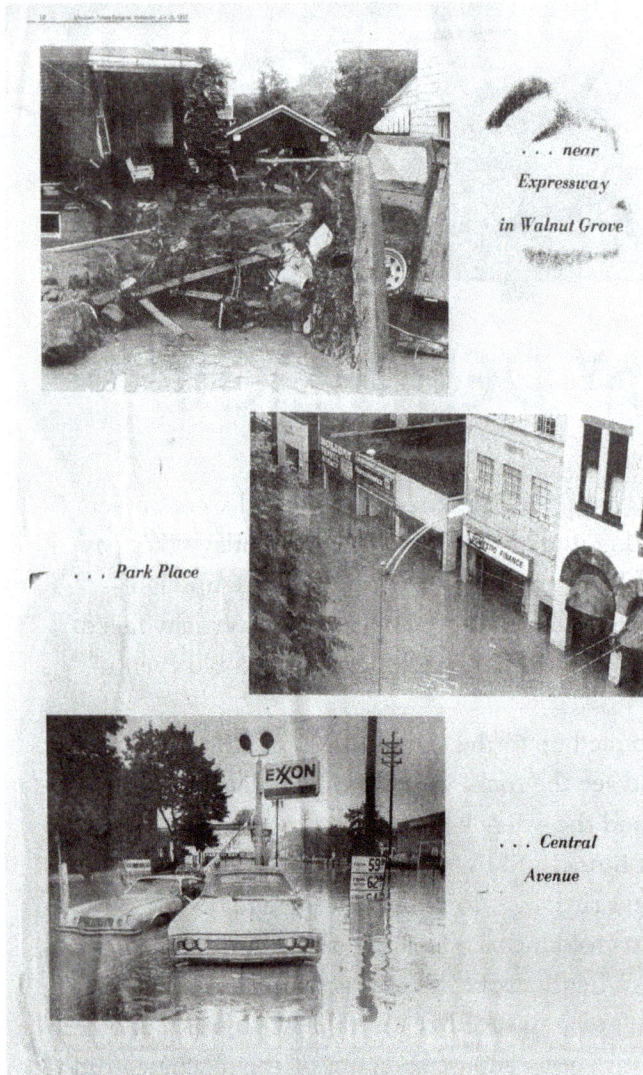

... *near*
Expressway
in Walnut Grove

... *Park Place*

... *Central*
Avenue

© *The Tribune-Democrat*

In July of 1977, we suffered enormous losses from the horrendous Johnstown flood. We were forced to close the store for approximately three weeks to clean up the basement and first floor. The basement supermarket was completely shut down and cleaned out, then turned into a bargain basement. The first floor of the building also had to be totally emptied. I vividly remember huge dump trucks parked behind the store, and all of the fixtures and merchandise being discarded and hauled away at a total loss. Somehow, in less than one month, we had the store back in business and reopened in time to take advantage of the final weeks of the back-to-school season.

I also remember our buying team meeting on Main Street in Central Park across from the store and having meetings right out on the sidewalk due to the store being closed at this time. As I peered into the store right after we were allowed to come downtown, the only thing I could think of was that it looked like a World War I or II picture. This was an event that living through on a daily basis truly aged us all and made us appreciate our lives that much more. I was so impressed with how the Glosser Bros. management dug into this catastrophe and were able to have their store reopened in such a short time to serve the people of Johnstown who were really hurting. I can really say that I was so proud to be part of this wonderful "Glosser Family!"

- *Jeff Diamond, Glosser Bros. employee 1966-1988 (and son-in-law of Sydney Ossip)*

Jeff Diamond and Steve Eiseman
(courtesy of Robin Eiseman)

The flood wiped out the entire first floor of the store in 1977. Racks of clothing were found miles away. The ground floor of the building was filled with thick mud and muck. When the other buyers and I were able to get in, we had to spend days working on the upper floors to box all the undamaged clothing and other merchandise, marking it and getting it out to our discount stores so it could be sold before the season ended. We worked in the humid musty heat and dimly lit conditions. After the store was cleaned up and life went on, our motto at Glosser's for everyone that worked there was, "We are wet, but not washed out!" We even had t-shirts made for everyone with this motto on them.

- *Chris Bittner-Italiano*

. . . *crossing on Horner Street near Sheesley's*

. . . *Horner Street at McMillen*

. . . *D Street and Fairfield Avenue*

. . . *Horner Street and McMillen*

. . . *walking up Bedford Street*

© *The Tribune-Democrat*

225

2 Johnstown Tribune-Democrat, Wednesday, July 20, 1977

City Flood Loss Expected to Top $100 Million

By JOHN McHUGH
Of The Tribune-Democrat

A massive flood struck the city Tuesday night. Two persons are known dead, five are missing and property damage is expected to top $100 million.

Johnstown Mayor Herb Pfuhl Jr. reported the toll Wednesday morning in the first official assessment of flood in the city. Reports that continued to filter in from flood-ravaged communities surrounding the city were expected to cause the casualty and loss figures to mount considerably.

Mayor Pfuhl said he expected the property damage to exceed the $100-million mark and issued pleas for federal and state aid. He declared the city a major disaster area at 2 a.m., at the height of the flooding.

"That's a conservative estimate," the mayor said of the damage figure. "The devastation is unbelievable —homes destroyed, automobiles washed away."

The flooding was caused by a series of summer rainstorms that official records show dumped 7¾ inches of water on the area in a 24-hour period. Overnight, the rainfall was recorded at 5.56 inches.

The huge volume of water poured down the Stonycreek and Little Conemaugh rivers that converge into the Conemaugh River in downtown Johnstown.

2 Major Fires

At least two major fires burned out of control during the night. The Robel Construction Co. in the city's Hornerstown section was destroyed and another fire burned a few blocks away.

Firemen were prevented by deep flood water from getting to the scene of the second fire.

In a radio broadcast, Mayor Pfuhl appealed for sightseers to remain away from the stricken city. He warned also about looting of flood-damaged stores in the downtown.

"Looters will be shot on sight," he said. "We aren't going to have a New York situation here."

However, despite the warning, looting was reported at a number of downtown stores, including James Jewelers, Weiser Music Store, Glosser Bros. and Acme Photo.

In addition to the downtown area, property damage was reported extensive in the city's West End, Moxham and Hornerstown sections and in adjacent Dale Borough.

Mayor Pfuhl, who said he had spent the night in the Meadowvale School in the Hornerstown neighborhood, reported that at one point a wall of water 15 feet high smashed through a nearby street. Its crest carried homes, automobiles, and small buildings.

At one point, lane-marker ropes were stripped from the school's indoor swimming pool to serve as lifelines for the rescue of persons trapped in their homes.

The force of the water finally blew out a rear wall of the school, causing evacuees to be relocated on the upper floors of the brick and steel building.

National Guard Asked For

Mayor Pfuhl said that arrangements were being made through the Cambria County Civil Defense organization to have National Guard units sent into the city for assistance in the cleanup and to help guard against looting.

Appeals for aid have been sent to President Carter and Gov. Shapp, he said.

A command post was being established in the WJAC Building in Upper Yoder Township to help consolidate what communications were still operating within the flood-stricken city. Field command posts also were being set up in the stricken neighborhoods, he said.

In an initial news conference, the mayor praised the many acts of heroism he encountered during the night.

"Neighbor worked with neighbor, often at risk of life and limb," he said. "It was a real team effort."

2 of Dead Mentioned

Mayor Pfuhl said that one of the known dead was an unidentified 10-year-old boy. Another was a man estimated to be in his 80s.

The mayor said police also were investigating a report that a compact car with several occupants was seen being washed away in the West End. Another of the missing was listed as a woman who reportedly fell into a flood-swollen stream in Moxham.

A spokesman for Peoples Natural Gas Co. said that there have been two line breaks in the area. Approximately 150 customers have lost service on Cooper Avenue while an additional 40 were without gas following the washout of a bridge in Elton.

At last report, the company hadn't been able to get to these areas to determine the extent of damage.

. . . Franklin Street Bridge from Haynes Street

Photos in this issue by:
Merle Agnello
Bob Donaldson
Kay Kusibab

An Editorial

City Faces Recovery Task for Third Time

Johnstown will do once again what people believed to be a never-to-be-repeated part of its history: Clean up and recover from extensive flooding.

Although not much of a definite nature is known about Wednesday's flooding following a storm spawned Tuesday night, the city of Johnstown is not the sole municipal victim. Outlying areas, including Franklin Borough, also were flooded.

Also sketchy is the extent of human suffering; there have been two confirmed drownings and five people are reported to be missing.

In terms of property loss and work stoppages in the area's industrial and business community, damage at the moment is incalculable. Considering contemporary costs of goods and services, the dollar value placed on the damage well may exceed that of Johnstown's other major floods. Mayor Herb Pfuhl Jr. has estimated property damage at $100 million; the figure could go much higher.

The comments of people atop Johnstown's Inclined Plane in the hilltop community of Westmont can be used to sum the attitude of reponse to the scope of the flooding

— Who would have thought it could happen again?

— Why, that river is coming over the approach to the Prospect Viaduct.

— We thought that the flooding was caused just because sewers backed up.

From the Westmont hillside, where other generation o Johnstowners had watched the major flooding of the valley, those remarks could but barely reflect what was happening in the Johnstown sector — to the buildings and to the people in them.

Still, as those high above the water watched, they also talked — even early Wednesday morning — about the task that lay ahead: Coming back from another disaster.

History, in short, was being relived. The specter of the Great Flood of 1889 and the St. Patrick's Daty flood of 1936 hovered as heavily over the city as did the fog that hid from time to time the evidence of Wednesday's flooding.

The history of those earlier major floods — and minor ones — is not composed simply of death and destruction; the history is not complete without the recounting of the massive and successful recovery efforts of those bygone days. So it was that while the Wednesday waters were receding slightly during the hours heading toward noon, people were beginning to wonder about the difficulties that lay ahead.

But the wondering what not cluttered bydoubts and despair; the city and its neighboring communities had been through it before, even if few of the people looking on were not here even for the 1936 flood. The people, even the young, knew that there was no need for doubt and despair. The cleaning up, the repairing, the getting Johnstown together again would be accomplished.

So although the Johnstown district has been proved by nature not to be flood free, as all of us had believed and hoped, there was the belief — the certainty — that the community and its spirit had been lainawash again but not destroyed.

City Waters Began to Build At Midnight

By SANDRA K. REABUCK
and
Cindy Burkett
Of The Tribune-Democrat

The "flood-free" City of Johnstown was paralyzed early today with swirling, muddy flood waters from the overflowing streams and rivers.

It was shortly after midnight when the word was first aired over the city police radio network that the city had been closed down to all incoming traffic because of the emergency situation.

That news made the Wednesday morning editions of The Tribune-Democrat, but just about nobody was reading it. Only a few thousand copies of the morning editions were gotten out of the downtown area before the rising water made the streets impassable.

25-30 Stranded

Approximately 25 or 30 people — employes, stuffers for the Conemaugh Township Area Band Boosters and stranded persons — were trapped in the newspaper office's second-floor.

Among the stranded were three city firemen, who had been trying to return to the Public Safety Building.

Before midnight, water was in the streets, but still passable in the vicinity of the newspaper office. But with the heavy electrical storm returning to the area and the river banks overflowing, the water level rose, and rose and rose . . . it covered cars and reached cab levels in pick-up trucks.

Fire hydrants and parking meters disappeared beneath the water.

The swiftly moving water could be seen in all directions — Washington, Locust, Main, Franklin and Market.

The emergency airways were jammed with messages. But at various points throughout the evening, Westmont Suburban Radio Network, the city fire radio network and eventually the city police radio network went down.

Water Begins to Subside

The waters began to subside at daybreak. The roofs of cars began to emerge, and to those stranded at The Tribune-Democrat building, they looked like the first flowers of spring.

It was about that time that a decision was made to publish a 12-page afternoon edition. But action didn't get started before all communication in and out of the office was ended.

Two girls swept by the raging currents made their way into the Glosser Bros. store, which adjoins The Tribune-Democrat building. They were noticed there by firemen, who also had spent the night marooned.

Beleaguered staffers and stuffers wearily climbed the steps leading from our second floor to Glosser's third floor and into their cafeteria, mouths watering for the cup of hot coffee or cold soda that awaited them there.

From the cafeteria windows, they could see the letters denoting the makes of cars begin to appear. Several were able to spot their cars several feet away from where they'd parked them before they began another routine workday.

Dwight Lehman, Tribune-Democrat purchasing manager, had parked his car in the alley beside the building when he came in about midnight.

About 7:30 a.m., the windshield of his car appeared, smashed into a pole at Locust Street and Park Place.

Receding water was checked periodically in the first-floor classified advertising department. The entire operation was flooded nearly to the countertops about 5:30 a.m. At 8:45 it had subsided several feet.

Out of a conference room window on the second floor, those still awake could watch bags of marshmallows, half gallon cartons of vanilla ice cream, tennis shoes or mannequins float by on Locust Street. The entire first floor of Glosser's seemed to be destroyed.

But perhaps the strangest thing of all to the marooned journalists was that they were sitting in the middle of the most sophisticated news-gathering agency in the area — and they knew only what they could see from the window or hear on the radio.

BES to Establish Temporary Offices

Of The Tribune-Democrat

Joseph Casale, manager of the local office of the state Bureau of Employment Security, announced Tuesday that temporary headquarters would be established as soon as possible to handle unemployment-compensation claims.

Mr. Casale said the downtown headquarters on Union Street were extensively damaged and may not be ready for business for several months.

Although unable to reach the office, Mr. Casale said that it appeared from the Inclined Plane that the water was 8 or 9 feet deep outside the one-story building.

He said that a search was under way for temporary headquarters, possible in Westmont Borough, and that the public would be informed as soon as the office is ready for business.

There is no doubt, he said, that the office will be receiving thousands of extra claims because of people thrown out of work by the flood.

According to Mr. Casale, he has contacted Harrisburg and extra equipment and supplies are being trucked here from the state capital for the temporary operation.

Chapter 25

Six Weeks of Hell

"Pulling a Penn Traffic" would have made perfect sense in '77. The Glosser company's losses from the flood were covered by insurance; closing The Store for good, as Penn Traffic had done, would not have been an unexpected business decision.

Glosser Bros., Inc. could have written off the downtown store and focused its attention elsewhere. It would have been a smart move, since everyone at the time knew the future of retail was closer to the Gee Bee model than the downtown department store. Not to mention, shuttering the ravaged old store would have saved a lot of people a lot of work.

But Glosser Bros.' leadership had only one option in mind. "Glosser's Department Store was still a profitable business," says Bill Glosser. "Why not reopen?"

In an interview with *The Tribune-Democrat*, company president Leonard Black was relentlessly upbeat. "We can't wait to restock after we get cleaned up. We'll reopen the store from the second floor on up just as soon as we possibly can.

"We're going to come back," said Leonard.

Leonard Black (photo © The Tribune-Democrat)

It was a fine sentiment, a strong commitment to rebuilding the store that had been the cornerstone of Glosser Bros.' business for over seven decades.

If only it hadn't meant going through weeks of pure hell to make it a reality.

Where To Begin?

As Leonard and his team were deciding to reopen the store, Fred Glosser was trying to decide where to begin the cleanup. There was so much destruction, it was hard to pick a starting point...but pumping out the basement was a pretty high priority. The raw sewage and spoiling food down there presented a health hazard and worse; the methane gas they produced was explosive, and would only get stronger as time passed.

When it came to pumping out the muck, though, there was a problem. Glosser's, and all of downtown Johnstown, had no electricity to power a pump.

So Fred's first task became clear. "A company in Ohio offered to loan us a big generator free of charge. They didn't even ask us to pay for shipping.

"The generator was capable of producing 110 volts of electricity continuously. That would give us more than enough power to pump out the basement."

As the generator was rushed to Johnstown, Fred turned his attention to clearing debris on the ground floor of The Store. The mess was staggering; just looking at it was disheartening.

Fortunately, Fred had plenty of help to clear it away.

It Was A Miracle

Even working with his right-hand men, Bill Zettle and Bill Sabo, along with other Glosser's employees, Fred knew it would take a long time to clean up the wreckage.

But a sudden infusion of manpower made the work go much faster.

"Young men and women just started showing up," remembers Fred. "They came in from out of town, and they pitched in and worked hard. And they didn't ask for a thing in return.

Photos by Fred Glosser

228

"It was a miracle. I saw these young people all over town, helping with the cleanup. We couldn't have done it without them."

Together, Fred's men and the out-of-town volunteers began the arduous task of hauling out ruined merchandise and piling it outside. It helped that the Glossers brought in earthmoving equipment to tackle the heaviest wreckage--several Bobcat loaders that could scoop up or push debris with a front-mounted hydraulic bucket.

Photo courtesy of Bill Glosser

A big conveyor belt--the kind used to transport rock out of mines--was brought in courtesy of Jack Creighton, a friend of Leonard's who owned the Creighton Coal Company in Beaverdale. The conveyor was set up to run from the basement to the first floor,

From The Happy Times newsletter, May 1978

traversing the basement stairs. Bobcat loaders and volunteers on foot dumped debris on the conveyor, which carried it up to the first floor. The debris was then unloaded and piled along Locust Street, where it was hauled away by trucks.

The Bobcats and volunteers put a real dent in the mess that first day, in spite of the dangerous conditions and accessibility issues inside The Store. Then, when the generator arrived from Ohio, Fred and his assistants wasted no time putting it to work. It was set up outside in the alley so the exhaust fumes wouldn't fill up the interior of The Store, where people were working.

"We strung lights on the first floor, powered by the generator, to better illuminate the work site," says Fred. "That would enable us to work effectively past sundown, into the night.

"We also brought in a big electric pump. We couldn't use the existing sump pump from the basement because it was underwater. Even if we could have reached it, the motor was ruined by the mud.

"Our electrical contractor, Andy Kindya, hooked the new pump up to the generator, and we started pumping water out of the basement and into the storm sewer. Some of the water had already started running out through basement floor drains into the city sewer, but the pump made the water level in the basement drop much faster."

But pumping out the water was only the first step in the battle for the basement.

Photo by Fred Glosser

229

The Glosser Bomb

Thanks to the buildup of methane gas in the basement, the Glosser Building had become a giant bomb.

"An inspector from the Federal Bureau of Mines came in and ran tests," recalls Bill Sabo. "He warned that the whole place could go up at any time. All it would take was a single spark."

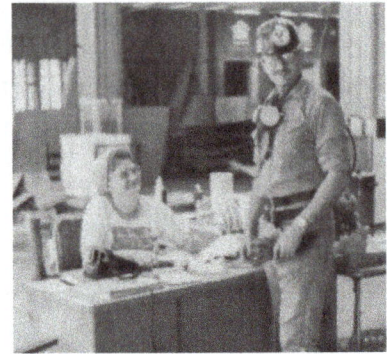

Fred Glosser at work
From The Happy Times newsletter, May 1978

Not only was the methane level high, but it was increasing as the contents of the basement continued to rot. "There were lots of packaged products in the supermarket, and they decayed slowly," says Fred. "There were stock rooms in the basement, too, loaded with sportswear, men's furnishings, shoes, and ladies' accessories. None of that was perishable, of course.

Photo by Fred Glosser

"But then there were two huge walk-in coolers full of produce and cheese, and an extra walk-in refrigerator and walk-in freezer full of meat from the meat department. The contents of those walk-ins just kept decomposing and adding to the level of methane."

No one could rest easy until the gas was evacuated...and no one could enter the basement for fear of igniting it. The next step in the cleanup was clear.

The company that had shipped the generator had sent along a giant exhaust fan to go with it. Fred and his team decided they would use the fan to suck out the fumes along the shortest route possible, through the freight elevator shaft.

Luckily, when the power had gone out the night of the flood, the freight elevator had been stuck on an upper floor of the building. That left the elevator shaft wide open from the basement to ground level, which was the path the gas would follow.

"We opened the freight elevator door in the alley, then sealed the exhaust fan in the doorway," explains Fred. "Then, we made sure the doors to the freight elevator shaft on the upper floors were all shut tight.

"We hooked the fan up to the generator and turned it on. The fan sucked the fumes up through the shaft, pulling them out of the basement and up one level to discharge in the alley.

"It worked great, though it still took a few days to clear out all the methane," says Fred. "There was a lot of gas down there, and some

Photo by Fred Glosser

of it was trapped in pockets behind closed doors."

According to Fred, the biggest pockets were trapped in the coolers, walk-in refrigerator, and walk-in freezer, which had been full of raw, unpackaged produce, cheese, and meat. As the methane cleared from the main section of the supermarket, members of the cleanup crew were able to enter the basement and open the doors to the coolers, refrigerator, and freezer, freeing the trapped gas so it could be drawn out by the fan.

"As an added bonus, the air flow from the fan helped dry the basement," says Fred.

After a few days, when Fred and the crew thought the basement might be clear of methane, they called in an inspector from the fire department. As the inspector performed tests in the basement, Fred held his breath; the lion's share of the cleanup in the supermarket couldn't be started unless the fumes were completely gone.

But when the inspector came up the steps, he gave the crew a big thumbs-up. "It was finally okay to send our people down to start cleaning up the mud and sewage and rotting food," says Fred. "And we could start working toward restoring power to the building, as well. We didn't have to worry that a stray spark might blow it to kingdom come."

Working in a Coal Mine

With the water drained and the methane cleared, Bill Glosser and his basement crew headed downstairs. When they got to the bottom of the stairs, they stood for a moment and stared, shaking their heads at the mess that lay before them.

"Everywhere you looked, there was muck and mangled wreckage and rotting food," says Bill. "There were mountains of it. An entire supermarket had been turned into a putrid compost pit.

"Insects were flying and crawling everywhere. We heard buzzing and sloshing and dripping noises from all directions. The whole place reeked of sewage and decompos-ing organic material."

Swallowing hard, Bill stepped forward and waved for his crew to follow. There were enough men to make some progress, at least--100 of them to start, descending into the pit with the promise of special hazard pay.

The earthmoving equipment that had made such a difference on the first floor was brought into play, too.

Photos courtesy of Bill Glosser

231

Bill Zettle--an assistant of Fred's from maintenance and construction--built a ramp over the stairs so one of the Bobcats could drive up and down it, hauling debris out of the basement.

But even with a Bobcat and all those men, the basement work was a challenge.

"It was like working in a coal mine," remembers Bill Glosser. "Back-breaking drudgery and filth. Sometimes we felt like we would never get it all done.

Photo courtesy of Bill Glosser

"It was six weeks of hell, plain and simple."

Downstairs, Upstairs

Even as work crews attacked the basement and first floor, chipping away at the waterlogged ruins, there was other work--office work--that couldn't wait. Certain key Glosser's employees had their own important roles to play in the flood's aftermath, including Arlene Goss, who was head stenographer at the time.

Photo by Fred Glosser

"There was correspondence that couldn't wait," explains Arlene. "Aspects of the business that had to keep going.

"For example, as a publicly held company in the midst of a crisis, it was crucial that we reassured our shareholders. We had to send out shareholder letters to let them know the state of their investment--our company--and how the flood might impact our profitability, if at all."

According to Arlene, she was able to get to The Store soon after the flood though access to downtown was limited...all thanks to Bill Glosser. "Bill was a federal magistrate, so all he had to do was show his badge to get us through the road blocks."

When Arlene entered the Glosser Building, she was stunned by the destruction all around her. "The windows were all broken, and there were mannequins out on the street. The amount of mud and guck everywhere was just unbelievable.

"And the stench was horrible. You had to wear a mask, you could hardly breathe," says Arlene.

From The Happy Times newsletter, May 1978

232

But Arlene--and fellow personnel, when they joined her upstairs--didn't let the conditions get in the way of their work. In the weeks after the flood, they completed a range of critical tasks and paperwork, including the preparation and mailing of the first letter to Glosser Bros. shareholders since the disaster.

In that letter, Leonard Black wrote about the status of the company, and the community, after the flood.

"Our Johnstown slogan is, "We'll Rebuild Together!" wrote Leonard. "The members of our organization, being optimistic by nature, are making plans to make your company a stronger and better one."

Today's Specials Are Baloney And Baloney

Though the office workers and cleanup crews worked on very different tasks at The Store, there was one thing they shared: free lunches provided on the house.

"Since the flood, there was nowhere downtown to get something to eat or drink," says Arlene. "The restaurants and stores were all closed and recovering.

"So the Gee Bee Richland store would put together lunches and send them down for us. Each

Photo by Fred Glosser

lunch included a sandwich, a piece of fruit, and a beverage...but the sandwiches were always the same. They were always baloney.

"We had baloney sandwiches every single day for lunch. By the time we were done, I didn't want to see another baloney sandwich for a while, let alone eat one."

The Rest of the Empire

While office workers got the word out and kept the company running on the upper floors, and cleanup crews slaved away downstairs, Fred Glosser had to steal able bodies from the effort at The Store and take them elsewhere. The Glosser Building wasn't the only part of the Glosser Bros. empire that demanded attention, and it was up to Fred to make sure the other bases were covered.

The Park Building, home of the Gee Bee and supermarket division accounting offices, had been taken on plenty of water itself during the storm. The owners of the first-floor Hello Shop were cleaning up their store, but it was up to the Glossers to clear the basement and get the electrical system ready for when power was restored to the city.

As for the warehouse headquarters of Globe Wholesale on Jackson Street, it had mostly been spared. There'd only been a few inches of water in the basement, and the merchandise stored down there had all been elevated on pallets, so it was undamaged. But someone still had to push out the muck that had washed in, mop the floors, and check the electrical system. Much of that work was left up to the warehouse crew.

The Gee Bee supermarket in the Center Town Mall on Walnut Street, six blocks from Glosser Bros. Department Store, had been hit hard, too. The store lost all of its stock and most of its fix-

Walnut Street supermarket 2014 (Photo by Philip Balko)

tures in the flood. Paul Glosser took charge of that cleanup, putting a crew of his own through their paces.

Windber warehouse (photo courtesy of Bill Glosser)

Then there was the Windber Gee Bee warehouse along state route 160. "The warehouse was located in a river valley, and the river topped its banks and rushed into the building," explains Fred. "We got two or three feet of water, and we lost a lot of merchandise."

As Fred led a team of warehouse employees in cleaning up the site and hauling out the ruined stock, he knew the damage could have been much worse. The original warehouse had had stability problems for years because there was abundant water under the three-foot layer of dirt on which it had been built.

Fortunately, Fred had recently overseen the construction of an addition with strong rein-forcement. "We sunk caissons all the way down to the bedrock," says Fred. "We had to drill down about 30 feet to hit solid rock, so the pilings would be firmly braced.

"It made a big difference when the river washed through. The new addition held fast, and the extra reinforcement steadied the original warehouse so it didn't shift at all."

There was still plenty to clean up at the Windber site, but it wasn't the worst or most dan-gerous of Fred's assignments. The Windber job wasn't likely to be a fatal one.

Though the same was nearly not true for his work back at the Glosser Building in John-stown.

A Brush With Death

Fred was not a late kind of guy. He made it a point to always be on time, in fact...but the morning of July 25th, 1977 was a different story.

Between cleaning up the Glosser Bros. Department Store, the Park Building, Globe Whole-sale, the Windber Gee Bee Warehouse, and the Landmark Building (his own personal piece of real estate), Fred had been working 15-hour days (at least) since the flood. By the fifth day of cleanup, on July 25th, all that overtime was catching up to him. He forgot to pick up his col-league, Isadore Suchman, on his way to town, and had to turn around to get him. As a result,

234

Fred ended up arriving at The Store 15 minutes later than usual.

When he got there, his favorite parking space had been taken. Fred pulled into the parking lot across Franklin Street from Glosser's and parked next to the sidewalk instead of next to the Royal Plate Glass Company building on the other side of the lot where he always parked.

It turned out to be a lucky move for Fred. Just as he was getting ready to get out of the car, it started shaking.

"I heard a rumbling sound, and the car shook harder," remembers Fred. "Then I heard a tremendous *boom.*

"I looked in my rear-view mirror and saw the Royal Plate Glass Company wall come toppling down, right on top of all the cars that were parked up against it...which was exactly where I usually parked."

Photo © The Tribune-Democrat

It was the very thing that Fred and the cleanup crews had been worried about earlier: buildings torn apart by an explosion. The blast might have been caused by natural gas fumes building up in the basement under Royal Plate Glass, though the cause was never officially determined.

Three Royal Plate Glass buildings were destroyed in the explosion that morning. It was a tragedy that left one man dead, another paralyzed, and 11 people hospitalized with injuries.

Fred knew all too well that he could have easily been among the injured...or worse. "I was fortunate that I was a little late that day. If I'd parked in my usual spot and had been getting out of my car, I would've been hit by the wall. I probably wouldn't be here today."

Photo courtesy of Bill Glosser

Shockingly Dangerous

Fred had narrowly escaped catastrophe when the Royal Plate Glass Company blew, but he didn't let it stop him from taking more risks during the cleanup. If anything, he put his life on the line in a way that was just as potentially lethal.

It had to do with restoring power to The Store. Though power was still out in the city of Johnstown, Penelec crews were working to bring it back.

The problem was, Glosser's electrical switches--which routed power from the transformer to the different parts of the building--were in no condition to handle the flow of current when it eventually returned.

Glosser's main electrical switches and fuses were located in a large electric switch control panel cabinet, a steel enclosure that had been fouled by flood waters and was still full of muck. The cabinet's interior, including the switches and fuses, had to be thoroughly cleaned before the electrical system could return to operation. The only other option was to replace it, which would have been exorbitantly expensive and time-consuming. With the company eager to reopen for business as soon as possible, cleaning the switches in the cabinet seemed to make the most sense.

But people weren't exactly lining up to do the job. Chief electrician Andy Kindya wouldn't even let his men do it, because the work was too dangerous.

"If someone was in that switch room, and Penelec turned on the electricity for the building in the underground box in the park, that person would be electrocuted," explains Fred. "He would die in that room in an instant.

"No matter how careful we were about notifying Penelec and the city and everyone involved, telling them not to flip the switch while we had someone in the switch room, we couldn't be sure it wouldn't happen. Electricity has a mind of its own sometimes, and it could have led to some poor fella getting fried by mistake."

With no volunteers coming forward, and the clock ticking as Penelec got closer to restoring power, Fred decided to take the risk himself. He'd already gotten a new lease on life when he'd escaped the Royal Plate Glass Company disaster; maybe he was meant to put it to use bringing Glosser Bros. back from the dead.

Fred notified Penelec that power must *not* be switched back on until he emerged from the switch room. Then, he gathered his cleaning equipment and went to work.

"I went in and hosed down the control switch panels," says Fred. "I also wiped the equipment down with lots of towels."

It took a whole day for Fred to hose and scrub away the muck, cleaning every surface so the switches wouldn't short out and blow up when the power returned.

"The whole time, I was soaked with sweat and water from the hose. Fortunately, I was in good physical shape, because I had to get on my knees and back a lot to access all the corners and crevices of the equipment.

"Meanwhile, I just kept praying that the power wouldn't accidentally switch back on. It would have been a hell of a way to go."

Luckily, the power stayed off as Fred finished the cleaning. It was still off at the end of the day, when he finally left the switch control panel cabinet.

The next day, Andy Kindya came to inspect the switches and install new fuses. When he'd finished, he notified Penelec it was okay to turn on the power.

When Penelec finally turned the power back on, the equipment worked fine. The transformer ran perfectly, and the Glosser Bros. Department Store lit up like a Christmas tree, like a sign that Leonard Black's promises were being kept and it was coming back to life after all. Fred's risk had been worth it.

From The Happy Times newsletter, May 1978

The Things That Went Away

As the cleanup continued in the weeks that followed, efforts slowly turned to rebuilding...which sometimes required major reconfiguring of The Store's former floor plan.

The destruction of the escalator, for example, forced the Glosser team to rethink the ground floor in a big way. Deciding not to replace the escalator was only half the battle.

With the escalator gone, the opening on the second floor that it had fed into had to be covered up. New steel and flooring had to be installed there, too, in order to fill the gap that had once been the top of the escalator.

Then there was the basement stairway that had been hidden under the escalator since its construction in 1936. That had to be closed up and covered over as well.

"We brought in contractors to do this work," remembers Fred. "The escalator left some big holes in our store, and we had to be sure that we filled them in properly."

Then there was the matter of the meat department, which had been located at the rear of the first floor for decades. Its fate was entwined with that of the supermarket...which might have just seen its last hurrah.

After all the devastation in the basement, all the toil and time and danger of cleaning it up, it was hard to think about putting another supermarket down there. It had been washed out twice, by the floods of 1936 and 1977; maybe enough was finally enough.

If the basement supermarket was done for, the meat department would probably go with it. By going that route, the Glossers would save themselves the trouble of rebuilding it, which would have been a challenge without the walk-in cooler and freezer storage space they'd once had in the basement. They could leave the grocery business for the Gee Bee chain, and let The Store do what it had always done best, from 1906 onward: be a department store with a reputation for quality discount merchandise.

Whenever the heck it finally got around to reopening, that is.

237

Johnstown Tribune-Democrat, Friday, August 19, 1977   23

July 19: Flash flooding in Morrellville

Stranded at Ash and McMillen

238

Chapter 26

Glosser's Shining Moment

"The whole town was excited," remembers Arlene Goss. "After everything that people went through, this was a highlight."

On the morning of September 26th, 1977, the sky was gray and cloudy, and drizzle was falling. In other words, it was typical Fall weather in downtown Johnstown.

But there was nothing typical about what was happening at the corner of Franklin and Locust Streets that day. Throngs of people mobbed the sidewalks, chattering and laughing and jostling as they waited for the magic moment.

The moment that was about to arrive.

Wet But Not Washed Out

"During the cleanup and rebuilding, the employees had t-shirts that said, 'We're wet but not washed out,' and 'We will be back,'" says Arlene. "Now we were finally back, and I would say we came back bigger and stronger than ever."

The buzz and fidgeting of the crowd increased as men in suits approached the big corner doors from inside the building. One of the men turned the latch, unlocking the doors, and pushed them open.

That man was Leonard Black, president of Glosser Bros., Inc.

The spectators tensed as the doors began to swing. It had been over nine weeks since any of them had crossed that threshold; now that they were finally about to do so again, they could barely restrain themselves.

Every one of them seemed to share that same eagerness. Every one of them seemed to feel exactly the same way about what was happening that morning.

"Thank God Glosser's is back," says Arlene. "That was the general feeling.

"Other stores decided they weren't coming back, but Glosser's didn't let us down. And with Glosser's coming back, there was still some hope for Johnstown."

Ready To Sell

If the city needed a symbol of the spirit of rebuilding, this was it. The structure that had been so ruined nine weeks ago looked as good as new on the outside. The walls and walks were as free of muck and mire as if they'd just been newly laid. New display windows covered what had once been jagged-rimmed gaps smashed open by telephone poles.

Through those gleaming new windows, the crowd glimpsed a bright and spacious new interior. Racks and counters and tables beckoned from inside, overflowing with new merchandise about to go on sale.

That merchandise had arrived thanks to Glosser's buyers, who'd been busy with their own rebuilding effort, rebuilding The Store's stock. Twenty-three of them had gone to New York City during the last week of August on a whirlwind buying spree, ordering merchandise to replace what had been lost during the flood.

Now the fruits of their search were displayed in The Store, price-tagged and ready to be swept out the door by shoppers. For the first time in nine weeks, the ground floor of Glosser's was stocked with merchandise.

And Glosser's employees were ready to sell it.

A Reunion As Much As A Reopening

Even as the swelling crowd leaned as one toward Leonard and the opening front doors, a small army of salespeople and cashiers waited inside the building to serve them. And if it was possible to feel any more excited than the crowd of shoppers, the army of employees certainly did so.

"It was so great to be back in the swing of things at Glosser's," says Arlene. "And it was especially great to see all the other employees.

"Only a minimal group of office staff had been working since the flood, so most of us hadn't seen each other for such a long time. Now we got to catch up and find out how everyone had made out during the flood.

"For us, it was a reunion as much as a reopening," says Arlene.

Photo © The Tribune-Democrat

Bigger And Better Than Before

Finally, the doors swung all the way open, and Leonard stepped forward, along with members of his staff and several dignitaries.

The crowd had to wait a few minutes more as Leonard offered some remarks on the occasion. "I think the spirit of our employees typifies the people of Johnstown," he said at one point, "in that they can't be licked and will come back bigger and better than before."

Johnstown Mayor Herb Pfuhl Jr. also spoke about the big day. "We're very proud of Glosser Bros.," he said. "Thanks for staying with us and helping us to come back strong."

Finally, when the speeches were over, Leonard spread his arms wide. "Welcome back!" He gestured for the crowd to enter. "Come on in!"

Photo from Glosser Bros. Annual Report, Jan. 1978

Grinning, Leonard stepped aside, holding one of the doors open as the mob surged into the store.

What the shoppers found when they got inside was a work in progress. Many of the fixtures had been borrowed from Gee Bee stores. The configuration of racks and displays wasn't intended to be permanent.

And the ground floor was the only one that was fully stocked. "It's somewhat temporary," Leonard explained in an interview with *The Tribune-Democrat* that day, "but our goal was to get the main floor open so we could open the rest of the store."

At least one part of The Store was still off-limits and in limbo at the time. The basement had been cleared out, but the fate of the supermarket was still undecided. "We're still assessing the damages as to what can be done to the basement," Leonard told *The Tribune-Democrat*.

Photo © The Tribune-Democrat

The World Was Our Family

As temporary and up in the air as the reopened store might have been, the customers didn't seem to mind. Employees wore ribbons in their lapels that read, "Welcome back! We missed you!"

From what Arlene could see, the shoppers felt the same way.

"The place was packed with people," she recalls. "You couldn't even move. And they all seemed to be happy to see us. They all seemed to be happy just to be back at Glosser's again."

Arlene's boss, Bill Glosser, was caught up in the excitement on the floor. He moved from one shopper to the next, greeting old friends and new ones alike.

"People could not wait to get into the store that day," remembers Bill. "Everybody was hugging and kissing everybody else."

To Bill, it was Glosser's shining moment, the absolute pinnacle of the place he'd known and loved so well all his life. The hard work of the cleanup and rebuilding had all been worth it; the weeks of hell had led to something beautiful.

"It was like the world was our family," he says.

Glosser Bros. Comptroller Sydney Ossip was also touched by the outpouring of support. "The way the people responded, I could tell they were very happy we were reopening.

"We had a lot of friends at the downtown store. They were all glad to see us open again, especially after Penn Traffic closed.

"It was very emotional," said Sydney. "For all of us."

A Brown-and-White Striped Bag

That day, and in weeks to come, messages of gratitude would shower Glosser Bros. from the community. People sent letters to The Store, praising Leonard and his staff for reopening.

One such letter, dated October 3rd and written by an anonymous patron, was typical of the outpouring of thanks. "How wonderful to have Glosser's back again!" it read. "Glossers do care! We know it!"

The letter went on to say, "Johnstown has a trustworthy friend in Glosser Bros. Years past have proven this factual. We are likewise as proud of you as you are of us."

Perhaps the anonymous patron who wrote that letter was part of the jubilant crowd filling Glosser's during the Grand Reopening on September 26th. He or she could have been any one of those happy shoppers who were hugging and shaking hands and purchasing merchandise from equally happy employees.

Because on that day, at least, everyone was united. The aftermath of the flood had left them all with a common desire, a vision to get back something they'd loved most and lost.

And that something came in a brown-and-white striped shopping bag with a "Glosser Bros." logo emblazoned across it.

Oct. 3, 1977
Johnstown, Pa

Dear Mr. Glosser,

How wonderful to have Glossers back again! It's beautiful!

Your people have once again rejuvenated the spirit in helping to ease the cloud of apathy that hangs over our community since the disastrous July 20 flood.

Glossers do care! We know it!

Your most recent announcement about the annual Halloween parade; your compassion and concern in that the people of Johnstown need this event now more than ever, touched more hearts than you can imagine.

Johnstown has a trustworthy friend in Glosser Bros. Years past have proven this factual. We are likewise as proud of you as you are of us.

"We will rebuild together." Some have forgotten -- but Glossers — never!

My name is not important. It speaks for so many.

Gratefully,
A patron

What we do for ourselves dies with us — What we do for our City will live on.

We **MUST** Rebuild Together.

HJI

Idzkowsky
opher Street
Pa. 15905

9-26
77

Ltr written
9/27

Dear Leonard:

Please extend our congratulations to your colleagues for their decision to continue the Glosser Brothers Department Store in downtown Johnstown. The Idzkowskys have been customers of Glosser's, and you can be assured that we will not only continue to buy at Glosser's, but that our interest as both Johnstowners and as customers will be expanded.

Thank you, and much continued success to you and to Glosser Brothers.

Sincerely
Henry

Courtesy of Johnstown Area Heritage Association

GLOSSER'S ALL-STARS

PAUL GLOSSER

In photos of the Glosser Bros. executives from back in the day, one man always stands out. One man, out of all the members of the Board of Directors, has a look that jumps off the page or screen. And it's all because he has one thing that no one else in the group has.

Facial hair.

Paul Glosser, the man with the beard, worked for Glosser Bros., Inc. for 36 years. For most of that time, he headed the company's supermarket division, running everything from Glosser's basement grocery store to the U-Save Food Warehouse discount markets.

Photo from Glosser Bros. Annual Report, Jan. 1978

Glosser Bros. was an important part of his life right from the start. Born in Johnstown on January 22, 1930, Paul spent many happy hours in The Store as a child.

"We used to play hide and go seek at night when the store was closed," he says. "We loved spending time in the candy and toy departments, especially."

Paul remembers watching his father, David--one of the original Glosser brothers--walk to work at Glosser Bros. "He walked to work from our house in Westmont every day. He took the Inclined Plane into town, then walked to the store. At the end of the day, I watched him coming home the same way, which was always nice."

Unfortunately, David Glosser died when Paul was just 24 years old. "I never got the chance to be as close to him as my sisters did," says Paul. "I only knew my father when I was a kid, and then I went off to college and the Army, and then he was gone."

Paul earned a Bachelor of Science degree in economics from the University of Pittsburgh, followed by a year of graduate school...and then he was drafted.

245

He went from Pittsburgh to Korea, where he served two years in the infantry during the Korean War. He fought in the first Battle of Pork Chop Hill, then the second one, and came away with a purple heart after taking some shrapnel.

Discharged from the Army in 1954, Paul returned to the U.S....and one of his favorite memories of his father. "I flew to Florida to see my dad," he remembers. "Our family had been spending the winters in Miami for many years.

"I hadn't had time to buy civilian clothes, so I still had my uniform on. When we were approaching Miami, the crew told me my father was waiting at the airport gate for me.

"When the plane landed, Dad ran out onto the tarmac. An attendant told him he couldn't go out there, and he just said, 'Oh yes, I can. My son just came home from the war.'

"He was so happy to see me, he ran out and threw his arms around me," says Paul. "I'll never forget that moment."

Soon after returning from Korea, Paul married Rita Gordon, a Squirrel Hill girl he'd met while in college in Pittsburgh. The newlyweds moved to New York City, where Paul planned to work...but they didn't live there very long. When Paul's father died, he and Rita decided to move to Johnstown so Paul could join the family business.

Paul started at Glosser Bros. as a manager in men's sportswear, then moved on to manage the meat department. In a little while, he took over from Meyer Silberstein as head of the company's supermarket division.

"That was when we had one grocery store," says Paul. "By the time I retired, we had 15."

The growth of the supermarket division began in earnest with the launch of the Gee Bee stores in 1962. The original Gee Bees included adjacent department stores and supermarkets, and Paul was in charge of setting up the supermarket side of each unit.

The added workload kept him jumping, but it all paid off for the company. "We were successful with Gee Bee," says Paul. "We were fortunate. The first new store we opened in Greensburg was a tremendous success. That led us to open lots more."

His busiest time might have been in 1979, though, when Glosser Bros. bought the leases on six Acme stores and converted them to Gee Bee supermarkets in one year. "It was pretty hectic, but I had very good help," says Paul. "I had three or four very trusted assistants. I had very good people working for me, and it made it wonderful."

Photo © The Tribune-Democrat

Paul also spearheaded the U-Save Food Warehouse discount markets, a group of bare bones supermarkets that achieved deeply discounted prices by stripping away frills and buying products in big lots when prices were lowest.

The years of success and expansion finally came to an end in the late 1980s, though. Glosser Bros. sold its supermarket division to the Penn Traffic Company, where it became part of the Riverside chain.

Photo courtesy of Paul Glosser

Paul moved over to work in Glosser Bros.' department store division for a year,

Photo courtesy of Paul Glosser

then retired in 1990. He and Rita moved to Long Boat Key, Florida, near Sarasota, where they still live today.

It's a long way--and a long time--from Glosser Bros., but Paul still looks back fondly on his time with the company. "I remember so many good times," he says. "My working days at Glosser's were such an important part of my life."

Paul's a true Glosser's All-Star because of his many years of Glosser and Gee Bee supermarket success. Also because of the innovations he helped create, like the conveyor belts at the Gee Bees that carried grocery purchases from inside the store to customers' cars outside, in the parking lot.

He's also forever an All-Star because of his support of Johnstown charitable organizations like Mercy Hospital.

And, of course, he's an All-Star for one other reason that really has nothing to do with his business acumen but has made him a standout nonetheless.

That *beard*.

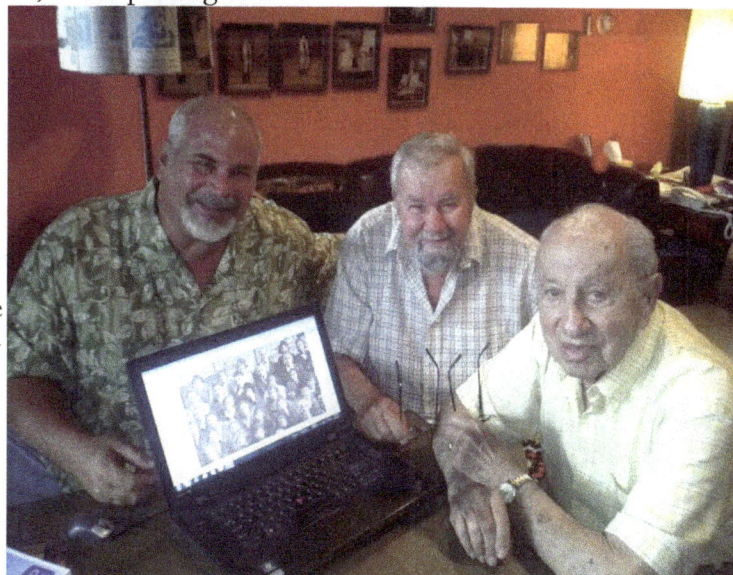

David and Paul Glosser and Sydney Ossip (photo courtesy of David Glosser)

Memory Department

Aside from the smell of cashews roasting upon entering the store and the twins working behind the counter in the restaurant, I have one particular lasting memory of Glosser's. In November 1978, I was pregnant. I went for a doctor's appointment and thought it would be a regular appointment. The doctor was not there, and the nurse wanted me to see the doctor, as I was having contractions. The nurse said it would be an hour or so. I decided to go to Glosser's to buy some baby clothes.

Not wanting to lose my parking space by the War Memorial, I walked to Glosser's. I did my shopping and walked back to the doctor's office. When the doctor examined me, he informed me that my baby's head was about to be born. He asked me where I went, and I told him. He told me that a few minutes more and my baby would have been born in Glosser's. I might have had to name him Glosser.

- Carol Moudy

My favorite Glosser's story is as a kid going to a bin table where no one was and grabbing things all excitedly like there was a huge sale, then stepping back and watching the lady shoppers go nuts grabbing up the items, thinking they were getting a huge deal.

- Becky Marie Glacken Buchko

My mother, Catherine Ludwig Duncan, remembers that Glosser's used to give coupon books out to help buy your school clothes. It was like money toward the clothes.

- *Carrie Duncan Walker*

Glosser's was known for its exceptional sales. Once, the coat buyer made a great buy on women's PVC coats (not real leather), buying boxes and boxes of them, all in the same saddle color. After the store closed, they were put on a large table by the front door for the sale that had been advertised for the next day. They were priced at just $5.00!

We were in our offices before the store opened, and I heard that women were outside in the pouring rain, forming a line around the store as they waited for it to open. We watched from the second floor as the doors opened, and women ran in, grabbing handfuls of the coats to try on in the corner. There was such a frenzy, I saw a few of the women get knocked in the head with umbrellas! What a show... and the coats sold out in less than 45 min.

Another sale was the "broken zipper" sale. This sale featured items that were slightly damaged and deeply discounted. They were put out on the famous sale tables on the main floor and sold briskly.

- *Chris Bittner-Italiano*

Photo from Glosser Bros. Annual Report, Jan. 1976

Chapter 27

The Art of Unsinkability

Just about everyone knew it was coming. Unlike the Flood of '77, which had taken Johnstown by surprise, most everyone in town expected the final fate of the basement supermarket that the flood had wiped out so thoroughly.

The news came in the form of a press release dated October 21, 1977. "Glosser Bros., Inc. announced today," said the release, "that the food market which was located in the basement of the downtown department store prior to the flood will not reopen."

It was the last big loss of the post-flood period...a loss that had almost happened once before, as it turned out. "This super-market has been in existence for almost 57 years, and many in the community have grown up with it," continued the press release. "In 1968 when the new Gee Bee Supermarket was opened in the Center Town Mall on Walnut Street, management had decided to close the Glosser Bros. market. However, strong sentiment against this decision prevailed and the food market remained open."

So the underground supermarket had dodged a bullet in '68... but the writing was on the basement wall this time. In the months after the flood, right up to the Grand Reopening and beyond, the company had made no effort to install new supermarket fixtures in the basement or stock groceries of any kind down there. To most folks--whether Glosser's shoppers or employees--it would have been more of a surprise if the leadership had announced that they were resurrecting the basement supermarket after all.

251

But the press release made it clear that the resurrection had been cancelled.

"Unfortunately," said the release, "because of the flood, all the equipment, refrigeration, electrical, and plumbing facilities were destroyed, and their replacement cost has proved to be exorbitant.

"As a result, management has been forced to make this difficult and emotional decision. The total number of employees in the downtown store will remain at approximately preflood levels with many of the food market employees being reemployed in the department store or in other area Gee Bee supermarkets."

So much for the legendary "Glosserteria." It was gone for good.

But that didn't mean the basement would stay empty for long. Remodeling was already underway, according to the press release. The brand-new basement would open to shoppers on October 31st, featuring "a new Toys and Sporting Goods Department, an expanded Trim-A-Tree Shop, a complete Phonograph Record Department, and a renovated Health and Beauty Aids Department." Other departments would be added after January 1st, 1978.

So once again, Glosser Bros. was turning a setback into a new opportunity. The company had turned its decision not to reopen the supermarket into a way to attract customers and build momentum.

Not that Glosser Bros. had ever really lost momentum because of the flood in the first place.

Record Disaster = Record Profits?

Remember what original Glosser Brother Sam used to tell his son, Fred? "Even in the worst of times, the store never lost money."

Well, if Sam had been alive in 1977, he might have changed it to, "Even in the worst of times, *the company* never lost money."

The flood of '77 had hammered the downtown department store, the Gee Bee supermarket on Walnut Street, and the Windber warehouse. All three had recovered in short order (three weeks for the warehouse, six weeks for the supermarket, two months for the department store), and the company had never stopped making money.

Most of the damage was paid for by Glosser Bros.' flood insurance and business interruption coverage. Any unreimbursed costs were offset by booming business in the rest of the company, which by late 1977 included 13 Gee Bee Department Stores and 2 free-standing Gee Bee supermarkets. (One of those department stores, in the North Hills of Pittsburgh, had opened just 48 hours before the '77 flood.)

Photos from Glosser Bros. Annual Report, Jan. 1976

According to Leonard Black's message to shareholders in the company's annual report for the fiscal year ended January 28, 1978, 1977 had been a record-setting year. Leonard wrote that Glosser Bros., Inc.'s volume increased 15% in '77, from $116,222,000 to $133,960,000.

"This is the 16th consecutive year that your company has shown an increase," wrote Leonard.

The growth in sales was good news for shareholders, he continued. "Record earnings were $2,986,000 or $2.32 per share, up 20.4% from the prior year's then record total of $2,480,000 or $1.93 per share."

Not bad for a flood year, right? Looking at the sales and earnings figures

and charts, it was as if the disaster had never happened.

Glosser Bros. was big enough now to absorb shocks like the flood without collapsing. Losses in one or two locations could be cushioned by profits in 15 others. It was the kind of financial insulation that could make the company even more of a survivor, and a player, in the retail industry.

Because being a large company, insulated against shocks, positioned Glosser Bros. for further waves of growth. The more money the company brought in from its many stores, the more it could spend on opening more stores.

Leonard wrote, in his shareholder message, that Glosser Bros.' objective, when it came to the company's 2400-plus shareholders, was "To successfully maintain our on-going growth program and thereby steadily increase yearly earnings..."

That was exactly what Glosser Bros. did, once the chaos of the flood had faded.

Data Consultants Domination

Computers were good for business. It was a lesson the Glossers had learned long ago, when they'd installed computerized cash registers in Gee Bee stores. And it was a lesson that had been reinforced through the years by the success of the Glosser Bros./H.F. Lenz co-venture, Data Consultants, Inc.

Launched in 1968 to process sales data from the Gee Bee chain and Glosser Bros. Department Store, Data Consultants had played an ever-increasing role in the Glosser business plan. Through the years, Data Consultants had even expanded to service financial institutions, hospitals, mining companies, schools, and other clients.

Photos from Glosser Bros. Annual Report, Jan. 1976

Data Consultants had developed a range of systems for area businesses, including Automated Payroll, Accounts Receivable and Payable, General Ledger, Inventory, and Sales Analysis.

The Glosser team knew that computer services would only become more important in years to come, both to Glosser Bros. itself and a host of other businesses. So the idea of buying out H.F. Lenz's interest in Data Consultants looked more and more like a shrewd investment in the future.

After negotiating and coming to an agreement with Lenz, Glosser Bros., Inc. bought up the remaining 63% interest in Data Consultants, giving them 100% ownership of the company.

According to Leonard Black, "Data Consultants was acquired to insure the continuity and expedite the expanding usage of the services provided by the company, including systems design, programming, and processing."

Data Consultants would operate as an independent subsidiary of Glosser Bros., Inc., directed by Frederick Mickel, who had helped found the firm back in the day. From that point on, Glosser Bros. would control 100% of the company that met 100% of its data processing needs.

Meaning Glosser Bros., Inc. was one step closer to launching the next phase of its expansion program.

Six New Stores in One Day?

One year after the flood, in July 1978, Glosser Bros., Inc. opened its first new Gee Bee stores since the disaster.

One of the new stores was located in the Lycoming Mall in Williamsport, Pennsylvania. The other opened the same day in Frederick, Maryland.

Though the next opening wouldn't occur for over a year, the Williamsport and Frederick stores signaled that the company was serious about continued growth. Glosser's was still in the business of expansion, though opening one store in a year did seem like a cautious approach.

When the next phase hit, however, it was anything but cautious, spurred on, perhaps, by another banner year. In fact, Glosser Bros., Inc. was named one of the top 83 discount retailers in the U.S. by *The Discount Merchandiser* magazine. Glosser Bros. was ranked 49th on the list, with total sales volume of $146,000,000 for the 1978 calendar year.

Published in May 1979, the list was the kind of recognition that got attention in the discount merchandising sector. Two months later, in July 1979, Glosser Bros., Inc. kept the good news coming by adding no fewer than *six* new free-standing supermarkets to the Gee Bee lineup...*all at the same time.*

It started when the sites of six recently closed Acme supermarkets in and near Johnstown became available at once. As Leonard Black wrote in a press release dated July 6, 1979, rental costs for the vacant supermarkets were "advantageous."

Leonard and his team saw an opportunity for significant expansion--and took it. Glosser Bros. negotiated and signed leases for all six properties and converted them to Gee Bee stores.

According to Leonard's press release, Glosser Bros. would take possession of the six stores on July 15, 1979. Paul Glosser, head of Glosser's supermarket division, expected to have all six of the stores open within 90 days.

Suddenly, the loss of one supermarket in the basement of the Glosser Building addition didn't seem like such a big deal. There were new Gee Bee supermarkets in Benscreek and Parkhill, plus a new, bigger location to replace the existing Gee Bee market in Westmont.

Photo by Albert's Photography

Photo courtesy of Bill Glosser

Ebensburg, Nanty Glo, and Somerset all got their own Gee Bee supermarkets, too. The landscape of grocery sales in Cambria and Somerset counties had shifted, and Glosser Bros. expected to reap the profits.

"This was an unexpected and unique opportunity to enlarge and strengthen our Supermarket Division," wrote Leonard. "By 'strengthening' I mean in the potential overall net profit. We view this as a considerable step forward for your company!"

What To Do For An Encore

As if the six new supermarkets weren't enough, Glosser Bros. opened another Gee Bee department store one month later. This time, the location was in Bethel Park, Pennsylvania.

Photo from Glosser Bros. Annual Report, Jan. 1978

That wasn't the last new store for the year, either. In October 1979, Glosser Bros., Inc. opened the first Gee Bee Jr. Family Apparel Center, a downsized spinoff of the Gee Bee department stores. This first Gee Bee Jr. took over the location of the original Gee Bee Supermarket in Westmont, in the vicinity of the Westwood Plaza. The space became available when the supermarket moved to the former Acme site in the main section of the plaza.

Gee Bee Jr. location, Westmont, 2014 (photo by Philip Balko)

So that made a grand total of eight new store openings in a year...a record for Glosser Bros., Inc. Would the company match that fast and furious pace in the year that followed?

It wouldn't, though the next streak of new stores that were planned would still be nothing to sneeze at. Three new Gee Bees were scheduled to open in 1980, on the heels of eight in '79.

If anyone had questioned Glosser Bros.' post-flood competitiveness, they had to know their concerns were misplaced. Glosser Bros., Inc. was on sound footing and well-positioned to meet the challenges of the future.

Black Out

If a company's president had retirement on his mind, could there be a better time go through with it? Could there be a better time to step down, let other hands take the reigns, and enjoy the golden years?

In the case of Leonard Black, the answer was no.

Leonard had been thinking about retiring for a while. As much as he loved Glosser's, he decided it might be a good time to step aside--if not out of the company entirely, at least out of the presidency.

Once his mind was made up, Leonard met with Glosser Bros., Inc.'s board of directors. The board accepted his resignation as president but asked that he stay with the company in a different capacity. To that end, they created a new position and voted to offer the job to Leonard.

He accepted. At the age of 61, Leonard ended his 21-year term as president and chief operating officer of Glosser Bros., Inc. and stepped into the role of chairman of the board and chief executive officer.

The change was effective on February 1, 1980, at which point the new president and chief operating officer of the company began his own term in office. For the first time in over two decades, the man in the president's chair would have Glosser blood in his veins. He was a son of Saul Glosser, one of the original Glosser brothers, and had actually been with the company longer than Leonard. Now, he was about to make his mark on Glosser Bros., Inc.

The Alvin Glosser era had begun.

GLOSSER'S ALL-STARS

ALVIN GLOSSER

Pittsburgh Steeler Terry Bradshaw and Alvin Glosser
(Photo courtesy of Saul Glosser)

Here's the kind of guy Alvin Glosser was.

His daughter, Diane Glosser Rosenthal, remembers him getting a call at home one Christmas Eve after The Store had closed for the night. Apparently, a customer was calling because he'd bought a bicycle at Glosser's for his child, but the bike was missing a part. Without that part, Christmas morning would be a big disappointment for the customer's kid.

What did Alvin do? He called the buyer for the department where the bicycle had been sold and met him at Glosser's. Alvin and the buyer went inside and worked together to track down a replacement part. Then, Alvin contacted the customer and told him the part was waiting for him at The Store. The customer picked it up and hurried home, where he was able to get the bike ready for his child in time for Christmas morning.

That was just how Alvin rolled.

Cynthia Eplett, a Glosser's buyer in the 1980s, remembers another story of his generosity. "Before my very first overseas buying trip, Alvin called me into his office and asked me if I was excited. I said yes, of course I am. He said, 'Well, I have something for you.' Then, he reached in his pocket and put his hand out, and I put my hand out, and he gave me $100.

257

"He said, 'The only thing I want you to do is tell me what you spent it on when you come back.' So I bought a camera, and I came back and showed it to him, and I was so proud. He was so nice. He didn't have to do that, you know? And it just meant a lot to me. He was a very good person," says Cynthia.

"I remember my dad as being someone who cared about everybody," says Alvin's son, Saul Glosser. "He always tried to see the good in everybody."

Alvin was born in Johnstown on March 4, 1923 and grew up in Westmont. His father was the original Saul Glosser, one of the founding fathers of Glosser Bros. Department Store.

After graduating from Valley Forge Military Academy in 1940, Alvin served in the U.S. Army. For several years during World War II, he was part of the Army's Medical Administrative Corps.

Following his discharge, he attended the Wharton School of Business at the University of Pennsylvania in Philadelphia. But he had to drop out in his junior year when his father died. With Saul gone, Alvin had to come to work at The Store and help put his brothers Bill and Morton through college.

From a humble start in the men's department at Glosser's, Alvin had a meteoric rise through the ranks. By 1946, he was a director and vice president of the company.

Throughout the 1950s, 60s, and 70s, Alvin was a key part of the leadership team that built Glosser Bros., Inc. into a powerhouse in the retail industry. He was influential in the creation and swift expansion of the Gee Bee chain of stores, as well as Glosser Bros., Inc.'s transformation into a publicly-traded company listed on the American Stock Exchange.

Later, when he inherited the presidency from Leonard Black, Alvin played an even more significant role in charting the company's course. During his time in the big chair, Glosser Bros. continued to grow at a fast pace, adding a host of new Gee Bees, Dollar Bargain Stores, and supermarkets. Even during the difficult economic times of the early-to-mid 1980s, he kept the company's earnings soaring.

He left the presidency--and Glosser Bros., Inc.--in 1988 (read on for the full story), but he had made a strong impression on the business world...and the local community.

He was recognized for it, too. On his 63rd birthday, on March 6, 1986, Johnstown's Mayor Herb Pfuhl renamed the passage between the Glosser Building and the Annex in his honor.

There was a ceremony along the Franklin Street side of the store, attended by Glosser's executives and a crowd of Glosser's employees. It was no wonder the employees turned out, because Alvin had always treated them with respect and friendship. "My father always said, 'the employees are vital to our success because they are our eyes and ears,'" remembers Diane. "'Without them, there would be no business,' he said."

During the ceremony, Mayor Pfuhl read a proclamation with Alvin by his side. "From this day forward this fine thoroughfare known as Good Place, which Alvin passes through each day to work, shall be known as Alvin's Alley," said Mayor Pfuhl.

The honor was bestowed to Alvin in recognition of his lifetime of service to the community. "Over the years Alvin has contributed much of his time and energy to improving the welfare of this city through such activities as the annual Halloween parade, the Christmas parade, and numerous other charitable promotions," said Mayor Pfuhl.

It was a big day for Alvin, complete with ribbon-cutting and a commemorative plaque...a day that meant a lot to the man for whom Glosser Bros. had always been so much more than a place of employment.

"Glosser Bros was not just a business but a place that my father considered home," remembers Diane. "He ate, slept, and walked Glosser Bros. 24 hours a day, seven days a week. It was his oxygen and meant everything to him."

Alvin passed away on Valentine's Day, 2012 from complications related to pancreatic cancer. But the echoes of the way he conducted his life, along with his business, continue to be felt today.

"My dad never raised his voice," says his son, Saul. "I never heard him swear. Even if he felt people wronged him at times, he never said a word. That's just the way it was. And he had a great sense of humor.

"That's what I remember most about my dad."

L. to R.: Bill Glosser, Leonard Black, Alvin Glosser, and Paul Glosser (photo courtesy of Bill Glosser)

Tribune-Democrat
THURSDAY

Study links suicide, Vietnam
Draft experience
2 A

Happy Birthday, Alvin Glosser

Singel gets nod for No. 2
Metro 1D

March 6, 1986 — Johnstown, Pa. — 25¢

Alley is renamed for Alvin Glosser

In recognition of a lifetime of service to the community, Mayor Herb Pfuhl officially renamed a Johnstown alley in honor of Alvin M. Glosser on his 63rd birthday Tuesday.

What was Good Place, a passage through the Glosser Bros. complex, will be known from now on as Alvin's Alley, according to the mayor's proclamation.

"From this day forward this fine thoroughfare known as Good Place, which Alvin passes through each day to work, shall be known as Alvin's Alley," the mayor proclaimed, while Alvin and fellow Glosser executives and employees looked on along the Franklin Street side of the store.

The dapper Mr. Glosser, known for his wry wit and pithy repartee, responded:

"Who's minding the store?"

"There are more people outside than inside."

> "From this day forward this fine thoroughfare will be known as Alvin's Alley."
>
> —Mayor Pfuhl

Then he joined the mayor in cutting a ribbon across the alley.

The mayor's proclamation noted that Alvin had been born in Johnstown March 4, 1923, the son of Saul and Eva Glosser; that on Oct. 28, 1956, he had married Joan Vertman; and that from this union came three children: Diane, Mindy and What's His Name (actually Saul).

"Over the years Alvin has contributed much of his time and energy to improving the welfare of this city through such activities as the annual Halloween parade, the Christmas parade and numerous other charitable promotions," Mayor Pfuhl said.

Norway snowslide kills 11

Oslo, Norway

The worst avalanche in Norway since World War II crashed down on its army ski patrol on NATO maneuvers Wednesday afternoon, killing at least 11 of the young draftees, police said.

No foreign soldiers were with the patrol, from the 2nd platoon of the army engineer corps near Elvegardsmoen Army Base, 22 miles north of Narvik.

6 missing

Narvik Police Chief Ivar L. Schroen, who is in charge of the rescue operation, said six soldiers were still missing Wednesday night, and 14 others survived with injuries.

Schroen told the Norwegian news Agency NTB late Wednesday that 31 soldiers, four more than originally reported by the army, were hit by the avalanche.

Schroen said on Norwegian radio station NRK that several hundred soldiers, six helicopters, civilian rescue teams and dogs were still searching for the missing soldiers through the night despite arctic darkness and strong wind that caused snowdrifts.

Lt. Col. Gunnar Mjell, information officer for the NATO winter exercise "Anchor Express," said injured soldiers were hospitalized in Narvik and Harstad, about 900 miles north of Oslo.

Reported by radio

NRK radio said surviving soldiers reported the accident by portable radio but that the connection had been so poor that the first reports were confusing and conflicting.

Sven Arne Simonsen, who survived with an arm injury, said on the radio that the first rescue team reached the scene one hour later. "It was terrible. I can't get over it. My pals are dead," he said.

Mjell said the maneuver in nearby Vassdalen was called off because of the accident. (AP)

Alvin and his alley

Throng observes special occasion

Contra aid rejected in its 1st tests

Washington

Two House panels voted Wednesday to recommend against giving $100 million to rebels fighting the leftist Nicaraguan government, President Reagan insisted that the money must be approved or the United States will not have to send "our own American boys" into the conflict.

The 9-2 vote by the House Intelligence Committee and 8-6 tally by the House Foreign Affairs subcommittee on the Western Hemisphere, both Democratic-controlled panels, were the opening salvos in legislative battles over the proposal. The issue, however, still must be considered by the full House and the Republican-controlled Senate.

Historic decision

The votes came shortly after Reagan said lawmakers faced "a historic decision."

None of the Intelligence committee's 10 Democrats voted against the proposal, with only Rep. Dan Daniel of Virginia joining with the Republicans. Despite the committee's opposition; however, the request for $70 million military aid and $30 million logistical aid must still go to the House floor.

The House Foreign Affairs subcommittee recommended defeat of Reagan's package in a strict party line vote.

Rep. Michael Barnes, D-Md., subcommittee chairman, said the two votes mean that "very likely the Reagan request will ultimately not succeed."

Earlier Wednesday, a House Democratic leadership task force issued a report contending that "U.S. policy toward Central America must be centered on diplomacy, rather than on the use of force or the quest for military victory."

However, at the White House, Reagan suggested that if the Congress does not support the rebels, called Contras, that decision could ultimately lead to use of American troops.

> The votes were the opening salvos in the battle.

"We must make sure they never are needed," Reagan told members of a Jewish organization. "We send money and material now so we will never have to send our own American boys."

"But if the members of Congress hide their heads in the sand and pretend the Nicaraguan threat will go away, they are courting disaster and history will hold them accountable," he said. "Nothing less than the security of the United States is at stake."

In an interview with reporters, Reagan reiterated he has no plans to send U.S. troops to Nicaragua, but said, "I don't go around shouting that because, frankly, while we have no intention of doing any such thing, it doesn't bother me at all if the Sandinistas go to bed every night wondering whether we're going to." (AP)

Cambria is shrinking

New York

A suburban Atlanta county was the nation's fastest growing county over the last five years, while Cambria County, Pa., was among the top 15 shrinking counties, according to a population study by a division of the Dun & Bradstreet Corp.

Cambria County, the site of the depressed industrial community of Johnstown, fell 4.2 percent to 175,693 on the list.

The study showed Georgia, Texas and Florida contained seven of the top 10 fastest growing counties. (AP)

4 killed as jets collide

San Clemente Island, Calif.

Two Learjets under contract to the Navy collided over the Pacific Ocean during radar training maneuvers on Wednesday, killing at least four people, the National Transportation Safety Board said.

The planes, owned by Flight International, were being used to help radar operators aboard the USS Gridley, a guided missile cruiser, learn to follow aircraft, said Petty Officer Rex Kramer, a Navy spokesman in San Diego.

"They (the planes) are the ships. They fly around and the radar operators say, 'There they are,'" Kramer said.

Searchers recovered some debris from the collision in waters about halfway between San Clemente Island and San Diego, about 60 miles to the southeast, but there was no sign of the planes' civilian crew members, he said. (AP)

Weather

Snow
High 30
Details on 1 D

INSIDE

News briefs	3 A
Opinion	4 A
Accent	1-5 B
Happenings	6, 8 B
TV	6 B
Comics	7 B
Sports	1-4 C
Scoreboard	4 C
Money	5, 6 C
Regional news	1, 2, 8 D
Obituaries	2 D
Classified ads	3-7 D
Lottery	8 D

© The Tribune-Democrat

Memory Department

Photos from Glosser Bros. Annual Report, Jan. 1977

GeeBee Mother's Day SALE
MENS' FAMOUS "RAPPER"
DENIM JEANS
8.77
MENS' FASHION COLOR PAINTER'S JEANS
7.88
MENS' SUMMER HAT RIOT
99¢
MENS' HANES® COTTON BRIEFS AND T-SHIRTS
4.79
4.97
Hanes®
MENS' SHORT SLEEVE FASHION KNIT SHIRTS
3.97
MENS' SHORT SLEEVE SHIRT SALE!
4.97
SHORTIE DRAPES
2.58
Famous Mills NO-IRON SHEETS
2.88
ANTIQUE SATIN INSULATED DRAPES
7.38
7.88
Famous Cannon "Santa Cruz" BATH TOWELS
2.88
COTTON QUILTED SPREADS
12.97
HIS or HER Print Polyester FILLED BED PILLOWS
4.28
CHATHAM ACRYLIC POLYESTER BLANKETS
5.97
Special Purchase
Famous Mills PRINTED COMFORTS
13.97
"Santa Cruz" 5 PIECE BATH SETS
8.44
Plaid Herculon Sofa and Chair THROW COVERS
60" WIDE SEEDED VOILE PANELS
32" and 42" DRESSER SCARVES
2 for $3
Printed Vinyl TABLECLOTHS
1.38
1.68
Striped Terry KITCHEN TOWELS
48¢
BROADLOOM RUNNERS
2.97
coupon
DACRON BATISTE TAILORED CURTAINS
WITH COUPON 3.18

GeeBee Mother's Day SALE
SUMMER NOVELTY KNIT TOPS
4.46 Each ONE GREAT PRICE!
SUMMER BLOUSES
4.46 to 7.76
FASHION SHORTS AT TREMENDOUS SAVINGS!
SAVE $1.21 on each pair!
3.76
SWIMWEAR SPECTACULAR
25% OFF
1 PIECE STYLES
2 PIECE STYLES
8.96
10.46
Great values at sun savings!
SUMMER SHELLS
3.96
4.46
Famous Maker SCOOTER SKIRTS
5.86
KNEE PANTS
3.46
SEERSUCKER SEPARATES
A Refreshing Summer Look!
SAVE OVER 20%
PANTS
SKIRT
SHIRT JACS
5.36
6.16
9.96

ANNIVERSARY
One Low Price
Buys A Lot
Of Style!
Trissi
SEPARATES
7.88
LADIES'
CO-ORDINATES
by
russ
50%
OFF
Use Our Convenient Layaway!
WALLETS and
ACCESSORIES
50% OFF
FAMOUS NAME WATCHES
25.88
Ladies' Famous
"TENNESSEE" HANDBAGS
5.94
Ladies'
DRIVING
GLOVES
2.22
Ladies' Folding
UMBRELLAS
2.66
EXPANSION BAND
WATCHES
9.88
L.C.D. DIGITAL
WATCHES
14.88

SALE!
Ready Monday 9 to 9
Tues., Wed., Fri. 10-5; Thurs. 10-9
SPECTACULAR
SAVINGS!
YOUR CHOICE
11.90
• VELOUR TOPS
• SUPER SWEATERS
• SOFT BLOUSES
All Perfect Quality!
VELOUR TOPS --
SUPER SWEATERS --
Lady Arrow® and
Ship 'n Shore®
BLOUSES --
Jovan Specials!
Cosmetic Specials

DON'T PAY MORE
SHOP Gee Bee SUPER SPECIALS
Gee Bee
SUPER MARKETS
STRICTLY FRESH
FRYING
CHICKEN
S-A-L-E!
DELI SPECIALS
MADE LOCALLY!
★ JUMBO BOLOGNA
★ PICKLE LOAF
★ OLIVE LOAF
★ CHEESE LOAF
99¢
FRYING
CHICKEN
LEGS
59¢
PICK of
the CHIC
89¢
Butcher's Trim
PORK
BUTT
ROAST
1.09
1.79
SAUER-
KRAUT
49¢
PORK
CHOPS
1.19
ARMOUR STAR
KULBASSY 1.69
GRAPE-
FRUIT
5 for 99¢
NAVEL ORANGES
TOMATOES
49¢
LARGE, SOLID, ICEBERG
LETTUCE
49¢
ONIONS
PEPPERS
MUSHROOMS
PRICES GOOD NOW THRU SAT., APRIL 26

THAN YOU HAVE TO...
EVERY WEEK AND SEE HOW MUCH YOU SAVE!
USE
ALL
3
SUPER
COUPONS
WITH ONE
$5.00
HEINZ KETCHUP
29¢
BOUNTY TOWELS
59¢
CALIFORNIA CARROTS
2
19¢
NO DEPOSIT...NO RETURN...2 LITER
★ COKE
★ SPRITE
★ TAB
★ FRESCA
99¢
Del Monte VEGETABLES
★ PEAS
WHOLE or CREAM
★ CORN
3 $1
Del Monte
FRUIT
COCKTAIL
49¢
POT PIES
FRENCH FRIES
1.39
FROZEN PIZZA
1.29
APPLE TURNOVERS
89¢
TOMATO
PASTE
CHICKEN
BROTH
TETLEY
TEA BAGS
1.69
IDAHOAN
MASHED POTATOES
LYSOL
BUNS

Photos from Glosser Bros. Annual Report, Jan. 1977

Chapter 28

The Age of Alvin

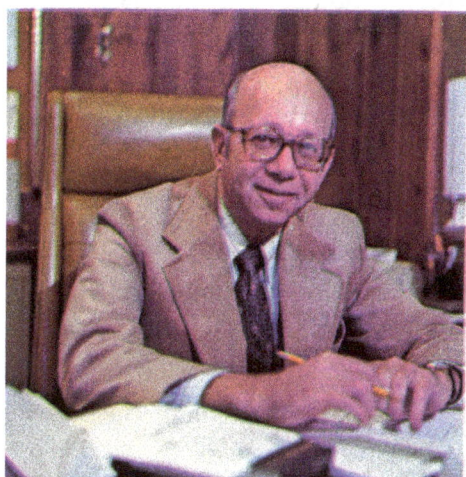

Photo from Glosser Bros. Annual Report, Jan. 1978

Imagine it's a sunny late-May morning in 1983, and you're watching the *Today* show on Channel 6, WJAC-TV in Johnstown. Willard Scott is hamming it up, as usual, with his corny jokes and birthday wishes to 100-year-old viewers.

The next thing you know, the show cuts from Willard to the studio, where host Jane Pauley introduces a story about a Buy American Festival in a Pennsylvania town. Jane starts talking to two guests on the set of *Today*... and you do a double-take. Maybe you even do a spit-take and lose your mouthful of coffee.

Because you recognize those two guests, don't you? And the town they're talking about is *your* town, Johnstown, isn't it?

One of the guests is the mayor of Johnstown, Herb Pfuhl Jr. He's telling Jane Pauley about the importance of buying American, and how the festival in Johnstown will help spread the word.

The other man does his share of the talking, too. And you know him as well as Herb Pfuhl, because he's nearly as famous a face around Johnstown. He's a top-level businessman in charge of a successful corporation that's listed on the American Stock Exchange.

And his name is Alvin Glosser.

The Road To *Today*

The *Today* show appearance was a milestone for Alvin--and Glosser Bros.--but it was hardly the only high point of his presidency up until then.

265

After taking office in February 1980, Alvin presided over two store openings in the course of a year. First, in April 1980, Glosser Bros. opened a Gee Bee department store in the Southland Shopping Center in Pleasant Hills, Pennsylvania. Shortly after that, a new Gee Bee department store popped up in Selinsgrove, Pennsylvania.

That made two new department stores in one year, on the heels of six new supermarkets the year before--a sure sign that the Glosser Bros. company was in good fiscal health.

Next, in September 1981, Glosser Bros. opened its first U Save Food Warehouse, the start of a new chain of no-frills supermarkets. This first U Save store opened in Greensburg, PA, in a building that until then had been home to a Gee Bee Supermarket.

U Save carried deeply discounted merchandise, purchased in volume from manufacturers and wholesalers. Brand names weren't always in stock, and selection was limited by whatever deals were available from suppliers at any given time.

U Save also kept costs low by slashing overhead--leaving out services like payroll check cashing and grocery bagging. It was a business model that in many ways was the ancestor of current discount chains such as Costco.

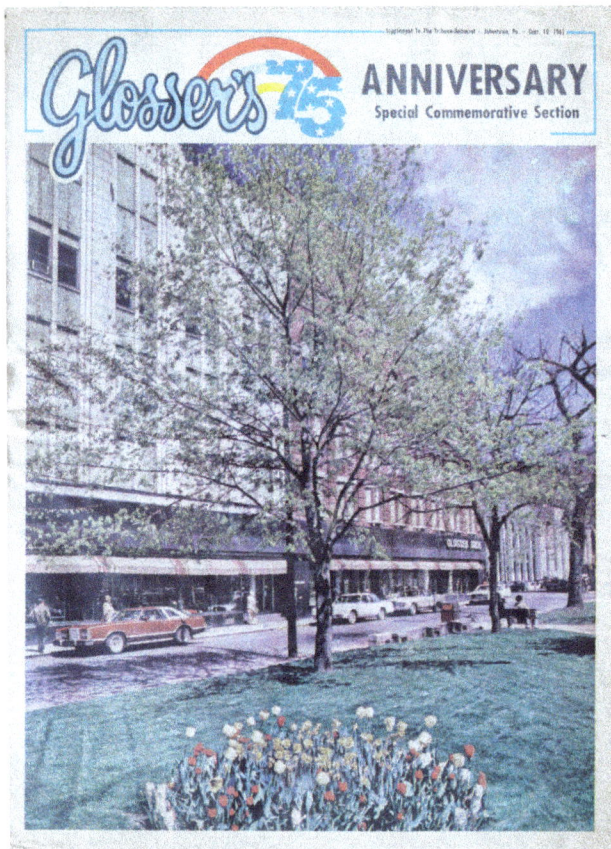

© The Tribune-Democrat

A 75¢ Breakfast Special in 1981?

The new store openings were a testament to the company's vitality as it celebrated a landmark occasion: the 75th anniversary of the opening of the Glosser Bros. Department Store.

As usual, Glosser's marked its birthday with a huge sale, promoted in plentiful newspaper ads and TV commercials. Gee Bee Supermarket gift certificates were raffled off to customers on Monday, September 14: five winners would receive $25 certificates at 6:45 p.m.; five more winners would walk away with $50 certificates at 7:45 p.m.; and five even luckier winners would take home $100 gift certificates after the drawing at 8:45 p.m.

The newspaper ad trumpeted, "It's Our Birthday, But You Get The Biggest Present Of All: SPECTACULAR SAVINGS!" Sure enough, there were lots of great deals in The Store, many featuring the number 75 in one way or another.

Many sale prices, for example, were rounded off to the nearest 75 cents. There was also a 75¢ anniversary breakfast special served until 11 a.m. including one egg (any style), toast and jelly, and coffee.

If shoppers wanted to stick around for lunch, they could enjoy a different 75¢ cafeteria lunch special each day. The week's 75¢ lunch menu looked like this:

Mon.: Egg salad sandwich & cup o' soup

Tues.: Spaghetti & 1 meatball, bread & butter

Wed.: Chicken Chop Suey, bread & butter

Thurs.: 1 wiener & sauerkraut, bread & butter

Fri.: Baked macaroni & cheese, bread & butter

Sat.: Baked ham w/pineapple sauce

Not bad for 75¢, eh? But the regular, non-75th anniversary prices were pretty good, too. None of them crossed the $2.00 mark. The highest, Chicken Chop Suey, had a regular price of $1.85. The least expensive was the egg salad sandwich and cup o' soup, at a mere $1.15.

Begin the Dollar Bargain

In October 1981, Glosser Bros., Inc. kept the 75th anniversary party going by launching a new Gee Bee Discount Department Store in the Manchester Mall in York, Pennsylvania. Also in October, the company rolled out the first store in a new chain--a Winners Ladies Off-Price Specialty Store located in a remodeled portion of the Pleasant Hills Gee Bee Department Store near Pittsburgh.

Another Gee Bee was christened soon after, in the Chambersburg Mall in Chambersburg, PA in March 1982. Two more U-Save stores also launched in Pennsylvania in '82--an Altoona location in February and a State College store in November.

Then there was the all-new Dollar Bargain Store chain, which also got its start in 1982. According to an annual report message to shareholders from Alvin and Leonard, "The concept of this store is cash sales of special purchase and close-out items at 'Nothing over $12.'" The first of these stores opened in Johnstown and served as a laboratory to test the viability of the Dollar Bargain concept.

A Plan for a Tough Economy

By 1982, Glosser Bros., Inc. was juggling *how* many discount merchandise and grocery chains? There were the Gee Bee Department Stores, of course, and Gee Bee Jr., plus Winners and Dollar Bargain. The supermarket division included the Gee Bee Supermarkets and U Save Food Warehouses. That added up to six groups, not even counting the original Glosser Bros. Department Store.

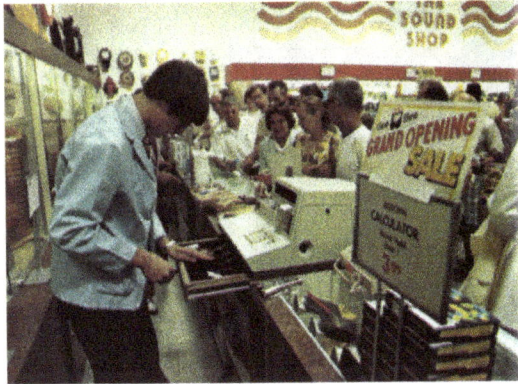

It was an aggressive growth strategy, especially given the grim economic conditions at the time. The country was in the midst of a widespread recession in the early 1980s, with rampant unemployment driving down consumer spending.

Glosser Bros. felt the squeeze in a big way during the 1981 fiscal year. The only record set by net sales that year was for the lowest percentage increase since the fiscal year ending January 29, 1972. The company still made money, but net sales only rose 4.3%, from $174,295,019 to $181,745,286.

The downward trend was discouraging, but not completely unexpected. What could you do as a retailer when unemployment was so high in your key marketing areas?

In Alvin's case, the answer was aggressive growth combined with targeted cost-cutting. That was why the company had so many chains and stores in play; losses from underperforming locations could be spread over a broader base and offset by gains elsewhere.

Photos from Glosser Bros. Annual Report, Jan. 1978

As Alvin himself wrote in the annual report for the year ended January 29, 1983, "Our merchandising requirements were tailored to the needs of the areas and economies served. Cost savings without reductions in efficiency were initiated.

"Energy control systems and new fixtures have been installed, along with the relamping of many of our stores to reduce our energy needs.

"Inventories were trimmed in all stores, and merchandise was purchased closer to the time of sale. Lower inventories meant increased turnover, and the ability to purchase special buys at considerable savings. Fringe items, normally a luxury, or that extra 'sale' item, were limited. Advertising programs were carefully screened for effectiveness."

Was the plan effective?

Could the expansion and cost-cutting possibly pay off in an era when Glosser Bros.' home town, Johnstown, was designated as the highest unemployment area in the United States?

The answer was a resounding yes.

Net sales in fiscal year 1982 were up a whopping *23.1%* over 1981's disappointing numbers--from $181,745,286 to $223,751,872. Not only had the company made up for the previous year's drop, but it had set a new Glosser Bros. record for net sales. It was also the highest percentage increase in net sales since 1973.

The plan was working, propelling Glosser's to new heights...and you know what that meant. More new stores would surely follow. Glosser Bros. wasn't about to stop growing anytime soon.

Though the possibility remained that the recession, if it deepened, might yet cause the company to lose ground. Unemployment in Johnstown stood at 24.6 in early 1983, with the potential to climb higher. The cycle of job loss leading to reduced consumer spending leading to more job loss could still create significant drag on Glosser Bros.' bottom line.

That was why local business leaders, including Alvin, came together in a series of brainstorming sessions to seek a remedy to the region's economic woes. One of the ideas that gained the most traction at these meetings was the creation of a Buy American Festival designed to encourage support of American-made goods over foreign imports.

Photos from Glosser Bros. Annual Report, Jan. 1978

Alvin said he got the idea while visiting Bloomingdale's department store in New York City during an American products promotion. "I said, 'I can improve on that,'" said Alvin in a newspaper interview. "You know, the town needs a lift. The merchants are down, the people are down and the unemployment rate keeps going up."

As part of the project, Alvin made sure that all American-made products at The Store were specially tagged and given extra attention in terms of display and marketing. He also bought Bloomingdale's own 27-foot by 34-foot red, white, and blue promotional banner and had it hung over Glosser's main entrance.

The first Buy American Festival was scheduled to run in Johnstown from May 11th through May 21st, 1983. According to Alvin, the event would feature crafts booths, balloons, music, and fireworks. The goal of the festival was to teach consumers and retailers that buying and selling American-made products was good for everyone in the local community.

Event backers quickly went to work making preparations, including getting the word out to the media on the local, regional, and national levels.

Photo from Glosser Bros. Annual Report, Jan. 1978

Local and regional news organizations had always been an easier sell--but there was national interest in those days, too. The recession was a big story, and Johnstown (the unemployment capital of the U.S.A.) was at ground zero. The battle over made-in-America goods versus foreign imports was a hot button issue that caught the eyes and ears of reporters and producers for shows like the nightly network news...

...or the *Today* show, whose staff was interested enough in the Buy American Festival to invite two of its chief boosters to appear live on its May 20th, 1983 broadcast.

Which is where we came in, remember...?

The Alvin Glosser Show

Let's return to the morning of that *Today* show broadcast once more. How cool must it be to see someone from Johnstown on such a popular national TV program?

Alvin Glosser is sitting right there, *right there* across from Jane Pauley. He is the ultimate local boy who makes good, a man from Johnstown--from *your* town--who is being watched by millions of viewers across the country as if he were some kind of celebrity.

Not only that, but he's making the case for Johnstown's interests in front of that national audience. He is putting the power of the media to work for you and all your fellow Johnstowners.

Maybe Johnstown will pull through the recession after all and come back stronger than ever. Things look grim, but maybe Alvin can help. It doesn't seem far-fetched, does it?

After all, he has that magical last name, doesn't he? The one from the store you've loved and trusted for your entire life, through good times and bad?

If anyone can help Johnstown, you've got to think it can't hurt to have a Glosser--and Glosser Bros.--in the picture.

MEMORY DEPARTMENT

I was hired as a part-time employee at the Gee Bee Department Store in Richland while attending high school at Greater Johnstown Vo-Tech in the early 1980s. I was enrolled through Vo-Tech's co-op program. I started out as a cashier and was quickly promoted to Ladies Sportswear. I remember coming in to work directly from school to find four rolling racks full of ladies' clothing which needed to be put away before closing time (which happened to be only a few hours away). This is where I learned how to work under pressure while remaining calm and yet muster an enduring amount of speed to complete the task at hand. I learned a lot from those days and have been successful throughout the years in my later endeavors. I am truly grateful for the opportunity and experience Glosser Bros gave me. Long Live Glosser's!

- *Carla Thomas Sorber*

When we had a family trip to Glosser's, my mom would shop, and my dad would buy popcorn and peanuts, and we would sit in the park and feed the pigeons. On Thursdays, my mom would take my sister and I to Glosser's to shop, and we would always look forward to eating in the cafeteria. I always had to get a dish of mushy broccoli...and a hot roast beef sandwich. I loved their teen floor when I reached that age. They always had cool clothes. When the store closed, my dad bought a display case from them. I think it was from the hat department. It is in my sister's basement.

- *Rebecca Siegrist Marsh*

I have memories as a very young kid, attending large family Passover Seders held in the store's cafeteria. But what stands out the most from those Seders was when the kids would leave the adults at the tables and run around the dark and quiet store, playing hide and seek or having elevator races.

Glosser's was like our own personal playground. And that extended to regular business hours. I knew people who worked in every department, and whenever we went to the store, I would go and visit my friends in the shoe department where they let me measure the size of my foot with an old metal measuring device; or I'd hang out with the ladies in the candy department, and they'd let me help them bag candy for customers. (Of course they'd reward me for my work with a few treats.)

But my favorite person to visit by far was Jackie, the seamstress. She worked in a room tucked back behind the children's department near the cafeteria, and she spent her days tailoring customer's clothing. Jackie would set me up on a sewing machine, with scraps of material, and let me sew lines into the fabric; or she'd let me help her press clothes with a giant clothing press that was frightening to watch at that young age for fear of getting burned by it. Jackie was such a warm and wonderful person, with a heart of gold. She always was interested in what I was up to and was happy to chat with me. I loved going to visit her.

The candy counter (photo courtesy of Kasey Hagens)

I think, looking back on it and thinking about Jackie and others...what I remember the most about Glosser's were the really warm and wonderful people who worked in the store.

- Greg Diamond (grandson of Sydney Ossip)

The store had an Annex where Christmas items were displayed, in addition to the second floor notions department. Mr. John Lipari was my first boss, and I would go to the Annex and work with setting up Christmas ornaments, light displays, and accessories.

- Paula Katie Buynack Becker

Photo from Glosser Bros. Annual Report, Jan. 1977

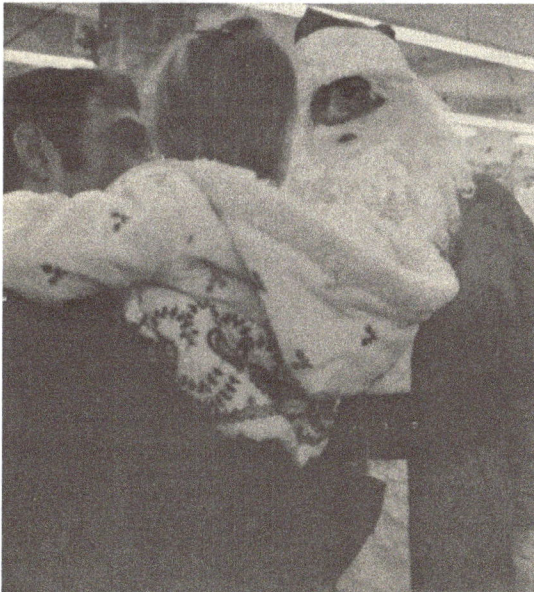

Photo from Glosser Bros. Annual Report, Jan. 1976

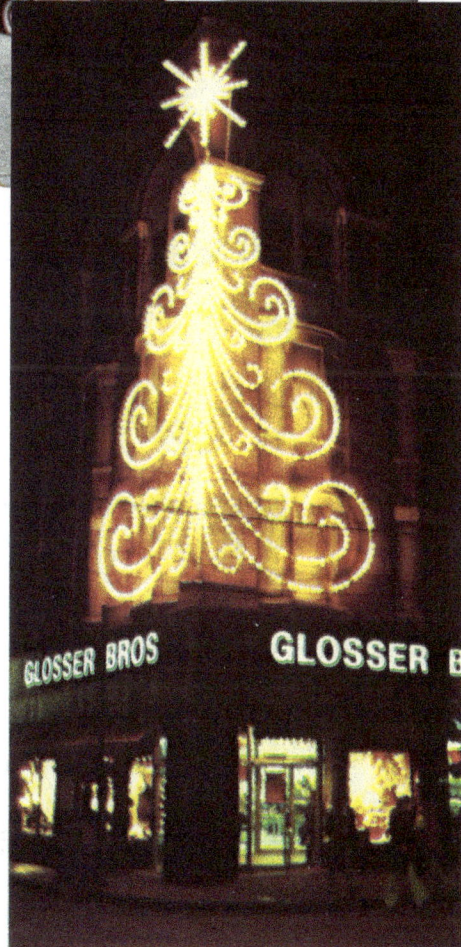

Photo from Glosser Bros. Annual Report, Jan. 1978

You Can Be A Lucky Prize Winner!
Glosser's
DOWNTOWN JOHNSTOWN
FREE! ALL-DAY METERED PARKING!
FREE! INBOUND BUS SERVICE FOR LADIES
LADIES' DAY
Saluting Great Women Of Show Business
THURSDAY ONLY
9 A.M. TO 9 P.M.
In Person: Rick Porter — Star of "Another World"!
9 A.M. RIBBON CUTTING
FREE! ALL-DAY METERED PARKING!
FREE! INBOUND BUS SERVICE FOR LADIES
EMPLOYEES IN COSTUME —
MYSTERY SHOPPERS —
with FREE GIFTS for You! Every hour on the hour — Watch for them!

Glosser's
DOWNTOWN JOHNSTOWN
LADIES' DAY
THURS. ONLY 9 to 9
rrrrrrruss
RUSS TOGS' VISA COORDINATES
SAVE 50%
NOW 6.98 to 13.98
Academy Award Winners
Ms. Chris Bittner President
Ms. Marcy Frank — Senior V. President
Ms. Kim Dick — Secretary-Treasurer
Ms. Evelyn Biber — Controller
Ms. Beth Korsh — Sales Promotion Director
Ms. Patty Macik — Advertising Director
Ms. Fritzie Shaffer — Store Manager

1906 to 1981 . . .
Glosser's 75 That's the Spirit!
Congratulations To Our Business Associate Of Over 43 Years
From Pepsi Cola Bottling Company Of Johnstown, Pa.
PEPSI 66
Catch The Pepsi Spirit
1915 to 1981 . . .
16
Pepsi
Pepsi-Cola
PEPSI

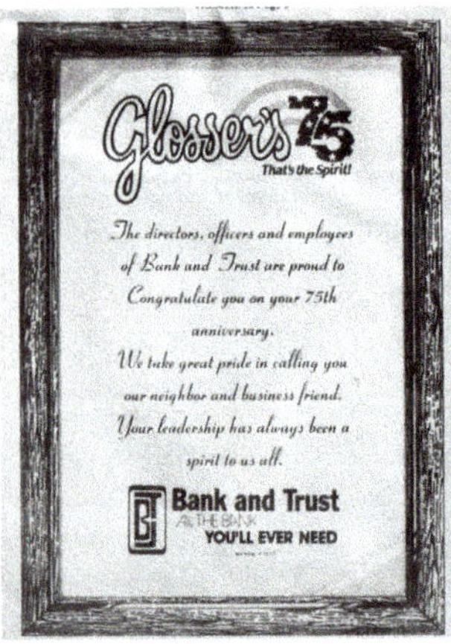
Glosser's 75 That's the Spirit!
The directors, officers and employees of Bank and Trust are proud to Congratulate you on your 75th anniversary.
We take great pride in calling you our neighbor and business friend.
Your leadership has always been a spirit to us all.
Bank and Trust
AT THE BANK YOU'LL EVER NEED

Old Friends . . .
We go back together
For 75 Years . . .
Let's go for 100.
Glosser's 75 That's the Spirit!
FOUNDED 1906
Sani-Dairy
FOUNDED 1902

SALUTING GLOSSER'S
For
75 YEARS
Of Service
J. PUMA CO., Inc.
709 Railroad St.
Johnstown, Pa. 15901
Phone: 536-8737
HAPPY ANNIVERSARY
AND CONTINUED SUCCESS TO OUR GOOD FRIENDS AT GLOSSER'S
DAVID BRETT, INC.
24-36 BINFORD STREET
BOSTON, MASSACHUSETTS 02210
GLOSSER'S and NCR
A Winning Combination Right from the Start!
Congratulations on 75 Years of Success
Best Wishes for the Next 75
In Greatest Appreciation
NCR
Retail Systems
Business Forms & Supplies
Field Engineering
355 Fleet St.
Pittsburgh, Pa.

Chapter 29

A Very Good Year

We almost never recognize the last perfect day while we're living it, do we? We don't realize until later, after things have changed for the worse, that there ever was such a thing.

Did Glosser Bros. have such a last perfect day? If so, it might have happened in 1984.

Flying High

When the year started, Glosser Bros. was flying high on its latest sales figures, which once again set a company record. Net sales for the fiscal year ending January 28, 1984 hit $252,879,770, a 13% increase over the year before. Net earnings for 1983 shot up 38.9% over the previous year, reaching a record $4,313,593.

To say the least, the numbers were impressive--especially considering that the economic recession wasn't quite over yet. Even in an economy that could still be characterized as tough, Glosser Bros.' strategy of cost-cutting and aggressive expansion was proving successful.

This wasn't to say there weren't a few adjustments along the way. At the end of June 1983, Glosser Bros. closed the Monroeville Gee Bee, citing declining sales volume and an oversaturation of the market in that area. "We view the termination of the lease as a positive step towards improving our net earnings," wrote Alvin and Leonard, "despite our natural reluctance to close one of our earliest locations."

There were other adjustments as well, such as moving the Winners store from Pleasant Hills to Altoona and converting the Gee Bee Department Store in Bethel Park to a Warehouse Outlet.

But these changes were only part of the big picture. Glosser Bros. was still bullish on expansion, opening new stores at a rapid clip.

The Dollar Bargain stores, in particular, were spreading fast. Between 1983 and 1984, Glosser Bros. only opened one new Gee Bee Department Store, an 80,000 square foot unit in the Fairland Village Mall in Pottsville, PA in July 1983.

But by March 1984, there were 13 Dollar Bargain stores, with five more on the way...and Glosser Bros. was actively studying new locations.

To keep these Dollar Bargain stores supplied with merchandise, Glosser Bros. rented and stocked a 30,000 square foot warehouse in the Geistown Cloverleaf, just off Route 56. This warehouse, located above the St. Benedict Church cemetery, was fully dedicated to the Dollar Bargain division. One hundred percent of the merchandise stored there was intended for distribution to Dollar Bargain stores across the region.

All in all, the company was in excellent shape. Profits were up, Dollar Bargain was booming, and shareholders were happy. Maybe the time was right to experiment a little, to take chances in search of diversification.

Maybe the time was right to try to break into broadcasting.

Geistown warehouse 2014 (photo by Philip Balko)

Glosser's, The TV Station

Had the *Today* show experience left Alvin with a new appreciation for television? After all, just a few months after his interview with Jane Pauley, Alvin and Glosser Bros. were in the running to start a new TV station in Johnstown.

Timing had more to do with it, actually. Glosser Bros. had applied for a TV channel license back in 1981, but the Federal Communications Commission (FCC) didn't render a decision until 1984.

Back in '81, the FCC had announced it would award a license for a new VHF TV station in the Johnstown area. Previously, the FCC had limited the proximity of TV signals in the region, and Channel 6 in Johnstown and Channel 10 in Altoona had cornered the market. But the new license, known as a "drop-in," would bend the rules just enough to carve out room for a third station, designated Channel 8.

When the Glosser Bros. team decided to go after the Channel 8 license in '81, they set up a wholly owned subsidiary called Laurel Television, Inc. to carry the ball forward. Laurel's officers were all Glosser Bros. directors or executives, headed by Louis Coppersmith in the president's chair. Herb Sinberg and Paul Glosser were named vice presidents of Laurel, and Bill Glosser was the new company's secretary-treasurer.

In its application for the license, Laurel said it planned to operate with a directional antenna on Laurel Hill, principally serving Johnstown and surrounding metropolitan Cambria County. Channel 8's signal would also reach Blair County, including Altoona, plus Bedford, Somerset, Indiana, and Westmoreland counties.

So how close did we come to having a Glosser Bros. TV station? Pretty close, actually.

Originally, four applicants had competed for the license--but the FCC dismissed one, leaving three in the running. After that, Laurel negotiated agreements that convinced the other two applicants to withdraw.

So by January 1984, it was all down to Laurel. An FCC administrative judge would decide whether to award the license to the sole remaining applicant.

On January 24, 1984, the judge announced his verdict...and the future of Glosser's TV looked grand indeed. In the judge's summary decision, he awarded a construction permit for a VHF TV station known as Channel 8 to Laurel Television.

Photo from Glosser Bros. Annual Report, Jan. 1983

The order became final on February 24, 1984, and Alvin and Leonard announced it in a March 1984 letter to shareholders. The stars seemed to have aligned; it seemed like it would only be a matter of time until local viewers would be watching a TV station owned by Glosser Bros.

But the station never happened. The project fell apart, and Glosser's TV faded to black forever. It could have been an exciting experiment with some very cool programming possibilities ("Glosser Twins Cooking Show," anyone?), but it just wasn't meant to be.

What The "GL" Stood For

At least there was one other broadcasting venture with the Glosser touch still on the air--a radio station owned by Fred and Betty Glosser. Though the station wasn't part of Glosser Bros., Inc., it shared the Glosser halo of success, attracting a sizeable young audience with an album rock format. It had been broadcasting in this format since Fred started it in August 1980, operating out of studios in the Landmark Building (which Fred and his wife Betty also owned) in downtown Johnstown.

You might have heard of it: WGLU, at 92.1 on your FM dial. Otherwise known as GLU 92.

Maybe you've wondered what the call letters stood for...but now you know. The "GL" in GLU 92 could only stand for one thing.

"Glosser," of course.

Stock Market Surge

Though the TV station bid fell through, Glosser Bros., Inc. continued to roar along, opening stores right and left and raking in tremendous net sales. The company continued to post dividends that kept its shareholders happy...and its performance by the middle of the year made them happier than they'd ever been.

Glosser Bros.' stock rose approximately 50 percent in value in a period of just a few weeks in mid-June 1984. Trading volume was relatively heavy at the time, as shares in Glosser Bros. soared.

Though the company was doing quite well financially at the time, that in itself might not have been enough to spur such an increase. Apparently, the main reason for the boost was speculation that a corporate takeover was in the works. Somehow, rumors had spread among investors that Glosser Bros. was being targeted for a buyout by another company.

Such buyouts were a fairly common practice in the mid-80s; in fact, the Penn Traffic company had nearly been drawn into one not long before the Glosser rumors. But the fact was, the speculation about Glosser Bros. was without merit.

Though, as is often the case, even the least accurate rumors can conceal a whisper of fact within them. A change to the stock status quo was in the wind for Glosser Bros....a *major* change. It would happen the next year, in 1985, and it would signal the beginning of the end of an era.

It would signal the beginning of the end of Glosser Bros.

L. to r.: Tom Zurilla, Bill Glosser, Fred Glosser, Alvin Glosser, Leonard Black, Herb Sinberg, Paul Glosser, and Sydney Ossip (photo © The Tribune-Democrat)

Memory Department

I worked at Glosser's for ten years, from 1975 to 1985. I went to airline school in Kansas, and after graduation, there was an energy crisis in the U.S., so I could not get a job in my field. As an alternative, I applied at Glosser's and got a job in the downstairs men's department. After I'd worked there for a few months, a buyer, Mr. Jess Ehrlich, told me he was looking for an assistant. That started my career as a buyer.

I started working with Mr. Ehrlich in women's daytime dresses and maternity. I was young and single, so I knew nothing about these areas, but learned quickly. Soon, Mr. Ehrlich decided it was time for me to go to New York for my first buying trip. Alvin Glosser, who was president of Glosser Bros. at the time, okayed it, and off we went.

I soon moved from assistant to getting my own departments. I was one of the youngest buyers for the company, in fact. During my career, I bought Better Dresses, Junior Sportswear, Large-Size women's clothing, and for a short time filled in on Bridals. I traveled with other buyers, usually in a company car (Glosser's owned a fleet of Oldsmobile 98s), and we drove to New York City. I also went to the Los Angeles market two times a year. In addition, I was required to visit my departments at the Gee Bee stores a couple days a week.

I had no formal merchandising schooling, but what I learned from the buyers for this wonderful family-owned company was not in a textbook. I truly worked my way up and gained valuable hands-on experience.

Fast-forward to 1985. One of my manufacturers in New York knew of a large company in Southern California that was looking for a buyer. Since I had such a good reputation with Glosser's, I got the interview, the job, and moved to Long Beach, California. Two years later, I learned that Glosser's had closed.

- *Chris Bittner-Italiano*

My mother worked in the credit department. When I was nine months pregnant with my now-26-year-old daughter, I got stuck in between floors on the elevator. I was on my way to meet my Mom to have lunch in the cafeteria when it happened. Needless to say, everyone was worried about me...but everything turned out okay.

- *Stephanie Vyhonsky Forosisky*

In 1980, I was promoted to the general merchandising manager of the hardlines division, which included housewares, hardware, automotive products, electronics, and furniture. This gave me an opportunity to see the other side of the business, and I enjoyed it immensely. It was much different than softlines, and I worked in that position until leaving Johnstown in late 1987. In the years that I worked at Glosser's, I saw big changes occurring due to the advent of the computer, specifically personal computers. We had always had our sales figures computerized at the store level, but in the early 80s, each buyer began to run their businesses almost totally by the computer. Our purchase orders were developed on the computer, and all inventories were totally managed by it. I worked hard to adjust to this new retail science, and by the time I moved on in late 1987, I was able to take advantage of some of the expertise that I had learned from my experience at Glosser/Gee Bee stores. By that time the company had expanded to 30 discount department stores, 25 dollar bargain outlets, and many supermarkets, and all of this growth had given me the opportunity to gain invaluable experience.

- *Jeff Diamond, Glosser Bros. employee 1966-1988 (and son-in-law of Sydney Ossip)*

There was once a promotion that Glosser's did where they mailed you a card. On the card was a discount. You went to the counter to make your purchase, the clerk scratched off the card (it might have been rub off, I don't remember now) and you got a discount. A kid got one in the mail. He held it up to the light and saw that the discount was 100%, so he went to the store and loaded up with electronics, etc. When they rubbed of the discount, of course it said 100%. The kid fessed up, though, and they still gave him some free stuff.

- *Becky Marie Glacken Buchko*

I worked for a buyer in the men's department, my mom worked for Alvin, my grandma was manager of layaway, and my great aunt worked in layaway. It was a family tradition to work at Glosser Bros.
- Lisa Tennis-Hughes

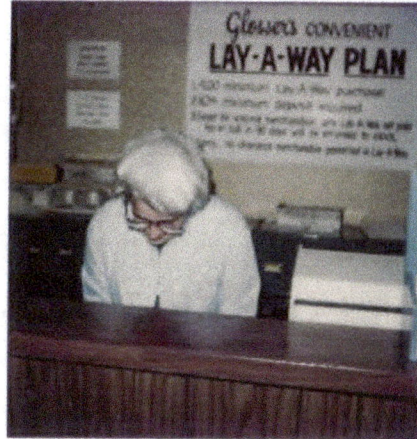

Photo courtesy of Jill Glosser

Photo from Glosser Bros. Annual Report, Jan. 1976

Photo from Glosser Bros. Annual Report, Jan. 1976

Photo from Glosser Bros. Annual Report, Jan. 1978

Gee Bee
SUPER MARKETS
SEE THE DIFFERENCE GENERICS CAN MAKE ON YOUR FOOD BILL!
Shopping With Us Has Its Rewards...
Exquisite Fine China
99¢
USE ALL 3 SUPER COUPONS WITH ONE $5.00 or more FOOD PURCHASE
CLOROX BLEACH 79¢
HI-DRI TOWELS 44¢
SLICED BACON 1.19
PEPSI
8 1.39
BEEF SALE!
ROUND STEAK
1.79
PRUNE PLUMS 29¢
KIDNEY BEANS 3 1.09
SOMERSET PARKHILL EBENSBURG WESTMONT NANTY GLO BENSCREEK RICHLAND WALNUT ST. OSBORNE ST.

OVER 300 WAYS TO SAVE
Gee Bee GENERICS
THERE'S A LOT BEHIND THE BLACK & WHITE LABEL
USE ALL 3 SUPER COUPONS WITH ONE $5.00 or more FOOD PURCHASE
Gee Bee KING SIZE BREAD 39¢
White Cloud BATHROOM TISSUE 99¢
MEDIUM YELLOW ONIONS 49¢
★ PEPSI (REG., DIET, LIGHT) ★ MT. DEW ★ HIRES ROOT BEER
8 1.39
OODLES of NOODLES 4 $1
CHAMP DOG FOOD 3.59
APPLE SAUCE 59¢
Potato CHIPS 99¢
GRAVY MIXES 6 $1
KRISPY
PIE CRUST MIX
QUICK OATS 69¢
Yogurt
SOMERSET PARKHILL EBENSBURG WESTMONT NANTY GLO BENSCREEK RICHLAND WALNUT ST. OSBORNE ST.

Gee Bee Jr.
Free Parking
Starts Today
GRAND OPENING SALE
5.97 MEN'S VELOUR SHIRTS
8.88 MEN'S HEAVYWEIGHT DENIM JEANS
3.97 BOYS' FLANNEL SHIRTS
4.97 MEN'S FLANNEL SPORT SHIRTS
$5 BOYS' WESTERN 4 PKT. JEANS
B.V.D.® DRESS SOCKS
$25 WRANGLER JACKETS
12.88 MEN'S COACH COATS
4.77 MEN'S WESTERN SHIRTS
OPEN 10 A.M. TO 10 P.M. Lyter Drive - Westmont

Gee Bee Jr.
FREE PARKING
Starts today
GRAND OPENING SALE
7.88 VELOUR TOPS
20% OFF ENTIRE SELECTION OUTERWEAR
7.88 WRANGLER® JEANS
6.88 COWL NECK SWEATERS
8.88 2-WAY STRETCH PANTS
One Week Only.
20% OFF DRESSES
5.66 PANTSUITS
USE OUR CONVENIENT LAYAWAY
OPEN 10 A.M. TO 10 P.M. Lyter Drive - Westmont

Chapter 30

End Times

It's complicated. That might be the simplest way to describe what went wrong with Glosser Bros., Inc.

There seem to have been many contributing factors, but how much or how little they played a role in the company's demise is hard to say.

There are plenty of theories around. Each might hold a grain, or many grains, of truth. But who can determine, 25 years later, which one carries the most weight?

For the purposes of our story, let's stick with the events that were best documented...those that were presented in the media.

And the words of the company president at the time. The words of the *last* president of Glosser Bros., Inc.

Risky Business

Little did Tom Zurilla realize, when he went to work for Glosser Bros. in 1971, that he would someday be president of the company. Little did he imagine that he would preside over Glosser Bros.' last days, and that he would be the one who would have to turn over its assets to another owner.

Born in Cresson, Pennsylvania in 1947, Tom worked at Price-Waterhouse in Pittsburgh after college...then went to work at Glosser Bros. in '71 as Chief Financial Officer (CFO).

"Tom loved it at Glosser's," says his wife, Anne Zurilla. "He loved the challenge of helping a company grow and develop."

Photo courtesy of Anne Zurilla

Tom served as CFO under Leonard, then Alvin. He was with the company for the good times, the great times...and then, the bad.

283

According to Tom, the trouble started with a risky business maneuver in the mid-80s. "In October 1985," he wrote in a 1989 letter to employees (after he'd become president), "Glosser Bros. was taken from a public corporation to a private company through a leveraged buyout which required the assumption of a very large debt."

Bill Glosser, who was also part of the company in the mid-80s, explains further. "There were six branches of the Glosser family who owned stock in the company, some more than others. They were getting modest dividends, and some family members decided it was time to cash out. They wanted to retire from the business, and a leveraged buyout seemed like a good way to make that possible."

To boil it down, the family members would get the money they wanted by selling their stock back to Glosser Bros., Inc. Glosser Bros. would pay for the stock with money borrowed from the investment banking firm Bear Stearns & Co. Then, Glosser Bros. would pay back the loan with future revenues, using the company and its assets as collateral (the "leverage" in "leveraged buyout").

Photo from Glosser Bros. Annual Report, Jan. 1983

It seemed like a simple plan, didn't it? The board of directors went along with it, and the stockholders approved it. There was just one catch: Glosser Bros. had to consistently bring in enough revenue to make the payments on the loan.

So guess what happened.

Glosser Bros. Is Falling Down

First off, a disagreement broke out within the family over the terms of the buyout. Bill Glosser opposed the structure of the plan and presented an alternative plan that required less debt...but it was rejected by the board of directors.

And so was Bill. "I was fired," he says. "I lost my company car and my key to the men's room."

It wasn't the end of the disagreement, though. The opposing factions ended up embroiled in a lengthy court battle.

Meanwhile, Glosser Bros., Inc. continued to post strong earnings. Alvin and his team kept up the push to build new stores, especially now that they had to keep revenue high to make the payments on the loan from the leveraged buyout.

Gee Bee Department Stores opened in Hazleton, Pennsylvania in 1985 and Manassas, Virginia and Meadville, PA in 1987. At the same time, the Dollar Bargain rollout continued to pick up steam. From 1985 through 1988, new Dollar Bargain stores sprouted up in numerous locations, everywhere from Gettysburg, PA to Fairmont, West Virginia to East Liverpool, Ohio.

Dollar Bargain seemed unstoppable. It was growing faster than any division in the company. By all rights, it should have been the salvation of Glosser Bros., Inc.

But it turned out to be the opposite. By 1988, Dollar Bargain had become part of the perfect storm that was taking down Glosser Bros.

Tom Zurilla, in his 1989 letter to employees, wrote, "Last year we began to experience serious difficulties due to store expansion in certain areas, inventory problems in the Dollar Bargain Division and the rising cost of money due to increased interest rates."

In spite of everything Alvin and his colleagues had done to keep Glosser Bros. roaring forward, the company was having money troubles by 1988. Tensions, which had never really gone away after the court battle, continued to rise.

Then, finally, they came to a head.

The Dark at the End of the Tunnel

On the surface, things looked good for Glosser's in early 1988. The company opened a new Gee Bee Department Store in Harrisonburg, Virginia in March and a second Gee Bee store in York, PA in April.

More Dollar Bargain stores launched that year, too, pushing the total over 40...ever closer to the 50-unit mark.

Things looked pretty good from the outside looking in. Most people probably had no idea there was any kind of strife going on at Glosser Bros., Inc.

But the numbers on the balance sheet told a very different story. Glosser Bros. was having serious cash flow problems...so serious that the company was having trouble making the payments on its leveraged buyout loan.

If something didn't change fast, Glosser Bros. would default on the loan, and drastic measures would be called for. Then, Glosser's might have to do the same thing that an average person sometimes must do when he or she can no longer pay the bills.

The company might have to file for bankruptcy protection.

Photos © The Tribune-Democrat

Thanks to tremendous customer acceptance, we're opening our 24th Dollar Bargain Store in 2 years!
GRAND OPENINGS
• Gettysburg
• State College
• Meadville
• Fairmont, W. VA
• Youngstown, OH
• East Liverpool, OH
Anniversary Sale
OUR PRICES ARE THIS LOW EVERYDAY!
•Manufacturer's Closeouts
•Manufacturer's Overstocks
•New Items Arriving Daily
•Special Buys
•Factory Odd Lots
•Prices in effect while quantities last
MEN'S & LADIES' WINTER OUTERWEAR
Assorted styles, fabrics and colors.
Selected slight irregulars.
$12
THE DOLLAR BARGAIN STORE
You'll pay $1, $2, $3, but seldom more than $15.

Affordable family fashions.
MEN
WOMEN
GIRLS
BRAXTON® DESIGNER STRETCH JEANS FOR THE FAMILY
MENS LADIES $12
GIRLS $10
ACTIVEWEAR FOR THE FAMILY!
MEN'S & LADIES' SWEAT TOPS $7
MEN'S & LADIES' FLEECE PANTS $5
CHILDREN'S TOPS $3
CHILDREN'S PANTS $4

Fashions priced right everyday!
LADIES' FASHION COORDINATES
WOMEN'S FULLER FIGURE COORDINATES
ALL FIRST QUALITY!
SKIRT $5
PANT $5
BLAZER $10
$8
$10
BLAZER $14
$3
$2
$1
$1
$3
$3
$2
LADIES' SWEATERS $5
MORE SWEATERS $8
LADIES' WOOL PLAID SKIRTS $8
MISSES' BLOUSES $5 and $6

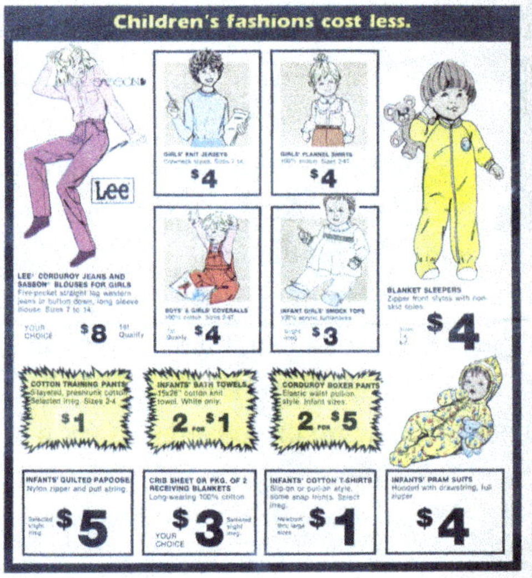
Children's fashions cost less.
Lee
$4
$4
$8
$4
$3
$4
$1
2 FOR $1
2 FOR $5
$5
$3
$1
$4

Great buys for men and boys!
MEN'S V-NECK SWEATERS $5
HEAVYWEIGHT SWEATERS FOR MEN AND BOYS $7 $8
MEN'S PLAID FLANNEL SHIRTS $5
MEN'S & BOYS' JEANS $6 $10
BOYS' THERMAL SHIRTS $4
Your Choice
•QUILT-LINED FLANNEL SHIRTS
•CORDUROY OR DENIM JEANS
$12
BOYS' CASUAL CORDUROYS $7
BIG MEN'S SIZES HOODED SWEATSHIRTS $12
MEN'S & BOYS UNDERWEAR $3
MEN'S & BOYS' CASUAL HOSE 2 FOR $1
MEN'S THERMAL TUBE SOCKS $1
MEN'S RIB V-NECK SHIRTS $2

Dollar for dollar, we've got more!
BIG SAVINGS
5 FOOT CHRISTMAS TREE
$12
HOLIDAY TREE GARLAND 2 FOR $5
CHRISTMAS WRAP $1
$2
HOLIDAY TRIMMINGS 2 FOR $1
CHRISTMAS CANDLES $2
CHRISTMAS CARDS $3
4 FOR $1
$1
3 FOR $1
THE DOLLAR BARGAIN STORE

SAT. 8 A.M. TO 10 P.M.
GLOSSER'S BIGGEST SALE EVER!

FREE 3-HOUR PARKING IN BOTH GLOSSER LOTS AND BOTH CITY GARAGES ALL DAY SATURDAY AND SUNDAY WHILE SPACE IS AVAILABLE

MANUFACTURERS BUYOUT!
FOAM-BACKED TEXTURED DRAPES

60% OFF AND MORE ON MANUFACTURER'S SUGG. RETAIL PRICES

12⁸⁸ PAIR

SPECIAL PURCHASE!
FOAM-BACKED SOLID COLOR **INSULATED DRAPERIES**

6⁹⁷ PAIR

YOUR CHOICE

BLANKET BONANZA

PRINTED PATTERNS **5⁵⁸**

SOLID COLORS **4⁵⁸**

SUPER VALUES!
Toasty, Warm Electric Blankets

Twin Single Control **19⁸⁸**
Full Dual Control **27⁸⁸**
Queen Dual Control **34⁸⁸**

COZY COMFORTERS AND BEDSPREADS
• TWIN • FULL • QUEEN
YOUR CHOICE
14⁹⁷
Reg. $19.97 to $26.98

DOMESTICS—SECOND FLOOR

THOMASTON MILLS' NO-IRON SHEET SETS **5⁹⁷** TWIN SET
COORDINATED FLANNEL SHEET SETS **8⁹⁷** TWIN SET
EVOLUTION BED PILLOWS **1⁸⁸** EA. STANDARD SIZE
FAMOUS MILLS BATH TOWELS **2⁸⁸**
LION BRAND JIFFY YARN **98¢**

Chapter 31

A Tragic Accident

Glosser Bros.' luck was turning bad, it seemed, and just kept getting worse. A cloud of misfortune seemed to hang over the company, bringing danger to its dealings...

...and, in June 1988, tragedy to several of its employees.

Wendy Dolges and Dottie McAlister

It all started when four female buyers set out for Pittsburgh in a leased station wagon. The women, all in their 30s, often traveled together for Glosser Bros., Inc., buying merchandise for the Dollar Bargain Stores.

On the morning of June 23, 1988, they were going to Pittsburgh on another Dollar Bargain buying trip. The skies were cloudy, and a light rain was falling; it seemed like just another June day in Western Pennsylvania.

Joyce Strushensky and Barbara Bienkowski

None of the four women could have known the tragedy that awaited them.

Wendy Dolges--Wendy McKee back then--was a passenger in the car. She remembers with painful clarity what happened next. The station wagon was traveling in the southbound lane of the Menoher Highway, about 300 feet north of the Cambria-Somerset county marker on Route 271. The time was approximately 9:15 a.m.

"As we entered the S-curve on Route 271, we saw a coal truck heading toward us," says Wendy. "The truck lost control on the rain-glazed road."

Photos courtesy of Wendy Dolges

Photo courtesy of Wendy Dolges

The truck's rear end swung into the southbound lane, and the station wagon was directly in its path. When the truck slammed into the station wagon, the driver's side of the car was instantly crushed.

"After that, there was just silence," recalls Wendy.

When emergency responders arrived, they pronounced the driver of the station wagon, Barbara Bienkowski, dead at the scene. Dottie McAlister, a passenger in the car, was taken to Conemaugh Valley Memorial Hospital, where she died in surgery.

Wendy's injuries were relatively minor, but the other passenger, Joyce Strushensky, was not quite so lucky. She was admitted to the intensive care unit of the hospital in serious condition with injuries to her head and spine.

Aftermath

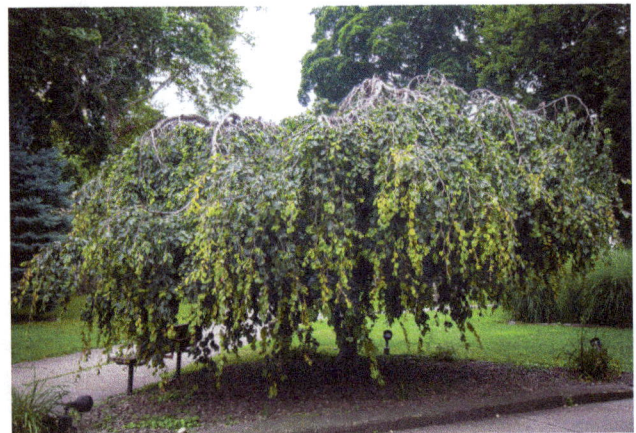

Photo by Philip Balko

The loss of her two friends left Wendy reeling. "The four of us had traveled together extensively," she says. "We'd gone on monthly buying trips to New York City and other areas when the need arose.

"We'd worked hard and always looked out for one another. Now two of us were gone."

But Wendy and Joyce were not alone in their grief. "There was an outpouring of support from the entire Glosser's family," remembers Wendy. "When you worked for Glosser Bros., you were part of one big family. When you lost somebody, it was like losing a family member."

The support extended throughout the Johnstown community, as well, and all the way to New York City. "As buyers, the four of us had met with hundreds of vendors on our monthly trips. Many of them reached out after the crash and extended their condolences."

The most lasting tribute came from Glosser Bros., Inc., though. In honor of Barbara and Dottie, the company planted a weeping cherry tree on the Locust Street side of Central Park in downtown Johnstown. The tree stands to this day, facing the Glosser Building across the street.

"The memorial tree was planted with thoughts of comfort, peace, and caring," says Wendy. "It's a living monument to the wonderful women we lost in the accident, women I still miss and think of often."

Photo by Philip Balko

Memory Department

There is no place like a department store in December. As I found out later in life, a substantial amount of family purchases happen in a few weeks at the end of the year. After a year of extending hamburger with a "helper" or adding a few extra cans of water to the frozen orange juice, it feels great to declare savings over and reach for the joy found in purchasing something that brings a smile to someone you love. From 5th Avenue in New York to Franklin Street in Johnstown, Pennsylvania, we open our pocketbooks and make former dreams into gifted realities. We all agree that there are not enough hours in December to get it all done. We pack elevators, squeeze past each other at doors, and even race into parking lots. We try to cram it all in.

One wintry day, a car zoomed into the tight little parking lot behind Glosser Bros. Department Store, intent on beating another customer to the entrance, just as I, the lot attendant, was backing a car out of a narrow two-deep car stack. That situation brought me into a "polar vortex" of turbulent December emotions. When metal met metal, a howl of pained protest arose that sounded primeval.

As an attendant in the Glosser's parking lot, my goal was to efficiently meet the time demands of potential shoppers in a very challenging environment. The lot was arranged to maximize the capacity of parked cars. This meant that there were multiple cars parked one in front of another in very narrow lanes. They were described as a "double stack" for two cars or a "triple stack" for three deep.

This productive arrangement meant that getting at least half of the cars out for a returning customer involved moving another car first. Once that blocking car or cars were moved, a long, narrow slot was created for backing the front car out. We did not allow the customers the opportunity to get their own car out of one of those narrow lanes. Backing out, perfectly straight with very small clearances on each side with falling snow was just not possible for a driver with normal skills. We were the proud car jockeys of Johnstown, who could pass the backup test that made us a valuable part of the Glosser's staff.

During the first few weeks of working in the parking lot, I took great pains to slowly perform the difficult backup procedure. Slow was not ideal. But, scraping another car's side was not acceptable with one of the owners watching the maneuver. Happily, after a week of parking hundreds of cars, my eyes and reflexes allowed me to get just about any sized car out of the narrowest of lanes quickly with no problem.

The normal spaces at the Glosser's parking lot were difficult. The spaces near the entrance with cars zooming into the lot from the street added a deeper layer of danger. Adding to the narrow space problem, varying widths of cars, frosted windows, skewed parking angles and vans to the sides, were the aggressive drivers darting in from the street. And then there was often a light dusting of lake effect snow on the back window of the car. The one-handed hand swipe of the rear window made for a very limited rear view. Backing out of those front spaces into active drive lanes, with inexperienced drivers sliding in, required a level of awareness that exceeded my skill.

The driver whose car I hit was no doubt on a mission to get a toy for his child or fragrance for his wife. Undoubtedly, he was cutting it close and knew that his most likely path to rapid gift-giving success was to be found in the sprawling floors of Glosser's Department Store. Through my narrow hand swipe of rear window snow, I looked back and did not see him. Suddenly, he was behind me. With foolish confidence, I was moving too quickly to stop on the hard-packed ice. I heard that crunch of metals colliding. I knew the result was not going to be pretty. When I heard the expletive from the customer, I knew that my day was about to go downhill.

He ripped open his door and glared at his crunched fender. He had the ferocity of a deeply wronged man who now knew that some of his limited December hours were going to be spent on a car repair. He towering frame said, "I make steel. You just bent my steel." His clenched fists required an immediate response. Somebody was going to have to pay for this. I knew that my usual calming smile was not of much use at this point. I kept out of swinging range. As instructed, I told the wronged man that we needed to "Call the Office." Those words did not do much to calm him. He just kept glaring at me, kicking the snow and snorting a pained growl.

It only took a few minutes, but it seemed like an eternity. The horns were blaring on Washington Street as shoppers could not imagine what event was blocking the entrance to the parking lot. Shoppers coming out of the store with packages waited in clusters. They milled about and kept their distance from the wronged man who kept muttering about idiots who ought to watch where they backed a car.

At last, the door by the receiving area at the rear of the five-story emporium opened. In an elegant long dark cloth coat stood Mr. Sydney Ossip, comptroller of Glosser's. He walked with steady assurance across the black ice of the parking lot. As he approached, you could see the assuring concern in his noble carriage and feel the winds around the turbulent vortex subside. The wronged customer offered no hand. But, Mr. Ossip exuded a presence that was overwhelmingly calm.

Photo from Glosser Bros. Annual Report, Jan. 1978

I stood a few feet away and knew that the storm had passed. In a short and sure phrase, he said that the problem was to be "fully covered by Glosser's." No questions on fault. No equivocations. No doubts. He simply made a reassuring statement taking full responsibility.

In an instant the Steel Man was placated. He was certainly not happy. But, he was satisfied enough that he went in to do some shopping. He did not look at me, but handed another attendant the key to park his car.

Photo courtesy of Ellen Ossip Sosinski

Like all of Johnstown, he knew that the word of an executive from Glosser's was the best assurance in town. He also knew that the best place to make his purchase was Glosser's. Like most of Johnstown, he was no fool.

The story might end there, but from my own standpoint, the story was certainly not over. If it was going to cost the store money, somebody was at fault. Mr. Ossip certainly needed to "manage" things and be sure that blame was assigned to the guilty party. I was certain that my job was at risk. Maybe my pay was going to be forwarded to the victim? Instead, Mr. Ossip turned to me and simply said, "Accidents happen." No recriminations, no blame, just an assuring comment. I kept parking cars and made it through the remainder of that stress-filled December with no accidents. I did move a bit slower, though.

I was very lucky that about five years later, I got to marry Sydney's daughter, Ellen Ossip. Along with Ellen, I got to enjoy 39 more years of being with Sydney at the eye of many storms until he passed in July of 2014 at the age of 97.

I've heard that he was calm at the end.

- *Tim Sosinski*

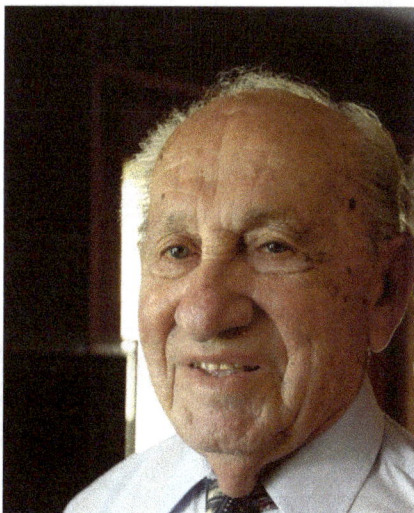

Photo courtesy of Ellen Ossip Sosinski

JUST SAY CHARGE IT! GLOSSER'S VISA MASTER CARD DISCOVER
SAT. 8 A.M. TO 10 P.M.
GLOSSER'S BIGGEST SALE EVER!
Ladies' Winter Outerwear
Selected Group! WINTER COATS AND SUITS
30% OFF AND MORE!
OVER 1,500 COATS
•ANNE KLEIN •MISTY HARBOR •FORECASTER •MACKINTOSH •DONNY BROOKE •TRILOGI •FREDDI GAIL •INTERNATIONAL SCENE •SUITS GALORE •FLEET STREET •PLUS MANY MORE!
$48
40% OFF AND MORE!
FULL LENGTH WOOL COATS
$84 TO $95
Glosser's

AND SUN. 11 A.M. TO 5 P.M.
20 SENSATIONAL HOURS — DON'T MISS IT!
Ladies' Winter Coats
FOUR FABULOUS GROUPS
50% OFF AND MORE!
Glosser's
FULL LENGTH LUXURY DESIGNER COATS
•HARVE BENARD •J. HOOK •MACKINTOSH •TRILOGI •GALLERY
50% OFF AND MORE!
SPECIAL GROUP
$110 TO $140
mackintosh
LADIES' 100% WOOL PANTCOATS
50% OFF AND MORE!
SPECIAL GROUP
$85 TO $90
50% OFF AND MORE! GENUINE LEATHER TRIM WOOL PANTCOATS
49.90 SPECIAL GROUP!
50% OFF AND MORE! WOOL AND WOOL BLEND BLAZERS
SPECIAL GROUP
29.90

JUST SAY CHARGE IT! GLOSSER'S VISA MASTER CARD DISCOVER
SAT. 8 A.M. TO 10 P.M.
GLOSSER'S BIGGEST SALE EVER!
BLACK&DECKER Small Appliance Bonanza!
Your Choice 11.97 EACH
Your Choice 19.97 EACH
BLACK&DECKER
Great Gift Ideas! PRESTO® APPLIANCES
9.97
14.97
34.97
"Country Design" PROCTOR-SILEX® APPLIANCES
19.97
14.97
WORLD FAMOUS HOOVER® VACUUM CLEANERS
Your Choice 59.97 EACH
HOOVER® SPIRIT™ POWERNOZZLE CLEANING SYSTEM
149.97
Glosser's

AND SUN. 11 A.M. TO 5 P.M.
20 SENSATIONAL HOURS — DON'T MISS IT!
MICROWAVE SAVINGS!
SAVE $70
SAVE $90
YOUR CHOICE 99.97
TOASTMASTER® MICROWAVE OVEN
With Turntable
99.97
CHEFTRONIC® MICROWAVE OVEN
99.97
Sunbeam® Express Meals™ Toaster Broiler Microwave Oven
169.97
Emerson® Refrigerator
87.97
FOREMOST® UTILITY CART
Perfect for your microwave!
$39
Your Choice ARMSTRONG® UTILITY CARTS
$39
Glosser's

Chapter 32

Under the Bus and Behind the 8-Ball

The Glosser Bros. family had suffered a terrible loss when two of its buyers died in a car crash in June 1988. But as the year wore on, a disaster of another kind, which had started months earlier, continued to take shape.

The company was still slipping financially, to the point that it was struggling to make the payments on its loans from the leveraged buyout. And there was no end in sight.

If something didn't change soon, Glosser Bros. might end up doing something it had never done before: defaulting on its debts.

The time had come to throw someone under the bus.

As the severity of the situation became increasingly apparent, the Glosser Bros. board of directors decided that drastic measures were necessary. If the company were to survive, they had to take some kind of action.

And they would start, as directors of companies in trouble often do, by cleaning house. They would get rid of the man in charge.

In November 1988, the board of directors voted to remove Alvin Glosser as president of Glosser Bros., Inc. Just like that, his eight-plus years at the top came to a screeching halt. His overall career at Glosser Bros., which spanned four decades, had come to an end.

Alvin was replaced by Glosser Bros. CFO Tom Zurilla, who immediately assumed the responsibilities of president. At the time, he must have known he was stepping into a minefield...but did he know just how bad things would get? Did he have any idea that he would be the last president the company would ever have?

More likely, he thought he could still save it somehow. Because in the months to come, and long after that, he kept working to bring the company around, one way or another.

Even as it slipped through his fingers like a handful of sand.

The Writing on the Wall

Tom and his team worked into the early months of 1989 on possible solutions. They met with advisors, researched options, crunched and re-crunched the numbers, and tried to think outside the box.

They worked with Bear Stearns & Co. "to explore various strategic alternatives," wrote Tom, "including the development of a business plan for future operation and restructuring of the Company's indebtedness."

But finally, they realized their efforts were in vain. By March 1989, time had finally run out. Glosser Bros., Inc. was no longer able to make the payments on the leveraged buyout loan.

At that point, all the possibilities had narrowed down to one. The board of directors voted, and the company's fate was set in stone.

Once the board had made its decision, Tom issued a letter to employees at the Glosser Bros. Department Store, dated March 27, 1989. "Due to present financial conditions and debt requirements," he wrote, "it has been

Photo courtesy of Anne Zurilla

determined by the Board of Directors to seek reorganization under the provisions of Chapter 11 of the Federal Bankruptcy Laws."

Not only was the company's fate set, but that of the downtown department store, as well. Glosser's had survived two floods, a Great Depression, and a constantly changing climate in retail merchandising...but it had finally reached the end of the road.

"As a part of the reorganization process under Chapter 11," wrote Tom, "several stores which are no longer economically feasible to operate will be closed, including the department store in downtown Johnstown.

"It is with deep regret and disappointment that I must inform you that the Glosser Bros. Department Store, located at Franklin and Locust Streets, Johnstown, PA, will close permanently at the end of the business day, Saturday May 27, 1989. Consequently, it is necessary to terminate your employment as of that day. Employees do not have transfer rights to other locations.

"I realize that this announcement comes as a great shock to you, particularly those who have spent many years with Glosser's and have faithfully served our loyal friends and customers.

"Arrangements will be made in the near future to assist you with pension eligibility, application for social security benefits, unemployment compensation and other related matters, during the period until closing," wrote Tom.

The story hit the newspapers the next day. The headline on the front page of *The Tribune-Democrat* read: "Glosser's closing downtown store," with the subhead "185 employees will be affected."

According to the article, Glosser Bros., Inc. had sales of $212,000,000 in 1988 and employed 2,500 people. One of those employees, 28-year Glosser's veteran Evelyn Mikas, was quoted as saying, "I can't believe it. It really was a shock. It brought tears to your eyes."

In the same article, Tom Zurilla said, "We are disappointed that we could not come to an agreement with our lenders. We do expect that we can operate profitably in Chapter 11 and continue implementing the restructuring initiatives begun last year."

Perhaps the company would survive, but the die was cast when it came to the store. Glosser Bros. Department Store, founded in 1906, was going to close in 1989, and there was nothing anyone could do about it.

Or was there?

© The Tribune-Democrat

2A The Tribune-Democrat, Tuesday, March 28, 1989

News in brief

at a prison farm in Guatemala on Easter, demanded an airplane Monday to take them to Cuba, a prison official said. At least seven people were killed — four guards and three inmates — and 21 were injured when 75 to 100 inmates seized much of the overcrowded prison farm Monday.

Machete attack — A mob with machetes attacked and seriously wounded seven U.S. missionaries in Haiti after a pickup truck carrying the Americans accidentally ran over two Haitians, Radio Haiti-Inter reported Monday. In Washington, a State Department official put the number of Americans injured in the Sunday incident at 11.

Rebuked — The White House on Monday rebuked C. Boyden Gray, President Bush's legal counsel, for raising an embarrassing challenge to a new agreement with the Congress on Central America. Gray suggested that the accord dilutes the constitutional powers of the president.

Prison standoff — Inmates who hold 426 hostages, most of them women and children who were visiting jailed relatives

Glosser's is closing its downtown store

Continued from 1 A

Oust-Mikula petitions

Continued from 1 A

Store thrived on novel approaches

Continued from 1 A

Glosser's started to advertise "The Largest One-Floor Store Between Pittsburgh and Harrisburg" in 1921, when it took over the entire first floor of the Franklin Building.

© The Tribune-Democrat

Tuesday, March 28, 1989

A tragic setback for Johnstown retailing

The decision by Glosser Bros., Inc., to close its downtown department store this spring is a devastating blow to the central business district.

For the 185 full- and part-time employees — many of them long-time workers — whose economic future has been dependent on Glosser Bros.' well-being, the closing brings deep and troubling uncertainty.

It will be difficult to overcome this setback, but the community cannot allow it to halt what's been great progress downtown.

Johnstown has been able to overcome seemingly insurmountable setbacks in the past; the community now must muster its collective energies to overcome this one.

Glosser Bros. has been a cornerstone of the downtown retail community for decades, and has anchored the city's retail trade since Penn Traffic Co. decided not to reopen its downtown store following the 1977 flood.

Meanwhile, Glosser Bros.' decision to file for reorganization under Chapter 11 of the Bankruptcy Code means the impact of the company's financial problems will be felt over a wide area, including Ohio, West Virginia, Maryland and Virginia.

While we regret bankruptcy action by any business, this one is particularly regrettable because of Glosser's dominant role in the downtown's resurgence.

It also was envisioned as the centerpiece of downtown retailing during this important flood centennial year.

It's hard to imagine downtown Johnstown without Glosser Bros.

Unfortunately, no hope was held out by Glosser officials that the store can be saved. By May 27 its doors will close for the last time.

Meanwhile, the full impact of the Chapter 11 filing remains to be seen: the company's announcement indicates that eight to 10 stores in the Gee Bee and Dollar Bargain divisions will be evaluated for possible future closing.

Glosser's operates 23 Gee Bee, 44 Dollar Bargain and two Gee Bee Jr. outlets, including at least four in the Cambria-Blair County area.

It's troubling that so many years of optimistic expansion have suddenly been halted by such unfortunate circumstances. No doubt many people felt that the

Glosser Bros. has been a cornerstone of downtown retailing for more than eight decades; for its 185 employees, economic uncertainty lies ahead.

Glosser-Gee Bee-Dollar Bargain names would eventually become household names throughout the eastern United States and possibly beyond.

Despite the setback, the current actions presumably will stabilize the company and eventually enable it to operate on solid financial footing once again.

But it won't be the same without the bustle at the corner of Franklin and Locust streets. The loss of a friend and neighbor after 82 years is never easy.

Can another retailer be found for the Glosser building?

Will the Glosser closing have any impact on Penn Furniture Co.'s plans to return to the downtown?

Will the Glosser action produce any changes in plans or strategy by businesses such as Meyer Jonasson Co. and the Step-In shoe store, both of which had set April opening dates for their downtown stores?

What about other businesses that may be pondering whether to move to the downtown or close?

It's imperative that Johnstown Area Regional Industries, Inc., and the Downtown Retail Division of the Greater Johnstown Chamber of Commerce begin working on the problem immediately. Likewise it's important for governmental officials to cooperate with the business community in making the negative impact from the Glosser closing as temporary as possible.

"To emerge from Chapter 11 successfully we need your help," wrote Thomas Zurilla, Glosser's president and chief executive officer, in a memo to vendors and landlords.

To emerge from the Glosser closing with the minimum amount of damage, Johnstown will need to do many things right.

Once again, the community must be up to the challenge.

Chapter 33

The Plan to Save the Store

"It was the unhappiest day of my life." That was how Bill Glosser described the announcement of the closing of Glosser's Department Store to *The Tribune-Democrat*.

Though Bill had been cut from Glosser Bros., Inc. in 1985, he still had a soft spot in his heart for The Store. Even as the company moved forward with plans to close it, releasing employees and shipping merchandise to other stores, Bill moved forward with his own plan to save it.

Photo courtesy of Jill Glosser

He was determined to do everything he could to keep Glosser's open, and he thought there might still be hope that he could help make that happen. He even thought he might find support within the Glosser Bros. organization. The decision to close the store was not unanimous, he told *The Tribune-Democrat*. He believed there were members of the board of directors who would still like to see Glosser's stay open in downtown Johnstown.

By the end of the week, five days after the closing announcement, Bill was meeting with local business and community leaders in his law office on Main Street to set the wheels in motion. Bill knew, given the situation, that he had to move fast, or it would be too late.

During that meeting, Bill spoke with representatives from the City of Johnstown (including Mayor Herb Pfuhl), the Greater Johnstown Chamber of Commerce, Johnstown Area Regional Industries, Inc. (JARI), and the Greater Johnstown Committee. He mapped out his plan, got the input of those attending the meeting, and resolved to forge ahead as soon as possible.

The key to the plan would be convincing Glosser Bros.' creditors to try to persuade the bankruptcy judge to keep The Store open. If the judge decided it was in the best interests of the creditors not to close Glosser's, he might order Glosser Bros., Inc. to stop the shutdown.

"The bankruptcy judge has it in his power to keep the store open," Bill told *The Tribune-Democrat*. "I want people who are creditors to stand before the court."

To give this part of the plan a chance of success, Bill would have to hire a bankruptcy lawyer in Pittsburgh to work on the case. The lawyer would facilitate presentations by members of the creditors committee to Federal Judge Bernard Markovitz, who had been assigned to the case.

Bill's goal was to convince the court to order the store to stay open until at least the end of the year. That would give Bill and his team the time they needed to seek a buyer for The Store.

If Bill managed to keep Glosser's open downtown, he hoped to increase business by changing The Store's focus back to selling lower-priced merchandise. He told *The Tribune-Democrat* that he wanted to return Glosser's to the days of being "Everyone's Store--Famous for Savings."

Turn It Upside Down

"We're going to turn this town upside down to keep Glosser's operating," Bill told *The Tribune-Democrat*.

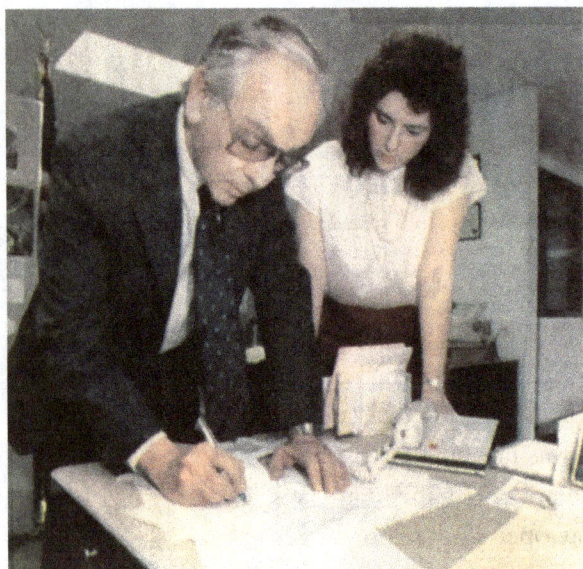

Photo © The Tribune-Democrat

In the weeks that followed, he did indeed push himself and his network of contacts and supporters to the limit. He reached out to members of the creditors committee, seeking support in making a case to Judge Markovitz. He asked local residents to sign a petition being circulated by the Greater Johnstown Chamber of Commerce. And he met with potential buyers, trying to drum up interest that would lead to a sale of the endangered store.

His efforts looked like they might pay off in April 1989 when he found a local buyer who seemed like a perfect fit. But the deal fell apart by the end of the month.

Bill wasn't ready to give up, though. When the buyer backed out, Bill started setting up his own limited partnership to purchase The Store. He would need time to pull it all together, but he was confident Judge Markovitz would give it to him.

Bill's belief in this impending reprieve stemmed from sales increases he predicted in coming months. For one thing, Johnstown was celebrating the centennial of the 1889 Flood, meaning there would probably be an increase in visitors--and tourist dollars--to Glosser's. Another boost would likely come during the third and fourth quarters, which were traditionally best part of the fiscal year for retailers. Increased sales would mean bigger payments to creditors, which Bill thought Judge Markovitz would want to see happen.

Bill also thought the petition would make a difference, along with letters of support from law-makers. By late April, Markovitz had already received letters from U.S. Sen. John Heinz, state Sen. William Stewart, and Lt. Gov. Mark Singel.

Still, the announced closing day for The Store--May 27th--was fast approaching. As much as Bill wanted to believe his plan would work, he knew the chances of success were dwindling with each passing day.

With each passing moment, Glosser Bros. Department Store got closer to the end.

The Last of the Glosser's Parades

By April 29, 1989, the petition to save The Store had 13,745 signatures. Bill hoped to have 50,000 signatures by May 12th, the date he had set for the end of the petition drive. He would present the signed petition that same day to Judge Markovitz at a hearing to determine the fate of Glosser's.

Bill planned to mark the occasion with a rally and parade. "It will either be a Save Glosser's rally or a We Saved Glosser's rally," he told *The Tribune-Democrat*.

The Greater Johnstown Chamber of Commerce was sponsoring and organizing the event, de-signing it for maximum impact. Scheduled speakers included Mayor Pfuhl, Cambria County Com-missioner Kathy Holtzman, state Sen. William Stewart, and Chamber president Ronald Budash. Edward Kane, chairman of the Chamber's retail division, would serve as the master of ceremonies.

As for the parade, it would feature the Bishop McCort High School marching band, a fleet of antique cars, and, hopefully, lots of supporters.

It was an ironic idea. Glosser Bros. had been holding parades downtown since the early days--all the way back to the 1920s, at least. Glosser's had used parades to mark anni-versaries, to draw attention to special sales, and to celebrate holidays.

Now, a parade was being planned in The Store's darkest hour, to help save it from a doom that seemed inescapable.

The Community Needs The Business

"Going Out of Business Clearance Continues...," said the full-page Glosser's ad in the May 7, 1989 edition of *The Tribune-Democrat*. "40% OFF ENTIRE INVENTORY."

Even as Bill Glosser and his supporters tried to keep The Store alive, the company that owned it proceeded with efforts to close it down. Glosser Bros., Inc. told *The Tribune-Democrat* that it had received an application of interest in purchasing the store from Bill's group of investors, but that alone was not enough to prevent the closing. The only way Glosser's would stay open after May 27th was if "a definitive agreement to sell the store is entered into by that date."

301

As the days zipped past, it seemed the company was sticking to its guns. By May 11th, a full-page Glosser's ad in *The Tribune-Democrat* trumpeted "50% OFF ENTIRE INVENTORY."

Meanwhile, the Save Glosser's petition kept gathering names, and Bill got ready for the Friday rally and parade, followed by the meeting with Judge Markovitz.

How would the meeting turn out? Could Glosser's Department Store still be saved?

On the morning of the meeting, *The Tribune-Democrat* published a story with the headline, "Glosser's: Most are skeptical." The piece quoted a former store official as saying "I think he (Bill Glosser) is just blowing smoke." The same official said that Bill was giving false hope to Glosser's employees and trying to play on the sympathy of the bankruptcy court.

In the same story, Bill said he knew that some people had doubts and questioned his motives, but "I could care less. Talk is cheap."

Bill insisted he was trying to save Glosser's "for the good of the community and to make the life of his father and brothers meaningful."

"The community needs the business," said Bill. "The business needs the community."

Raining on the Parade

It was raining in downtown Johnstown on the morning of May 12, 1989...raining hard enough by 8 a.m. that the organizers of the rally and parade decided to cancel both events.

It wasn't exactly the high-powered lead-in Bill had imagined for the hearing that day. The parade would have passed the Federal Building in time for Judge Markovitz, who would be inside, to see it before the hearing. Now, the big demonstration of local support would be nonexistent.

But that was all right with Bill. He was ready to make his case.

When the time came, Bill presented two petitions on behalf of one of Glosser Bros.' creditors, Conrad Wholesale Co., Inc. In the petitions, Conrad, a Johnstown-based candy distributor, asked that Judge Markovitz order Glosser Bros., Inc. not to close the downtown store.

In addition to those documents, Bill handed over the Save Glosser's petitions, which by then included more than 17,000 signatures.

The formal motion, however, would not be made until the middle of the following week in Pittsburgh. Bill would have to wait at least until then to find out what the judge would decide. The people of Johnstown would have to wait at least that long to find out if Glosser's would live or die.

In the meantime, another full-page Glosser's ad appeared in *The Tribune-Democrat*. This time, it read, "60% OFF OUR ENTIRE IN-VENTORY."

Photo © The Tribune-Democrat

302

The Waiting Game

At the May 17, 1989 hearing in Pittsburgh, Bill made a motion that asked Judge Markovitz to keep The Store open at least until the end of the year. Doing so "...would preserve the asset and make it available for sale to a third party interested in acquiring the same and continuing to operate."

Then, when the hearing was over, there was nothing to do but go home to Johnstown and wait. It would take some time for the judge to make his decision.

Would there be anything left to save when he finally did, though? The shelves at Glosser's were being emptied fast as shoppers took advantage of the deep discount clearance sales.

And as the days raced past, the discounts got even deeper. On May 21st, Glosser's full-page ad in *The Tribune-Democrat* announced "70% OFF ENTIRE INVENTORY."

Still, there was no word from Judge Markovitz. Still, Bill was constantly on pins and needles, wondering how the decision would go.

And then, when he finally found out, he might have wished he could have waited a little longer.

Seven Pages, Eighty-Three Years

By Thursday, May 25th, Glosser's merchandise had been stripped to the bone. The upper floors of The Store had been picked clean and closed; only the ground floor and part of the second floor were still open.

By then, the fate of The Store seemed inevitable. How could Glosser's possibly come back after being reduced to a shell of its former self?

Only Judge Markovitz knew the answer...at least until that Thursday, when a clerk in the bankruptcy court released the judge's decision to the public.

In the space of seven pages, Markovitz sealed Glosser's fate forever. He ended whatever hope there had been that the 83-year-old department store could somehow survive its latest trial.

According to the judge's written opinion, it was not feasible to keep The Store operating any longer. He denied Conrad Wholesale's motion to force Glosser's to stay open through at least the end of the year.

The miracle that Bill--and Glosser's 185 employees--had been hoping for had not come to pass. Bill's grand plan had failed. Even in the face of defeat, though, Bill refused to surrender. "I'm going to explore every other avenue," he told *The Tribune-Democrat*. "I'll have to see the decision and see if it's economically feasible to keep the store open."

But by that point, Bill had already played his best cards. He had thrown his hand down on the table...and lost the game.

A sign went up at Glosser's, announcing that the cafeteria would close to customers for good at 5 p.m. Thursday. The final menu included grilled pepper steak, breaded veal with tomato sauce, and roast chicken with filling.

It would be open the next day for one last meal, a free lunch for employees. And that would be the end of it. The cafeteria--and Glosser's entire department store--would close forever at 5 p.m. on Friday, May 26th, 1989.

The Tribune-Democrat

25¢ Friday, May 26, 1989 Johnstown, Pa.

Judge: no Glosser's stay

By Jeff McCready
The Tribune-Democrat

Judge Bernard Markovitz has denied a motion by Conrad Wholesale Co. Inc. to keep Glosser Bros.' downtown department store open at least through the end of the year.

Glosser Bros., which is reorganizing under Chapter 11 of the Bankruptcy Code, announced at the time of the March bankruptcy filing that it would close its 82-year-old downtown store

by May 27.

William Glosser, a Johnstown lawyer and former store executive, then began an effort to keep the store open. The effort included asking people to sign petitions and the Conrad motion.

Conrad, a Glosser creditor, is located at 111 Adams St.

A clerk in the bankruptcy court reported that the approximately seven-page opinion said, in essence, that it was not feasible to keep the store op-

● Downtown retailers to offer longer hours
— Metro 1 C

erating.

The store, Johnstown's only department store, will close Saturday.

"I'm going to explore every other avenue," Glosser said Thursday when informed of the decision. "I'll have to see the decision and see if it's eco-

nomically feasible to keep the store open."

Glosser had hoped that the judge would order the store to stay open to give him time to put together a limited partnership to buy the business.

The Conrad petition argued that the

store should not be closed at a time when tourists will be coming to town for the flood centennial.

Each day, there has been less merchandise in the store. By Thursday, only the first and part of the second floor were open.

What's left is being sold at 70 percent off the lowest ticket price.

A sign said that the second-floor cafeteria would close permanently at 5 p.m. Thursday.

Lunchtime patrons were saying their goodbyes and thank yous to the staff, some of whom have worked there for years.

Grilled pepper steak, breaded veal with tomato sauce and roast chicken with filling were on the final menu.

The cafeteria will be open today, but only to serve employees a free lunch.

It will be closed Saturday, the final day for the store.

Chapter 34

The Last Day of the Glosser bros. Store

What was the last item sold at the Glosser Bros. Department Store? Who was the customer who bought it? Who was the cashier who rang it up?

No one seems to know anymore. All that matters now is that there *was* a last item sold, and a final customer.

And then Glosser's was gone.

It had had a good run, all the way from 1906. It had fallen and risen again and again, like Johnstown itself. It had been a gathering place, a shelter, an institution, and the greatest show in town. In so very many ways, it had been a *home*...and now, that home was finished.

Friday, May 26th, 1989 was the end of its era.

One Last Cup of Coffee

The closing actually happened a day earlier than Glosser Bros., Inc. had originally announced.

Maybe it didn't matter. Maybe it didn't make that much difference in the grand scheme of things that The Store closed on May 26th instead of May 27th.

Or maybe it just made it that much tougher to take. Maybe it made it that much harder for the employees and patrons who already had precious little time to say goodbye.

Still, they did the only thing they could, going through the last scenes of the tragedy together. They smiled sadly, they shook hands, they hugged, they laughed, they cried. They reminisced about days gone by and wondered how the good times had gotten away from them so fast.

Some customers had said their goodbyes earlier, avoiding the sadness of the last day. Those who'd wanted one last visit to the cafeteria, for example, had had to come Thursday, the last day the cafeteria was open to customers. One of those final cafeteria visitors, Albert Zawallah of Upper Yoder Township, had come for one last cup of coffee after having one in the cafeteria every day for the past 50 years.

Chances are, he might have nursed that last cup of coffee and had a refill or two.

One More Time Together

Glosser Bros. employees gathered in the cafeteria on Friday for a free lunch, courtesy of the company. It was a somber occasion, as men and women who'd spent so much time together through the years came together once more to share a meal.

When would they all be together in the same place like that again? Maybe never, though people talked about staying in touch and keeping up friendships.

Soon enough, the last of the lunch guests trickled back to their work stations in The Store, leaving the cafeteria employees to clean the place up...one last time.

Leaving them to share their own memories and hopes and regrets as the little world in the Annex they'd known so well for so long continued to darken around them.

Hunt Room Mary Locks Up

After the last meal had been served, one of the managers handed a set of keys to Mary Schuster--aka Hunt Room Mary. "He gave me the keys to the Hunt Room, the freezers, everything," remembers Mary. "He said, 'Give the girls anything they want, get rid of everything, then lock up.'

"So that was what I did. The employees in the Hunt Room and cafeteria took all the food that was left, so it wouldn't go to waste.

"I gave the window curtains to the girls, too," says Mary. "The manager had given me the clock off the wall and a special plaque, so I took those myself."

When the place was empty, Mary did as she'd been told and locked it up. Then, trying not to think about how much her life was about to change and how hard it would be for her, she handed the keys to the doorman and walked off down the street.

The Last Shopper

Who was the last shopper to walk out of The Store? Did he or she stop on the way out and turn for one last look around? Did he or she brush away a tear at the thought that it was all coming to an end forever?

Who closed and locked the front door the last time? Who turned out the lights and walked off into the shadows, footsteps echoing across the deserted ground floor?

Maybe, when that last person was gone, the lights flickered up once more, and the past came to life again. Who's to say it didn't?

Maybe the big room filled with bustling shoppers again, shoppers from all the years, all the ages of The Store, mingling in a giddy, ghostly swirl.

Maybe holiday music filtered from the P.A. system, and the sound of laughter rippled through the shimmering air. Maybe the display windows flowed like kaleidoscopes with Halloween paintings and Christmas decorations--maybe even a monkey or two.

Maybe it all danced and swirled for a while, a gossamer calliope of price tags and cellophane and starlight. Maybe the elevators rose and fell of their own accord, doors opening and closing to admit spectral passengers. Maybe the escalator returned, built of silvery moonbeams and mist, carrying customers up and down, up and down.

Maybe, in the heart of it all, four men stood and smiled, surveying the scene...four familiar faces, four brothers from Antopol. Maybe they smiled wistfully, or proudly, or sadly, arms around each other's shoulders, eyes glistening more brightly than any of the flickering, otherworldly lights that spun and twinkled like pinwheels through the room.

And then, maybe a car's headlights blazed through the windows, dispelling that glorious whirl of times gone by like dust in a Johnstown wind.

Leaving only the sweet smell of roasting cashews to linger in the air within those silent walls.

Photo courtesy of Johnstown Area Heritage Association

12 A   The Tribune-Democrat, Saturday, May 27, 1989

Glosser Bros. Department Store
1906   1989

Thanks
for the
memories
We'll miss you

The Glosser Bros. store in 1906 featured a varied selection of men's, women's and children's clothing.

Shoppers took advantage of 70 percent savings during the store's final days.

The "Glosserteria," added in 1916, is believed to have been the nation's first self-service supermarket within a department store. It marked Glosser's entry into the food business.

Jeff McCready
The Tribune-Democrat

Glosser Bros.' downtown store on Friday went the way of Penn Traffic and Gable's.

Johnstown's lone department store passed into history at the close of business Friday. The store follows the Penn Traffic Co., which closed its Johnstown department store after the 1977 flood, and the William T. Gable Co., which closed its Altoona department store in 1980.

Glosser's, too, has become only a memory.

What long-time resident doesn't remember the smell of popcorn, the rides on the escalator or eating in the store cafeteria? Many recall shopping in the store's food market.

The second-floor cafeteria was a gathering place at lunch time. Until the end, there was spaghetti on Tuesday and fish on Friday.

The friendly, familiar faces of long-time employees helped to make the store what it was.

The Shaffer twins, Ruby and Ruth, had been waiting on people at the second-floor soda fountain since 1951. Their late father, Edward, was a night watchman at the store.

Mothers took their children to Glosser's to buy school clothes. Shoppers flocked there for Old Fashioned Bargain Days and other promotions for which employees, dressed for the occasion, would be waiting on customers inside as well as outside the store.

And who can forget Christmas shopping at Glosser's?

In the days before shopping centers and malls took their toll, shoppers would trudge through the downtown snow looking for that special gift.

Glosser's almost always was one of their stops.

The store bustled with activity as children, their faces beaming, looked at toys or greeted Santa Claus.

For years, Glosser Bros. made possible Johnstown's Halloween parade. Glosser family members always were there to play an active role in the community.

The decision to reopen the store following the 1977 flood was perhaps not a sound business move. But the Glosser family knew what the store meant to the city and did not want to abandon the downtown.

Glosser's, organized as a partnership in 1906, was incorporated in 1946. It had gone from a one-store operation to one that today consists of Gee Bee Discount, Gee Bee Jr. and Dollar Bargain stores in five states.

It remained a family-operated business until 1985 when it went private through a leveraged buyout. Glosser stock had been traded on the American Exchange.

The buyout brought in outside interests and split family members.

Financial problems developed and in late March the fears of many became reality — Glosser Bros. filed for reorganization under Chapter 11 of the bankruptcy code and announced that it would be closing the downtown flagship store.

William Glosser, a former store executive, launched an effort to try to keep the store open. He says he'll continue to work to reopen the store.

At 5 Friday afternoon, store personnel locked the store just as they had done before hundreds of other holiday weekends.

But come this morning, the business community reopened without Glosser's.

A billboard advertises one of the many promotions Glosser's held over the years.

Glosser's
DOWNTOWN JOHNSTOWN

GOING OUT OF BUSINESS CLEARANCE!

NOW **70% OFF** ENTIRE INVENT...

Photos by Pete Vizza of The Tribune-Democrat and through the courtesy of Glosser Bros., Inc., and William Glosser.

You can save 25 per cent on all Men's, Women's and Children's Wear at

GLOSSER BROS.
Out of the High Rent District,
118-120 Franklin St., Near Main

The Tribune-Democrat
Judge: no Glosser's stay

The slogan, "We're all going to Glosser's," has held through the years.

FREE RIDE!
Courtesy of GLOSSER BROS.

Joseph Slonka of Edgewood peers into a nearly empty store.

This is one of the floats Glosser Bros. entered in the Halloween parades that it sponsored for so many years.

Non-Tobacco Items
50% Off
All Sales Final

Albert Zawalish of Upper Yoder Township enjoys a last cup of coffee in the second-floor cafeteria. Zawalish says he's had coffee there every day for the past 50 years.

Chapter 35

One Last Tour of the Store

How would you like to go back in time to the last days of the Glosser Bros. Department Store? What if you could magically open a window on those days and have one last peek at The Store's final moments?

Thanks to Izzy Glosser, you can.

Izzy had the foresight, amid the sadness and stress of The Store's last hurrah, to photograph everything he could before it was gone forever. "I thought it was important to have a historical document of Glosser Bros. at the end," he says. "I wanted to capture it for future generations."

That was why, on two separate occasions, Izzy went on a tour of Glosser's with camera in hand. He took the first tour on a day in late April 1989, when there was still a good bit of merchandise on display in The Store. He took another tour in late May 1989, right after Glosser's had closed for business for the last time.

Between the two visits, Izzy managed to capture a large portion of The Store--from the ground floor to the departments and offices upstairs. He photographed everything from the basement to the cafeteria in the Annex to the receiving department on the fifth floor.

In so doing, he created a unique photo essay of Glosser Bros...the most complete snapshot of The Store at *any* time in its existence. If anyone at any point in the life of Glosser's did anything comparable--capturing much of The Store in a series of photos--that work has been lost in the mists of history.

So what we have here is the closest you'll ever get to a trip back in time, a floor-by-floor tour of our beloved Glosser's Department Store. The photos, though shot on different days in April and May 1989, are arranged side by side, sorted according to floor, to recreate the experience of walking through Glosser's one department at a time.

It's a vision of a legendary place at a pivotal point...one last glimpse of familiar rooms and racks and fixtures and decorations. We can almost imagine, as we gaze at each image, that we are back there in that final magic moment, taking the tour of a lifetime through a place we never thought we'd see again. A place we thought we'd never return to outside of our dreams.

These photos will bring back memories, and they might even bring you to tears. Best of all, they'll take you back again and again, as often as you like, because they're all yours now, in the pages of this book, complete with the original captions that were written on the back of each print.

And you have the one and only Izzy Glosser to thank for that.

BASEMENT

Budget Basement
Paint, hardware, health and beauty aids, ready-to-wear. Izzy with employee Guelda (Midge) Kane

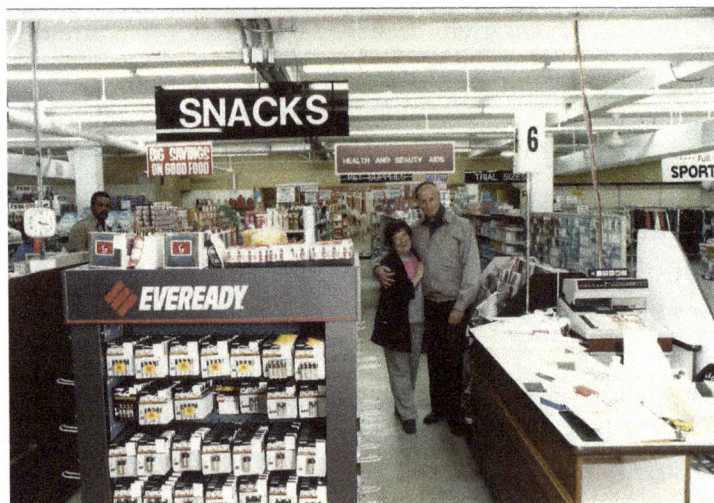

Photos courtesy of Izzy Glosser

Basement Incinerator
This is where we disposed of store trash. One of my first jobs was firing this furnace and also trimming produce in the nearby produce receiving department.

Basement Sales Area
This was a supermarket up to the 1977 flood. Many happy times were spent working down here before I went off to college. In recent years, a variety of department store merchandise was sold in this space.

Photos courtesy of Izzy Glosser

FIRST FLOOR

Main Floor, Ladies' Accessories
Franklin/Locust Street entrance in corner at rear of photo

Men's Furninshings
*Franklin Street entrance at
right of photo*

Photos courtesy of Izzy Glosser

Men's Furninshings
From Franklin Street entrance

Shoe Department
*Tobacco department at
rear in corner*

Men's Clothing Department

Photos courtesy of Izzy Glosser

313

FIRST FLOOR

Photos courtesy of Izzy Glosser

Photos courtesy of Izzy Glosser

SECOND FLOOR

Budget dresses in rear and lingerie beyond.
Lamps in this shot were brought down from the fourth floor, which was being cleared.

Domestics Department

Budget Dresses & Lingerie

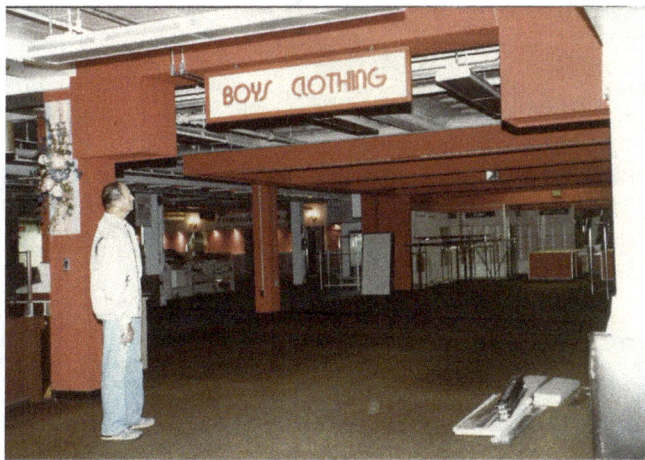

The second floor included the boys' department, men's tailor shop, budget dresses, lingerie, notions, domestics, school supplies, greeting cards, and the entrance to the cafeteria with its adjoining Hunt Room.

Photos courtesy of Izzy Glosser

THIRD FLOOR

The third floor housed the women's ready-to-wear, girls', infants, and women's sportswear. The layaway department was also here, along with an entrance to rented office space in the Tribune-Democrat building.

Better Dresses, Suits, and Coats

Women's Ready-to-Wear

Photos courtesy of Izzy Glosser

Girls' Wear

Photos courtesy of Izzy Glosser

FOURTH FLOOR

Cashier, Housewares

Home Furnishings
Almost cleared out

Housewares

Check Cashing, Cashier Office

Photos courtesy of Izzy Glosser

Stenographers' Office
I picked up lots of mail here and in other steno offices we had over the years.

The Money Office
Checks were cashed here and cashiers brought their receipts here. The rest of the floor included housewares, home furnishings, and electronics. In the early days, we had paint and wallpaper departements here also.

Inside the Money Office
My Dad opened the safes here for many years, as did I and Syd Ossip to start the store's daily activity.

Photos courtesy of Izzy Glosser

FOURTH FLOOR

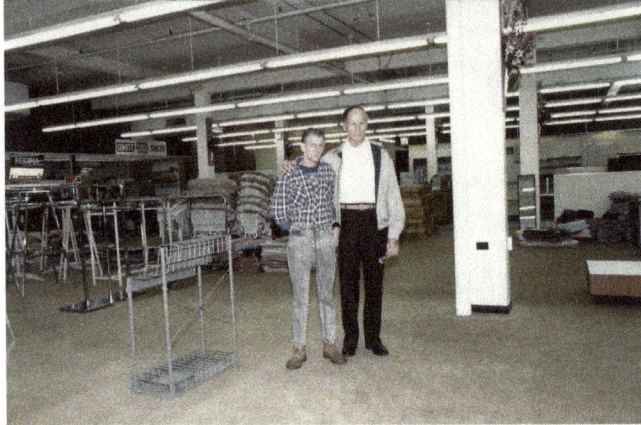

Home Furnishings
About all cleared out. With Ted Swanson, an employee.

The Board of Directors Room
*I attended many a meeting here as corporate
secretary and director, along with many of our
Glosser family who also served.*

Photos courtesy of Izzy Glosser

FIFTH FLOOR

Receiving Department
One of my first jobs was running this freight elevator.

Receiving Department

Shipping Department

Photos courtesy of Izzy Glosser

FIFTH FLOOR

Shipping and Delivery Department
*I worked on the delivery trucks in the early days.
(Izzy is sitting with a mannequin who took up
residence in the department.)*

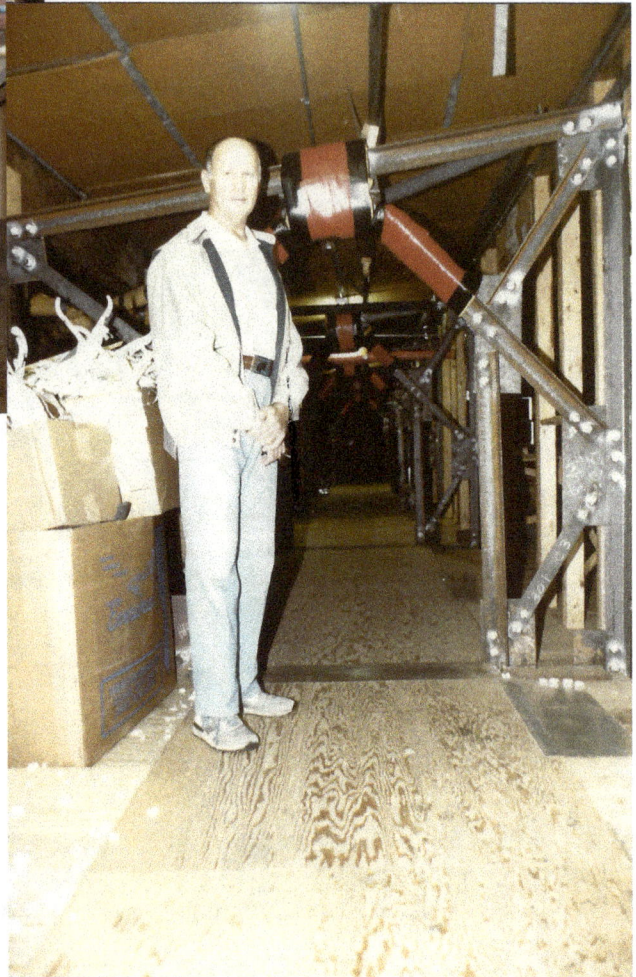

Storeroom Space
*Located in the old part
of the fifth floor*

THE ANNEX

Sporting Goods/Toys

Outdoor Furniture

Photos courtesy of Izzy Glosser

THE ANNEX

Cafeteria
With employee Ted Swanson

Cafeteria

Photos courtesy of Izzy Glosser

Cafeteria

The Hunt Room
*The Hunt Room adjoined the cafeteria. Small groups from around town
and in the store would lunch here and settle cosmic problems.*

Photos courtesy of Izzy Glosser

Photos courtesy of the Library of Congress

328

GLOSSER'S ALL-STARS

ARLENE AND JACK GOSS

Arlene Goss must have made a good impression on her boss at Glosser Bros. back in the 1970s. She still works for him today.

"I was Bill Glosser's personal secretary," says Arlene. "That was in the early 70s, and I was fresh out of high school. Now here I am, all these years later, and I'm *still* his secretary."

Arlene started working at Glosser Bros. Department Store in 1971. She'd taken the secretarial course at Bishop McCort High School and was hired to work in the stenographers' office at Glosser's. (Her starting wage was $1.60 an hour.)

"There were four of us in the stenographers' office," remembers Arlene. "We worked for all the executives--Alvin Glosser, Leonard Black, Sydney Ossip, and Bill Glosser. We also worked for the buyers and merchandise managers."

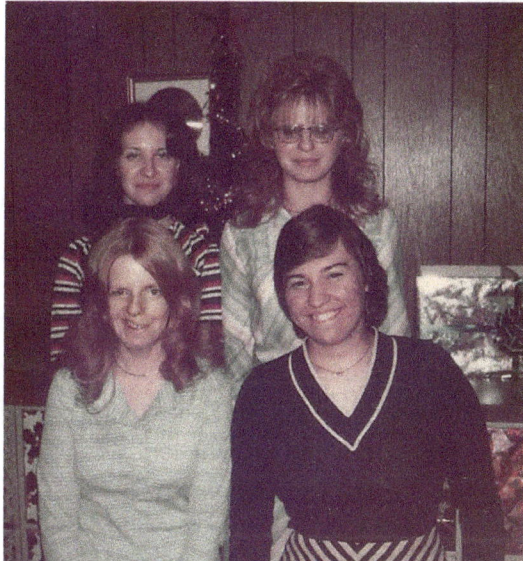

Arlene Goss in front row, at right (photo courtesy of Arlene Goss

Life as a Stenographer

Arlene and the other women in the stenographers' office took dictation, sorted the mail, made phone calls, and typed letters and other documentation. One of their most challenging assignments, however, was preparing and mailing the shareholder letters.

"We'd type up the letters, give all the executives a copy, and then we'd have to apply whatever changes they made," says Arlene.

"Back then, we didn't have computers to make editing easy. If the executives wanted changes, we had to type the entire letter *all over again*. If we made a mistake in the process, we had to pull it out and try again.

"Not to mention, we used those stencil machines where you cut the stencil and duplicated it," says Arlene. "Oh my gosh, it was wild.

329

Arlene Goss and Sydney Ossip (photo courtesy of Arlene Goss)

"You'd pray to God that Leonard Black or Alvin didn't change something, because you were ready to pull your hair out if you had to redo it all over again."

Whatever the frustrations, Arlene did well enough in her job to be promoted after a year to head stenographer. The promotion came with a pay increase, and her store discount doubled from 10% to 20%.

It was a position she didn't leave until her first child was born in 1984. She loved the job so much, she didn't have a reason to leave until then.

Sales Upon Sales Upon Sales

"The people I worked with made it fun," says Arlene. "My co-workers were great, and so were the executives.

"The bosses were really nice and took care of us. They gave us Christmas bonuses and gifts, and every year we had a Christmas dinner. One year, it was down at the Golden Key restaurant on Main Street, where the Szechuan is now. They'd even sing Christmas carols with us, though they were Jewish.

"They considered our suggestions, too," says Arlene. "We'd put them in a suggestion box, and Bill would look at them. If he liked one, he'd give you a little postal card with a discount on it."

Arlene got to meet famous people who came to The Store, too, including Franco Harris of the Pittsburgh Steelers. And she had a ringside seat to the filming of *Slap Shot* in 1976.

"Bill's office overlooked Central Park, where they were shooting the movie," says Arlene. "Bill would be sitting there, and I'd push him aside and look out his window so I could see Paul Newman in the park."

Franco Harris and Arlene Goss (photo courtesy of Arlene Goss)

Arlene loved a lot about Glosser's, but she always had a special place in her heart for one aspect of The Store in particular: its sales.

"Glosser's had great sales," says Arlene. "The men's suit sale, for example. The suits were so cheap, people would buy dozens of them at a time. The place was just packed.

"The women's dress sale was unbelievable, too. Then there was the big coat sale and the white elephant sale in January for the domestics department.

"They had sales upon sales upon sales, and you got some incredible buys."

A Glosserite for Life

Arlene left Glosser's in 1984 after her first baby, but she couldn't stay away for long. Six months after she left, Bill convinced her to come back part-time.

A year later, Bill lost his own job in the upheaval that followed the leveraged buyout. Arlene, who by then was expecting her second child, left two weeks later.

Arlene Goss 2014 (photo by Philip Balko)

But she found herself working for him again in his law office on Main Street, which is where she still works to this day. And she kept up her Glosser Bros. connection in another way, through someone close to her who continued working for the company.

Her husband, Jack Goss.

Jack Goss 2014 (photo by Philip Balko)

From the Big Time to the End Times

Jack Goss is the man who helped to launch 300 stores--though he did all that after he left Glosser Bros.

Long before that, in 1980, he was hired as the energy manager of Glosser Bros., Inc. His job was to cut energy costs at the Gee Bee stores in every way possible.

"We changed the lighting systems and installed energy management computers," says Jack. "Whatever we could think of to reduce energy consumption."

Eventually, he went to work for Fred Glosser, assisting with maintenance for the Gee Bees and Dollar Bargains and helping open new stores.

"It was fun back then," remembers Jack. "There was always something to do.

"I was involved in putting in the infrastructure for anything new that came along, like new wiring systems, lighting systems, cash register systems. I enjoyed that kind of work.

"I also enjoyed working with Fred. He became a mentor of mine, and I learned a lot from him."

The Man of 300 Stores

Jack ended up staying with Glosser Bros. for 14 years, through the bankruptcy and into what would become the Schottenstein era. He was instrumental in designing and constructing the new headquarters building in Richland...and helped find a new tenant (H.F. Lenz) a few years later when Glosser Bros. shut down its local operations.

In 1993, as Glosser Bros. ceased to exist, Jack moved on...only to be pulled back in by Schottenstein. "The Schottenstein organization contacted me in 1994 about working for one of their divisions, American Eagle Outfitters," says Jack. "I decided to give it a try.

"At the time, American Eagle Outfitters was in the midst of an aggressive nationwide expansion. They were opening stores wherever they could.

"So that's what I worked on. While I was with the company, we opened 300 stores in malls across the country. For every store we opened, we looked at three.

"That was a lot of air travel and nights in hotels. We used to fly all over the country like we owned the place. I'd leave home on Monday, come home on Friday, then do it all over again the next week."

Eventually, though, Jack left the company and explored other options. Today, he works for the Johnstown Housing Authority.

But like his wife, Arlene, he looks back fondly on his time with Glosser Bros. "It was a great company to work for. The people who ran it really knew their stuff.

"They knew how to sell, they knew how to make money, and they knew how to create excitement about retailing. They were always innovative and looking for ways to expand.

"That was fun, being part of that. Helping and learning from some of the best in the business."

Arlene and Jack Goss 2014 (photo by Robert Jeschonek)

Chapter 36

Aftermath

Just because the Glosser Department Store had closed its doors, that didn't mean Glosser Bros., Inc. didn't have some life left in it.

The company was in Chapter 11, not exactly in the best of health, but it was still in business. Its supermarket division was sold to the Penn Traffic Company, but people were still shopping at the Gee Bee and Dollar Bargain stores. Employees were still going to work at those stores and getting paychecks.

And maybe there would still be hope for survival if a buyer could be found. Maybe the stores would stay open and the employees would keep their jobs. Maybe Glosser Bros., Inc. would become something new and more agile, better suited to the modern era of retail merchandising.

That was the hope as Glosser President Tom Zurilla searched high and low for a buyer.

Bill Glosser kept searching, too, trying to find someone who might be willing to reopen the Glosser Bros. Department Store. In July 1989, according to *The Tribune-Democrat*, he sought financial assistance from Moxham National Bank...though it was starting to look like his efforts would be too late to help The Store.

Tom Zurilla, on the other hand, was having better luck finding interest in buying the company. He found a potential buyer in Schottenstein's Stores Corporation of Columbus, Ohio. Schottenstein already owned the Value City chain of discount retail stores, so the purchase of Glosser Bros. seemed like a perfect fit.

Glosser retains hopes for store

By Kirk Swauger
The Tribune-Democrat

7-24-89

William Glosser still believes he can open a new store in the vacant Glosser Building.

Thomas J. Zurilla, president and chief executive officer of Glosser Bros. Inc., said Glosser has sought financial assistance from Moxham National Bank.

"Bill Glosser and I met about a week or so ago," Zurilla said. "He's trying to put together something in the neighborhood of a retail store here, but we don't have anything definite yet."

Glosser, a Johnstown lawyer and former Glosser Bros. executive, declined to discuss for the record whether he has spoken with the bank. Bank officials also would not comment.

"I don't want to raise any false hopes, but we are working on the possibility of reopening the store," Glosser said. "Nothing is concrete."

The Glosser Bros. department store closed May 26 after the corporation filed for reorganization under Chapter 11 of the bankruptcy code. It had been a community fixture for 83 years.

Since April, William Glosser has tried numerous ideas to keep a store at Franklin and Locust streets — among them a limited partnership and a petition asking the bankruptcy judge to order the store to remain

Continued on 7 A

The Schottenstein Heard 'Round the World

In late November 1989, the Glosser Bros. board of directors agreed in principal to accept a proposal from Schottenstein to acquire all the outstanding stock of G.B. Holding Corporation, which was formed during the leveraged buyout. Zurilla sent a letter notifying Glosser Bros. employees of the plan, which would allow Glosser Bros. to continue to operate some of its Gee Bee and Dollar Bargain stores as a subsidiary of Schottenstein.

For the deal to go through, however, it would have to be approved by the U.S. Bankruptcy Court for the Western District of Pennsylvania. Once again, the fate of Glosser Bros. would be in the hands of Judge Bernard Markovitz in Pittsburgh.

The situation was complicated further, though, when Johnstown-based mall developer Crown American Corporation attempted to acquire Glosser Bros. during the proceedings. Even as Glosser Bros. sought permission from Markovitz to notify the creditors' committee of the details of the Schottenstein plan and put it to a vote, Crown American filed its own plan and presented it to the same committee.

Glosser's accepts merger proposal

By Jeff McCready
The Tribune-Democrat

The Glosser Bros. Inc. board of directors has selected Schottenstein Stores Corp. of Columbus, Ohio, for a possible merger.

A letter sent to employees earlier this week told them that Glosser's board of directors has agreed in principle to accept a proposal allowing Schottenstein to acquire all the outstanding stock of G.B. Holding Corp.

The holding corporation was formed when Glosser Bros. was taken private in 1986 through a leveraged buyout. A story in The Tribune-Democrat last week told of the Schottenstein offer.

The merger is subject to a definitive agreement and must be approved by the shareholders. It must be approved by the U.S. Bankruptcy Court for the Western District of Pennsylvania.

In late March, Glosser Bros. filed for protection under the federal bankruptcy laws. In the meantime, Glosser Bros. has closed permanently a number of stores, including its downtown Johnstown department store.

The plan would make Glosser Bros. a subsidiary of Schottenstein, the parent of Value City, which has stores in Richland and Altoona.

Glosser Bros. would continue to operate its Gee Bee Discount Department and Dollar Bargain Outlet divisions, the letter said. Current management group and employees would be retained and the headquarters would remain here.

There was no answer yesterday at Schottenstein's corporate headquarters in Columbus, Ohio.

"We just can't comment yet," said Thomas J. Zurilla, Glosser Bros. president and chief executive officer.

The letter to employees was signed by Zurilla.

"It's better than a lot of other scenarios," said a source who asked not to be identified.

Another proposal had come from Heck's Inc. of Nitro, W.Va., and reportedly would have involved the liquidation of some stores.

The source said that it will be up to management and the employees to see that the stores perform well. Schottenstein also would provide Glosser Bros. with a line of credit.

The plan could be approved by early next year.

The Zurilla letter asks employees to do all they can to make certain that customers return, that the stores are stocked with quality merchandise and that costs are reduced and profits improved.

© The Tribune-Democrat

Crown wants Gee Bee, not Bargain unit

By Jeff McCready
The Tribune-Democrat

Crown American Corp.'s proposed acquisition of Glosser Bros. Inc. — which was disclosed last week — calls for the continued operation of an undisclosed number of Gee Bee stores, but the closing of the Dollar Bargain Division's 36 stores.

Under another plan, currently being voted on by Glosser's creditors, the Dollar Bargain Division would continue to operate.

Crown, under terms of a plan filed last week with the Bankruptcy Court in Pittsburgh, said it would pay unsecured creditors 65 cents on the dollar — 10 cents more than is being offered in a plan calling for the acquisition of Glosser's by Schottenstein's Stores Corp. of Columbus, Ohio.

Glosser Bros. is reorganizing under the Bankruptcy Code.

The Crown proposal came on Jan. 25 as Glosser's was mailing out copies of the Schottenstein plan and disclosure statements to creditors

Please turn to Page A 2

© The Tribune-Democrat

In short, Crown American's plan would liquidate the Dollar Bargain stores and keep only the Gee Bee Discount Department Stores in business, while Schottenstein proposed to keep both divisions active.

Zurilla, however, said that Crown's true motive was to liquidate the entire Glosser Bros. corporation, leaving none of its stores still open. In that way, Crown would gain control of the leases for Gee Bee stores in malls and shopping centers owned by Crown.

Whatever Crown's intentions might have been, the creditors voted in favor of Schottenstein, and Judge Markovitz approved the merger at a confirmation hearing in March 1990. By then, Glosser Bros. had laid the groundwork to meet Schottenstein's terms, closing 20 stores--three Gee Bees and 17 Dollar Bargains--in five states. The reorganized Glosser Bros. company would operate 17 Gee Bees and 18 Dollar Bargains in its new role as a Schottenstein subsidiary.

A New Nerve Center

Once the merger was approved, Tom Zurilla went to work on seeing it through to completion. He traveled regularly to Schottenstein headquarters in Columbus to manage the consolidation of Glosser Bros. assets with Schottenstein's.

It was not a simple, quick process. By 1991, Tom and his wife, Ann, a former ladies' sportswear buyer for Glosser's, were traveling weekly to Columbus and returning to Johnstown on weekends.

Meanwhile, changes continued to shake up the Glosser organization. In the summer of 1990, for example, the headquarters of Glosser Bros. and all its divisions moved from the Park Building

Photo © The Tribune-Democrat

downtown to a brand new building in the University Park Shopping Center, the same plaza that was home to the Richland Gee Bee store.

Jack Goss, who was working for Glosser Bros. at the time, was involved in

Photo by Norma Balko

the design and construction of the new headquarters. "One of Schottenstein's first orders to our company was to get it all under one roof, instead of scattered among several locations," says Jack. "So that's exactly what we did.

"I remember working with Hal Cooley, our vice president of operations, to select the site. We picked one in the University Park Shopping Center, because Glosser's already owned that property."

Former Gee Bee Headquarters, Richland
(Photo by Philip Balko)

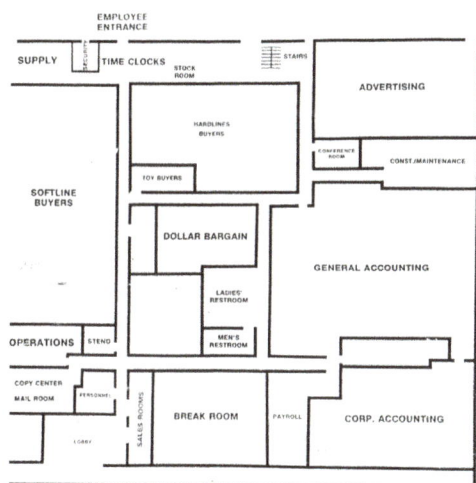

GB Stores
Corporate Headquarters
1407 Scalp Avenue
University Park Shopping Center
Johnstown, Pa. 15904

Courtesy of Norma Balko

According to Jack, Schottenstein's in-house architect designed the building itself, which was meant to accommodate future expansion. It could also be converted to a department store. "You could knock out the front walls, and the reinforcing was there to put in store windows," says Jack.

As for the floor plan, that was up to Jack and the Glosser Bros. team. They got to choose where to put the various offices and facilities to make the headquarters as efficient as possible.

The new nerve center was meant to carry Glosser Bros. forward into the Schottenstein era, enabling the reorganized subsidiary to meet the parent company's expectations. The focus was clearly away from downtown Johnstown now--and away from the Glosser family that had started the company in the first place.

Soon, in fact, there was only one Glosser left working in the organization.

The Last Glosser Standing

David Glosser, son of former supermarket division chief Paul and grandson of founding Glosser Brother David, had been working for Glosser Bros. for years. He'd originally worked in the supermarket division that his father had helped build and headed, though that changed when the division was sold.

After a stint working for the Dollar Bargain division, David worked at the Gee Bee department store in Richland, then in store operations. After Alvin Glosser left the company, David moved into the buying area of headquarters as the candy and tobacco buyer, dealing with many local vendors including Hershey.

When Glosser Bros. eventually closed its Richland offices, he realized that he was the only person with the last name "Glosser" to be working for the company. "I was the last Glosser standing, in a way," says David. "So many

David and Paul Glosser (Photo by Philip Balko)

Glosser family members had been part of the company through the years, it was sad to see the entire operation and its roots in western Pennsylvania closed up and shuttered forever."

Following the Schottenstein merger, David was offered a position in Columbus and ended up working with Schottenstein's Value City hardlines division. But he didn't stay with the company for long. "Working for Value City wasn't a good fit for me," he says. "It was the beginning of the end."

After six months in Columbus, he knew that there was no future for him with Value City as a castoff from one of their acquisitions. As Glosser Bros. continued to lose ground, David left the organization.

Glosser Bros. R.I.P.

In the years that followed, the Gee Bee stores were converted to Value City stores. Glosser Bros. was completely absorbed into Schottenstein, and Gee Bee ceased to exist as a brand.

As president of the Glosser Bros. subsidiary, Tom Zurilla completed the conversion process he'd begun in 1989. By 1993, it was finished...and there was no more Glosser Bros. for him to be president of, nothing left for him to do. The man who'd led the company through its final hours had worked himself out of a job. The last president of Glosser Bros. was a president no longer.

And the Glosser Bros. company, which had been in business in one form or another since 1906...which had been listed on the American Stock Exchange and grown to encompass 24 department stores, 18 supermarkets, and 44 dollar stores...which had survived all manner of economic and natural disaster yet had still gone on serving thousands of devoted customers for decades...

AFTERMATH

That company, at last, was at an end.

Though some would say it had been over since May 26th, 1989.

Some would say it had been over since the Glosser Bros. Department Store had closed its doors for the last time, and the company's truest, strongest heart had ceased to beat forever.

Photo © The Tribune-Democrat

Photo courtesy of Bill Glosser

SHAKER SQUARE CREATES THE PERFECT SUMMER WARDROBE FOR EVERY MOTHER
ALL STYLES AVAILABLE IN SIZES 12 to 20 and 14½ to 24½
6⁹⁵
8⁹⁰
6⁹⁵
7⁹⁵
13⁹⁰
13⁹⁰
13⁹⁰
GLOSSER BROS., JOHNSTOWN, PA.
SHOP TODAY NOON to 9 TUES. 9:30 to 5
Glosser bros
USE YOUR GLOSSER'S CHARGE CARD! NEW ACCOUNTS INVITED! CREDIT SERVICE DEPT.-3rd Fl.

Shopping With Us Has Its Rewards...
Exquisite Fine China
by EKCO INTERNATIONAL, "A Truly Magnificent Offer!"
Gee Bee
SUPER MARKETS
Complete Selection of Accessory Pieces Available
SUGAR BOWL and COVER $2.00 off
Western Grain Fed BEEF SALE
BONELESS BOTTOM ROUND ROAST
1.89 LB.
SUPER LEAN
Strictly Fresh Young Tender WHOLE FRYING CHICKEN
49¢ LB.
WHOLE BONELESS BOTTOM ROUND 1.69
Fresh lean Gee Bee Quality GROUND BEEF 1.19 LB.
Armour Golden Star Butter Basted YOUNG TURKEYS
79¢
SUPER LEAN PORK SALE
PORK BUTT ROAST 1.29
PORK BUTT STEAK 1.39
PORK BUTT STEAK 1.59
CITY CHICKEN 1.69
SLICED BACON 1.39
LUNCH MEAT SALE 1.39
POLSKA KIELBASA SMOKED SAUSAGE 1.99
COOKED HAM 1.89
CALIFORNIA SUNKIST LEMONS 10 for 89¢
ROASTED PEANUTS 1.29
AVOCADOES 39¢
CALIFORNIA New - Crop Sweet Delicious RED EMPEROR GRAPES
69¢ LB.
BARTLETT PEARS 10 for 99¢
CALIFORNIA ORANGES 15 for 99¢
RED, RIPE TOMATOES 49¢

ANNIVERSARY
One Low Price Buys A Lot Of Style!
Trissi SEPARATES
7⁸⁸ each
LADIES' CO-ORDINATES by russ
50% OFF
Use Our Convenient Layaway!
WALLETS and ACCESSORIES 50% OFF
FAMOUS NAME WATCHES 25⁸⁸
Ladies' Famous "TENNESSEE" HANDBAGS 5⁹⁴
Ladies' DRIVING GLOVES 2²²
Ladies' Folding UMBRELLAS 2⁶⁶
EXPANSION BAND WATCHES 9⁸⁸
L.C.D. DIGITAL WATCHES 14⁸⁸

SALE!
Ready Monday 9 to 9
Tues., Wed., Fri. 10-5; Thurs. 10-9
SPECTACULAR SAVINGS!
YOUR CHOICE
11⁹⁰
• VELOUR TOPS
• SUPER SWEATERS
• SOFT BLOUSES
All Perfect Quality!
VELOUR TOPS
SUPER SWEATERS
Lady Arrow® and Ship 'n Shore®
BLOUSES
Jovan Specials!

Memory Department

The two words, Glosser Bros., conjure up countless treasured memories. Growing up I viewed the store as one of the anchors of the town and my family. Indeed, in the off-hours, our family held special family events in the cafeteria, including holiday dinners and sundaes after the parades.

When I was old enough, I worked many a Saturday at the store. Everyone in my immediate family worked there at some point in time, including my younger brother Jon, who was shorter than the candy counter when he started selling candy and nuts! While every visit to Glosser Bros. was akin to a family reunion, the employees were also a part of my extended family. Long-term employees were the rule, not the exception. I knew employees in all the departments, from the grocery in the basement all the way up to the top floor where shipping and receiving was tucked away.

I bonded with and appreciated all of my mentors at the store, who gave me invaluable life skills (to this day I will not leave clothing in a dressing room): Mrs. Psinakis, Molly, Chris, Fritzie, and Candy to name a few. I worked in a variety of departments: cosmetics/drugs, notions, women's coats, jewelry, junior sportswear, credit (for the Glosser's credit card and layaway), telephone operator (loved plugging and unplugging the wires in the switchboard) and the highlight, bridal, complete with the annual fashion show.

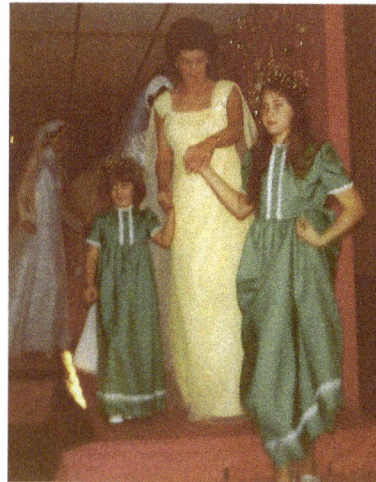

1977 Bridal Show (courtesy of Robin Eiseman)

Each shift also meant an anticipated visit to the cafeteria, where I would order a tuna fish sandwich and a chocolate milkshake made by one of the twins. I genuinely enjoyed working in the store.

As an adult, I realize what a truly unique environment Glosser Bros. was on so many levels: the vast variety of departments, the number of family members involved, the sense of community both among the entire staff and with the town, and the extraordinary loyalty of the employees. In fact, Arlene and my father, Bill Glosser, are still working together as a team.

I still get a warm feeling inside when I look at the watercolor painting in my entryway which depicts the exterior of Glosser Bros. at Halloween, complete with ghoulish designs on the windows. I choose to remember Glosser Bros. at its height, and I am forever grateful for its place in my youth.

- Jill Glosser (daughter of Bill Glosser)

Loyal employees: 11 members were inducted into Glosser's 25-Year Club in 1976. Front row, l. to r.: Ruth Shaffer, Ruby Shaffer, Florence Williams, Rose Kawchak, and Guelda Kane. Back row, l. to r.: Elaine Mae Long, Nellie V. Slonaker, Joseph Kovach, Lilly Mae Cox, Ann Matyuch, and Margaret Chose. (photo © The Tribune-Democrat)

Santa Claus Sydney Ossip and friends
(photo courtesy of Ellen Ossip Sosinski)

Chapter 37

Where Are They Now?

After The Store closed and Glosser Bros., Inc. ceased to exist, the stars of our story--like John, Paul, George, and Ringo after The Beatles broke up--never really came together again. Their shared adventure in Johnstown was over; they would remain forever family, but their lives carried them in different directions.

The Old Guard

The "second generation"--the children of the original Glosser brothers--began new phases of their lives beyond The Store and the company.

Fred Glosser had always dreamed of being a cowboy. After retiring in 1986, he and his wife Betty moved to Austin, Texas, to be part of the West that had always been close to his heart.

Fred's brother, Izzy, and his wife Ruth ended up moving to Los Angeles, California after retirement. They love the sunny weather, though Izzy sometimes misses living in the close-knit community of Johnstown.

Leonard Black, on the other hand, continued to live in Johnstown, though he and his wife Betty spent a good bit of time in Palm Beach, Florida. He passed away in 2007.

Alvin Glosser also stayed in Johnstown and died a few years later, in 2012. Sydney Ossip, Glosser Bros.' comptroller for so many years, stayed in Johnstown, as well. He died in July 2014 at the age of 97...one day after being interviewed for this book.

Herb Sinberg and his wife Freda (Fred and Izzy's sister) moved to Lake Worth, Florida, near Palm Beach, where Herb died in 2007.

Paul Glosser also moved to Florida--to Long Boat Key, near Sarasota--where he still lives with his wife, Rita. Rita has a company called Reminkie Bears, which turns old fur, fabrics, neckties, and other materials into keepsake teddy bears.

As for Bill Glosser, he might be the only member of the old guard

Glosser Bros. team who has not yet retired. Now in his mid-80s, he continues to practice law in downtown Johnstown--and travels to the Caribbean twice a year to vacation among the islands with friends.

The Third Generation

The "third generation"--the grandchildren of the original Glosser brothers--fanned out across the country, carving out unique destinies all their own. Their numbers include doctors, dentists, lawyers, entertainment executives, real estate moguls, and businessmen and women of every stripe.

Fred's son, Daniel, for example, is the director of music clearance for syndicated programming for CBS Television in Los Angeles. Bill's daughter, Jill, is a Senior Vice President, Employee Relations Legal Services for Paramount Pictures, also in L.A., where she has worked for 25 years.

Izzy's youngest son, Dr. David Glosser, lives in Yardley, PA and is director of neuropsychology at Virtua Health System.

As for David, the "last Glosser standing" from the Value City era, he built his own horticultural maintenance company in Sarasota, Florida.

Fate of a Building

There is just one other major player left unaccounted for, perhaps the biggest star of our story: the Glosser Building.

Photo courtesy of Fred Glosser

After The Store closed and the company's offices moved elsewhere, the Glosser Building sat empty for years. The Glosser family searched high and low for a new tenant or owner, but had no success for years.

By late 1993, options were running out for the building. The family couldn't even *give* it away... and the costs of maintaining it continued to mount. Taxes had not been paid on the building for quite a while, and it had gone unsold at a delinquent tax sale in 1992.

Finally, Bill Glosser made an offer to the Cambria County Redevelopment Authority. The Glosser family would hand over the building and two parking lots as a gift, and the Redevelopment Authority could use them as they saw fit.

At first, it looked like even this plan would fail. Several Cambria County Commissioners opposed the donation, saying they didn't want to take over what they considered to be a white elephant. The Redevelopment Authority wasn't sure what to do with the structure, or if funds even existed to demolish it.

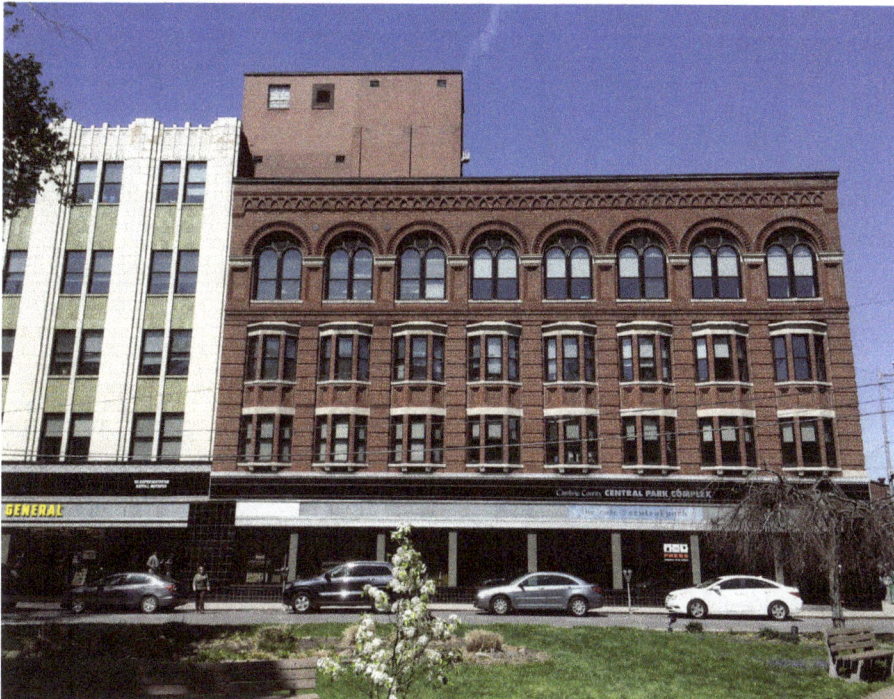

Photo by Robert Jeschonek

Ultimately, though, the County accepted the donation and remodeled the building. It became the home of the Penn Highlands Community College for a while, along with the offices of multiple Cambria County agencies. When the community college moved out, the open space was quickly occupied by additional County offices, and the college's lecture auditorium became a meeting room open to local organizations.

To this day, Bill and Fred are happy to see the building still standing and put to good use. The outside, in fact, still looks much the same as it did during the Glosser Bros. days.

Though inside is a very different world, one that few of us would ever get to see in its entirety...

...if not for the next chapter of this book.

The Tribune-Democrat
GLOSSER'S HAS SO MUCH to CHOOSE for SPRING and EASTER . . . for so very, very little!
Glosser bros
JOHNSTOWN, PA.
SHOP THURSDAY 9:30 'til 9:00
Stuffed EASTER BUNNIES!
American Girl
PUMPS and MORE PUMPS!
EASTER CANDY!
BOYS Permanent-Press SPORT and DRESS TROUSERS
3.99
5.00
5.99
her's
9.99
BOYS' 10-WAY EASTER SUITS
$12
OMEGA . . . the last word in BIBLES!
15.99
Li'l Girls' EASTER DRESSES
Just arrived . . .
EASTER DRESSES
5.95
8.80
2.99

Maxwell House
COFFEE
2-LB. can
1.29
Domino
SUGAR
5-LB. bag
55¢
WE RESERVE THE RIGHT TO LIMIT QUANTITIES!
PRICES GOOD thru SATURDAY!
Easter Parade of GREAT Food Values
Argo
SLICED
PEACHES
4 $1
Royal
GELATIN
All Flavors
8¢
Burn's WHOLE BEETS
10¢
KRAFT
OIL
gal.
1.89
Gee Bee
WHITE GRADE 'A'
LARGE EGGS
53¢ doz.
Easter EGGS
Chef's Delight
PIMENTO CHEESE
49¢
CLIP & SAVE!
VALUABLE COUPON
CANNED POP
5¢
SPRY SHORTENING
49¢
Cinderella FLOUR
29¢
IVORY LIQUID
39¢
SLICED PINEAPPLE
4 89¢
KRISPY CRACKERS
25¢
HORSERADISH
2 29¢
KETCHUP
19¢
PROCESSED DILL PICKLES
39¢
STUFFED OLIVES
3 $1
ALUMINUM FOIL
4 $1
CIDER VINEGAR
19¢

GLOSSER'S and GEE BEE Auto Centers Bring You
SEIBERLING'S NEW SPEED BREED of TIRES
at SPECIAL SALE PRICES
★NO TRADE-IN NEEDED!
★FREE MOUNTING NOW or LATER!
★WE NEVER SELL A "SECOND", BLEMISHED or REJECT TIRE!
THE TIRES of TOMORROW TODAY
SUPER WIDE SPORTS TIRE
24.77
SEIBERLING 110 NYLON 4-PLY
13.97
14.97
15.97
16.97
18.97
SEIBERLING 120 . . . the "PLUS" PERFORMANCE QUALITY TIRE
15.97
16.97
16.97
18.97
18.97
20.97
22.97
24.97
16.97
SEIBERLING Premium SUPREME 170 TOX
24.97
25.97
26.97
28.97
31.97
39.97
GeeBee and GLOSSER BROS.
CHARGE IT or USE LAYAWAY

Glosser's Ladies' Day
DOWNTOWN JOHNSTOWN
Thursday, April 26--9 to 9
Lady Arrow® and Ship'n Shore®
BLOUSE SPECTACULAR!
Regular
$12.00 to $28.00
50% OFF
JUNIORS' and MISSES' SUMMER
T-SHIRTS
50% OFF
FAMOUS MAKER LADIES' SUMMER
SHELLS
4.44

Chapter 38

Revisiting the Glosser Building

What does the interior of the Glosser Building look like today? How has it changed, a quarter-century after the closing of The Store?

Normally, you wouldn't be able to see much of it--just the businesses that operate on the first floor, and a lobby area where guards control access to the county offices located on the floors above. Unless you have a good reason to go upstairs--appearing in court, for example, or meeting with personnel from a county agency--you aren't likely to get past the guards. Even then, you probably won't get to see much beyond your specific destination. Left to your own devices, you'df never get the full picture of what has become of the fabled Glosser Building.

But thanks to Fred Glosser, you get to boldly go where so few members of Glosser Nation have gone before, or ever will go. You get to see what has become of your favorite parts of The Store, from the basement all the way to the attic. You get to peer into nooks and crannies and secret places you might never have known existed.

And you get to see what traces remain of the Glosser Bros. Department Store you knew and loved.

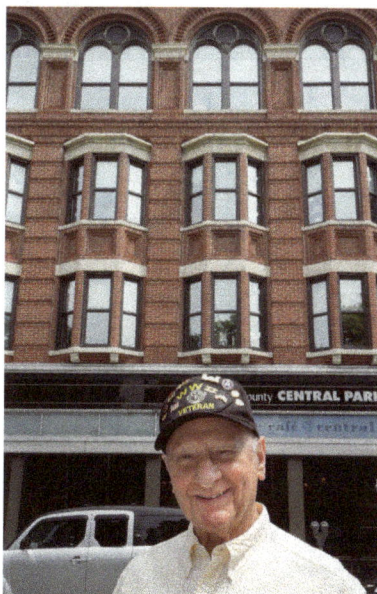

Photo by Philip Balko

So much of the building looks so different, but Fred knows it better than anyone else. He knows exactly how to find where everything was, even after all the renovations that have been layered overtop it. You could not ask for a better guide on this very special tour.

Back to the Future

Just as his brother Izzy photographed The Store's last days before him, Fred toured the Glosser Building 25 years later, helping to capture the current state of the place in a series of remarkable photos by *Long Live Glosser's* Photo Editor and Photographer Philip Balko.

Accompanied by *Long Live Glosser's* author Robert Jeschonek, who shot footage for a video documentary about Glosser Bros., Fred started on the ground floor, in the lobby area that was once part of the main floor of The Store. There's a restaurant, the Press Bistro, at the corner of Franklin and Locust Streets now...plus a Rent-a-Center on the Franklin Street side. The local office of Congressman Keith Rothfus is down there, too, along with other assorted offices. And the first floor of the Locust Street Addition, where the entrance to the tobacco and magazine department was once located, is now occupied by a Dollar General store.

Photos by Philip Balko

Photos by Philip Balko

From the ground floor of the Glosser Building, Fred took the elevator to the second floor, where the notions and women's departments have been replaced by Cambria County offices, including the Probation office, the Emergency Operations Center (auxiliary 911 center), and an auditorium that was once used by Penn Highlands Community College.

A Peek at the Cafeteria

The second floor also provided a glimpse of the fabled cafeteria in the Glosser Annex. Though the Annex building is vacant and locked up (empty since Conemaugh Engraving moved out), Fred was able to peek out a second floor window and see the exterior of the old cafeteria. The walkway leading to it is closed, boxed in on the Glosser Building side, but the outside of that brick-covered passage can still be seen, linking the second floors of the main structure and the Annex.

Photos by Philip Balko

Remnants of Times Past

When Fred got to the stairwell to head for the upper floors, he got a pleasant surprise: the stairs, railings, and sprinkler system are almost the same as they were 25 years ago. Lovely wrought iron scrollwork affixed to the railings was left over from The Store's glory days, repainted but otherwise unchanged.

The stairwell also brought other memories to life for Fred. On the third floor landing, he found the space that was once his office. He took a moment to sit in a chair there and gaze out at the view from his old office, looking over the treetops of Central Park.

Photos by Philip Balko

Photos by Philip Balko

Into the Heights

On the third floor, Fred found blocks of County offices that had once been part of the Infants and Children Under 6 department, the layaway department, the women's suit, coat, and dress department, the women's tailor shop, and the nurse's station.

Photos by Philip Balko

Next, Fred journeyed straight to the fifth floor, where Sheriff's Department personnel opened a locked attic area that had once been Glosser Bros' stockrooms. Now converted to storage for County files, this part of the building had original structural details that hadn't changed since the days of The Store. The original steel support braces that had been installed on Fred's watch in the old days were still in place, as were the red foam pads mounted on the overhead braces to protect the heads of people passing under them.

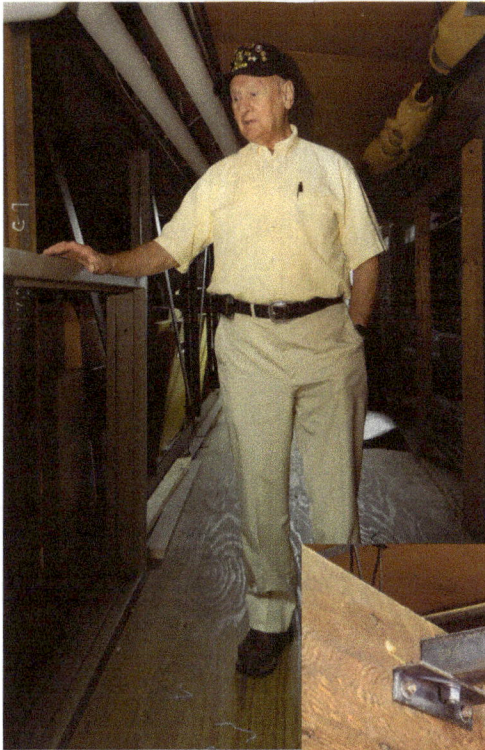

Photos by Philip Balko

Photos by Philip Balko

354

Fred also got to wander through the County courtroom which is now located where Glosser's display department once resided. Next, he toured the halls and offices where the receiving and shipping departments had been.

Photos by Philip Balko

Fourth Floor to the Basement

When Fred was done on the fifth floor, he took the elevator back down to the fourth, where he found the former locations of the furniture department, toy department, advertising department, switchboard, executive offices, and the money office, where cash from The Store's daily receipts was kept, counted, prepped, and shipped out to the bank.

Fred also pointed out the door to the old board room where Glosser Bros. board of directors had held its meetings (a room he'd once soundproofed by lining it with lead) though he wasn't able to go inside for a closer look.

Photos by Philip Balko

Finally, Fred made his way to the basement, where Glosser stockrooms had been replaced by the offices of the Cambria County Public Defender and District Attorney. Here, too, he found traces of the old Glosser Bros. store--massive columns installed after the 1936 Johnstown Flood to reinforce the structure of the building.

Photos by Philip Balko

Fred also continued his tour outside, surveying the exterior of the Annex and the alley where trucks had once backed in to make deliveries of merchandise to The Store.

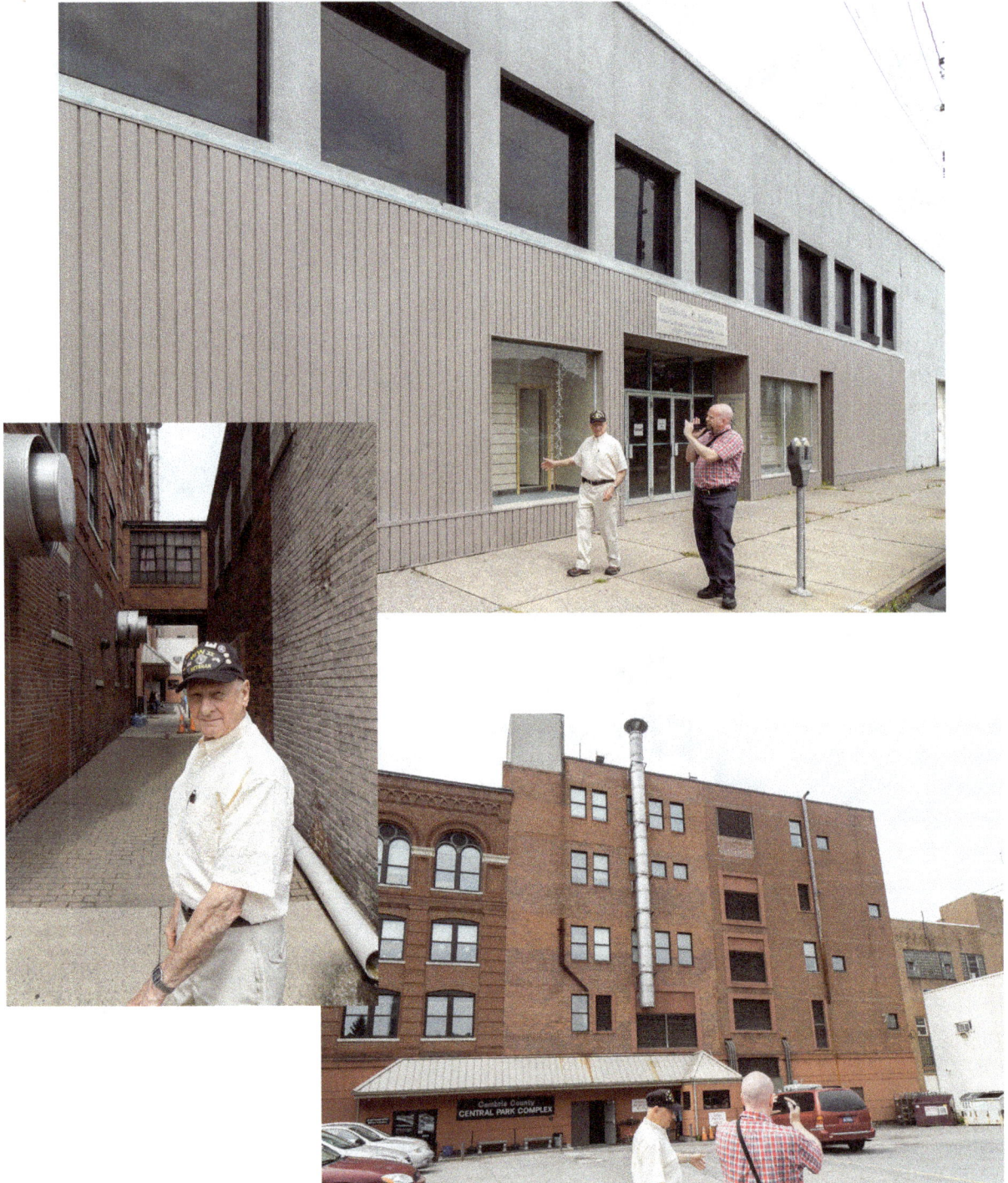

Windows on Yesterday?

In the end, Fred stood on the sidewalk out in front of the Glosser Building--now known officially as the Cambria County Central Park Complex--and stared up at what had been his home away from home for decades. On the outside, it didn't look all that different from the way it had looked for all those years. Maybe, if he blinked hard enough and looked through those windows one more time, he might see the displays and offices of The Store again, brought back to life on the other side. Maybe he might see friends and family hard at work, greeting and serving shoppers as if no time had passed at all. As if the past 25 years had never happened, and Glosser Bros. was still in business as it had been since 1906.

Or maybe, as happened that day, he would simply smile and shake his head, then walk off down the street into the future, whatever it might hold.

Photos by Philip Balko

FRED'S FLOOR PLANS

Fred Glosser sketched these plans from memory, exclusively for *Long Live* Glosser's, based on the layout of the Glosser Bros. Department Store from the 1950s until the 1977 Flood. Things changed here and there through the years, but the basic layout stayed essentially the same.

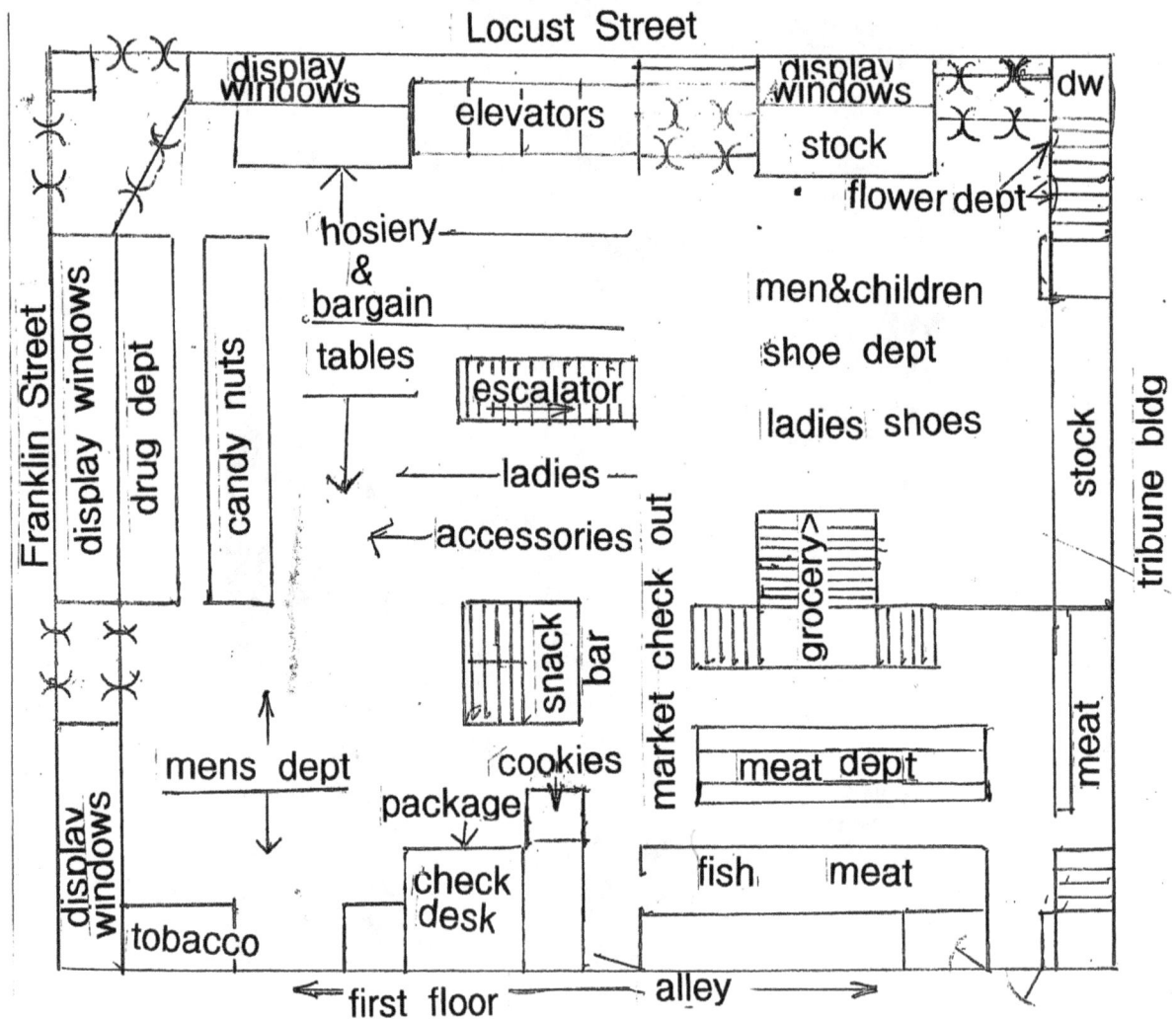

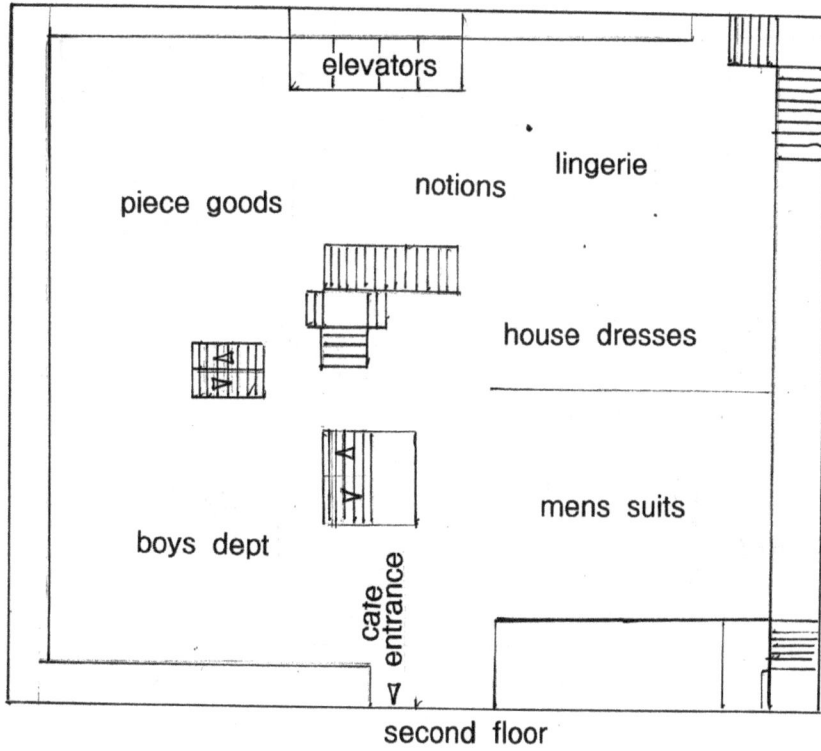

second floor

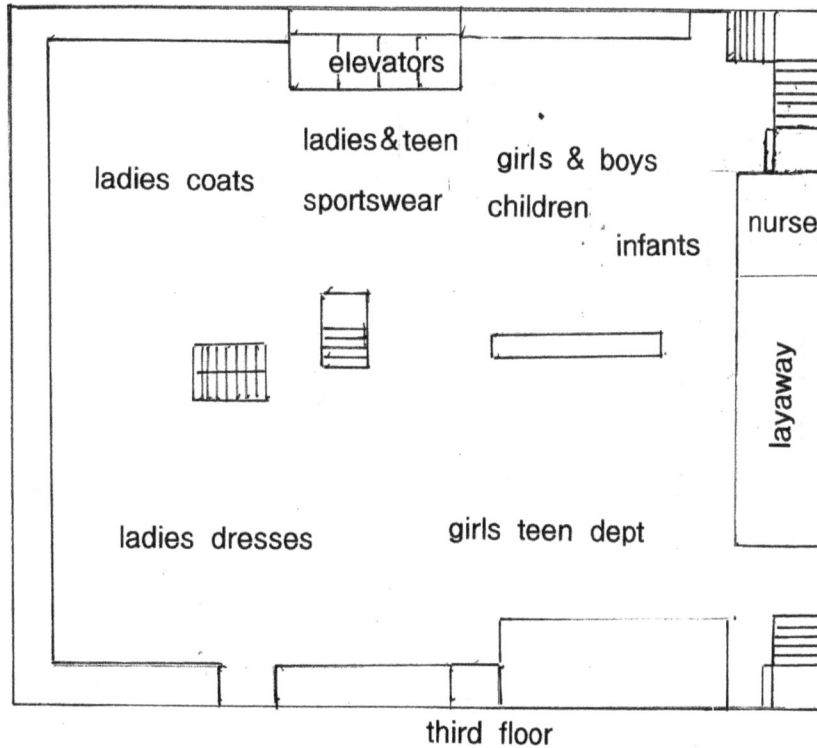

third floor

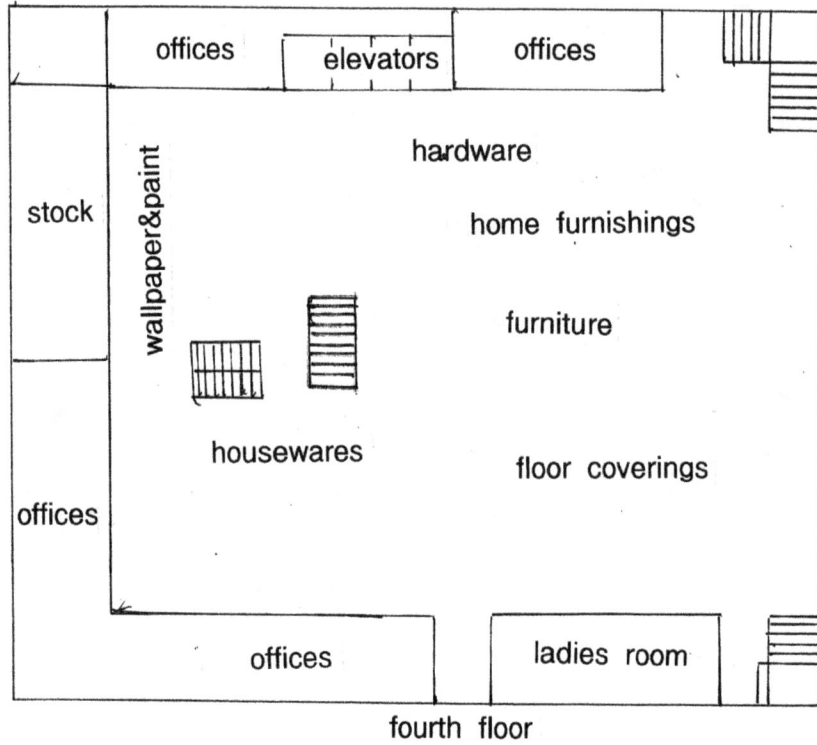

fourth floor

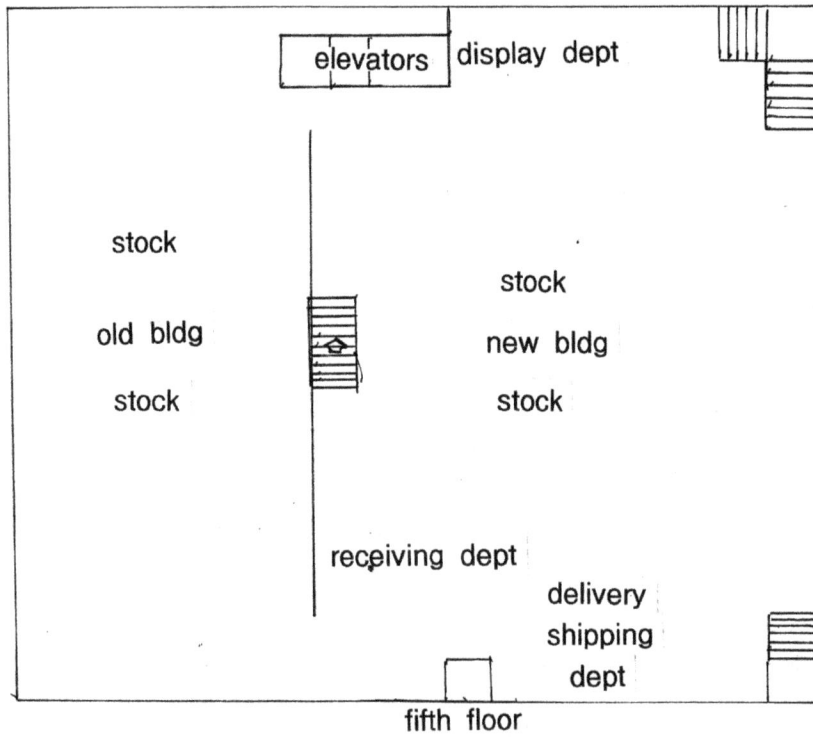

fifth floor

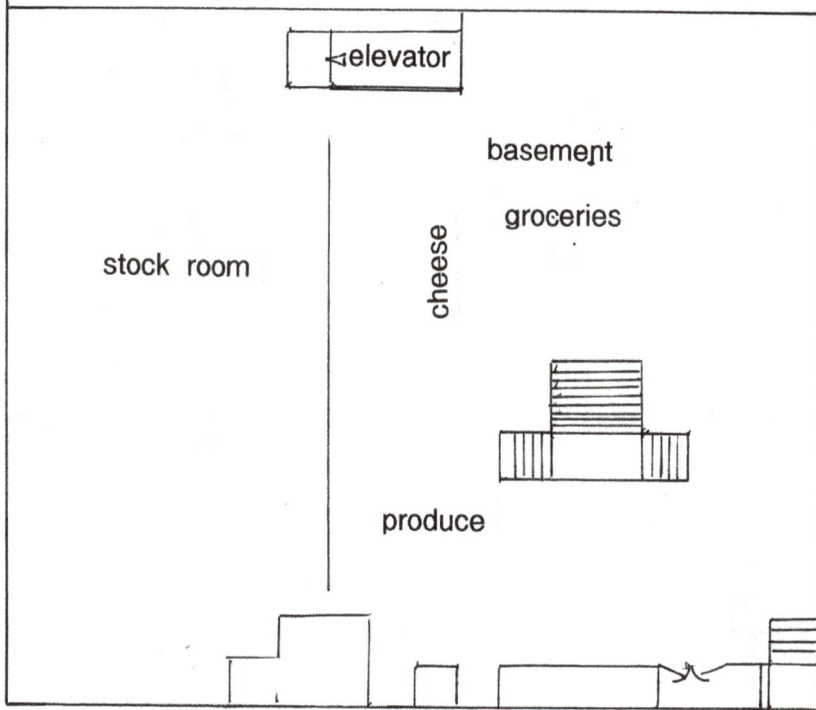

elevator

basement

groceries

cheese

stock room

produce

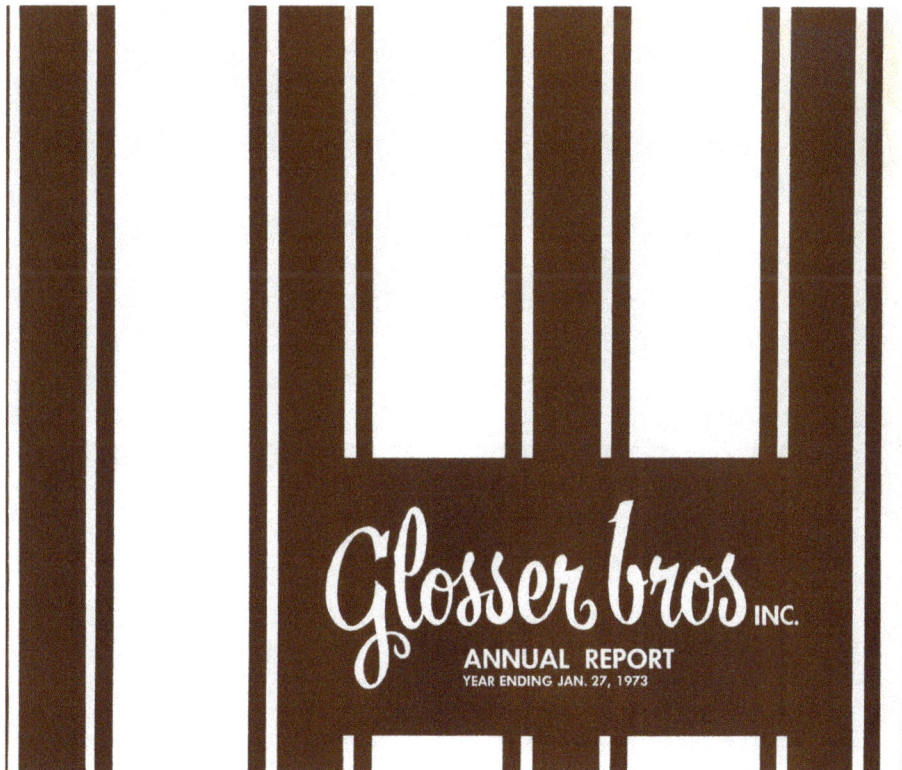

Glosser bros INC.

ANNUAL REPORT

YEAR ENDING JAN. 27, 1973

GROWTH OF AN EMPIRE
1973-1983

Chapter 39

Carrying the Torch

In the years that followed the closing of Glosser Bros. Department Store, the hardcore heroes of Glosser Nation kept the memory of the place alive.

The Glosser Bros. Breakfast Club is one of the best examples. For years, this group of former Glosser's employees has gathered for breakfasts at Harrigan's Café in the Holiday Inn in downtown Johnstown.

Hunt Room Mary (Schuster) is a regular attendee, along with her son, Mark. So are John and Sally Hudak, a husband and wife who both worked at Glosser's back in the day. Then, there's Agnes Siska, who worked for Glosser's for 25 years, right up to the end...and another Agnes, last name Detrick, who worked there even longer, for 35 years. The two Agneses are both members of Club 25, an organization set up by Glosser Bros. to honor employees who'd worked 25 years or more for the company.

The Breakfast Club carried the torch for decades, then took a brief hiatus in early 2014...only to come back stronger than ever later in the year, reenergized by the excitement surrounding the 25th anniversary of The Store's closing.

They met again on July 1st, 2014, to share stories of the old days, laugh about the crazy things that happened way back when, and enjoy the company of co-workers who were more like family than friends.

365

Photos by Philip Balko

Agnes Times Two

Agnes Siska

Agnes Siska, like many of the other Breakfast Clubbers, says she would still be working at Glosser Bros. if it was still open.

"It was a nice place to work, and the Glossers were so nice to us," says Agnes, who worked in the domestics department. "They were really nice people. It was great being a part of their store."

What about the other Agnes, Agnes Detrick? She feels the same way. "We had a lot of fun at Glosser's. All my years there, I enjoyed my job."

Agnes Detrick started her 35-year career as a teenager, stocking shelves in the grocery department. "We loaded the food on a big cart, and then I rode the cart up the aisle to the shelves. When we put the stock on the shelves, we used a crayon to mark the price on it."

Agnes Detrick

Next, Agnes became a grocery cashier, which required her to know prices by heart. "When you ran one of those old, black registers, you had to know the prices. In those days, there was no such thing as looking up prices. You had to memorize your prices all the time. When someone brought some items up and said they were seven for a dollar, you had to know that was only 15 cents for one. You had it figured out and had to know it."

Eventually, Agnes Detrick became a grocery secretary, then went to work in the accounting department of the supermarket division in the Park Building. The whole time, she loved her work and her co-workers. "We got along real well together," she says. "We were like family."

Hunt Room Mary and Son

Mary Schuster

Mary Schuster, who worked in the Hunt Room for 28 years and was known as "Hunt Room Mary," has fond memories of her time at Glosser's. One of her favorite events was Old-Fashioned Bargain Days, when employees dressed up in costumes.

"I used to wear an old-fashioned dress and a hat with a big feather in it," remembers Mary.

Her son, Mark, who worked in various departments at Glosser's from 1975 to 1989, always liked Old-Fashioned Bargain Days, too. "It was fun, and the crowds really turned out," says Mark. "We had tables lined up along the sidewalk around the store, and they were jam-packed with shoppers. You couldn't even get in the store."

Like Mary, Mark enjoyed working at Glosser Bros. "They treated us like we were people," he says. "They knew us by name and didn't treat us condescendingly. We were not numbers to them."

Mark Schuster

Photos by Philip Balko

Almost Golden

When it comes to longevity at Glosser's, Florence Williams takes the cake. She started working at The Store in 1941, when she was a sophomore in high school...and she worked right up until the end, in 1989.

That works out to a 48-year Glosser Bros. career, just shy of a golden anniversary.

During her time at The Store, Florence worked in almost every department, selling everything from

Florence Williams

butter and eggs to cakes to wallpaper. She followed in the footsteps of her mother, who worked as a cashier in the grocery department.

When Florence started, she made just 90 cents an hour. "We went up to get our pay from Miss Lewis at the office," she remembers. "You told them your name, and they would hand you the envelope, and it was full of cash...no checks."

Though she didn't make much money at Glosser's, Florence loved her job--especially the customers. "The customers were always so nice to us," she says. "They remembered us and they missed us when we weren't there, and it was really nice."

She still misses The Store and its great selection. "If you couldn't find something you were looking for, you could always find it at Glosser's. Today, I can't find anything that I like because it's not from Glosser's."

Marilyn Weaver

Good, Kind People

Marilyn Weaver didn't work at Glosser's as long as Florence (spending nine years as an assistant buyer for jewelry and handbags), but she had a similar appreciation for the people she met there.

"Everybody was nice," says Marilyn. "You never dreaded going to work. I always remember how kind all the other employees were. Everybody seemed to be pleased with their jobs and happy with their circumstances.

"As for the Glosser executives, they knew every employee. They knew our families, our circumstances, when we were ill, when we were off work. It was common for Sydney Ossip or Alvin Glosser or another Glosser to walk through the store and ask us, 'How are you feeling? Are you feeling better?'

"Once, when I was going through a divorce, I talked to Alvin. I said the job was going to be more important to me since I was on my own, and he gave me a better position.

"They were good, kind people to work for, which was wonderful," says Marilyn.

Photos by Philip Balko

The Rest of the Club

Olga Kohan (call her Ollie) worked in the accounting department from 1976 through 1987. She took care of travel expenses and made travel reservations for the buyers.

Ollie Kohan

"I enjoyed all the people," says Ollie. "I also liked being able to get some shopping done during my breaks."

Helen Luberto

Helen Luberto worked 35 years in the candy and maintenance departments at Glosser's. "I saw it all," she says.

Alice Guizio started one year later than Helen, in 1955, and stayed until The Store closed in '89. She worked in the supermarket until the '77 flood, then moved to the shoe department.

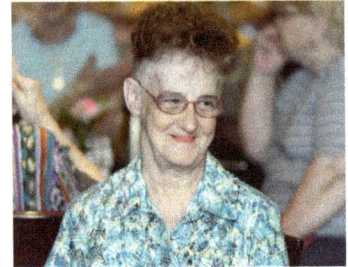

Alice Guizio

"The Glossers used to take us places," she says. "We had picnics, went to the Ice Capades, all sorts of things."

She still misses The Store today. "That was the only place we knew. That was our home away from home."

There are many other members of the club, each with a wealth of wonderful stories: Paulette Balog, Theresa Conway, Janet Felix, Esther Gerber, Madeline Lauper, Nita Prossen, Peggy Varholak, and more.

They share a bond, the kind that comes from working together for so many years...and carrying the torch of Glosser Bros. long after its closing. With their breakfasts, they've helped make sure that Glosser's--and the memories it made possible--are not forgotten.

There's another group, too, a group of women who get together regularly to reminisce over drinks at a local watering hole. Like the Breakfast Clubbers, they've kept it going all these years, sharing stories and laughter.

As long as these groups, and others like them, continue to meet, Glosser Bros. Department Store--though it might be closed forever--will never truly die.

Glosser Bros. Employees at the Boulevard Grill, December 2013
Front row, l. to r.: Sally Hohman, Peggy (Mirolvich) Beppler, Brenda (Brezensky) Lawhead, Susie Johns
Back row, l. to r.: Ronnie Washington, Linda Banko, Patty Bernat, Debbie Moehler, Ruth Pozun, Linda Eash, Robin Kibler

Photos by Philip Balko

The Breakfast Club

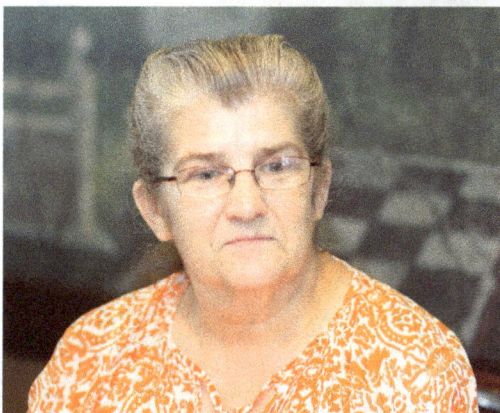

Photos by Philip Balko

Photos by Philip Balko

Chapter 40

The Ad Gang
(Buyer Included)

What would Glosser's reunion year be without a get-together of the people who were most responsible for the company's image on a daily basis?

Since the closing of The Store 25 years ago, stalwart members of the advertising department--and a loyal friend who was an international buyer--have met periodically to relive favorite memories and keep their bond alive.

They came together again this year to mark the anniversary of the closing--fittingly, meeting at the Press Bistro in the Glosser Building. They sat at the bar along the Franklin Street side, ten feet from the very same doors at the corner of Franklin and Locust that they'd walked through hundreds (thousands?) of times in their careers.

As they told their favorite stories of the old days and cracked each other up, it almost seemed like no time had passed for them at all.

Photo by Philip Balko

Under a Bridge in Altoona

Once upon a time, when Judy Crookston was working in the advertising department at Glosser Bros., thousands of dollars' worth of work got lost under a bridge.

"We had shipped a package to the printer, containing what we called 'assemblies,'" remembers Judy. "An assembly was a pre-printing version of a page from an advertising tabloid, with photo transparencies glued onto it.

"This one time, FedEx lost the package. This package contained maybe $65,000 worth of work, and it was just *gone*. And the clock was ticking. It had to reach the printer soon, or we wouldn't make our deadline.

"So we leaped into action. We started calling in the team, saying we're going to have to work Sunday because we have to redo this whole job.

"But then word reached us that the package had turned up after all," says Judy. "FedEx found it *under a bridge in Altoona*, of all places. How it had gotten there, I'll never know."

Judy started working in the advertising department at Glosser's in the early 1970s, joining a team she refers to as "a well-oiled machine." "We all went out of our way to help each other," she says. "It was like, 'I'm done with this, can I help you with that?'

"Other people came and went through the years, but the core group of us were still friends. And we still get together to this day."

Cranking Out Pages

Judy became head layout person for the Glosser Bros. division, helping to generate a staggering amount of advertising output. "The department put out dozens of pages of material every week for years," she says.

"Between Glosser's and Gee Bee, we put out a new tabloid every Sunday. Plus the ROPs-- the 'run of press' display ads in the daily papers.

"The tabloids would be either 24 or 36 pages of ads," says Judy. "So we were cranking out a lot of pages. And this was all done manually, without computers."

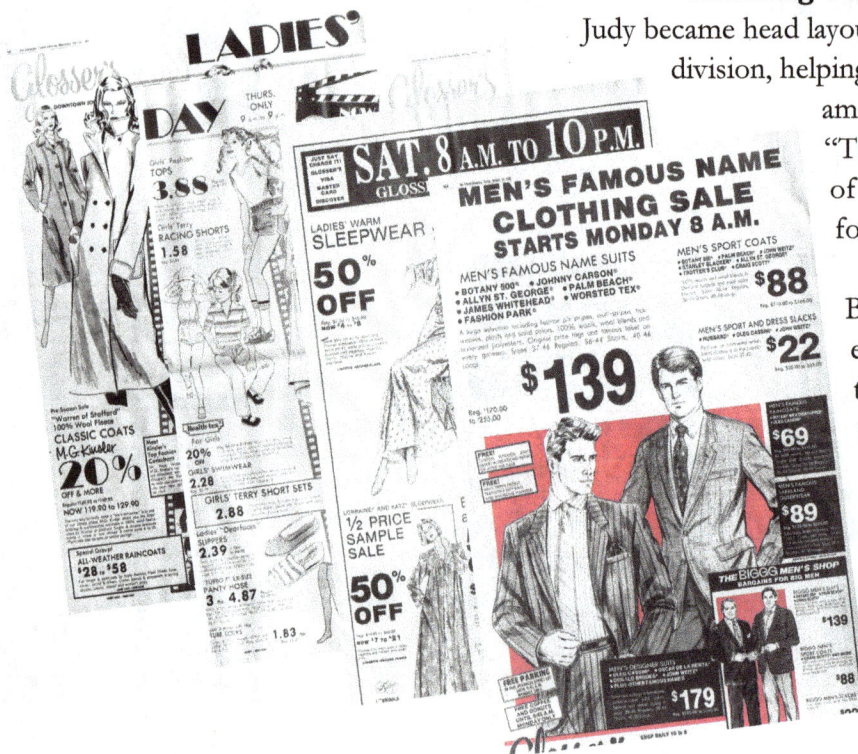

Photos by Philip Balko

372

It was a tough schedule to maintain, complicated by the fact that multiple projects were underway at the same time.

"We had to work four to six months ahead to keep things moving," says Judy. "Our tabloids were 12 weeks out, and we had six or seven of them in the works at any given moment, in different stages of completion.

"So while we were laying out one tabloid, another one was being proofed by the buyers, and another one was in the second proof stage. It was just this constant churn of organized chaos."

In addition to her other responsibilities, Judy handled all the photography for print advertising. She prepared detailed instructions on how to shoot each item for the tabloids or ROPs, then shipped them with samples of the items to photographers in New York City.

But sometimes, the items didn't make it on the truck as scheduled. "There were times when I had to take the train to New York," says Judy. "I had to carry stuff with me that didn't get shipped and absolutely had to be shot for an upcoming ad."

Life With Lazy Lucy

Like Judy, Sally Fink used to work in "advertising alley" at Glosser's...so named because the office was so narrow.

"We sat at slanted drawing tables on hard stools that weren't even close to being ergonomically correct," recalls Sally. "Good thing I was in my 20s and didn't have any back trouble at the time."

Sally, who was trained at the Art Institute of Pittsburgh, worked as a fashion illustrator at Glosser's from 1972 to 1976. In those pre-digital illustration days, the work was much more challenging than it is today.

"It was all hands-on," says Sally. "I actually drew the clothing freehand. A buyer would bring it to the department, hang it up, and I would draw it.

"The problem was, if the buyer didn't like the end result for some reason, I couldn't just revise an electronic file using graphic design software. I had to totally redraw the whole thing from scratch."

If Sally had an existing image to work from, she broke out the Lazy Lucy--a device that allowed her to trace the image and use it as the basis of a new drawing.

"I'd put the original illustration on a light table, so it was illuminated from below," says Sally. "Then I'd put the Lazy Lucy device over that. The Lazy Lucy would project a copy of the image on the table, and I could reduce or enlarge the projection using manual controls. Then, I just traced it onto a sheet of paper."

The resizing process didn't end there, though. Sally had to send the image next-door to the *Tribune-Democrat*, where staff members shot it with a special sizing camera. The resized image was printed on glue-backed paper called velox, which was cut and pasted onto a page to create the finished ad.

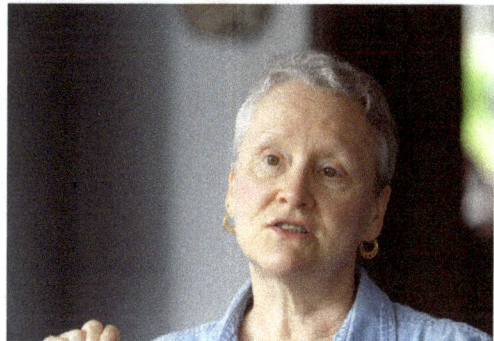

Photos by Philip Balko

It was a far cry from layout and design in the digital age, and the heavy workload kept up the pressure. "It depended on the day as to how many ads ran in the paper," says Sally. "Wednesday was the big day, with lots of full-page ads.

"On a day like that, it wasn't unusual to have to generate 6 to 10 pages of advertising."

Mr. Teddy Bear

What was Ed Craine's favorite thing about working as the advertising layout manager for the Gee Bee division? You name it.

"I enjoyed coming to work," says Ed. "I loved just working with the crew. It was the best time I ever had."

Ed never made a lot of money at Glosser Bros., but the people more than made up for it. Like so many other employees, he says the Glosser's team was like a family. They looked out for each other.

All the way to the top. "There was a guy who tried to get me fired once," he remembers. "He just didn't like me for some reason."

"You were a teddy bear," interjects Judy. "What's not to like?"

Ed smiles and shrugs. "Anyway, he went in to talk to Alvin Glosser. He told Alvin he wanted me out.

"And guess what? It didn't work. Because Alvin was looking out for me. My last name wasn't Glosser, but I was part of the Glosser Bros. family," says Ed.

Clockwork Drunks

Like Sally Fink, Marcia Martyak attended the Art Institute of Pittsburgh and came to work as an artist at Glosser's. She remembers those days well, especially the first of the month.

"The ad department was located by the men's bathroom on the fourth floor," says Marcia. "On the first of the month, the alcoholics would come in, and they'd be drunk because they'd gotten their monthly relief checks. It was like clockwork. Naturally, they'd stop at the bathroom at some point, and we could hear them yelling all kinds of crazy stuff at each other."

Marcia remembers other characters from those days, too, like the homeless lady who collected cans from the dumpster out back.

"She would put items on layaway on the fourth floor, near our office," says Marcia. "She'd get them almost paid off, and then she'd tell the layaway staff she didn't want them. It was like a little savings account for her, a place where she could keep her money safe for a little while."

Photos by Philip Balko

Globetrotting for Glosser's

Cynthia Eplett never worked in the advertising department at Glosser's, but she's part of the ad gang just the same. She befriended them back in the day, and they stuck together from then on.

Cynthia started as a buyer's secretary in 1983, then became an assistant and finally a full-fledged buyer in 1986. That was when she started traveling the world.

"I was an import buyer, traveling primarily to Hong Kong and Taiwan," says Cynthia. "The idea being that we could find much better deals overseas in person than if we stayed in the U.S."

The trips lasted six weeks at a time, and Cynthia worked long hours...but she loved the experience. And as time went on, she got to see much more of the world than just Hong Kong and Taiwan.

"My boss was very good at getting more miles out of the company," says Cynthia. "He even got them to pay for a trip that was literally all the way around the world."

For that around-the-world journey, Cynthia and her fellow buyers started in Frankfurt, Germany, then traveled on from Europe to the Far East. "We went to Hong Kong, Taiwan, Macau, Korea, Japan, and more. I don't even remember everywhere we went without checking the stamps on my passport. There were so many."

Cynthia got to see plenty of the U.S., too--from New York to New Orleans to California to Hawaii.

She hasn't traveled as much since she left Glosser's in 1988, but she still treasures her memories of going around the world...and the lasting friendships she made with the gang from the advertising department.

The Road to Now

What roads did the ad gang and Cynthia follow after the closing of Glosser's? What have they done in the 25 years since then?

Sally worked in the art department at *The Tribune-Democrat* for 24 years, eventually becoming art director. Marcia worked several jobs and has a business painting portraits and designing custom glassware. Cynthia sells real estate in Johnstown.

Photos by Philip Balko

As for Judy and Ed, they stayed with Glosser Bros. through the closing of The Store, the sale of the company to Schottenstein Stores, and the swan song of Gee Bee and Dollar Bargain. Judy, in fact, helped close down the last remnants of Glosser Bros., traveling back and forth to Columbus, Ohio for eight weeks in 1992.

Today, she has her own photography studio, and her Glosser's days bring her plenty of happy memories.

"They did not pay a lot," she says. "Nobody got rich working there. But they were just really nice to you. If they liked you, they treated you like gold. They treated you like family."

Photos by Philip Balko

Memory Department

I remember that Glosser's started and sponsored the annual Halloween parade every year. They also allowed students to paint the windows at holiday time. I remember the escalator in the middle of the store; my first time up it, I dropped all my popcorn while trying to grab onto something. I also remember Glosser's being the place to transfer buses (since all the buses stopped there) before the transit center. I remember the grocery store in the basement (and Gee Bee ice cream) before the 1977 flood and the basement becoming the toy department after the flood.

At Christmas time, you were almost certain to be able to get Christmas work at Glosser's if you wanted it. I remember working at the wrapping station on the top floor (outside the office), wrapping customers' purchases for Christmas presents. I remember the cashiers on the main floor sending your credit card purchase (bill) through the pipes to the office for approval.

On Thursday nights, Glosser's was open; it was closed on Sundays. I remember shoppers gathered at the main door (which was an entrance inside the outside doors) waiting for the store to open for sales.

- Joanne Vernalli

I loved entering Glosser's at Christmas time and seeing the beautiful lit Christmas tree on the building. It never failed to put a smile on my face. I also loved how beautifully the store was decorated inside. Glosser Bros. had class. I sure miss that store.

- Carol Lutz

Christmas 1976 (courtesy of Johnstown Area Heritage Association)

The windows of Glosser Bros store were a true work of art, and the eyes of the store. Jim Reed was in charge of decorating them and changing them for the new seasons or special sales. There were about 13 or 14, I think. Mostly, they lined the Central Park side of the building. How they showed off the store, especially at Christmas shopping time with the snowflakes falling.

- Chris Bittner-Italiano

I worked in the men's department and cameras for years. The one thing I remember most about Glosser's is that we shared laughter, tears, and sorrow (too many times), life beginnings and life endings, but most of all WE WERE A FAMILY!

- Maxi Prucnal

Glosser Bros. offered employee discounts to all employees, and the discount could also be used in all the Gee Bee stores. There was very nice merchandise to be had, including groceries, clothing, hardware, toys, electronics, televisions, cameras, and candy. You could also use your discount at the cookie counter or lunch counter.

- Paula Katie Buynack Becker

Ah, the cafeteria! So underappreciated at the time. Who can forget the twins at the snack bar? After they gave you your order they would say, "And what else?" every single time.

- Jen Lehman

I worked in the credit department, and I remember we used to have to take turns staying in Glosser's at night when the store was closed until 10:00 P.M., to approve individual credit charges from Gee Bee. I was just out of high school. The cleaning crew was there but that was it.

- Mary Ann Kamler DiMauro

When Glosser Bros. had a bridal department, I organized, produced, and did the commentary for some bridal fashion shows. My daughter Amy modeled, as did Mindy Glosser, Alvin's daughter.

- *Rita Glosser (wife of Paul Glosser)*

1978 Bridal Show (courtesy of Robin Eiseman)

Gee Bee Richland, 1970 (courtesy of Johnstown Area Heritage Association)

Courtesy of Maria Reavel Wengert

Pete Vizza/The Tribune-Democrat

The board of directors Members of the board of directors of Glosser Bros., Inc., are (left to right) Isadore Glosser, Herbert Sinberg, Sydney Ossip, Alvin M. Glosser, Leonard J. Black, William L. Glosser, W. Louis Coppersmith, Samuel B. Roth, N. Gwynne Dodson, Richard L. Van Horn, Fred Glosser and Clarence A. Peterson. Paul L. Glosser was absent.

20   The Johnstown Tribune-Democrat, Thursday, September 10, 1981

Chapter 41

A Family Reunion, Part 2

Sometimes, the very best stories end where they began, don't they? So let's go back to where *our* story started...

On a sunny Memorial Day morning in May, more than 70 former employees of Glosser Bros. gathered in front of the old department store building. They came to the corner of Franklin and Locust Streets to be part of a reunion and photo shoot commemorating the 25th anniversary of The Store's closing in 1989.

But this reunion was the furthest thing from a somber affair. Everyone present was grinning and hugging and shaking hands. They could barely stop talking and laughing long enough to have their photos taken.

Some of them hadn't seen each other in years...or decades. Some of them lived far away and had come to town just for this event...while others lived in the same nearby homes where they'd lived in Glosser Bros. days.

Photo by Philip Balko

But all of them came together again on this special day. They broke out their biggest smiles and warmest hellos for the occasion; they also broke out those prized possessions that had always been the best things to come out of Glosser's, right from the start until the finish and beyond.

They had broken out their best *stories*.

Everybody's Psychiatrist

Rose Samuels Reed worked for years as the elevator operator and head cashier in the shoe department at Glosser's. But the work she loved the most wasn't part of her official job description.

"Every morning on the elevator, everybody thought I was a psychiatrist," remembered Rose. "They'd come and tell me all their problems."

She laughed. "If I'd been paid like a psychiatrist, I'd've been rich back then."

"Ring Bell for Help"

William Chase worked in the basement grocery store from 1961 until 1977 (then worked at a Gee Bee supermarket until 1989). It never ceased to amaze him that Glosser's customers were so faithful that they put up with the inconvenience of underground grocery shopping.

"They couldn't just wheel in a shopping cart, fill it up, and wheel it back out again," remembered William. "First, they had to walk down the steps into the basement. Then, after putting their groceries in a basket, they had to walk back up the steps carrying what could be a very heavy load."

When the going got heavy, though, Glosser's employees came to the rescue, thanks to a special bell. "We had a little bell down there, and a sign that said, 'Ring Bell for Help.' When a customer rang the bell, we would hurry over and carry their purchases up to the cash registers on the ground floor.

"Sometimes, it was a single basket we had to carry. Other times, it was a couple baskets, and it took a couple employees to carry them up. It could be a lot of work, but it was worth it. We loved helping our customers," said William.

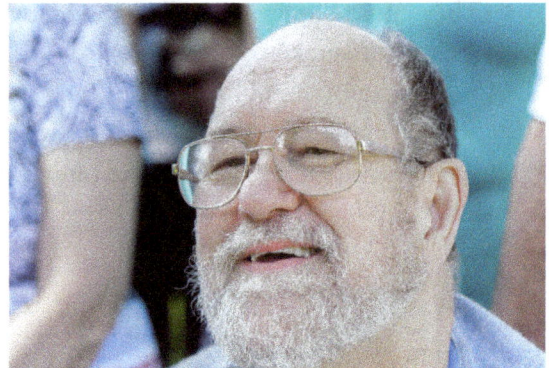

Photos by Philip Balko

A Tip of the Hat

Old-fashioned Bargain Days was Debbie Moeller's cup of tea. She loved how local vendors set up booths in Central Park, selling food and crafts.

But she especially loved how Glosser Bros. got into the spirit of things. Employees got to wear costumes to work, often based on a common theme. "One year, we had a carnival, like they did in the movie *Pollyanna*," said Debbie.

Photo by Philip Balko

And sometimes, there were prizes given out for the best costumes...or *parts* of them, at least. "I'll never forget the hat contest we had. People wore the craziest, most elaborate hats you could think of. It was so much *fun*.

"Especially because *I* won the prize for best hat that year." Debbie swirled her hand over her head as if to conjure the winning hat from thin air. "You should have *seen* it."

Ups and Downs

The award for biggest prize winner might just go to Linda Hockenberry, though. When she was a little girl in 1950, her family won a car during Glosser's anniversary sale.

"The winning numbers were posted in Glosser's window," says Linda. "My mother wrote them down and checked them against our numbers when she came home. 'I think we won the car,' she said, and then she sent my father down to the

Al and Linda Hockenberry

store to check and see if we really did win.

"So my dad ran down to Glosser's, and sure enough, the numbers matched! He was so excited, he pounded on the side door, and the night watchman ran over to see what was happening. Dad just kept waving his prize-winning ticket and shouting about the car he'd just won."

But the biggest prize Linda won at The Store wasn't a car or any kind of object. It was a *husband*.

"Margie the elevator operator introduced me to Al in the elevator in 1961," says Linda. "He worked in the men's department for Alvin Glosser, and I worked on the fourth floor in advertising.

"We got married in 1963, two years after meeting on the elevator. We always tell people we've had a lot of ups and downs since then."

Al and Linda Hockenberry's Wedding Day

The Welcome Back Sale

The stories went on and on that day, among the fluttering bright green leaves enfolding Central Park. How many of those tales had been retold dozens of times through the years, or even hundreds? How many had twists and turns and punchlines that were so well-worn, everyone in that crowd could quote them by heart?

And how many of those stories featured people who were no longer in this world? Employees, bosses, and shoppers who had passed away down through the decades? Remarkable characters in their own right, who had helped--each in his or her own unique way--to make Glosser Bros. the store, the institution, and the *dream* that it was?

In the telling of those stories, they came back that day. They mingled in the warm summer sun among their co-workers, customers, survivors...*family*.

The park and sidewalks around Glosser's were so much more crowded than they appeared to be. As long as those memories and voices brought life to the missing, all was overlaid with a diaphanous double-image, a shimmering outline of faces past and present.

If you listened hard enough to the stories and cocked your head *just right* and squinted a little, maybe you could have made them out: Leonard Black and Alvin Glosser looking out a window on the fourth floor. Ruth Shaffer on her way to the soda fountain to serve ice cream sundaes and banana splits. Paul Newman filming *Slap Shot* by the windows on Locust Street. Kids taking potshots at a hot-air balloon on the roof.

The lights of the Christmas tree draped around the corner at Locust and Franklin, twinkling in a swirl of lacy snowflakes.

The doors at the corner glide open and people wave for you to come in, *come in*, just look at the glow of the silver and glass, breathe in the smell of the

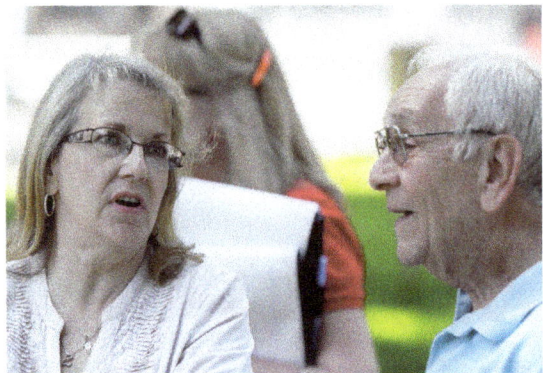

Photos by Philip Balko

386

roasting peanuts and cashews, it's the Welcome Back sale you've always dreamed of, you've been here hundreds of times and you're always *always* welcome, just as welcome as you were the first time you ever set foot in The Store.

Is someone calling your name over the loudspeakers? Do you recognize that man trying on a raincoat? That woman in the shoe department, that child scampering up the escalator?

Your eyes burn a little; you think you might cry. And your feet start to move, almost of their own accord. There's never any doubt about where they will take you.

A marching band passes, brass flashing in the everlasting sunlight, and then the marchers and crowd part just enough so you can cross the street to the beckoning threshold.

And you go in...

Photos by Philip Balko

Photos by Philip Balko

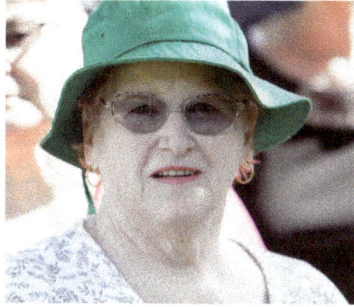

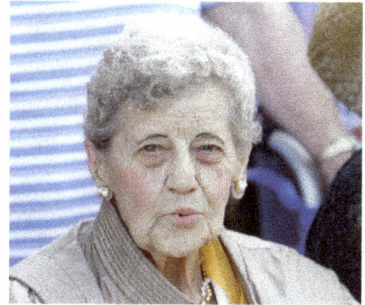
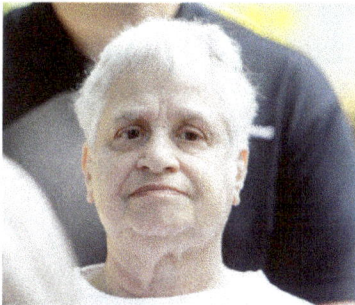

Photos by Philip Balko

Photos by Philip Balko

Photos by Philip Balko

Photos by Philip Balko

Acknowledgements

In many ways, this book is a true group effort. Many people have contributed to it in one way or another, their generosity fueled by the same motivation that made me want to write it in the first place: a desire to hold the finished product in their hands, to capture the story of Glosser Bros. before it could be lost forever.

These contributors include the many individuals who donated photographs and artifacts from their personal collections (see photo credits throughout the book for their names); the many Facebook members who provided anecdotes about their personal Glosser's experiences; the many Glosser Bros. employees who participated in the reunion celebrations; and, of course, the folks who provided the oral histories that formed the backbone of *Long Live Glosser's*. These living repositories of Glosser Bros. history gave generously of their time in helping me record and shape the narrative of the book. They all deserve special recognition, including: Fred and Betty Glosser; Izzy and Ruth Glosser; Sydney Ossip; Bill Hritz; Ruby Shaffer; Betty Black; Mary Schuster; Bill Glosser; Paul and Rita Glosser; Saul Glosser; David Glosser; Daniel Glosser; Arlene and Jack Goss; and everyone else who gave of their time in providing interviews or anecdotes for the book.

Thanks also to Chip Minimeyer, executive editor of *The Tribune-Democrat*, for generously allowing me to include photos from that publication in this book.

I also appreciate the efforts of Kaytlin Sumner of the Johnstown Area Heritage Association; she assisted me in obtaining images from JAHA's archives for use in *Long Live Glosser's*. Marcia Kelly at JAHA provided top-notch image digitization services. Miriam Meislik at the University of Pittsburgh also provided support in locating and obtaining clearances for archival materials.

While we're on the subject of research, Jennifer Pruchnic at the Cambria County Library supplied first-class research support in the development of this project. The entire reference library staff deserves kudos for their able and prompt assistance.

Pat DeRubis, chief fiscal officer of Cambria County Human Services, also merits special thanks. Pat made it possible for Fred Glosser and I to tour the Glosser Building, now known as the Central Park Complex.

For meritorious service above and beyond the call of duty, I have to give a huge shout-out to Phil Balko, the official photographer and photography editor on this project. This man truly loves Glosser's and went out of his way to help make this book a reality. Do me a favor and shake his hand when you see him, because he really came through for Glosser Nation.

Thanks as well to Linda Hudkins, legendary *Altoona Mirror* writer/reporter/editor, for providing editorial services.

Of course, the highest commendation goes to my wife, Wendy Jeschonek, for her infinite support and understanding. Her contributions and sacrifices throughout the development of this book are too many to count. And her love of Glosser's, which exceeds that of anyone I know, helped to inspire me to write this book in the first place.

Special thanks goes to my grandparents, Bernard and Margaret Heinrich, for all the times they took me to Glosser's when I was a little boy. Without them, and their deep appreciation of the world within The Store, this book would not have happened.

Finally, thank you to all the members of Glosser Nation out there, who kept the story alive long after The Store was no more, therefore making this book possible. There are too many of you to name, but you know who you are. Now say it with me, won't you? One more time:

Long Live Glosser's!

October 10, 2014, Johnstown, PA

About the Creators

Robert

Author and editor Robert Jeschonek grew up in Johnstown and spent many happy hours as a kid in the Glosser Bros. Department Store. Since then, he has gone on to write lots of books and stories, including *Christmas at Glosser's, Fear of Rain,* and *Death By Polka* (which are all set in and around Johnstown). He's written a lot of other cool stuff, too, including *Star Trek* and *Doctor Who* fiction and *Batman* comics. His young adult fantasy novel, *My Favorite Band Does Not Exist*, won a Forward National Literature Award and was named a top ten first novel for youth by *Booklist* magazine. His work has been published around the world in over a hundred books, e-books, and audio books. You can find out more about them at his website, www.thefictioneer.com, or by looking up his name on Facebook, Twitter, or Google. As you'll see, he's kind of crazy...in a *good* way.

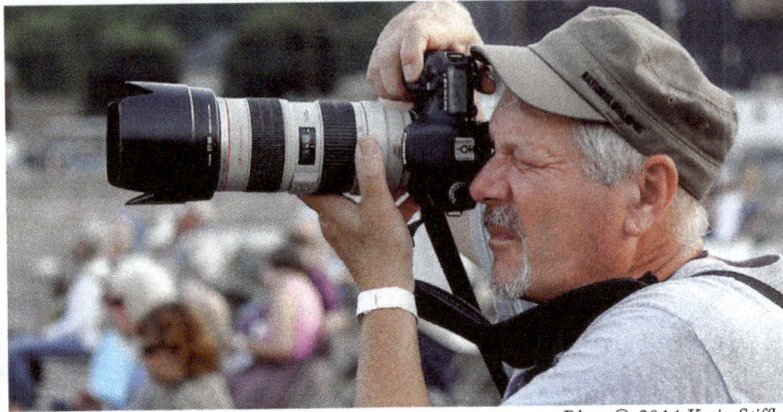

Photo © 2014 Kevin Stiffler

Phil

Photo editor Philip Balko is an award-winning photographer whose work has been published in newspapers and magazines across the state, and internationally. Phil specializes in portrait, wedding, and landscape photography. His scenes of the Allegheny Highlands can be viewed at www.laurelight.com. He can be contacted through his studio website at www.philipbalko.com.

Phil says, "My fondest memories of Glosser's include the bouquet of diesel busses, the blind man and his guide dog selling Hershey Bars at the entrance, the aroma of roasted cashews, the magic of the escalator at Christmas time, and the occasional Vanilla Smash in the cafeteria. I am especially grateful to Bob for this opportunity and for the people met, the stories shared, and the sights seen."

Ben

Cover artist and graphic designer Ben Baldwin is a self-taught freelance artist who lives in the UK and works with a combination of traditional media, photography, and digital art programs. He has been shortlisted for the British Fantasy Award for Best Artist for the last four years and has also been shortlisted for the British Science Fiction Association Award for Best Artist. Last year, he won "Best Artist of the Year" in the annual This Is Horror Awards. You can find out more about Ben and his work at www.benbaldwin.co.uk and https://www.facebook.com/pages/Ben-Baldwin/343132594365

Bibliography

"1936 & 1977 Floods." JAHA. http://www.jaha.org/FloodMuseum/1936.html

"And 47 Years Later...Another Disaster." JohnstownPA.com. http://www.johnstownpa.com/History/hist20.html

Black, Betty. Phone interview by Robert Jeschonek. Digital recording. August 17, 2014.

Black, Leonard. "Glosser Bros., Inc. Announces Purchase of Data Consultants, Inc." News release, February 8, 1978.

Black, Leonard. "Glosser Bros., Inc. Announces Two New Gee Bee Department Stores in Pittsburgh & York, Pennsylvania." News release, October 26, 1979.

Black, Leonard. "Glosser Bros., Inc. Leases Six Former Acme Supermarkets." News release, July 6, 1979.

Black, Leonard. *Letter to Shareholders.* Johnstown, August 1977.

Black, Leonard and Glosser, Alvin. *First Quarter Report.* Johnstown, 1983.

Black, Leonard and Glosser, Alvin. *Letter to Shareholders.* Johnstown, March 1984.

Breakfast Club at the Holiday Inn. Video interview by Robert Jeschonek. Digital recording. July 1, 2014.

Crichton, Jean. "Music and Lights of Main Street." *Johnstown: The Story of a Unique Valley.* Johnstown. 1985.

Craine, Edward M., Judy Crookston, Cynthia Eplett, Sally Fink, and Marcia Martyak. Video interview by Robert Jeschonek. Digital recording. May 27, 2014.

Disaster's Wake: A Retrospective of the 1977 Johnstown Flood. Johnstown: *The Tribune-Democrat,* 2007.

Drahuschak, Greg M. "Glosser Brothers latest target of buyout rumors." Taking Stock. *Pittsburgh Business Times,* June 18-24, 1984.

Ferrell, Jesse. "1936 Johnstown Flood - How Much Rain?" Accuweather, March 17, 2009. http://www.accuweather.com/en/weather-blogs/weathermatrix/1936-johnstown-flood-how-much-rain/18454

Ferrell, Jesse. "What Caused the Johnstown Floods?" Accuweather, July 17, 2007. http://www.accuweather.com/en/weather-blogs/weathermatrix/edu-what-caused-1/10046

Flood '77. Johnstown: *The Tribune-Democrat,* 2002.

Glosser, Alvin. "Glosser Bros., Inc. To Open New Gee Bee Department Store in Plaza Shopping Center, Selinsgrove, Pennsylvania." News release, March 20, 1980.

Glosser, Alvin. *Letter to Shareholders.* Johnstown, March 1982.

Glosser Bros., Inc. *Annual Report of Glosser Bros., Inc.: Fiscal Year Ending January 27, 1973.* Johnstown, 1973.

Glosser Bros., Inc. *Annual Report of Glosser Bros., Inc.: Fiscal Year Ended February 1, 1975.* Johnstown, 1975.

Glosser Bros., Inc. *Annual Report of Glosser Bros., Inc.: Fiscal Year Ended January 31, 1976.* Johnstown, 1976.

Glosser Bros., Inc. *Annual Report of Glosser Bros., Inc.: Fiscal Year Ended January 29, 1977.* Johnstown, 1977.

Glosser Bros., Inc. *Annual Report of Glosser Bros., Inc.: Fiscal Year Ended January 28, 1978.* Johnstown, 1978.

Glosser Bros., Inc. *Annual Report of Glosser Bros., Inc.: Fiscal Year Ended January 26, 1980.* Johnstown, 1980.

Glosser Bros., Inc. *Annual Report of Glosser Bros., Inc.: Fiscal Year Ended January 29, 1983.* Johnstown, 1983.

Glosser Bros. 25th Anniversary Reunion. Video interviews by Robert Jeschonek. Digital recording. May 26, 2014.

"Glosser Bros. Baby Derby Is Popular." *The Tribune-Democrat*, April 18, 1953.

"Glosser Brothers Grows With The Community." *The Tribune-Democrat*, April 18, 1953.

Glosser, Bill. Interview by Robert Jeschonek. Digital recording. April 7, 2014.

Glosser, Dan. Phone interview by Robert Jeschonek. Written notes. August 22, 2014.

Glosser, David. Phone interview by Robert Jeschonek. Written notes. July 17, 2014.

Glosser, Fred. Phone interview by Robert Jeschonek. Digital recording. June 13, 2014.

Glosser, Fred. Video interview by Robert Jeschonek. Digital recording. July 29, 2014.

Glosser, Freda. Phone interview by Robert Jeschonek. Digital recording. July 16, 2014.

Glosser, Izzy. Phone interview by Robert Jeschonek. Digital recording. June 18, 2014.

Glosser, Izzy. Phone interview by Robert Jeschonek. Digital recording. July 17, 2014.

Glosser, Morton. Phone interview by Robert Jeschonek. Written notes. August 20, 2014.

Glosser, Paul. Phone interview by Robert Jeschonek. Digital recording. September 9, 2014.

Glosser, Ruth. *A Precious Legacy: Louis Glosser and Bessie Greenberg Glosser 1854-1929*. Johnstown. 1998.

"Glosser rally off; some marchers turned up anyway." *The Tribune-Democrat*, May 15, 1989.

Glosser, Saul. Phone interview by Robert Jeschonek. Digital recording. August 19, 2014.

"Glosser's Early Self-Serve Food Market Was One of the First of Its Kind in Country." *The Tribune-Democrat*, April 18, 1953.

Goss, Arlene and Jack. Video interview by Robert Jeschonek. Digital recording. September 6, 2014.

Horton, Linda. "Johnstown, PA Flood, Mar 1936." Gendisasters, November 13, 2007. http://www3.gendisasters.com/pennsylvania/2806/johnstown,-pa-flood,-mar-1936

Hritz, Bill. Phone interview by Robert Jeschonek. Written notes. July 17, 2014.

Mamula, Kris B. "Crown ups Glosser's bid." *The Tribune-Democrat*, February 8, 1990.

Mamula, Kris B. "What Glosser's closing means to Johnstown." *The Tribune-Democrat*, May 8, 1989.

McCready, Jeff. "Crown wants Gee Bee, not Bargain unit." *The Tribune-Democrat*, February 4, 1990.

McCready, Jeff. "Glosser bankruptcy developments a legal first?" *The Tribune-Democrat*, February 9, 1990.

McCready, Jeff. "Glosser closing's still on." *The Tribune-Democrat*, May 11, 1989.

McCready, Jeff. "Glosser's fate up to judge." *The Tribune-Democrat*, May 15, 1989.

McCready, Jeff. "Glosser has new plan for store." *The Tribune-Democrat*, April 27, 1989.

McCready, Jeff. "Glosser's accepts merger proposal." *The Tribune-Democrat*, November 25, 1989.

McCready, Jeff. "Glosser's closing downtown store." *The Tribune-Democrat*, March 28, 1989.

McCready, Jeff. "Glosser's earnings surge; stocks at new highs." *The Tribune-Democrat*, March 19, 1983.

McCready, Jeff. "Glosser's is closing 20 stores." *The Tribune-Democrat*, December 28, 1989.

McCready, Jeff. "Glosser Bros. Department Store 1906-1989." *The Tribune-Democrat*, May 27, 1989.

McCready, Jeff. "Judge: no Glosser's stay." *The Tribune-Democrat*, May 26, 1989.

McCready, Jeff. "Potential buyer for Glosser's." *The Tribune-Democrat*, April 21, 1989.

McCready, Jeff. "Save-Glosser's bid." *The Tribune-Democrat*, March 31, 1989.

McCready, Jeff. "The keys to saving Glosser's." *The Tribune-Democrat*, April 3, 1989.

McHugh, John F. "FCC action looms on Laurel TV's bid for new channel here." *The Tribune-Democrat*, January 20, 1984.

"Merchandising With Color Marks Store's History." *The Tribune-Democrat*, April 18, 1953.

Ossip, Sydney. Phone interview by Robert Jeschonek. Digital recording. July 17, 2014.

Phyrillas, Tony. "No Frills at U Save Warehouse." *The Daily Collegian*, January 7, 1983.

Reabuck, Sandra K. "New Glosser proposal eyes." *The Tribune-Democrat*, August 31, 1993.

Sabo, Bill. Phone interview by Robert Jeschonek. Written notes. August 27, 2014.

Schuster, Mary. Phone interview by Robert Jeschonek. Digital recording. September 22, 2014.

Shaffer, Ruby. Video interview by Robert Jeschonek. Digital recording. August 24, 2014.

Siehl, James W. "Glosser parade, rally set Friday." *The Tribune-Democrat*, May 9, 1989.

Swauger, Kirk. "Glosser retains hopes for store." *The Tribune-Democrat*, July 24, 1989.

"The top 83 companies in sales." *The Discount Merchandiser*, May 1979.

Whittle, Randy. *Johnstown, Pennsylvania: A History, Part One: 1895-1936*. Charleston: History Press, 2005.

Whittle, Randy. *Johnstown, Pennsylvania: A History, Part Two: 1937-1980*. Charleston: History Press, 2007.

Zurrilla, Thomas J. *Letter to Co-Workers, Store #41*. Johnstown, March 27, 1989.

Photo © The Tribune-Democrat

Old World traditions make fabulous fashion innovations for today. Here are some of our favorites from Michael Murray and Coco Creations.

72A — Imported Pakistan leather gaucho vest. Multicolor hand-sewn embroidery and tassel trim. Red, black. S-M 25.00

72B—Imported Moroccan hand-tooled leather shoulder bag. Earth tones 8.00

72C—20-inch all-silk imported Indian squares. Hand-blocked paisley, foulard patterns, hand-rolled edges. Assorted holiday tones 3.00

72D—Pure silk imported Moroccan braided thread cords to wear as a belt or jewelry. Black and jewel tones 3.00

72E—Imported Pakistan black velvet vest with silver or gold embroidery 25.00

72F—Imported Pakistan velvet bag with silver or gold embroidery. Holiday colors 8.00

GLOSSER BROS, INC.
Franklin & Locust Sts.
Johnstown, Pa. 15901

BULK RATE
U. S. POSTAGE
PAID
Permit No. 46
Johnstown, Pa.

Pants Plus—the fashion answer for holiday!

62A—Alex Colman's sleeveless, washable Dacron® polyester diagonal knit vest. Coral, violet. Sizes 10 to 18 .... 21.00

62B—Matching pull-on pant with elasticized waist, stitched crease 16.00

62C — Geometric print acetate overshirt. Coral/brandy, violet/blue. 10 to 18 ... 15.00

62D—Belted tunic and straight-leg pant by Spertempo in 70% wool/30% Dacron® polyester knit. Aqua, beige. Size 8 to 16 . . 48.00

62E—Puccini by Tiffany Manor teams this full-fashioned, cable-trim sweater tunic with a double-knit straight-leg pant. Both 100% wool. Flame, periwinkle. Sizes 8 to 16 . . 48.00

What's the fashion word for holiday? The answer is Pants-Plus!

63A—Echo Bay's short sleeve jumpsuit in machine-washable double-knit acrylic. 8 to 16, eggplant, black 26.00

63B—Dacron® polyester waffle-textured knit tunic with tri-color border stripes by Devon. Machine washable and dryable. Sizes 8 to 18. Flax, black 16.00

63C—Matching straight-leg pull-on pant 14.00

63D—Robert Alan's washable 70% acetate/ 30% Fortrel® polyester belted jumpsuit with zip-front convertible turtleneck. Sizes 8 to 16 in red, navy 32.00

Knit toppings for holiday!

65A—Helen Harper's space-dyed Acrilan® acrylic ribbed body sweater with long sleeves, mock turtleneck, industrial zipper. Monsanto's Wear-Dated® guarantee, too.* Brown/grey/white/brass, navy/red/white/yellow. Sizes S-M-L . **12.00**

65B—Long sleeve ribbed acrylic knit turtleneck sweater by Miss Gotham. Yours in white, navy, red. Sizes S-M-L **8.00**

65C—Penrose's short sleeve Orlon® acrylic chain-stitch sweater with jewel neck. 3-button shoulder. Egg shell, gold. Sizes S-M-L **7.00**

65D—Zip-front Orlon® acrylic boucle stitch sweater by Penrose with short sleeves, mock turtleneck. Sizes S-M-L in eggshell, navy **9.00**

* Wear Dated®—"Guaranteed for one full year's normal wear, refund or replacement when returned with tag and sales slip to Monsanto."

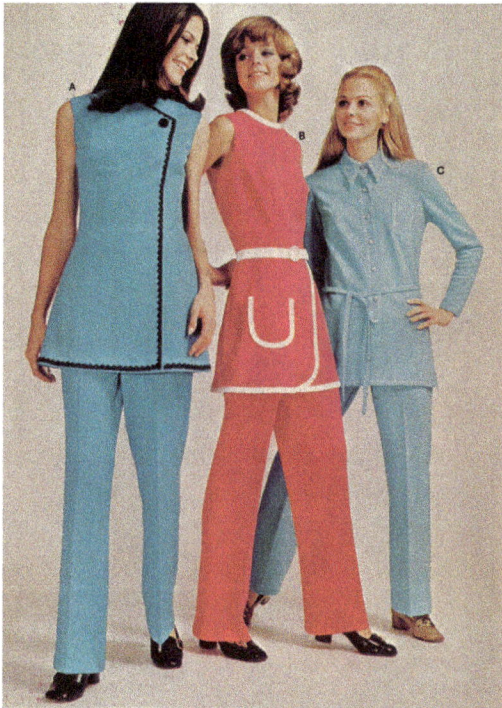

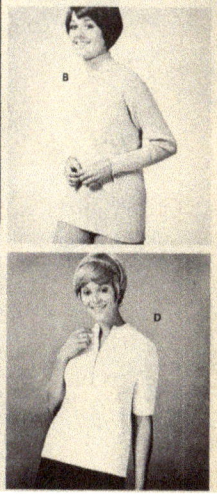

Kay Windsor's sensational Dacron® polyester double knit pant dresses look great for holiday and cruise time.

64A—Sleeveless top with braid and button accents. Matching pant. Coral, aqua, black. Sizes 10 to 18 . . . . **34.00**

64B—Sleeveless top with contrast trim and belt, wrap-effect skirt. Matching pants. Sizes 8 to 16 in coral, aqua, black . . . **34.00**

64C—Long-sleeve shirt top with placket-front and contrast stitching. Matching pants. Aqua, green, black in sizes 10 to 18 . . **38.00**

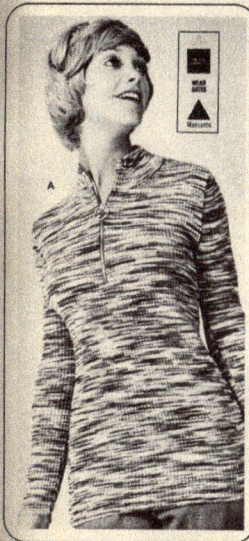

Sheffield tells holiday time!

10A—Link bracelet watch with white stick dial. Gold, silver tone **20.00**

10B — Pendant watch with Roman numerals. Gold, silver **15.00**

10C—La Regale's "beetle bead" evening pouch with snake chain handle. Iridescent white, gold, silver **11.00**

10D — "Knirps" by New York Umbrella. 12½ inch nylon telescopic umbrella. Frame guaranteed for life. Black, red, navy **8.00**

K. Gimbel designs great fashion luggage for holiday giving.

10E — Krinkle vinyl patent nested luggage with two-tone fashion accents. Black / red, red / navy, black/amber, amber/black.
16", 17" sizes **7.00**
18", 19" sizes **8.00**
20", 21" sizes **9.00**

10F — Soft vinyl, double-handle travel tote. Black, brown, amber **6.00**

10F1—Same tote in cotton corduroy. Fashion colors **7.00**

COLLECTOR'S CORNER

Choose from charming fashion accessories for holiday gifts.

11A—Burmel's imported acetate chiffon print oblong scarf. Hand rolled, 15 x 63" size. Blue, green, orange, shocking pink **5.00**

11B—Dyed rabbit headband earmuff by Madamoiselle Specialities in fashion colors **2.50**

11C—David E. Schwab's Dacron® polyester 15-inch initial handkerchief. All white, pastels on white **1.25**

11D—Pure silk 28-inch square print scarves by Baar & Beards **3.50**

Bueno does the suede thing in two great shoulder bags.

18A—Triple-tier fringe shoulder bag in shag suede. Flap closing. Camel, brown 7.00

18B—Suede and leather hobo short shoulder bag, full top zipper. Camel/cognac, black/black, brown/walnut. 9.00

David D works sensational fashion ways with shag suede fringe and things.

18C—The suede fringed poncho ... 17.00
18D—The long fringe cuff 5.00
18E—The fringe and disc headband that's also bracelet, belt, choker 3.00
18F—The newest multi-color embroidered waistlette belt 8.00
18G—Shag suede and earthstone choker. Amethyst, ruby, topaz, emerald in golden setting on suede 5.00
18H—Matching bracelet 5.00

FRINGE BINGE

19A — Fourth Additions presents this Caprolan® nylon tricot ensemble for holiday. Sheer pleated short coat tops opaque satin gown and bikini panties. White, black, blue. Sizes P-S-M-L. 13.00

19D—Siren's brushed nylon/acetate "Love" tunic with long pants. P-S-M-L in ivory/tomato red, pink/shocking pink 9.00
19D1—Matching Mini-shift and bikini panties 7.00

Here are two great footed bunny sleepers for you from Barad in 100% cotton flannel with reinforced non-skid soles.

19B—Ticking stripe one-piece sleeper with drop seat, eyelet trim. Pink, Navy. P-S-M-L 11.00
19C — Scandinavian print one-piece sleeper with drawstring neck. Red. P-S-M-L 10.00
19C1—Matching 2-pc sleeper 11.00

Who's got the greatest pant coat looks? Swingles by Character, that's who ... in sizes 5 to 15 and 6 to 16.

68A—Sculptured Regina "super wale" cotton corduroy pant coat with the four-pocket safari look. Fashion belt, warm acrylic pile lining. Pumpkin, brown 34.00
68B—Double-breasted wool melton pant coat with knit accents on collar. Flap patch pockets. Quilt lined, polyester fiberfill. Coffee, camel 42.00
68C—Make-believe beaver pant coat in acrylic pile with quilt lining and polyester fiberfill. Lots of "wet look" fashion accents. Brown, sand 38.00

RAINPAKA Travelers by David Smith —the anywhere coats that travel in their own pockets. A fabulous rain-or-shine coat that folds easily into its own pocket for travel, town or just toting around.

69A—Leopard-print acetate jersey coat with notch collar, wet-look buttons and tie belt. Wrinkle-proof. Natural, sizes 8 to 18 .... 45.00
69B—Nylon matelasse coat with side-button closing. Washable, wrinkle-proof. Bone. 6 to 18 .... 36.00
69C—Ladies' Petite Nylon Umbrella from New York Umbrella with crushed vinyl patent case. Black, navy, red 6.00

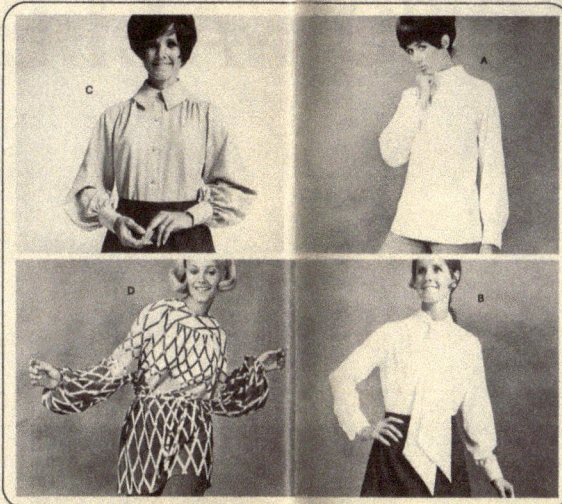

66A—Weber's Arnel® triacetate crepe tunic with long, full sleeves, elasticized wrists. Embroidered ribbon trim on square neck and separate sash tie. White with gray/black tone ribbon, pink with pink/purple tone ribbon. Sizes 8 to 16 .... 14.00
66B—The 28-inch, double-knit acetate print tunic by Mardi Modes with long sleeves, 3-button placket front, pointed collar. Blue, gold. Sizes 8 to 16 . 14.00
66C—Lady Arrow's long sleeve tuck-in shirt in fabulously washable Ultressa® texturized polyester. White, beige, navy. Sizes 8 to 16 .... 13.00
66D—Long sleeve, diamond pattern 30-inch tunic by Monique in Arnel® triacetate. Elasticized wrist, self sash tie. Lilac/purple, brown/black. Sizes 8 to 18. .... 13.00

67A—Judy Bond's long-sleeve turtleneck blouse in machine washable Arnel® triacetate crepe. Shirred-shoulder detailing. Sizes 10 to 18 in white, bone. 6.00
67B—Long sleeve, ascot tie blouse with button-front by Oak Hill in a machine washable blend of acetate/nylon crepe. Shirred shoulder detailing. White, blue. Sizes 10 to 18 .... 9.00
67C—Kelita's cotton challis print peasant tunic with wide laced belt, long full sleeves. Sizes 5 to 13 in assorted prints 14.00
67D—Mock turtleneck tunic by Fairfield in Blue C® nylon knit with Monsanto's Wear Dated® guarantee. Long sleeves, braid rope belt. White, poppy red, navy. Sizes 34 to 40 .... 10.00
* Wear Dated®—"Guaranteed for one full year's normal wear, refund or replacement when returned with tag and sales slip to Monsanto."

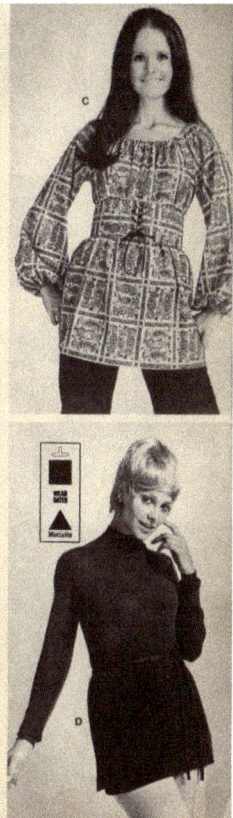

70A—Sally Gee's acrylic knit fringed triangle shawl. American-made. White, natural 8.00
70B—Fringed triangle shawl from Baar & Beards in Orlon® acrylic/wool jersey. American made. Black, red, white 10.00
70C—Sally Gee's imported acrylic Chanel sweater, lined. S-M-L. White only 8.00
70C1—Same in XL 9.00
70D—Acrylic plaid 5' scarf by Baar & Beards 2.50
70E—Baar & Beards long acrylic stripe scarves. Assorted colors, stripes 3.50
70F—Sally Gee's American-made acrylic cloche hat and scarf set. Natural, red, brown ... 5.00

Robinson & Golluber designs these beautiful "SILLOOK" scarves in machine washable silk-like polyester.
71A—22-inch scarf, assorted prints 2.50
71B—28-inch scarf, assorted prints 3.50
71C—16x48-inch scarf/sash, assorted prints 3.50
Glentex presents "Glen Challis"—American-made sheer acrylic challis that's completely washable and yours in a fabulous collection of print accessories.
71D—3x30-inch bias tie 2.00
71E—Charming mini-bolero 6.00
71F—45-inch square shawl/scarf 6.00

PHOTO GALLERY

Photo courtesy of Johnstown Area Heritage Association

Photos by Bill Glosser

PHOTO GALLERY

Photos by Bill Glosser

PHOTO GALLERY

Photos courtesy of Bill Glosser

PHOTO GALLERY

Above—Gee Bee's "Action Alley" features the newest in junior sportswear in a boutique setting.

Right—Glosser Bros. new gift-ware department highlights unusual, colorful glassware and gifts.

Our seventh Gee Bee unit in Uniontown, Pennsylvania, which opened August 1972, anchors one end of a large enclosed mall.

Garden fresh produce, attractively displayed, is a daily feature at all Gee Bee Supermarkets.

Wide aisles, clean stores, excellent selections make for satisfied customers.

Photos from Glosser Bros. Annual Report, Jan. 1973

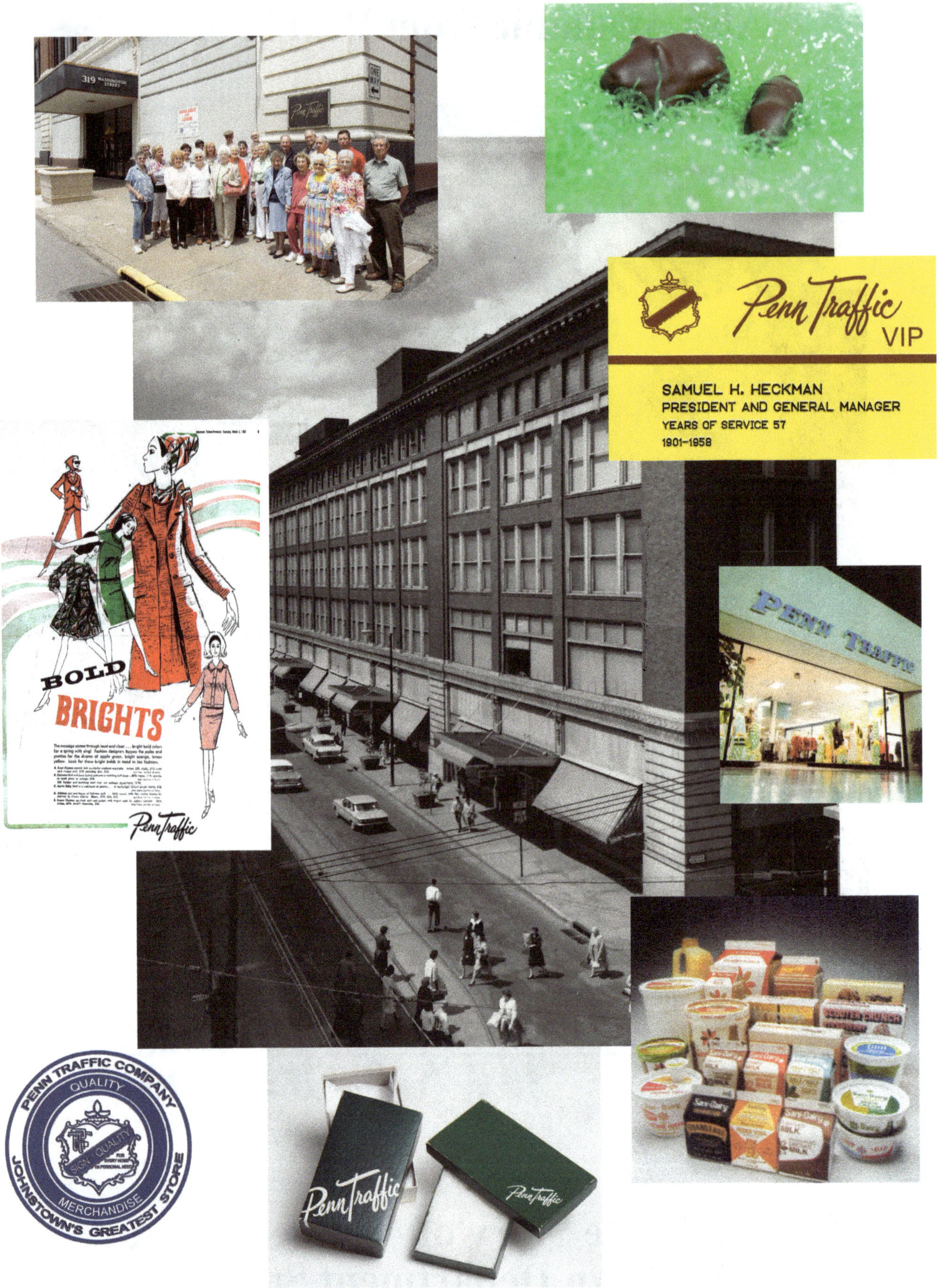
319 WASHINGTON STREET
ONE WAY
Penn Traffic
Penn Traffic
VIP
SAMUEL H. HECKMAN
PRESIDENT AND GENERAL MANAGER
YEARS OF SERVICE 57
1901–1958
BOLD
BRIGHTS
Penn Traffic
PENN TRAFFIC
PENN TRAFFIC COMPANY
QUALITY
SIGN OF QUALITY
MERCHANDISE
JOHNSTOWN'S GREATEST STORE
Penn Traffic
Penn Traffic

Meet you on the mezzanine...

The Penn Traffic Department Store is back in business in the pages of this one-of-a-kind book. Now's your chance to revisit this Johnstown, Pennsylvania landmark or experience its magic for the very first time. The whole true story of the legendary store, its employees, and the shoppers who loved it is right here, complete with all your favorite treats and traditions. Help yourself to Penn Way candies...have a burger and fries in the Penn Traffic restaurant...relax on the mezzanine...and wait on the sidewalk on a cold winter's night for the grand unveiling of the most spectacular Christmas window in town. You'll never forget this trip through history, from the store's pre-Civil War beginnings to its dramatic finale 123 years later, with three devastating floods, an epic fire, and a high-stakes robbery in between. Hundreds of photos, never before gathered in one place, will whisk you back in time to the people and events that made Penn Traffic great...and carry you forward for a special tour of the Penn Traffic building as it stands today, complete with traces and treasures from the store's glory days. You'll feel like you've returned to the store of your dreams, especially when you cook up the authentic goodies in the Penn Traffic recipe section, handed down from the store's own bakery and candy kitchen all-stars. If you've ever longed to go back to the magical department store where you always felt at home, or you just long for a simpler, sweeter place where the air smells like baking bread and the customer is always right, step inside. Welcome to the grand reopening of the store that comes to life every time we shout the magic words...

Penn Traffic
Forever

Other Johnstown and Pennsylvania Books
By Robert Jeschonek

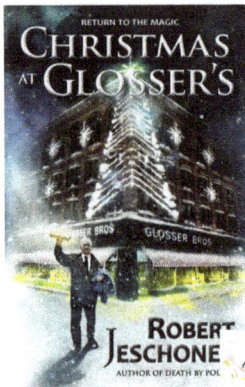

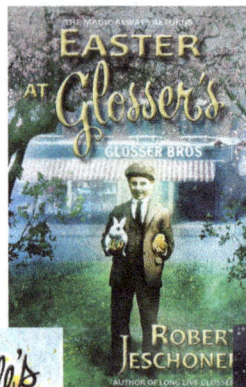

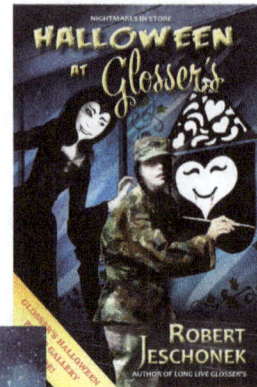

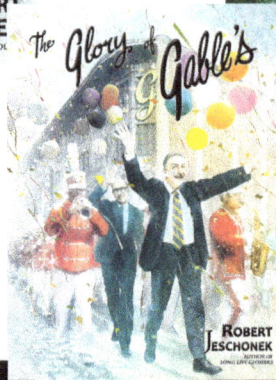

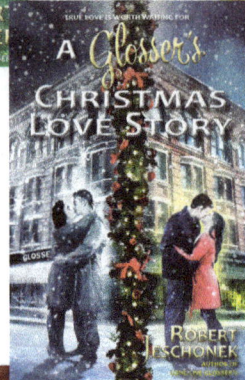

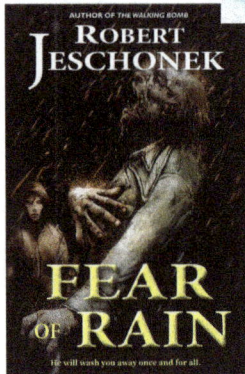

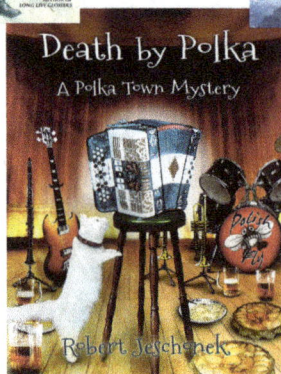

(A Johnstown Flood Story)　　　(A Johnstown Mystery)　　　(A Cambria County Adventure)

**Order from Amazon, Barnes and Noble, Books-A-Million,
or any bookstore or online bookseller.**

Ask your book dealer to search by title at Ingram or Baker and Taylor.

**Also available from Pie Press at www.piepresspublishing.com
or call (814) 525-4783**

PIP

pie press publishing

www.ingramcontent.com/pod-product-compliance
Lightning Source LLC
Chambersburg PA
CBHW062023090426
42811CB00005B/934